The Wordsworth Dictionary of
Culinary & Menu Terms

The Wordsworth Dictionary of
Culinary & Menu Terms

Compiled by
Rodney Dale

Wordsworth Reference

This edition published 2000 by Wordsworth Editions Ltd
8b East Street, Ware, Hertfordshire SG12 9HJ

2 4 6 8 10 9 7 5 3 1

ISBN 1 84022 300 6

Typeset by Antony Gray
Printed and bound in Great Britain
by Mackays of Chatham plc, Chatham. Kent

Compiler's Notes

Putting this book together has been rather like assembling some giant recipe, containing all the ingredients in all their varieties known to humankind. I must begin by expressing sincere thanks to 'the team' – Zoë Dale, Sarah Barrett-Jolley, Matthew Pettitt and Vicki Morrison – who got all the material together, trawling through shelves of books, and articles collected from newspapers and periodicals since the dawn of the project.

Zoë also contributed a great deal to the editing of the material once it had been got together, but I must in the time-honoured fashion – and rightly – confess to any errors as being my own.

I would also like to thank Marcus Clapham, Clive Reynard and designer Antony Gray for their help and support.

The text needs two words of explanation: 'BM' stands for 'Bazaar Malay', a language developed many years ago to help English-speakers in that far-off land. Beyond that, I trust that everything is self-explanatory, and will be pleased to receive your comments to put by for a second edition.

Rodney Dale
Haddenham, Cambridgeshire

A

a caballo	steak topped with eggs SPANISH
à la	in the style of, or manner of FRENCH
am	mango INDIAN
a punto	medium (cooked) SPANISH
A1 sauce	commercially bottled, highly spiced sauce ENGLISH
aal	eel DUTCH, GREEK
aalbes	black, red and white currant DUTCH
aamiainen	breakfast FINNISH
aardappel	potato DUTCH
aardbeien	strawberry DUTCH
aarfugl	small, black game bird NORWEGIAN
abacate	avocado pear PORTUGUESE
abacaxi	pineapple PORTUGUESE
abalone	ormer, sea-ear; single-shelled (univalve) mollusc found in warm waters off the Californian coast AMERICAN
abatis de volaille	chicken giblets FRENCH
abats	offal FRENCH
abatte	from 'battre'; thick double-edged knife used to tenderise and flatten meat FRENCH
abbacchio	grilled lamb ITALIAN
abbachio al forno	roast baby lamb, usually cooked with rosemary ITALIAN
abbaise	thinly rolled pastry used as a base; biscuit or sponge cake to be topped with jam, icing or cream FRENCH
abbore	perch DANISH
abborre	perch SWEDISH
Abendbrot, Abendessen	evening meal; supper GERMAN
Aberdeen crowdie	soft cheese made with soured milk curds or buttermilk SCOTTISH
Aberdeen crulla	plaited cake, similar to a doughnut SCOTTISH
Aberdeen sandwich	sandwich made with curried chicken, ham or tongue, cut into small rounds and fried SCOTTISH
Aberdeen sausage	long sausage made from minced beef, bacon fat, oatmeal and seasonings SCOTTISH
Aberdeen softies	soft buns made from baker's dough, butter and sugar SCOTTISH

Aberfrau cake	cake from a seaside village in Anglesey, made from butter, sugar, flour and milk, baked in a scallop shell WELSH
Abernethy biscuit	plain, sweet biscuit flavoured with caraway WELSH
abertam	hard ewe's milk cheese CZECH
abji l'amid	cold soup of mashed potato, yoghurt and lemon juice TURKISH
ablette	bleak; a type of fish FRENCH
abóbora	pumpkin; squash PORTUGUESE
abrestir	rare Icelandic dish; 'beestings' milk is coagulated over hot water, and served with cream, sugar and cinnamon ICELANDIC
abricot	apricot FRENCH
abricoter	to coat a cake or flan with apricot jam – inspissated, flavoured with liqueur and strained FRENCH
abricotine	apricot brandy FRENCH
abrikoos	apricot DUTCH
abrikos	apricot DANISH
abruzzese	method of cooking from the Abruzzi region; soups containing large amounts of fiery red peppers ITALIAN
acacia	a shrub whose flowers are used for making fritters FRENCH, ITALIAN
açafrão	saffron PORTUGUESE
acajou	cashew nut FRENCH
acanthe	acanthus, whose young leaves are eaten as a salad in southern France FRENCH
acará	portion of fritters PORTUGUESE
acarne	local name for sea bream FRENCH
acave	variety of small edible snail FRENCH
acciughe	northern Italian name for anchovy ITALIAN
accolade, en	arranging meat, poultry or fish on a dish; whole birds or joints arranged back to back FRENCH
accote-pot	small piece of iron placed on the stove under a pot or saucepan to tilt it FRENCH
accoub	edible thistle with a flavour between that of asparagus and globe artichoke
accuncciatu	lamb, goat or mutton stew with potatoes CORSICAN
acedera	sorrel SPANISH
aceite	oil SPANISH
aceite de oliva	olive oil SPANISH

aceituna	olive SPANISH
acelga	Swiss chard PORTUGUESE
acelga	spinach beet; chard SPANISH
aceline	fish of the perch family FRENCH
acepipes	hors d'œuvres PORTUGUESE
acetabula	algae with broad cupola similar to a mushroom
acetic acid	essential constituent of vinegar
aceto	vinegar ITALIAN
aceto-dolce	fruits preserved in a syrup of vinegar and honey ITALIAN
acétomel	sweet-sour syrup made of equal parts honey and vinegar
acetosella	sorrel ITALIAN
achard	pickle of chopped fruits and vegetables in a spicy sauce
ache des marais	wild celery; known as smallage in England FRENCH
achicoria	chicory SPANISH
achillée	wild herb, similar to the milfoil or goose tongue
achinoi, ahinoi	sea urchins GREEK
acid drops	boiled sweets made from sugar flavoured with citric acid
acidulate	to make acid by adding lemon juice, vinegar or other acid
acini di pepe	small squares of pasta for garnishing soups
acitron	candied cactus, used as stuffing for meats MEXICAN
ackee	bright red tropical fruit
acompanhamento	vegetables; side dish PORTUGUESE
açorda	thick soup or side dish whose main ingredient is bread PORTUGUESE
açorda alantejana	thick bread and garlic soup, often served with a poached egg PORTUGUESE
açorda com amêijoas	thick clam bisque PORTUGUESE
acorn barnacle	small shellfish
acorn coffee	roasted acorns with a little butter added
acquacotta	Tuscan soup made with vegetables and sweet pepper poured over bread brushed with beaten egg ITALIAN
acquacotta	soup of bread and vegetables ITALIAN
actinia	sea anemone, eaten in parts of southern France FRENCH
açúcar	sugar PORTUGUESE

adana soup made from beef stock with small pastry shapes filled with meat floating in it, and garnished with yoghurt, thyme and mint TURKISH

additive any substance added to processed food to prevent spoilage, or enhance texture, flavour or appearance

adèle clear chicken broth with peas, cubed carrots and chicken quenelles FRENCH

Adelina Patti clear chicken broth garnished with tiny pieces of baked egg custard, carrot and puréed chestnuts
FRENCH

adeline salad of chopped cooked salsify with mayonnaise, garnished with sliced tomato and cucumber FRENCH

Adirondack bread speciality bread of ground maize, wheat flour, butter and egg yolks, with beaten egg whites folded in
AMERICAN

adlon salad salad of raw celery hearts, cooked potatoes, beetroot and raw apples; corn salad is served round the outside

adobo a la madrilena marinade for pork chops of vinegar, white wine, herbs and seasoning SPANISH

adobo, al marinated SPANISH

adoucir to reduce bitterness by prolonged cooking; to dilute with milk, stock or water to reduce saltiness FRENCH

adulterant substance added to another to increase bulk and reduce cost, with intent to defraud

advocaat liqueur made from fresh egg yolks and brandy DUTCH

adzuki bean small, round, reddish-brown bean CHINESE, JAPANESE

aeble apple DANISH, NORWEGIAN

aeg egg DANISH

aegir sauce hollandaise sauce flavoured with mustard

aeglé ugli fruit FRENCH

aerated flour self-raising flour

aert pea DANISH, NORWEGIAN

affettati sliced cold meat, ham and salami ITALIAN

affriander to tempt by making the food look attractive FRENCH

affumicato smoked ITALIAN

áfonya blueberries HUNGARIAN

africaine, à la garnishing to imitate a style of cooking from Africa
FRENCH

African snub variety of chilli similar to jalapeño KENYAN

afronchemoyle Norman–French form of haggis

aftensmad dinner DANISH

agar-agar	tasteless white powder derived from seaweed used as a vegetarian substitute for gelatine
agaric	fungus family
agerhøne	partridge DANISH
agerkesalat	sliced cucumber in vinegar dressing. DANISH
ägg	egg SWEDISH
äggplanta	aubergine SWEDISH
agliata	garlic sauce ITALIAN
aglio	garlic ITALIAN
agneau	lamb FRENCH
agnello	lamb ITALIAN
Agnes Sorel	soup named after the mistress of Charles VII of France made from chicken stock, cream and puréed mushrooms, diced chicken and ox tongue, garnished with small pastry tarts filled with chicken mousse, mushrooms and diced ox tongue, and served with chicken or turkey FRENCH
agneshka churba	Easter dish of whole young spring lamb, stuffed with rice mixed with offal and raisins BULGARIAN
agneshka soup	Easter soup of lambs' liver, heart, sweetbreads and kidneys, garnished with onions, noodles, hot red pepper, eggs and yoghurt BULGARIAN
agnolotti	type of ravioli filled with a vegetable or meat stuffing ITALIAN
agoni	small, flat, freshwater fish found in Lake Como ITALIAN
agoursi	ridge cucumber FRENCH
agrafa	ewe's milk cheese resembling Gruyère GREEK
agrest	gooseberries POLISH
agrião	watercress PORTUGUESE
agrimony	perennial of the rose family, whose yellow flowers may be used for making tea
agro	lemon juice and oil dressing ITALIAN
agrodolce	sweet-sour sauce/dressing of sugar, vinegar, garlic, chocolate and gravy ITALIAN
aguacate	avocado SPANISH
aguglie	variety of garfish ITALIAN
agurk	cucumber DANISH, NORWEGIAN
agurku salotas	cucumber salad LITHUANIAN
agyvelö	brains HUNGARIAN
ahumado	smoked SPANISH

ahven — perch FINNISH

ahvenmuhennos — stewed perch FINNISH

aida salad — salad of green peppers, tomatoes, artichoke hearts, curly endives, and hard boiled eggs, served with vinaigrette

aiglefin — fresh haddock FRENCH

aïgo bouïllido — Provençal soup made with garlic, olive oil, bay leaf and water – once boiled it is poured over raw eggs FRENCH

aïgo-sau — Provençal fish and root vegetable soup, poured over garlic bread FRENCH

aigre de cèdre — citron tree FRENCH

aigre-doux — sweet–sour sauce (like agrodolce) FRENCH

aigrefin — fresh haddock FRENCH

aigrette — small, very light biscuit, made of fried flaky pastry FRENCH

aigroissade toulonnaisse — dish from Toulon of assorted warm vegetables with cooked dried beans or chickpeas and garlic sauce FRENCH

aiguillat — dogfish FRENCH

aiguille — needle (à brider: for trussing; à piquer: for larding) FRENCH

aiguillette — thin strip of cooked poultry, meat or fish; (de boeuf) a cut of beef FRENCH

aiguiser — to sharpen cream or liquid with lemon juice or citric acid; strongly spiced dish FRENCH

aïl — garlic FRENCH

aïle — wing FRENCH

aileron — terminal segment of bird's wing FRENCH

aïllada, l' — sauce for snails from Gascony and Bordeaux FRENCH

aillade — includes garlic in the preparation of the dish FRENCH

aioli, aïoli — garlic mayonnaise

aipim — cassava root PORTUGUESE

aipo — celeriac PORTUGUESE

airelle — berries such as bilberry, whortleberry and blueberry FRENCH

aish el sarya — dish eaten at the Muslim feast of Id-il-Fitr, made from honey, sugar, butter, cream and breadcrumbs ARABIC

aisy cendré — Burgundian cow's milk cheese the colour of ash FRENCH

aitch-bone — bone of the rump; the cut of beef lying over it

ajada	sauce of bread steeped in water and garlic SPANISH
aji	an aromatic chilli often eaten raw in salads and salsas, *see* aji amarilo BRAZILIAN, PERUVIAN
ajiaceite	garlic mayonnaise SPANISH
ajiaco bogotano	chicken soup with potatoes SPANISH
aji amarilo	dried aji
ajmooda	equivalent of parsley INDIAN
ajo	garlic SPANISH
ajonjoli	sesame seed SPANISH
ajowan	spice seed with strong thyme-like flavour – closely related to caraway
ajwan	equivalent of thymol INDIAN
ajwan-ka-patha	equivalent of celery INDIAN
akee	bright red pear-shaped Caribbean fruit, poisonous when unripe or over-ripe
akhni, yakhni	aromatic, clear vegetable stock which probably originated in ancient Persia and is now used all over the Middle east and as far east as Thailand
akola	a variety of small chillies from Thane, near Bombay IINDIAN
ål	eel DANISH, NORWEGIAN, SWEDISH
al cuarto de hora	soup containing mussels, onions, ham, parsley and rice, garnished with finely-chopped hard-boiled egg SPANISH
al dente	'to the tooth'; slightly firm to the bite – the perfect consistency of cooked pasta ITALIAN
ala	wing SPANISH
alacha	large fish, like a sardine SPANISH
aladåb	aspic SWEDISH
Alant	chub GERMAN
alar	chemical spray to regulate apple growth
alati	salt GREEK
albacore	long-finned species of tuna
albahaca	basil SPANISH
albaricoque	apricot SPANISH
albele	coconut pancakes INDIAN
alberchigo	peach SPANISH
albert	French name for English hot horseradish sauce FRENCH

albertine	poached fish with white wine sauce, served with mushrooms, truffles and parsley FRENCH
albicocche	apricot ITALIAN
albigensian soup	soup of calf's foot, goose, sausage, root vegetables and cabbage, served with bread FRENCH
albigeoise, à l'	garnish of stuffed tomatoes and potato croquettes FRENCH
albion	fish soup with lobster quenelles and truffles, thickened with tapioca; chicken broth with truffles, asparagus tips, chicken liver quenelles and cock's combs FRENCH
albóndiga	spiced meat or fish ball SPANISH
albondiguillas	walnut-sized meat or poultry rissoles, served with tomato sauce SPANISH
alboni	sauce for venison, of stock, pine kernels and redcurrant jelly ITALIAN
albran	very young wild duck FRENCH
albuféra, d'	suprême sauce with beurre pimenté flavoured with port; poultry stuffing of rice, chopped liver and truffles; garnish of tartlets filled with truffle balls and forcemeat balls; short pastry flavoured with arrack, with chopped almonds; (duckling à la d'albuféra) duckling roasted with bayonne ham, herbs, onion, cloves and Madeira FRENCH
albume	egg white ITALIAN
albumen powder	commercially-produced form of egg white
albumin	soluble protein found in blood, milk and egg white
alcachofa	globe artichoke SPANISH
alcachofra	artichoke PORTUGUESE
alcaparra	caper PORTUGUESE, SPANISH
alcarab	capon SPANISH
alcaravea	caraway seed SPANISH
alcazar	tart filled with icing sugar, egg whites, ground almonds and kirsch, garnished with marzipan and nuts FRENCH
alcide	white wine sauce with chopped shallots and grated horseradish FRENCH
alcobaca	farmhouse variety of serra cheese PORTUGUESE
alcohol	liquid – particularly ethyl alcohol – produced by fermentation and distillation of sugary substances
alcool	alcohol FRENCH

Alderman's Walk London name for the longest, finest cut from a haunch of venison or lamb

ale alcoholic drinks brewed from malt and hops

ale soup soup of ale, lemon and cinnamon GERMAN

alec herrings in brine LATIN

alecost aromatic herbaceous plant, similar to mint

alecrim rosemary PORTUGUESE

alénois species of cress, known as 'garden cress' FRENCH

alentejo partridges braised in olive oil, onions, parsley, garlic, white wine and vinegar, served on fried bread; ewe's milk cheese PORTUGUESE

aletria vermicelli, thin noodles; dessert made with vermicelli PORTUGUESE

alewife fish of the herring family AMERICAN

alexander member of the cow parsley family

alexandra suprême sauce with truffles; mayonnaise with mashed hard-boiled egg, mustard and chervil; Mornay sauce with fish, garnished with poached truffles and asparagus; slightly thickened chicken broth with lettuces, chicken quenelles and julienne of chicken; cold poached eggs on pastry tarts filled with lobster mousse; salad of lettuce, artichoke hearts, beetroot and celery, with mayonnaise FRENCH

alface lettuce PORTUGUESE

alfajor gingerbread SPANISH

alfalfa European leguminous plant with clover-like leaves, primarily used as fodder, though it can be used in salads or as a garnish

alföldi marharostélyos steak with rice sauce and stewed vegetables HUNGARIAN

alföldi saláta salad alföldi-style; sausage sliced in vinaigrette sauce HUNGARIAN

älg elk SWEDISH

algérienne garnish for steak of tomatoes or green and red peppers simmered in oil; fried eggs with puréed tomatoes, peppers and aubergine in fresh tomato sauce; salad of courgettes and sliced cooked sweet potato with mixed garlic mayonnaise; sautéed chicken and fried aubergine with tomato, onion and garlic sauce; cream soup made from sweet potato with filbert nuts FRENCH

alhambra
garnish of artichoke hearts, green or red peppers and sautéed tomatoes; salad of beetroot, celery, artichoke hearts and lettuce with mayonnaise

alheira
garlic sausage made of breadcrumbs and minced meats PORTUGUESE

alho
garlic PORTUGUESE

ali
wing ITALIAN

alice
southern Italian anchovy; cream, potato and turnip soup; French fruit and vegetable salad; eating apples filled with diced apples, redcurrants and walnuts
ITALIAN, FRENCH

alicot, l'
ragoût from south western France made from poultry giblets and carcasses, garlic, herbs, onions, tomatoes and white haricot beans FRENCH

alig sütve
very rare (cooked) HUNGARIAN

aligot, l'
dish from south western France served as a first course, of cream, butter and garlic added to puréed potatoes, with tomme de cantal cheese melted over the top FRENCH

aliñado
seasoned SPANISH

alioli
garlic mayonnaise SPANISH

ali-oli
garlic sauce SPANISH

alise
fruit of the amelanchier tree, which is similar to rowan or mountain ash FRENCH

alivenci
dish of cabbage, maize flour, milk and seasoning
ROMANIAN

alkali
the most common alkali used in cooking is bicarbonate of soda; it reacts with acids giving off gases which have a leavening effect

alkanet
small evergreen plant, *Anchusa officinalis,* whose thick leaves were once eaten as a vegetable in France and Germany, and which is used as a medicinal herb in the British Isles; *see* ox-tongue

alkanna
borage indigenous to the Mediterranean and South East Europe, once eaten as a vegetable, but its most common use today is the red food dye extracted from the roots

alkekénge
strawberry tomato; a variety of Cape gooseberry
FRENCH

alkermes
old-fashioned sweet cordial FRENCH, ITALIAN

alkupala
appetiser; starter FINNISH

allemande, à la	dish garnished with German specialities such as sauerkraut, smoked sausage or potato dumplings; dish with 'sauce allemande'; method of preparing game FRENCH
Allgäuer Bergkäse	cow's milk cheese similar to Emmental GERMAN
alliance	sauce of white wine, tarragon vinegar and egg yolk, beaten until thick; garnish of demi-glace, artichoke hearts, onions and carrots FRENCH
alligator	genus of saurian reptiles, eaten in North and South America
allodola	lark; often served grilled, as other small birds ITALIAN
alloro	bay leaf ITALIAN
allspice	spice made from Jamaican pepper, myrtle pepper and pimento, flavoured with cloves, cinnamon, and nutmeg WEST INDIAN
allumettes	fried 'matchsticks' of potatoes; sweet or savoury pastry fingers FRENCH
alma	apple HUNGARIAN
Almacks preserve	compote of fruit; apples, pears and sugar, served in slices
almaleves	apple soup HUNGARIAN
almamártás	apple sauce HUNGARIAN
almás palacsinta	apple pancake HUNGARIAN
almeja	clam, cockle SPANISH
almejas a la marinera	cooked in hot pimento sauce SPANISH
almejón	scallop SPANISH
almendra	almond SPANISH
almíbar	basic syrup used in the preparation of puddings SPANISH
almoço	lunch PORTUGUESE
almond	nut of the peach family from hot, dry climates; oils and essences are extracted from bitter almonds, which are poisonous if eaten in quantity; sweet almonds can be eaten whole, split, flaked, chopped or ground
almond essence	fermented and distilled from bitter almonds
almond oil	pressed from bitter almonds
almond paste	marzipan – firm, sweet paste made from ground almonds, used in cake decoration to stuff dried fruits
almôndega	ball of fish or meat PORTUGUESE

almondija   oven-poached minced beef, tomatoes, onions and hard boiled eggs SPANISH

almorta   flour from the beans of the common vetch SPANISH

almuerzo   lunch SPANISH

aloe   plant of the genus Aloe; an extract is used to flavour alcoholic drinks, gelatines and baked goods

alondra   lark SPANISH

aloo   potatoes INDIAN

alouette   lark FRENCH

alouette sans tête   slice of veal rolled and stuffed with minced meat, garlic and parsley FRENCH

aloyau   sirloin FRENCH

aloyau de boeuf   sirloin of beef FRENCH

alperce   apricot PORTUGUESE

alpestra   hard, dry, lightly-salted, golden cheese from Briançon and Gap FRENCH

alphée   a crustacean like a crawfish FRENCH

alphonse   garnish for meat of sauce màdere with artichoke hearts and mushrooms FRENCH

alsacienne, à la   garnished with smoked sausages, ham and peas FRENCH

Alsen   shad GERMAN

Altenburger   mild, soft, goat's milk cheese GERMAN

altitude   the higher the altitude the lower the boiling temperature of water; this affects cooking times and temperatures

alubia   french bean SPANISH

alum   astringent mineral salt used in pickling

aluminium   strong, light, metal which is a good conductor of heat; used to make cooking pans, utensils, food and drink cans and kitchen foil

alverde   local name for farmhouse-made variety of serra cheese PORTUGUESE

alverof   a dish from Rhodes of lentils mixed with noodles, served with chopped fried onion GREEK

amande   almond FRENCH

amandel   almond DUTCH

amandel broodje   sweet roll with almond paste filling DUTCH

amandine   variety of almond-flavoured French cakes and pastries; American dish containing chopped almonds, especially grilled or fried fish or poultry;

dried apricot paste pressed into sheets, used in Middle Eastern cuisine FRENCH, AMERICAN, MIDDLE EASTERN

amaranth plants of the genus *Amaranthus* with edible green leaves, also known as bayam, calaloo, Chinese spinach

amaretti macaroons ITALIAN

amarettini small macaroon flavoured with apricot kernels ITALIAN

Amaretto di Saronno liqueur flavoured with almonds ITALIAN

amargo bitter PORTUGUESE

amarilla, salsa yellow sauce made from eggs, Madeira, stock, mustard and seasoning SPANISH

amasette palette knife FRENCH

amazone meat garnish of lentil fritters filled with morels and chestnut purée

ambassadeur haute cuisine garnish of pommes duchesse and artichoke hearts filled with puréed mushrooms and horseradish; clear chicken broth with puréed truffles, chopped mushrooms and slivers of chicken breast FRENCH

ambassadrice suprême sauce with pounded chicken and whipped cream; garnish of asparagus tips and lambs' sweetbreads larded with truffles, served with barquettes of pastry filled with chopped chicken livers, cocks' combs and truffles; garnish for steaks of pounded chicken livers, with sautéed mushrooms, pommes Parisienne, kidneys and braised lettuce; clear chicken soup garnished with cubes of chicken, mushrooms, truffles and peas FRENCH

ambelopoùlia small bird, a figeater

amber fish tropical and sub-tropical fish

ambigu mixed cold collation, not eaten at a regular meal time FRENCH

ambrosia mythical food of the Greek gods

amêijoas small clam or cockle PORTUGUESE

ameixa plum PORTUGUESE

amelanchier shrub whose fruit is called alise FRENCH

amélie fish garnish of white wine sauce with tomato purée, diced truffles, mushrooms and potato croquettes FRENCH

amêndoa almonds PORTUGUESE

amendoim   peanut PORTUGUESE

americaine, à la   various methods of preparing meat, game, fish, vegetables and eggs FRENCH

American cheddar   pasteurised milk cheese similar to English cheddar AMERICAN

American cherry   bush-like tree with tart fruit used for pies and sauces AMERICAN

American crab apple   species of crab apple admired for its pink blossom AMERICAN

American cress   land cress; useful as winter salad, it grows without running water AMERICAN

American frosting   cake icing which forms a crust on the outside but is never hard throughout AMERICAN

American mysost   cheese made from the whey from the manufacture of other cheeses AMERICAN

American partridge   related to the quail, but slightly larger AMERICAN

American quail   sometimes called partridge; there are many varieties AMERICAN

American sage   cheese made from cow's milk and flavoured with sage AMERICAN

American woodcock   smaller than the British woodcock; cooked as a snipe AMERICAN

amino-acid   basic constituent of proteins, essential in a healthy diet; the full range of amino-acids is contained in egg yolk, milk, liver and kidney

amiral   sauce for boiled fish, with anchovies, capers and lemon zest; scrambled eggs with lobster sauce; garnish for fish of oysters, mussels, crayfish and sauce normande; fish consommé with fish quenelles, diced lobster, mushrooms, oysters and truffles FRENCH

ammocète   a cross between eel and lamprey FRENCH

amora   blackberry; mulberry PORTUGUESE

amou   cow's milk cheese from the Béarn region FRENCH

amourettes   calves' bone marrow FRENCH

amuse-bouche   little pre-hors d'œuvres FRENCH

amydon   cornflour NORMAN-ENGLISH

amygdalin   foods containing almonds FRENCH

amygthala   almond GREEK

amygthalota   almond 'pears' – a dish from Hydra; ground almonds, sugar, egg whites, vanilla and breadcrumbs are made into pear shapes, with a clove in the end as

	the stalk, baked, cooled, dipped in orange flower water and rolled in icing sugar GREEK
anacard	vinegar from fermented pulp surrounding cashew nuts
anaheim	a variety of chilli cultivated in California for canning AMERICAN
ananas	pineapple DUTCH, FRENCH, GERMAN, INDIAN, ITALIAN, NORWEGIAN, POLISH, SWEDISH
ananás	pineapple PORTUGUESE
ananaskrem	pineapple cream dish NORWEGIAN
ananasso	pineapple ITALIAN
ananász	pineapple HUNGARIAN
anari	ewe's or goat's milk cheese GREEK
anatto	tree with salmon pink fruits which produce an orange dye, used to colour confectionery and cheese SOUTH AMERICAN
ancho, ancho chino	aromatic and fruity dried Poblano chilli, the most popular dried chilli in Mexico MEXICAN
anchoa	anchovy SPANISH
anchoïade	anchovies, tomatoes, almonds, herbs and olive oil pounded to a paste, spread on bread and baked FRENCH, CORSICAN
anchois	anchovy FRENCH
anchova	anchovy PORTUGUESE
anchovy	small round, salty, oily fish, of the genus *Engraulis* and related genera, especially *E.encrasicolus*
anchovy butter	served with grilled fish and meat or on canapés
anchovy essence	strong essence from cured anchovies
anchovy paste	pounded salted anchovies, vinegar, spices and water
ancien impérial	cow's milk cheese of the Neufchâtel type FRENCH
ancienne, à la	'old style'; usually with garnish of sliced onions and button mushrooms FRENCH
and	duck NORWEGIAN, SWEDISH
anda	eggs INDIAN
andalouse, à la	dishes containing tomatoes and rice FRENCH
andijvie	endive DUTCH
andithia	chicory GREEK
andouille	large black-skinned sausage from Normandy made from pig stomach and intestines, usually sliced and served cold as an hors d'œuvre FRENCH
andouillette	similar to andouille, but smaller and coarser in texture FRENCH

andruty	wafer similar to a waffle POLISH
âne	haddock NEWFOUNDLAND
aneth	dill FRENCH
angel cake	classic pale sponge cake, light and delicate in texture AMERICAN
angel fish	fiddlefish; shark-ray; monkfish; its thick, meaty tail contains few bones.
angelica	tall plant of the parsley family; the hollow green stalks are candied and used in cake decoration
angelot	angel fish FRENCH
angels on horseback	oysters rolled in strips of bacon, grilled and served hot on fried bread croutes
ang-gor	grape BM
anginares	artichokes GREEK
anglaise, à l'	'English style'; plainly cooked food, usually boiled in stock or water FRENCH
anglerfish	frogfish or monkfish; the tail meat is firm, resembling lobster
angolna matróz módra	eels marinière HUNGARIAN
angostura bitters	very bitter, reddish brown liquid containing gentian, cloves, cinnamon, nutmeg, citrus peel, prunes, quinine and rum; used in cocktails and as flavouring in casseroles
Angoulême	town famous for partridge pâté FRENCH
angouria	cucumber GREEK
angrest	gooseberries CZECH
angu	cassava-root flour or maize boiled in salted water PORTUGUESE
anguila	small eel (not conger eel) SPANISH
anguilla	eel ITALIAN
anguille	eel FRENCH
anguille de mer	conger eel FRENCH
angula	baby eel SPANISH
anguria	watermelon ITALIAN
anho	lamb PORTUGUESE
anice	aniseed ITALIAN
anijs melk	aniseed milk, traditionally associated with ice skating – where there is an ice rink, aniseed milk can be bought DUTCH
anijszaad	aniseed DUTCH
animelle	sweetbreads ITALIAN

animelles	testicles, particularly rams' FRENCH
anis	aniseed FRENCH, GERMAN, SPANISH
anise	cow's milk cheese flavoured with aniseed FRENCH
anisé	aniseed GREEK
anise pepper	hot aromatic spice from dried, roasted red berries of a Chinese tree; also known as Chinese pepper or Szechuan pepper
aniseed	anise, small seeds from the sweet cumin plant
anisette	colourless aniseed-flavoured liqueur FRENCH, SPANISH, ITALIAN
anitho	fresh dill GREEK
anitra	duck ITALIAN
ánizsmag	aniseed HUNGARIAN
anjou	game consommé with asparagus tips and quenelles of game, garnished with rice FRENCH
anjovis	anchovy SWEDISH
anka	duck SWEDISH
ankerias	eel FINNISH
ankerstock	spiced rye flour loaf with currants SCOTTISH
ankka	duck FINNISH
annegati	sliced meat in white or marsala wine ITALIAN
annos	portion FINNISH
anodonta	freshwater mollusc with large thin shell
anodonte	anodonta FRENCH
anolini	oval pasta with meat or vegetable stuffing
anon	fish of the genus *Gadus*; a variety of haddock
Anona	annona GERMAN
anone	annona FRENCH
anonna	genus of custard apple, a fleshy tropical fruit
ansjos	anchovy; marinated sprats NORWEGIAN
ansjovis	marinated sprats SWEDISH
antelope	collective name for deer-like ruminant mammals which live all over the world
antholyti	round, yellow cheese with thick mottled rind GREEK
anthotyro	Cretan goat's milk cheese GREEK
antibiotic	a substance capable of killing organisms, particularly bacteria
antiboise	sauce from Antibes of mayonnaise with tomato purée, anchovy essence and chopped tarragon FRENCH

anticucho beef heart grilled on a skewer with green peppers SPANISH

antin sauce madère with shallots, mushrooms, truffles and parsley, cooked in white wine sauce FRENCH

antioxidant organic or synthetic substance added to foods to prevent oxidation and resulting deterioration

antipasto 'before the meal'; selection of hot or cold foods served as an appetiser or starter ITALIAN

antoine scrambled eggs with chopped fried bacon, herbs and capers, covered in melted butter FRENCH

antoinette poached fish in herb sauce with anchovy essence, mixed with butter, capers and shrimps FRENCH

antrykot rib steak POLISH

anversoise, à l' meat garnish of small pastry shells filled with creamed hop shoots and plain boiled potatoes; eggs or calves' sweetbreads, with hop shoots and fried potatoes; beef consommé thickened with tapioca, and hop shoots, FRENCH

Anzac biscuits eggless biscuits, which originated in Australia during World War I AUSTRALIAN

Anzio pie flat pastry pie filled with macaroni or spaghetti and a layer of minced beef ITALIAN

ao in the style of PORTUGUESE

apelsin orange SWEDISH

apéritif drink served before a meal, differing from a cocktail as it is fairly mild and often bitter FRENCH

aperitiv aperitif CZECH

Apfel apple GERMAN

Apfelsine orange GERMAN

aphie small round fish from the Mediterranean, prepared as whiting

apio celeriac; celery SPANISH

aplatir flatten, usually by beating with a mallet to tenderise FRENCH

apo aravosito, soupa Cretan village soup; dried sweetcorn mixed with dried milk, kept for use in the winter GREEK

apogon cardinal fish FRENCH

apokreo means 'fast from the meat'; the many days of fasting ordained by the Greek Orthodox Church GREEK

Apostelkuchen brioche-like bun, usually made in one large loaf, rather than the small buns more popular in France AUSTRIAN

appareil	ingredients used in a particular dish FRENCH
appel	apple DUTCH
äppel	apple SWEDISH
äppel kaka	apple charlotte; apple pudding SWEDISH
äppelmos	apple sauce SWEDISH
appelsiini	orange FINNISH
appelsin	orange NORWEGIAN
appenzell	full-fat cow's milk cheese from the canton of Appenzell SWISS
appetiser	hot or cold food served before a meal
appétit	common name for chives FRENCH
Appetithäppchen	appetiser GERMAN
appigret	old French word for gravy, juice or essence seasoning FRENCH
apple	popular snack and dessert fruit
apple, dried	usually sold as rings, apples are one of the few fruits that don't lose vitamin C in the drying process
Applewood	type of Cheddar cheese smoked over apple tree branches and coated with paprika
apprenti	apprentice FRENCH
après	after FRENCH
apricot	fruit with velvety yellowish-orange skin and soft juicy flesh, originally from China but now cultivated in many warm countries
apricot, dried	the flavour is often better than that of the fresh fruit; dried apricots that have not been sulphur-treated are dark brown in colour rather than golden-orange
apricot, glaze	glaze of apricot jam
aprikoosi	apricot FINNISH
aprikos	apricot SWEDISH, NORWEGIAN
Aprikose	apricot GERMAN
apró uborka	gherkins HUNGARIAN
apron	small freshwater fish, prepared as perch
aquavit	national drink made from grain, rye and potato, flavoured with caraway, aniseed or dill SCANDINAVIAN
arachide	peanut FRENCH
arachide	peanuts ITALIAN
aragosta	spiny lobster ITALIAN
araignée de mer	spider crab FRENCH
Aran isenach	bannock from the Outer Isles SCOTTISH

araña	weaver or dragon fish SPANISH
arancia	orange ITALIAN
arancini alla Siciliana	rice balls with veal filling, rolled in breadcrumbs and fried SICILIAN
arandano	blueberry SPANISH
aranygaluska	sweet dumpling filled with jam HUNGARIAN
arapède	univalve shellfish found off Provence, cooked as cockles FRENCH
arasídy	peanut CZECH
arbenne	variety of grouse; snow partridge FRENCH
arborio rice	short oval variety of rice ITALIAN
arbouse	arbute FRENCH
arbute	fruit of the strawberry tree, used in Spain and Italy in confectionery, and in France to make a liqueur FRENCH, ITALIAN, SPANISH
arbuz	water melon POLISH
arca	edible bivalve mollusc with the common name arch FRENCH
arcanette	small, non-migratory teal from Lorraine FRENCH
archiduc, à l'	dish seasoned with paprika and blended with cream FRENCH
archiduchesse, à l'	hard boiled or scrambled eggs with diced ham, mushrooms and paprika, garnished with potato croquettes and asparagus tips FRENCH
arcing	blue spark produced when a metal object is used in a microwave
Arctic flounder	small flounder found in the Bering sea
ardennaise, à l'	soup of leeks, endives and potatoes simmered in milk; pheasant soup with port and kidney beans; small birds cooked in a cocotte with juniper berries; pork chops fried or grilled with junipe berries FRENCH
Ardense pastei	rich pork mixture in a pastry crust, served cold in slices DUTCH
ardoise	slang for bill or check (only used in cheap restaurants); FRENCH
	Andorran method of cooking on a red hot roof slate heated over a wood fire ANDORRA
aremberg, d'	clear beef soup with carrots, peas, turnips and truffles; clear chicken broth with diced carrots, turnips, truffles and chicken quenelles FRENCH
arenque	herring PORTUGUESE, SPANISH

arepa	flapjack made of maize SPANISH
Argenteuil	garnish for fish of white wine sauce with asparagus tips; cream soup with asparagus, cream and chervil FRENCH
argol	hard crusty deposits in casks or tanks of maturing wine
Argyll	vessel or well in a carving board, to catch juices
ariégeoise, à l'	all dishes from the Ariége region (famous for pork, geese and ham); dishes garnished with cooked green cabbage, pickled pork and sometimes kidney beans FRENCH
aringa	herring ITALIAN
arista	loin of pork ITALIAN
arista fiorentina	Florentine method of roasting pork in a little water with garlic, rosemary and cloves ITALIAN
arista perugina	Perugian method of roasting pork with fennel and garlic ITALIAN
Arles, saucisson d'	lean pork and beef sausage, flavoured with pepper, garlic, paprika and saltpetre FRENCH
arlésienne	garnish of cooked aubergine, onions and tomatoes; garnish of tomatoes with pickled chicory hearts; garnish of tomatoes stuffed with rice and large olives – themselves stuffed with minced chicken and anchovy butter – and boiled new potatoes FRENCH
armadillo	large family of edentate mammals; the three-banded armadillo is edible
armagnac	fine French brandy, second only to cognac FRENCH
armand, d'	garnish of soufflé potatoes, red wine sauce with chopped cooked goose liver and truffles FRENCH
arme riddere	sliced bread soaked in a salt and cinnamon flavoured mixture of milk and egg, and fried DANISH, NORWEGIAN
Arménonville	garnish for joints of pommes cocotte with cooked artichoke hearts and tomatoes; dish of pommes anna and morels; thick soup of green peas and chervil FRENCH
armoise	mugwort FRENCH
armoricaine, à l'	dish served with shellfish sauce FRENCH
arnaki sti souvla	Easter lamb as eaten in towns, where it cannot be cooked on the spit and must be cut into pieces and cooked in the oven GREEK
arni	lamb roasted on a spit, rubbed with lemon salt and pepper; one of the most traditional of dishes GREEK

arnissia paithakia riyanata   lamb cutlets in marjoram sauce GREEK

aromatics	fragrant plants which add flavour to a dish, such as herbs, garlic, onions, mushrooms, celery and carrots
aromivoi	herb butter FINNISH
aromsmör	herb butter SWEDISH
árpa	barley HUNGARIAN
arpenteur	plover FRENCH
ar-ra	fig BM
arrack	(arak, raki, rakia) Eastern spirit made from fermented palm sap, often flavoured with aniseed
Arran cheese	hard, moist, close-textured, rindless dunlop cheese ARRAN
arrigny	cow's milk cheese from the Champagne region FRENCH
arroche	orach, cultivated in French gardens and eaten as spinach FRENCH
arrosé	diluted with wine FRENCH

arrostino annegato alla milanaise   calf's liver dish from Milan, cut lengthwise and rolled in a boned loin of veal ITALIAN

arrosto	roast ITALIAN
arrosto di maiale	roast pork cooked with rosemary ITALIAN
arrowhead	Chinese water-plant with leaves shaped like arrowheads
arrowroot	light, white odourless powder, the starch from the pith of the roots of the maranta, used as a thickening agent in liquids WEST INDIAN
arroz	rice PORTUGUESE, SPANISH
arselle	clam ITALIAN
arsenic	a poison found in trace amounts in our diet
ärt	pea SWEDISH
Artagnan, d'	clear beef broth with essence of game, garnished with heathcock or blackcock and peas; garnish of ceps in béarnaise sauce, stuffed tomatoes and potato croquettes FRENCH
ärter	peas SWEDISH
artésienne, à l'	thick soup of cooked dried haricot beans, white sauce and tapioca FRENCH
artichaut	globe artichoke FRENCH
artichoke, Chinese	small tubers similar to the Jerusalem artichoke; also known as Japanese artichoke, crosnes
artichoke, globe	North African thistle now grown as a vegetable; the bud of the flower is eaten and the rest discarded

artichoke, Jerusalem knobbly tuber with nut-like taste; indigenous to America

articsóka avocado HUNGARIAN

Artischocke artichoke GERMAN

Artishokenboden artichoke bottom GERMAN

artisjok artichoke DUTCH

artiskok artichoke DANISH

artois, d' garnish of tart-shaped potato croquettes filled with green peas covered with sauce madère; garnish flavoured with Madeira of glazed carrots, onions and artichoke hearts FRENCH

artycok artichoke CZECH

arvi artichoke INDIAN

arzavola teal ITALIAN

asado roast SPANISH

asado de cerdo roast pork SPANISH

asafœtida pungent spice from the resin of a plant native to Afghanistan and Iran, which tastes a little like spicy garlic – use it sparingly

Äsche grayling GERMAN

ash keys seeds of the ash tree, used in early English times for pickling

ashberry jelly jelly made from the berries of the mountain ash, served with mutton and venison

Ashley bread rice flour bread from the deep south; eaten hot it has a distinctive rice flavour AMERICAN

asiago a skimmed milk cheese ITALIAN

asie kind of large cucumber, seeded and pickled DANISH

asparago asparagus ITALIAN

asparagus cultivated form of the lily family; blanched (white) variety cut below the soil; green asparagus cut at soil level

asparagus bean similar to the French bean, eaten whole when young; black-eyed beans are mature beans removed from pod

asparagus lettuce variety of cos lettuce with no head; boiled, the inside leaves are eaten with melted butter

asparagus pea thin green rectangular pod; should be eaten young

asparges asparagus DANISH, NORWEGIAN

aspargo asparagus PORTUGUESE

aspartame low-calorie sugar substitute

asperges	asparagus FRENCH, DUTCH
asperges à la Flamande	Flemish asparagus; popular vegetable in Belgium BELGIAN
asperula	woodruff SPANISH
asperule	woodruff FRENCH
aspic	savoury jelly made from clarified meat stock
Aspik	aspic GERMAN
ass	member of the horse family
assado	roast PORTUGUESE
assaisonnement	seasonings; salad dressings FRENCH
assiette anglaise	assorted cold meats, usually ham, beef and tongue FRENCH
assorti	assorted FRENCH
assortito	assorted ITALIAN
astako	lobster GREEK
Asti Spumante	sparkling wine combining the champagne method with the 'cuve close' (closed seal) method of production ITALIAN
asticciole alla calabrese	beef rolls stuffed with mozzarella and pork sausage ITALIAN
astice	lobster ITALIAN
astroderme	saltwater fish found along the Mediterranean coast, used in soups such as bouillabaisse
asturias	strong, fermented cheese SPANISH
aszalt szilva	prunes HUNGARIAN
ateria	meal FINNISH
athénienne, d'	garnish of thick aubergine slices stuffed with duxelles and fried in oil; dishes flavoured with aubergine, fried onion, tomatoes and peppers FRENCH
atherine	small fish resembling smelt
attelet	pin or skewer with ornamented top, threaded with truffles, crayfish and cocks' combs FRENCH
attendu	postpone eating a dish or food to allow it to improve – for example, by hanging FRENCH
ätter ock fläsk	yellow split pea soup with pickled pork SWEDISH
attereau	skewer threaded with ingredients, dipped in a sauce, rolled in breadcrumbs and deep fried FRENCH
ättika	white vinegar SWEDISH
ättiksgurka	pickled gherkin SWEDISH
attorta	flaky pastry filled with fruit and almonds ITALIAN
atum	tuna fish PORTUGUESE

atún	tuna fish SPANISH
Atzem Pilauf	meat or poultry, onions, herbs and rice cooked as a pilauf GERMAN
auber, d'	garnish of artichoke hearts stuffed with pounded chicken, covered with sauce madère FRENCH
aubergine	a member of the tomato family; native to South East Asia
Audit ale	strong ale originally brewed at Oxbridge and drunk at the Audit Day festivities
Auerhahn	black cock; capercaillie GERMAN
Auflauf	soufflé; a dish which is oven browned GERMAN
Aufschnitt	cold meat GERMAN
augelot	a Pont l'Evêque type of cheese
Augsberger Würste	sausages of coarsely chopped lean pork with diced bacon fat, seasoned with cloves, nutmeg, salt, saltpetre and pepper GERMAN
augurk	gherkin (US: pickle) DUTCH
augusta, d'	garnish for fish poached in white wine of sliced boletus and chopped shallots covered with a Mornay sauce FRENCH
aulagnier, d'	clear beef soup garnished with peas and cabbage FRENCH
aumale, d'	scrambled eggs with ox tongue and sliced truffles, served with grilled veal kidneys and a sauce madère FRENCH
Aura	blue cheese FINNISH
auriol	Marseillaise name for mackerel FRENCH
aurone	southernwood FRENCH
aurora sauce	béchamel sauce flavoured with tomato purée, often served with fish DANISH
aurore, à la	dish served with tomato-flavoured 'sauce aurore'; dome-shaped yellow dish, suggesting the rising sun FRENCH
Ausone	a St-Emilion wine FRENCH
Auster	oyster GERMAN
Austern Krabbe	oyster crab GERMAN
auszpik	aspic POLISH
Auszug	extract or essence GERMAN
autocuiseur	pressure cooker FRENCH
autrichienne, à l'	Hungarian-style dishes seasoned with paprika, fennel and soured cream FRENCH

autun	cow's milk cheese produced in Burgundy FRENCH
auvergnate, à l'	pig's head broth with lentils, leeks and potatoes, garnished with strips of pig's head and served with rye bread FRENCH
avec	with FRENCH
avefria	plover SPANISH
aveia	oats PORTUGUESE
avelã	hazelnut PORTUGUESE
aveline	filbert FRENCH
avellana	hazelnut or filbert SPANISH, ITALIAN
avena	oats SPANISH, ITALIAN
avern jelly	wild strawberry jelly SCOTTISH
aves	fowl PORTUGUESE
aves de corral	fowl SPANISH
avga	egg GREEK
avgolémono	sauce of egg, lemon and stock; soup with the same ingredients and rice GREEK
avgotaraho	grey mullet roe purée, also known as 'red caviar' GREEK
avies koja	roast leg of lamb, marinated in vinegar, spices and juniper berries LITHUANIAN
aviyal	traditional mixed vegetable curry INDIAN
avocadella	a small squash resembling avocado in taste and shape
avocado	(alligator pear) tree fruit grown in sub-tropical regions; most varieties are pear-shaped with smooth green or bumpy purple-brown skin and pale green oily flesh, with the consistency of butter and high calorific value
avocat	avocado FRENCH
Avocatobirne	avocado GERMAN
avocette	avocet, a wading bird with a slightly fishy flavour, eaten mainly in the Poitou region FRENCH
avoine	oats FRENCH
avokádó	avocado HUNGARIAN
avondeten	dinner, supper DUTCH
axolotl	larval salamander from the lakes of southern Mexico and the southern States of America MEXICAN, AMERICAN
axonge	high quality lard from round a pig's kidneys FRENCH
aydes, les	cow's milk cheese FRENCH

ayran	iced drink of yoghurt, iced water and salt, decorated with mint leaves TURKISH
äyriäinen	shellfish FINNISH
aythya	pochard duck FRENCH
azafrán	saffron SPANISH
azarole	hawthorn berry, used to make confectionery, liqueurs and jam
azeda	sorrel PORTUGUESE
azedo	sour PORTUGUESE
azeitão	a variety of farmhouse-made serra cheese PORTUGUESE
azeite	olive oil PORTUGUESE
azeitona	olive PORTUGUESE
azerole	azarole FRENCH
azijn	vinegar DUTCH
azúcar	sugar SPANISH

B

B and B	drier version of Bénédictine, the liqueur is mixed with half brandy
bażant	pheasant POLISH
baars	perch DUTCH
baba	light-textured yeast cake, sometimes containing raisins FRENCH
babá de moça	egg yolks poached in coconut milk and syrup PORTUGUESE
baba ghannouj	dish made with eggplant MIDDLE EASTERN
babaco	large tropical fruit shaped like a fat banana; when ripe the flesh is pale orange
babbaluci	snails in olive-oil sauce with tomatoes and onions ITALIAN
babérlevél	bay leaf HUNGARIAN
babeurre	buttermilk FRENCH
babi ketjap	pork strips simmered with onions in diluted soy sauce, served with rice DUTCH East Indian
babi pangang	roast suckling pig served with sweet-and-sour sauce DUTCH
babka	grated potatoes or carrots mixed with flour and baked; Polish cake similar to the French baba but without yeast BYELORUSSIAN, POLISH
babka drożdżowa	yeast cake with a hole in the centre POLISH
babok	beans HUNGARIAN
bábovka	cake CZECH
bacalao	dried, salted cod SPANISH
bacalao fresco	fresh cod SPANISH
bacalhau	cod, usually dried and salted PORTUGUESE
bacalhau fresco	fresh cod PORTUGUESE
baccalà	stock-fish; dried cod. ITALIAN
baccalà fresco	haddock ITALIAN
bàckai káposzta	cabbage and pig's knuckles HUNGARIAN
Backerbsen	garnish for soup of batter mixture poured through a colander into hot fat; when the 'peas' are cooked they are ladled out AUSTRIAN, GERMAN
Bäckerei	biscuit; there are many varieties AUSTRIAN
Backforelle	baked trout GERMAN

Backhänchen   (Backhendl, Backhühn) fried chicken GERMAN

Backobst   dried fruit GERMAN

Backpflaume   prune GERMAN

Backpulver   baking powder GERMAN

Backsteinkäse   Bavarian cow's milk cheese GERMAN

baclava   traditional a nut-filled pastry, sweetened with honey
GREEK

bacon   cured fresh pork, sometimes smoked

bacon bits   small pieces of imitation bacon made from soy products

baconer   pig weighing between 83 and 101kg, from which bacon is cut

bacoreta   dark meat variety of tuna fish

ba-dam   almonds BM

badami   almonds INDIAN

badderlocks   edible seaweed from the Faroe Islands and the northern coasts of the British Isles; known as honeyware in Scotland

bagel   traditional ring-shaped roll made from plain or sweetened yeast dough JEWISH

baghaar   dropping whole spices into hot oil to change their characteristics INDIAN

bagna cauda   hot dip of anchovies, garlic and olive oil served with crudités ITALIAN

bagozzo   hard, sharp, pungent cheese of the caciotta variety
ITALIAN

bagration   salad of cooked artichoke bottoms and celeriac with macaroni, mixed with mayonnaise flavoured with tomatoes; meat or fish soup prepared from a velouté sauce, garnished with macaroni FRENCH

bagt kartoffel   baked potato DANISH

baguette   bread stick; French bread FRENCH

baharat   the Arab version of garam masala

bahmi   Chinese noodles served with shredded leeks, chopped celery, minced garlic, bok choy and bean sprouts, pork, shrimps or prawns, and soy sauce
DUTCH INDONESIAN

baila   salmon trout SPANISH

Bailey's Irish cream   commercially-made coffee liqueur made from Irish whiskey and double cream

baingan   brinjal, aubergines INDIAN

bain-marie	low sided container half-filled with water, kept just below boiling point, in which food containers are placed to keep warm or gently cook FRENCH
baisan	sweet fudge made with chickpea flour INDIAN
baiser	two small meringues joined together with thick cream or jelly FRENCH
bajai halászlé	fish and potato soup HUNGARIAN
bajaina	local name in Grasse for the small garden snail FRENCH
bakad	baked SWEDISH
bakaliaros	salt cod GREEK
bakalie	exotic or non-Polish fruits such as raisins POLISH
bake	cooking food by dry heat, usually in an oven
bake blind	partially pre-baking a pastry case filled with dried beans or similar
baked Alaska	ice cream on sponge cake, covered in meringue, browned in a very hot oven for a short time without melting the ice cream
bakelse	pastry; fancy cake SWEDISH
baker's cheese	skimmed milk cheese, finer grained and with less moisture than cottage cheese AMERICAN
Bakewell pudding	(Bakewell tart) buttery mixture flavoured with almonds and baked in a pastry case
baking powder	a mixture of various simple chemicals used as a substitute to yeast in bread and cake making
baking soda	alternative name for bicarbonate of soda
baklażany	aubergine POLISH
baklava	filo pastry sandwiched with chopped nuts in honey GREEK
baklazán	aubergine CZECH
baklazhany	aubergine RUSSIAN
bakonyi betyárleves	'outlaw soup'; richly spiced soup with chicken, beef chunks, thin noodles, mushrooms and vegetables HUNGARIAN
bakonyi gombamártás	mushroom sauce HUNGARIAN
bakpoeder	baking powder DUTCH
bakpulver	baking powder SWEDISH
bakt	baked NORWEGIAN
balachan	important Indonesian dish containing shrimps or prawns INDONESIAN
balachaung	South Indian pickle made from salted prawns INDIAN

balandėliai	cabbage rolls stuffed with minced lamb and rice LITHUANIAN
balane	acorn barnacle FRENCH
baldpate widgeon	perhaps the best known bird in North America, with a white crown and short narrow bill AMERICAN
baleine	whale FRENCH
baleron	large ham sausage POLISH
balik pilâki	traditional fish dish amongst Turkish Jews TURKISH
baliste	triggerfish FRENCH
balka	cake rather like pannetone, usually eaten at festivals POLISH
ballon	brandy glass FRENCH
ballotine	galantine of meat, poultry, game or fish, which is boned, stuffed, rolled into a bundle and usually served hot FRENCH
balm	lemon-scented herb
Balmoral tin loaf	rounded, fluted loaf tin
balnamoon skink	old Irish soup of boiled chicken, herbs, chives, celery, lettuce and green peas, thickened with egg yolk and mixed with cream IRISH
balorine	minced beef, spring onions, beetroot and caraway seeds FRANCO-RUSSIAN
balsamic vinegar	rich, dark-coloured vinegar
balti	bucket; now the pan in which a balti dish is cooked; method of marinating and simmering cubes of meat in a sauce INDIAN
bambelle	small fish of the carp family FRENCH
bamboo shoot	conical shaped shoot of a bamboo plant
bami goreng	casserole of noodles, vegetables, diced pork and shrimps DUTCH
bámia	okra HUNGARIAN
bamies	okra GREEK
bamya	okra TURKISH
banaan	banana DUTCH
banaan	banana DUTCH
banaani	banana FINNISH
banan	banana DANISH, NORWEGIAN, SWEDISH
banán	banana HUNGARIAN
banana	tropical fruit with a bright yellow skin and pale, sweet, soft flesh

banana flour   nutritious flour made from dried, ground bananas, used to make cakes and biscuits

banana pepper   *see* Hungarian yellow wax

banana split   banana split in two lengthways, arranged with scoops of ice cream, and topped with sauces, nuts, cherries and whipped cream

banana, dried   dried whole or sliced, can be eaten as they are or soaked

Banane   banana GERMAN

banany   banana POLISH

Banbury cake   flat, oval cake of flaky pastry filled with dried cake

ENGLISH

bande   pastry base, slice FRENCH

bangers   colloquial name for sausages ENGLISH

Bangladeshi   fairly hot style of cooking INDIAN

banilia   vanilla GREEK

banilles   long tapering pods of plant similar to vanilla FRENCH

bànitsa   paper-thin pastry tart with a variety of fillings

BULGARIAN

bank cress   alternative name for American cress AMERICAN

bankebiff   slices or chunks of beef simmered in gravy

NORWEGIAN

bankekød   stewed beef, peppercorns, onions and bay leaves

DANISH

banketletter   puff pastry roll with almond paste filling, shaped into a letter of the alphabet DUTCH

banmirchi   capsicum INDIAN

banneton   receptacle with holes used in France to keep fish in a tank, pulled up when the fish is needed for cooking; a baker's basket FRENCH

bannock   large round scone made from barley flour, oatmeal or barley meal, baked on a griddle SCOTTISH

bano de azúcar   icing SPANISH

baño maria   bain marie SPANISH

banon   Provençal ewe's milk cheese wrapped in chestnut leaves or flavoured with a variety of wild savory called poivre d'âne FRENCH

banquière, à la   suprême sauce coloured with tomatoes and blended with butter and veal with a little Madeira wine; garnish of braised quenelles and truffles FRENCH

bantam   small, brightly-coloured fowl

bap	flat, oval breakfast roll made from yeast dough containing a little fat SCOTTISH
bar	dog fish
Bär	bear GERMAN
bär	berry SWEDISH
barščiai	beetroot soup LITHUANIAN
bara brith	'speckled loaf'; cake made with yeast or baking powder containing currants and caraway seeds WELSH
baranina	lamb POLISH
baranina	mutton RUSSIAN, POLISH
baranka	cake like a round, unsweetened, unsalted doughnut sprinkled with poppy seeds RUSSIAN
bárány	lamb HUNGARIAN
bárányhús	lamb HUNGARIAN
baraquilles	hot hors d'œuvre of pastry shells filled with a salpicon of game birds, sweetbreads, foie gras and mushrooms, bound with sauce allemande flavoured with Madeira FRENCH
barashek iz masla	traditional symbolic lamb used for the ritual Easter table, made from butter moulded to the shape of a lamb RUSSIAN
barbabietola	beetroot ITALIAN
barbada	dab SPANISH
barbadine	edible fruit of the elderflower or grenadilla tree FRENCH
barbarin	surmullet; fish of the mullet family FRENCH
barbarine	variety of American squash AMERICAN
Barbe	barbel GERMAN
barbeau	barbel FRENCH
barbecue	outdoor cooking over coals, giving it a smoky flavour
barbecue sauce	sauce spread on meat before cooking on a barbecue
barbe-de-capucin	wild straight endive FRENCH
barbel	fish of the carp family found in many European waters, and in Africa and Asia where it grows three times larger; eaten in France grilled, fried or cooked in white wine, but not eaten much in England
Barberey	(or Troyes – the name of the region where it is made) soft Camembert-like cheese made from fresh warm rennetted cow's milk FRENCH
barberon	the name in southern France for salsify FRENCH

barberry	thorny shrub with sour red berries used to made jelly or pickled for use as a garnish
barbo	barbel SPANISH
barbotine	tansy or mugwort, used as a flavouring in cakes FRENCH
barbounia	red mullet GREEK
barbue	brill FRENCH
barbuta	brill ITALIAN
barcelonesa	mutton broth flavoured with tomatoes, thickened with white breadcrumbs and garnished with small minced mutton meatballs SPANISH
barding	covering breast of poultry with pieces of bacon to prevent drying out during roasting; rashers of streaky bacon used to line a pâté or terrine
barding fat	slices of bacon fat or fresh or salt pork cut very thin to wrap round food
barge	godwit, prepared like woodcock FRENCH
barigoule	mushroom from the south of France; globe artichokes stuffed with mushrooms FRENCH
bärkräm	fruit cream made with raspberries, gooseberries, strawberries or currants SWEDISH
Bar-le-Duc	town in Lorraine famous for its redcurrant preserve FRENCH
barley	one of the earliest cultivated cereals, used in Scotch whiskies, malt drinks, malt extracts and as fodder
barley sugar	hard toffee flavoured with lemon
barley water	infusion of pearl barley in water, cooled, strained and often flavoured with lemon
barm	the yeast formed on the top of malt liqueur when fermenting; a form of yeast used in bread making
barm brack	yeast cake containing dried fruits soaked in tea Irish
barnacle	species of crustacea, some of which are edible
barnacle goose	wild goose from Arctic regions, not as succulent as domesticated goose
baron of beef	two sirloins of beef left uncut at the backbone and roasted; in France 'baron' describes the same cut of lamb ENGLISH, FRENCH
barquette	small, filled boat-shaped pastry case FRENCH
barracuda	vicious pike-like sea fish
barrot	small barrel containing anchovies FRENCH
Barsac	wine from the region of Bordeaux FRENCH
Barsch	perch GERMAN

barse	old name for perch (from bass) ENGLISH
barszcz	traditional soup; there are many varieties, but the basic ingredient in many of them is beetroot POLISH
barszcz czerwony borsch;	beetroot soup POLISH
bartavelle	rock-partridge FRENCH
Bartlett pear	William pear AMERICAN
Baseler art	'Basel-style'; Swiss sauce; garnish for fried fish SWISS
Baseler leckerli	small biscuits from Basel SWISS
basella	green vegetable prepared and cooked as spinach, also known as Malabar spinach, Ceylon spinach, Indian spinach
baselle	basella FRENCH
basil	herb with a distinctive pungent taste and aromatic scent
basilic	basil FRENCH
basilico	basil ITALIAN
basilico	basil SPANISH
basilicum	basil DUTCH
Basilikum	basil GERMAN
basmati	long-grained rice
basquaise, à la	garnish of fried ceps and dariole moulds of pommes anna, sprinkled with Bayonne ham; beef broth garnished with peppers and tomatoes; a method of serving potatoes FRENCH
bass	round sea fish similar to salmon in shape
basse venaison	the meat of hare or wild rabbit FRENCH
bassine	hemispherical copper bowl for beating egg whites FRENCH
bastable oven	iron pot with a lid, handles and three short legs, suspended by chains over a turf fire IRISH
bastardue	bustard FRENCH
basting	moistening meat, poultry or game during roasting by spooning over the juices and fat from the tin
bastion	method of arranging dishes in aspic; applied mainly to fish and especially eels FRENCH
bastourma	ham of Armenian origin, heavily-spiced with garlic and cayenne pepper TURKISH, EGYPTIAN
basturma	marinated beef fillets threaded onto skewers RUSSIAN
bat	the tail of a fish FRENCH

ba-ta-clan a rich pastry including almonds and rum, invented by Lacam, a famous 19th-century Parisian pastry-cook FRENCH

batalia pye traditional pie filled with young chickens or pigeons, cock's combs, sweetbreads, lamb's stones (testicles), oysters, gizzards, tongues, spices and butter ENGLISH

bâtarde butter sauce made from a roux, boiling salt water, the yolk of an egg, butter and lemon juice FRENCH

batata potato PORTUGUESE

batata sweet potato; yam SPANISH

bateaux small boat-shaped containers of china or glass, used for serving cold hors d'œuvres FRENCH

batelière, à la fish garnish of mushrooms, silver onions, fried eggs and crayfish; fish fillets with small pastries filled with shrimps and mussels in wine sauce, and gudgeon coated with breadcrumbs and fried FRENCH

Bath bun yeast bun topped with coarse sugar crystals ENGLISH

Bath chap the lower half of a pig's head, cured like bacon ENGLISH

Bath cheese cow's milk cheese now no longer made ENGLISH

Bath Oliver plain cracker, usually served with butter and cheese ENGLISH

bâton loaf in the form of a long stick FRENCH

bâtonnets biscuits and pastries in the form of sticks FRENCH

battelmatt an Italian copy of the Swiss cheese of the same name ITALIAN

Battelmatt Käse a Swiss cheese made from cow's milk GERMAN

Battenburg cake oblong sponge cake, square in cross sections, with the square further divided into four smaller squares, two pink and two yellow, assembled with jam, the whole with marzipan on the outside; perhaps named after Battenburg, a Prussian village covered

batter thick liquid mixture of flour, eggs and milk

battuto recipe for the first preparation of a soup or stew ITALIAN

baudroie angler fish FRENCH

Bauernbrot rye or wholemeal bread GERMAN

Bauernfrühstück 'peasant's breakfast'; scrambled eggs, cooked meats, bacon, mixed vegetables, fried potatoes and fried tomatoes GERMAN

Bauernklösse farmhouse dumplings GERMAN

Bauernomelett diced bacon and onion omelette GERMAN

Bauernschmaus	pork chops, bacon, and sausages cooked in beer with sauerkraut, cumin seeds, grated potatoes and onions AUSTRIAN
Bauernsuppe	thick soup of sliced frankfurters and cabbage GERMAN
baume	various plants of the mint family FRENCH
baume de coq	alecost FRENCH
Baumnuß	walnut GERMAN
baunilha	vanilla PORTUGUESE
Bavarian blue	rich, soft, blue pasteurised cow's milk cheese GERMAN
bavarois	crème bavarois is a cold custard-based dish containing whipped cream, served with various flavourings and garnishes
bavaroise	hot drink of eggs, sugar and boiling milk flavoured with vanilla or liqueur FRENCH
baw-wong	onion BM
baw-wong poo-tay	garlic BM
bay	herb with a strong spicy flavour
bayam	*see* amaranth, calaloo, Chinese spinach
bay salt	rock salt
bayonnaise, à la	garnish of cooked macaroni in cream sauce with julienne of Bayonne ham; macaroni croquettes with Bayonne ham and tomato-flavoured sauce FRENCH
Bayonne	the town where the wine-cured Bayonne ham, usually eaten raw in thin slices, is prepared FRENCH
Bayrische griesklösse	Bavarian soup dumplings GERMAN
Bayrische Leberknödel	veal and liver dumplings, served with sauerkraut GERMAN
Bayrisches kraut	Bavarian method of cooking cabbage braised with bacon GERMAN
bazsalikom	basil HUNGARIAN
bean	leguminous plant of which there are many varieties; the seeds and sometimes the pod are used as a vegetable
bean sprouts	the shoots of germinated dried beans – an interesting addition to salads, sandwiches and stir-fry
bean, broad ·	thought to be the original bean; cultivated in pre-historic Egypt, it has a tough pod with a furry lining
bean, curd	(tofu) pressed purée of soya beans; available in various forms
bean, French	annual of South American origin; the beans are small, thin and available all year

bean, paste	very salty paste made from fermented soya beans, used in cooking and as a condiment
bean, runner	fast-climbing perennial introduced from Mexico, usually grown as an annual
beard	gills of an oyster; which can be removed before consumption; the byssus of a mussel, which it uses to cling to rocks, should always be removed before cooking
béatilles	'titbits'; a dish of small ingredients such as cocks' combs, sweetbreads, liver and mushrooms, cooked in Madeira and butter FRENCH
beating	incorporating air into a mixture by agitating it vigorously with a spoon, fork or whisk
béatrix	garnish for meat of morel mushrooms fried in butter, or quartered artichoke bottoms with small young carrots and pommes fondantes FRENCH
Beaufort	hard cow's milk cheese from the highlands of the Jura and Savoy mountains. FRENCH
beauharnais, à la	béarnaise sauce with tarragon but without chervil; garnish for meat of stuffed mushrooms and quartered artichoke hearts; chicken broth with paupiettes of lettuce, asparagus and truffles FRENCH
Beaujolais	light, short lived, fruity red wine made from grapes grown in the Lyon region FRENCH
Beaumont	cow's milk cheese FRENCH
Beaupré de Roybon	cow's milk cheese from the Dauphiné region FRENCH
beauvilliers	garnish of stuffed tomatoes with purée of brains, salsify and spinach; a cake almost identical to bonvalet FRENCH
beaver	large semiaquatic rodent, no longer common in Europe and now eaten only in Germany; the American beaver was once enjoyed by North American Indians and by trappers but not often eaten today; when skinning, the musk glands must be avoided – if they are damaged, the meat is completely spoilt
becada	woodcock; snipe SPANISH
bécard	'hooked nose'; term used for old salmon FRENCH
bécasse	woodcock FRENCH
bécasse de mer	local name in the south of France for red mullet FRENCH
bécasseau	young woodcock until they are eight months old FRENCH

bécassin	great snipe FRENCH
bécassine	snipe FRENCH
bécassine la sourde	jacksnipe FRENCH
becatses	woodcock GREEK
beccabunga	brooklime FRENCH
beccaccia	woodcock; snipe ITALIAN
beccafico	figeater ITALIAN
bec-figue	figeater or figpecker FRENCH
béchamel	white sauce used as the basis for a number of dishes and other sauces FRENCH
bécisiszelet	fried veal fillets. HUNGARIAN
bec-plat	spoonbill FRENCH
bec-pointu	small white skate from the Atlantic FRENCH
bécsi heringsaláta	herring salad HUNGARIAN
bécsi szelet	Wiener schnitzel HUNGARIAN
bedgi	an aromatic variety of chilli from Goa INDIAN
bediening	service DUTCH
bedstraw	plant with yellow flowers used to curdle milk and to make Cheshire cheese
beech nut	small triangular nut from the beech tree; similar in taste to the hazelnut; it makes a fine oil
beef	meat of bullock, cow or bull
beef olive	thin slices of beef topside rolled around a stuffing of breadcrumbs and cooked in stock in the oven
beef tea	concentrated beef stock
beef Wellington	dish made with a cut of tender beef
beef, corned	beef cooked and preserved in salt
beef olives	thin slices of beef filled with a stuffing, rolled up, secured (sometimes rashers of bacon are rolled round the outside of the beef) and braised with root vegetables in stock
beef stroganoff	slices of beef cooked with onions, mushrooms, seasoning and served in a sour-cream sauce (after the 19th-century Russian displomat Count Paul Stroganoff)
beefburger	minced beef patties usually served in a roll, often with cheese, salad and relishes (a false analogy with Hamburger)
beer	alcoholic beverage produced by fermentation of malted barley and hops
beer bread	bread made with beer instead of yeast

Beere	berry GERMAN
beestings	the first milk from a cow after calving, not normally sold
beet	vegetables grown for their fleshy roots
beetroot	vegetable with bulbous, dark red edible root and leaves which can be eaten like spinach
befsztyk	beefsteak POLISH
begun bahar	mild northern sauce of blended spices, bananas and cream INDIAN
béhague	chicken broth with poached egg and chopped chervil FRENCH
beigli	cake traditionally eaten at Christmas time HUNGARIAN
beignet	small ball-shaped doughnut; small vegetable, poultry or meat fritter coated in batter and deep fried FRENCH
Beilage	side dish; garnish GERMAN
békacomb gombával és rákkal	frogs' legs with freshwater crab and mushrooms HUNGARIAN
békacomb paprikásan	frogs' legs in paprika sauce HUNGARIAN
bekasy	snipe POLISH
bekkasin	snipe, often braised with sour cream DANISH
bekkasin	snipe NORWEGIAN
bekkørret	river trout NORWEGIAN
Bel Paese	smooth cheese with a delicate taste ITALIAN
belegd broodje	roll with variety of garnishes DUTCH
belegen kaas	pungent-flavoured cheese DUTCH
belegte Brot	open sandwich GERMAN
beli sir	cheese pickled in brine YUGOSLAVIAN
bell pepper	the mildest and most popular member of the capsicum family; also known as capsicum, sweet pepper, pimiento, simla mirch, red and green pepper
belle Hélène	garnish of grilled mushrooms stuffed with cooked tomato or green peas, young carrots and potato croquettes; pears poached in vanilla-flavoured syrup, served with vanilla ice cream FRENCH
belle-alliance	winter pear, yellowish on one side and red on the other FRENCH
belle-angevine	very large winter dessert pear FRENCH
belle-chevreuse	bright red variety of peach FRENCH
belle-de-berry	variety of pear FRENCH
belle-et-bonne	variety of cooking pear FRENCH
belle-garde	pear with firm flesh FRENCH

Bellelay cheese	whole cow's milk cheese with a delicate flavour SWISS
bellona	very large fig grown in Provence. FRENCH
beluga	white sturgeon from the Black and Caspian seas; its roe is the beluga caviar RUSSIAN
belyashi	Siberian meat tarts RUSSIAN
ben cotto	well cooked; rusk, biscuit ITALIAN
bénari	a kind of ortolan found in the Langedoc region FRENCH
bénédictin	almond-flavoured sponge cake sprinkled with the liqueur of the same name FRENCH
Bénédictine	herb-based liqueur first created by an Italian Bénédictine monk FRENCH
bénédictine, à la	garnish for fish or eggs; method of serving potatoes
Bengali	hot and spicy INDIAN
benløse fugle	slices of veal or beef stuffed with bacon, parsley and onions DANISH
benløse fugler	rolled slices of veal stuffed with minced meat NORWEGIAN
bentoo no tomo	seasoning from coarsely ground dried fish, salt, soy sauce, seaweed and monosodium glutamate JAPANESE
beolas	fritter, sometimes sprinkled with cinnamon sugar, lemon zest and water JEWISH
berberecho	cockle SPANISH
berbigão	type of cockle PORTUGUESE
berce	cow parsnip FRENCH
Berchoux	sauce allemande with herb butter and cream; game broth garnished with quail, chestnut royale, mushrooms and truffles FRENCH
bercy	fish sauce of white wine and shallots; meat sauce of white wine, butter and shallots and meat marrow FRENCH
berebere	a variety of scarlet chilli ETHIOPIAN
berenjena	aubergine SPANISH
Bergkäse	hard cheese from western Austria AUSTRIAN
bergamot	small citrus fruit (*Citrus bergamia*) grown mostly in Sicily and Calabria; a fragrant essential oil is extracted from its rind and the candied fruit is used as decoration
beringela	aubergine PORTUGUESE
Berliner kranser	small, glazed pastry rings NORWEGIAN

berlingot   hard, sweet toffee, usually flavoured with peppermint FRENCH

bernard-l'ermite   hermit crab FRENCH

Berner platte   dish from Berne of thin slices of beef, sauerkraut, chopped pig's trotter, bacon and Würst, served with potatoes SWISS

berny   mashed potatoes with chopped truffles, rolled in almonds and fried; garnish of berny potato croquettes and pastry tarts filled with lentils and chestnuts; beef broth with pommes dauphines, almonds and truffles FRENCH

berraza   parsnip SPANISH

berrichonne, à la   garnish of glazed button onions, chestnuts, bacon and braised balls of cabbage; method of serving potatoes FRENCH

berro   watercress SPANISH

berry   small fruit without a stone

berry, in   fish eggs in roe; a hen lobster carrying eggs

bertiche   perch ITALIAN

bertines mandelbunn   very rich apple meringue pie NORWEGIAN

berza   cabbage SPANISH

besamel   white sauce CZECH

besan   chick peas INDIAN

besan flour   pale yellow flour made from dried chick peas INDIAN

besan roti   bread made from chick pea flour INDIAN

besciamella   béchamel sauce ITALIAN

besi   several varieties of pear; in the Jura region it means salted, fried cow's meat FRENCH

bessensoep   traditional soup of vermicelli, potato flour, redcurrant juice and a little sugar BELGIAN

besugo   sunfish; type of seabream PORTUGUESE

besugo   sea bream SPANISH

betasuppe   thick mutton soup NORWEGIAN

bête de campagne   wild boar between one and two years old FRENCH

betel leaf   leaf from the betel vine used in Indian cooking INDIAN

betel nut   hard, small nut, stimulant added to Indian pan, chewed after a meal as a digestive stimulant and narcotic; slightly poisonous in its untreated state INDIAN

beterraba   beetroot PORTUGUESE

betony	weed thought to have magical properties; the leaves and flowers make a tea
betterave	beetroot FRENCH
beurre	butter FRENCH
beurré	dessert pear FRENCH
beurre composés	fresh butter worked with herbs or other foods, served as a garnish FRENCH
beurre manié	paste of butter and flour; used to thicken soups, stews and casseroles after cooking is complete FRENCH
beurre noir	'black butter'; sauce of butter cooked until dark brown and mixing with warm vinegar and flavouring FRENCH
beurre noisette	sauce of butter cooked until golden brown with a nutty aroma, flavoured with lemon juice and seasoning FRENCH
beurre, au	cooked in or served in butter FRENCH
Beuschel	lights; lungs. GERMAN
beveca	coconut pudding INDIAN
beverage	any liquid other than water consumed as a drink
bezy	meringue POLISH
břnenskýrizek	thin veal fillets stuffed with scrambled egg, butter, green peas and chopped ham CZECH
bhaji, bhajee	'fried'; fried vegetable dish served as a starter or as an accompaniment to a curry INDIAN
bhare	stuffed INDIAN
bhindi	okra; ladies' fingers INDIAN
bhoona, bhuna	fried dry dish of medium spiciness INDIAN
bhooni	crisp INDIAN
biała kiełbasa	pork sausage POLISH
białko	egg white POLISH
bianchetti	small white fish found especially off the Tuscan coast ITALIAN
Biberschwanz	beaver's tail GERMAN
bicarbonate of soda	white powder used as a raising agent when added to an acid
biche	female deer FRENCH
biešu sakņu saláti	beetroot salad flavoured with caraway, sugar, and vinegar or lemon juice LATVIAN
biefstuk	rump steak DUTCH
bien cuit	well cooked FRENCH

bien hecho	well done SPANISH
bien me sabe	pudding made from grated coconut an its milk; Spanish custard-like pudding eaten cold PUERTO RICAN
Bienenstich	honey and almond cake GERMAN
Bierkaltsuppe	cold soup made using light beers, currants, brown breadcrumbs, cinnamon and lemon juice AUSTRIAN, GERMAN
Bierplinse	batter made from dark beer instead of milk GERMAN
Bierrettitch	black radish, generally cut, salted and served with beer GERMAN
Biersuppe	soup of mild beer, cinnamon, spices and peel, garnished with pieces of fried bread GERMAN
Bierwürst	dried spiced pork sausage, sometimes flavoured with garlic GERMAN
bieslook	chives DUTCH
bieten	beetroot DUTCH
bietole	beetroot leaves ITALIAN
bifana	slice of pork tenderloin usually served in a bun PORTUGUESE
bife	steak, escalope PORTUGUESE
biff	beefsteak NORWEGIAN, SWEDISH
bifinhos de vitela	slices of veal fillet served with Madeira wine sauce PORTUGUESE
bifshtek	beefsteak RUSSIAN
bifstik	beefsteak BM
biftec, bistec	beefsteak SPANISH
bifteck	from 'beefsteak', a slice of beef taken from the fillet, sirloin or contre-filet; minced beef eaten cooked or raw FRENCH
bigarade, à la	cooked or served with orange or orange sauce FRENCH
bigarreau	a hard-fleshed cherry FRENCH
bighorn	wild sheep found in the Rocky Mountains AMERICAN
Big Jim	the world's largest chilli, developed in 1975 by Dr Makayame; specimens up to 17 inches have been grown
bigné	kind of fritter eaten in Rome on St Joseph's Day (19 March) ITALIAN
bigorneaux	periwinkles FRENCH
bigos	layered casserole of sauerkraut, cooked meat, game, pork sausages, apples, ham, lard, flour, tomato essence, onions, vodka, and wine POLISH

bijane	cold soup containing crumbled bread steeped in sweetened red wine FRENCH
biksemad	leftover meat, fried with slices of potato and onion and gravy DANISH
bilberry	small dark blue berry with a distinctly acid taste
biltong	seasoned, dried strips of meat SOUTH AFRICAN
bindaloo	*see* vindaloo INDIAN
Bindenfleisch	very thin wafers of air-dried beef, dressed with vinaigrette SWISS
binding	holding a mixture together with liquid, gelatine, egg or fat
Birchermüesli	uncooked oats with raw, shredded fruit and chopped nuts in milk or yoghurt GERMAN
bird	very small, hot, wild chilli which grows all over African, and which attracts birds who eat them and distribute the seeds via their droppings
bird's-foot trefoil	small plant with yellow spiky flowers, thought to have magical properties; used as a herb in France
bird's-nest soup	speciality made from the outer part of the nest of South East Asian swifts, genus *Collocalia* CHINESE
birkahús	mutton HUNGARIAN
Birne	pear GERMAN
birsalma	quince HUNGARIAN
biryani	basmati rice with meat or fish, coloured with turmeric or saffron and flavoured with cumin, cardamom, coriander and other spices INDIAN
Bischofsbrot	'bishop's bread'; a cake made with dried fruit, nuts, peel and candied fruit AUSTRIAN
Bischofsbrot	fruit and nut cake GERMAN
biscoito	biscuit PORTUGUESE
biscotins	small biscuits served with ice cream FRENCH
biscotte	rusk FRENCH
biscuit	small flat, baked, sweet or savoury cake with crisp dry texture
biset	rock pigeon; wading bird not unlike a wild duck FRENCH
bishop	favourite drink of the Middle Ages described as 'port wine made copiously potable by being mulled and burnt with the adenda of roasted lemons studded with cloves and bristling like angry hedgehogs'
bishop's hat	a cut of halibut

Biskuitrolle	Swiss roll; jelly and butter-cream roll GERMAN
Biskuitschöberisuppe	very rich beef broth, garnished with lozenge-shaped biscuits AUSTRIAN
biskupsky chlebíček	fruit cake CZECH
biskut	biscuit BM
Bismarckheringe	Bismark herrings, scaled, cleaned, soaked in vinegar, seasoned, layered with onion and left for 24 hours before eating GERMAN
Bismarcksuppe	strong port-flavoured consommé, garnished with diced mushrooms and grated cheese GERMAN
bison	American bison, buffalo, much-hunted North American cattle (*Bison bison*)
bisque	rich, creamy soup consisting mainly of a thick purée of shellfish or game FRENCH
Bisquit	a brandy FRENCH
bistecca	beefsteak ITALIAN
bístola de roca	fish (called forkbread in English) belonging to the cod family SPANISH
bistort	perennial plant with pink flowers and astringent properties, used in traditional Easter puddings
biszkoptowe ciasto	sponge cake POLISH
biszkopty	fancy biscuits POLISH
bit	piece SWEDISH
bita śmietana	whipped sour cream with sugar, flavoured with vanilla pods POLISH
bite size	marketspeak for an undersized fruit, *etc*
bitki	traditional meatballs POLISH, RUSSIAN
bits	local name for a herb believed only to be found in north Cornwall ENGLISH
bitter melon	cucumber-like melon from South East Asia
bitterbal	sharp-flavoured meatball, eaten hot with mustard as an appetiser DUTCH
bittern	nocturnal water-bird, highly prized during the 16th and 17th centuries
bitters	apéritifs made from distilled spirits flavoured with roots, herbs and barks
bitto	cheese made from a mixture of cow's and goat's milk ITALIAN
bivalve	shellfish with two shells hinged together
bizcocho	sponge cake SPANISH
bizcotela	glazed biscuit SPANISH

bizet	chicken consommé thickened with tapioca and garnished with chicken quenelles and chopped herbs FRENCH
björnbär	blackberry SWEDISH
bjørnebær	blackberry NORWEGIAN
blåbær	bilberry DANISH, NORWEGIAN
blåbær	bilberry NORWEGIAN
blåbär	bilberry or blueberry SWEDISH
blachan	prawn paste
black bean	dried beans with a shiny black casing and white flesh
black bean, Chinese	fermented, salted soya beans, used as flavouring CHINESE
black bryony	climbing gourd; the young shoots are edible but must be soaked before boiling in salt water
black bun	spiced plum cake with a pastry case, eaten at Hogmanay SCOTTISH
black cumin	an umbelliferous plant whose seeds are used as a spice
black duck	*see* ringneck AMERICAN
Black Forest Gâteau	layers of rich chocolate sponge cake soaked in kirsch-flavoured syrup, filled with whipped double cream mixed with black cherries
black gram bean	small dried bean with black outer casing; available whole or split
black pudding	type of sausage made of pig's blood, suet, breadcrumbs, oatmeal, onions and seasoning
black radish preserve	traditional jam eaten during Passover, especially popular in Russia JEWISH
blackberry	small soft fruit, dark red to black in colour, available wild and cultivated
blackbird	song bird of the thrush family usually served in a pâté or a terrine
blackcock	game bird resembling grouse in taste
blackcurrant	black, juicy fruit of a northern European shrub
black-eyed bean	cream-coloured dried bean with a black spot
black-eyed pea	also known as the cow pea
blackfin	chavender, or chub AMERICAN
blackfish	collective name for various dark or black fishes
black-throated diver	fish-eating bird, inferior to wild duck but prepared in the same way
bladder	membranous sac in which certain dishes may be cooked

bladsalat	lettuce NORWEGIAN
bladselleir	celery DANISH
bladspenat	spinach SWEDISH
blanc, au	dish, often chicken or veal, white in colour or cooked in white stock FRENCH
blanch, to	brief immersion of food in boiling water to whiten it or to aid removal of skins
blanchaille	whitebait FRENCH
blanche de volaille	boned breast of fowl FRENCH
blanchir	to blanch FRENCH
blancmange	traditionally an almond-flavoured dessert, but today made with milk and cornflour and flavoured with chocolate, strawberry or vanilla
blandad	mixed, assorted SWEDISH
blandede grønnsaker	mixed vegetables NORWEGIAN
blando	soft SPANISH
blanquet	variety of French pear mainly used for compotes FRENCH
blanquette	stew made from white meat cooked in white sauce enriched with cream and egg yolk FRENCH
Blarney cheese	cow's milk cheese IRISH
blåskjell	mussel NORWEGIAN
Blätterteig	puff pastry GERMAN
Blau	freshly poached fish GERMAN
Blaubeere	bilberry (US: blueberry) GERMAN
Blaufisch	'blue fish'; boiling tarragon or wine vinegar is poured over unscaled fresh water fish and left to stand – this gives it a blue shimmer GERMAN
Blaukraut	method of cooking shredded red cabbage GERMAN
blaundesorye	mediaeval dish of curd mixed with minced white meat and almonds ENGLISH
blawn fish	'wind blown'; traditional dish of cleaned, skinned fish hung in a current of air, rolled in flour and grilled with butter ORKNEY ISLANDS
blazinde moldovenești	cheesecake ROMANIAN
blé noir	buckwheat FRENCH
bleak	small European fish of the carp family
blender	electric machine with rotating blades, used to purée wet mixture and grind dry ingredients
blending	mixing flour, cornflour and similar ground cereals to a smooth paste with cold liquid before adding to a boiling liquid

blennie cagnette	European freshwater fish of the blenny family FRENCH
blenny	small European and American sea fish, prepared like whitebait
blette	chard or spinach beet FRENCH
bleu d'Auvergne	cow's milk cheese of the Roquefort type FRENCH
bleu de Basillac	blue mould cheese of the Roquefort type FRENCH
bleu de Bresse	quite recent subtle-flavoured creamy blue cheese FRENCH
bleu de Laqueuille	bleu d'Auvergne cheese from the Puy-de-Dôme region FRENCH
bleu de Sassenage	blue-veined, semi-hard cow's milk cheese from the Isère department FRENCH
bleu naturel de L'Aveyron	blue-veined cheese made in small quantities in the Millau and Sainte-Afrique districts FRENCH
bleu, au	fish cooked in white wine with herbs, or in water containing salt and vinegar, immediately it is caught FRENCH
blewitt	edible fungus with a lilac stem
blinchki s tvorogom	small, thin pancakes cooked on one side and rolled up with a cheese mixture RUSSIAN
blinde vinken	stuffed veal fillets (veal bird) DUTCH
blini	buckwheat pancake SWEDISH
blintz, blintze	pancake fried on one side, filled with cream, cottage cheese or pot cheese, apple, cinnamon, fruits and preserves or minced meat, and fried JEWISH
blinut	bliny eaten at Shrovetide FINNISH
bliny	Russian-style pancakes POLISH
bloater	gutted herring, salted and smoked without being flattened like a kipper
blødkogt æg	soft-boiled egg DANISH
blodpølse	black pudding (US: blood sausage) DANISH
blodpudding	black pudding (US: blood sausage) NORWEGIAN, SWEDISH
bloedworst	black pudding DUTCH
bloedworst met appelen	black pudding with cooked apples DUTCH
bloemkool	cauliflower DUTCH
blomkål	cauliflower DANISH, SWEDISH, NORWEGIAN
blomme	plum DANISH
blond de veau	concentrated veal broth used for mixing with soups and sauces FRENCH

blond de volaille   blond de veau made with chicken FRENCH

blonde, sauce   velouté sauce beaten with egg yolks, served with white meats and poultry FRENCH

blondiner   sliced onion fried in butter until pale yellow, described by Alexandre Dumas FRENCH

blondir   to brown very lightly FRENCH

blood   enriching and thickening agent in traditional English country cooking

bloodwort   red-veined variety of dock, used as a herb and cooked as spinach or sorrel

Bloody Mary   cocktail of vodka and tomato juice, seasoned with Worcestershire and tabasco sauce, served over crushed ice

bløtkake   rice sponge layer cake NORWEGIAN

blue Castello   blue cow's milk cheese with soft creamy texture DANISH

blue Cheshire   red Cheshire to which blue veins are added ENGLISH

blue Dorset   white, crumbly blue cheese with a sharp strong flavour, made in Dorset ENGLISH

blue grouse   large member of the grouse family, found in North America

blue Shropshire   mild cheese with a misleading name, because it is orange and comes from Leicestershire ENGLISH

blue veined cheese   cheese with veins of blue-green mould culture

blue-back, or red salmon   species of salmon from the waters of the Pacific; not a true salmon, nor as tasty

blueberry   small, round and black, similar to bilberry but a little larger

bluefish   medium-sized blue fish from the North Atlantic and the Mediterranean

Bluefort   blue-veined cow's milk cheese DUTCH

Bluefort cheese   trade name of a 'blue' cheese of the Roquefort type CANADIAN

Blumenkohl   cauliflower GERMAN

Blutwürst   sausage made from pig's blood and pork and bacon fat, flavoured with herbs, spices and onions GERMAN

boar   wild pig, extinct in Britain (though attempts are being made to reintroduce it) but living elsewhere in Europe; only the young animal is considered edible

bób   broad bean POLISH

bobkovy list   laurel CZECH

bobó
a dish made from dried shrimps, onions, cassava root, fish stock, palm-oil and coconut milk, served with bananas and grated coconut PORTUGUESE

bobotie
baked meat or vegetable pie with a baked egg topping, it is one of South Africa's national dishes SOUTH AFRICAN

bob-white
quail found in America, from Canada to Mexico; its name comes from its call AMERICAN

bocadillo
sandwich; sweet SPANISH

bocal
wide-mouthed glass jar used in France for bottling or pickling fruit or vegetables FRENCH

bocconcini
diced meat with herbs; thin slices of veal with slices of Gruyère cheese and fresh tomato sauce ITALIAN

boccone squadrista
cutlets of fish cooked between two slices of apple, sprinkled with rum and ignited when served ITALIAN

bochník
loaf CZECH

böckling
small Baltic herring SWEDISH

Bockwürst
boiled sausage GERMAN

boczek
spare ribs; bacon POLISH

boerenkool
kale DUTCH

boerenkool met worst
kale mixed with mashed potatoes, served with smoked sausage DUTCH

boerenomelet
omelette with diced vegetables and bacon DUTCH

boeuf
beef FRENCH

boeuf Stroganoff
beef stroganoff POLISH

bøf
fillet of beef or beefsteak DANISH

bog myrtle
once a popular aromatic herb, with a flavour similar to bay

bogavante
lobster SPANISH

boghvedegrød
porridge of buckwheat and milk, with butter, beer, sugar and cinnamon added to taste DANISH

bogue
Mediterranean fish; two species are known

bohémienne
mayonnaise with cream and tarragon vinegar; garnish of pilaff rice, tomatoes and fried onion rings; method of serving potatoes; method of serving chicken FRENCH

böhmische Dalken
yeast dough cut into rounds and when risen indented with the finger before baking; served hot with plum jam or redcurrant jelly in the hollow AUSTRIAN

Bohne
bean GERMAN

boi
beef PORTUGUESE

boïeldieu	chicken consommé with quenelles of foie gras and chicken with truffles FRENCH
boiled dressing	type of cooked mayonnaise
boiled sweets	various hard-textured sweets made by boiling sugar, glucose, an acid and fruit
boiling	cooking in liquid, usually water, at 100°C; applied for example, to vegetables, rice and pasta
bois de Sainte-Lucie	cherry tree with sweet-smelling wood FRENCH
boitelle	garnish for fish of sliced raw mushrooms cooked with the fish FRENCH
bok choy	leafy vegetable with thick white stalks *see* Chinese leaves, headless Chinese cabbage michihili, pe-tsai, wong bok
bokking	bloater DUTCH
bol	bowl FRENCH
bola	yeast cake JEWISH
bola	semi-hard cow's milk cheese PORTUGUESE
bola de Berlim	doughnut PORTUGUESE
bolacha	biscuit PORTUGUESE
bolacha de bacalhau	deep-fried croquette of dried cod and mashed potatoes flavoured with eggs and parsley PORTUGUESE
bolet	boletus FRENCH
boletus	genus of fungi with tube-shaped features under the cap rather than gills; there are wild and edible varieties
bolinho de bacalhau	deep fried minced salt cod fritter made from sieved potatoes, herbs and seasoning mixed with egg white PORTUGUESE
bolitas	fritter SPANISH
bolle	bun; meat or fish ball DANISH
boller	dumpling DANISH, NORWEGIAN
bollito	rich stew made from several different sorts of meats and poultry boiled in one pot and served with vegetables ITALIAN
bollito, bollo	roll, bun SPANISH
bollo maimón	biscuit shaped like a bull ring SPANISH
bolo	cake PORTUGUESE
Bologna sausage	(bolony; polony) large smoked sausage made of seasoned mixed meats AMERICAN
bolognaise sauce	thick meat and tomato sauce served with pasta
bolognese, alla	beef and vegetable sauce traditionally served with spaghetti ITALIAN

bolonaise	in the style of Bologna
bo(u)lting	passing milled grain through a sieve to grade it as part of the milling process
bomba	ice cream made with thick whipped cream, like the French bombe POLISH
Bombay cherry	small chilli from central India INDIAN
Bombay duck	gelatinous fish (*Harpodon negereus*) from Indian and South Asian waters, which is dried, salted, impregnated with asafœtida (which makes it unpalatable to some Western palates) and eaten with curry; now unobtainable in UK through some absurd regulation; also called bommaloe fish INDIAN
Bombay potatoes	potatoes cooked in curry and tomato sauce INDIAN
bombe	metal mould, usually copper with tightly fitting lid, used for shaping ice cream; once turned out the ice cream is also known as a bombe FRENCH
bomboline di ricotta in brodo	broth with ricotta cheese dumplings ITALIAN
bommaloe fish	*see* Bombay duck
bonaparte	chicken consommé with chicken quenelles FRENCH
bonaventure potato cake	mashed potato baked in a flat cake tin, served hot and buttered CANADIAN
bonbons	various kinds of sugar confectionery FRENCH
bonbóny	sweets (US: candy) CZECH
bon-chrétian	pear, usually used for cooking; there are two varieties, one summer and one winter FRENCH
bondart	cow's milk cheese from Normandy FRENCH
bondbönor	broad bean SWEDISH
bondepige med slør	apple pudding, consisting of layers of apple and a mixture of rye and breadcrumbs, topped with grated chocolate or jam and whipped cream DANISH
bondiola	cured shoulder of pork from the provinc of Parma ITALIAN
bondon	small, soft, whole-milk cheeses from Neufchâtel-en-Bray FRENCH
bone(s)	bones from raw or cooked meats can be used to make stock; meat cooked on the bone in dishes such as stews and casse roles are enriched by the collagen that dissolves from the bone to form gelatine; tubular bones contain marrow, a fatty, nutritious substance
boning	removal of bones from meat or poultry, cutting as little of the meat as possible so it can be rolled or stuffed

bonito	oily fish of the genus Sarde found in the Atlantic, Pacific and Mediterranean
bonnach grùan	cod liver bannock, traditionally made on the Isle of Barra SCOTTISH
bonnag	traditional Manx soda bread MANX
bonnag arran oarn	traditional Manx barley meal bread MANX
bønne	bean NORWEGIAN
bonne femme	dish prepared in a simple way, often served in the dish in which it was cooked FRENCH
bonne-bouches	canapés or small items of savoury food served as an appetizer or as a savoury course at the end of a meal FRENCH
bonne-dame	orach(e) FRENCH
bonnefoy	bordelaise sauce with tarragon and with white wine instead of red; it may be garnished with beef marrow FRENCH
bonner	bean DANISH, NORWEGIAN
bonnet turc	variety of pumpkin known in English as Turk's cap FRENCH
bönor	beans SWEDISH
bonvalet	cake created in Paris in the 19th-century, almost identical to beauvilliers but topped with kirsch icing and filled with chantilly cream FRENCH
boo-ah	fruit BM
boo-ah chen-kay	cloves BM
boo-ah soo-soo	passion fruit BM
boo-bor	porridge BM
boo-loo	bamboo BM
boon	bean DUTCH
boondi	type of deep-fried batter crouton INDIAN
boquerón	anchovy; whitebait SPANISH
boquerones	fresh anchovies joined at the tail, floured and pan-fried in the form of a fan SPANISH
boršč	borsch; vegetable soup with meat and sour cream, which may be served hot or chilled CZECH
borage	herb with slightly hairy leaves and bright blue flowers, both of which have a flavour of salt and cucumber
boraggine	borage ITALIAN
bordaloue	plain or garnished beef consommé FRENCH
bord-de-plat	small dish to protect the border of a dish on which food is served FRENCH

Bordeaux	range of quality wines produced in the Bordeaux region FRENCH
bordelaise, à la	dish incorporating wine sauce, bone marrow, ceps, or a garnish of artichokes and potatoes FRENCH
bordure	mixture of ingredients, especially cooked vegetables, arranged in a ring around a dish to contain the other ingredients in the centre FRENCH
börek	fried or baked filo pastry rolls with a savoury filling, commonly of cheese TURKISH
borjúhús	veal HUNGARIAN
borjúmirigy	sweetbreads HUNGARIAN
borjúpörkölt	stew of veal chunks, onions, tomatoes and pepper rings, seasoned with paprika and garlic HUNGARIAN
borlotto bean	speckled, pinkish, dry bean ITALIAN
børnemenu	children's menu DANISH
boro chingri	king prawns INDIAN
boronía	soup of aubergine, pumpkin and tomato, flavoured with garlic, salt, allspice and caraway seeds SPANISH
borowiki	boletus mushrooms POLISH
borówki	bilberries, blueberries POLISH
borracho	young pigeon PORTUGUESE
borrego	lamb PORTUGUESE
borrelhapje	appetiser DUTCH
bors	pepper HUNGARIAN
borsch, borscht, borshch	soup containing beetroot, cabbage and perhaps other vegetables and diced meat – brilliant red in colour EASTERN EUROPEAN
borschok	soup of shredded cabbage, root vegetables and red beetroot, cooked in meat stock; always coloured red and served with soured cream RUSSIAN
borsó	pea HUNGARIAN
borssikeitto	borscht; soup of beetroot, butter, flour, vinegar, served with frankfurter sausage or chopped pieces of ham FINNISH
borstplaat	sweets traditionally eaten on St Nicholas's Eve DUTCH
borststuck	breast, brisket DUTCH
borůvky	bilberries (US: blueberries) CZECH
bosanski lonac	casserole of pork, beef, lamb, vegetables and white wine; lonac is the deep earthenware cooking pot in which it is cooked BOSNIAN
bosbes	bilberry (US: blueberry) DUTCH

bossons   cow's milk cheese from Provence. FRENCH

Boston baked beans haricot beans baked with salt pork, brown sugar, molasses, salt and water for 6 to 8 hours AMERICAN

Boston brown bread bread made from rye flour, cornmeal and whole wheat flour, steamed before baking AMERICAN

Boston fish chowder fish soup with onions, green pepper and celery
                                                                    AMERICAN

Boston scrod   famed delicacy in the fish restaurants of Boston, MA

boszorkányhab   pudding of sieved, baked apples mixed with egg yolk, lemon and sugar HUNGARIAN

bot   flounder; bone DUTCH

botargo   salted, pressed and dried tuna or grey mullet roe

boter   butter DUTCH

boterham   slice of buttered bread DUTCH

botermèlk   buttermilk BELGIAN

boti kebab   marinated cubes of lamb cooked in the tandoor
                                                                      INDIAN

bottling   preserving food in glass jars under sterile conditions

bottomless   marketspeak for continuous refilling of tea or coffee cup

botvinya   traditional cold herb soup RUSSIAN

botwina   beet greens POLISH

bouchée   small, round piece of cooked puff pastry served hot with a savoury filling; small pieces of sponge cake filled with rich cream or jam filling, coated in fondant icing FRENCH

boudin   black pudding FRENCH
                        (also the song of the Foreign Legion)

boudin blanc   creamy white sausage made of finely minced veal, pork, rabbit or chicken mixed with cream, egg, onions and flavourings FRENCH

boudin noir   blood sausage made from pig's blood, pork fat, cream, onion and spices FRENCH

boudy   an apple mainly used for cooking or decoration
                                                                      FRENCH

bouffoir   bellows used by butchers to force air under the skin and into the tissue of carcasses FRENCH

bougon   soft goat's milk cheese from Pitou FRENCH

bougras   soup from the Périgord region, made of cabbage, leeks, onions and potatoes cooked in the same water that has cooked black puddings FRENCH

bouillabaisse	fish stew from the south of France made of a variety of Mediterranean fish cooked with olive oil, spices and herbs FRENCH
bouillade	Catalonian sauce of snails and fish cooked with garlic, red peppers and white wine, sometimes served over diced potatoes SPANISH
bouillant	puff pastry patty filled with salpicon of chicken, served very hot – which is why it is called 'boiling' FRENCH
bouillante	old name for soup served boiling hot FRENCH
bouille, la	cow's milk cheese from Normandy; vessel for carrying milk FRENCH
bouilleture	matelote of various types of fish, especially eels, garnished with toast, mushrooms, onions and sometimes hard-boiled eggs FRENCH
bouilli	boiled beef, especially cooked with pot au feu; soufflé made from milk, sugar and flour FRENCH
bouillie	porridge made from a variety of grains FRENCH
bouillnada	Catalonian version of bouillabaisse with equal proportions of fish and potato SPANISH
bouillon	plain, unclarified meat or vegetable stock, served as soup FRENCH
boula boula	soup originally from the Seychelles – turtle soup with puréed green peas AMERICAN
boulangère, à la	garnish of sliced raw potatoes and onions baked with a little stock in the same dish as the joint FRENCH
boulbett	sweet pastry and cheesecakes RUSSIAN
boule de neige	ball-shaped sponge cake covered with whipped cream; iced bombe covered with whipped cream; local name for an edible agaric FRENCH
boulette	alternative name for cheese cassata; minced meat and onion shaped into small balls, rolled in breadcrumbs and fried FRENCH
boulettes de viande	small pastries; bouilli from a pot au feu enclosed in pastry FRENCH
bouquet garni	small bunch of herbs tied together, used to add flavour to stews and casseroles FRENCH
bouquetière	garnish of pommes château, artichoke bottoms filled with white turnips and carrots, French peas, beans and cauliflower in hollandaise sauce FRENCH
bouquetin	ibex FRENCH
bouquets	prawns FRENCH

bourbon robust whiskey from Kentucky, distilled from maize and flavoured with malted rye and barley AMERICAN

bourdaines, les apples filled with plum or quince jam, wrapped in short crust pastry and baked FRENCH

bourekia filo pastry patties filled with a savoury filling GREEK

bourgain cow's milk Neufchâtel-type cheese FRENCH

bourgeoise, à la homely, appetizing style of cooking not to a set recipe, often garnished with carrots, onions and bacon FRENCH

bourgogne burgundy FRENCH

bourguignonne dish containing burgundy and button mushrooms FRENCH

bourride, la Provençal fish soup made with monkfish, flavoured with garlic FRENCH

Boursin fresh cream cheese flavoured with garlic or herbs or rolled in crushed peppercorns FRENCH

bourtheto speciality dish of baked fish with sliced onions, tomatoes and cayenne pepper CORFIOTE

boutargue salted grey mullet or tuna fish roe FRENCH

bovine spongiform encephalopathy BSE, commonly known as 'mad cow disease' has infected many British cattle; tissues that might contain the agent which causes the disease, such as brain, spinal cord, spleen, thymus, tonsils and intestines are banned from human food

Bovril™ from bos (Latin: ox) and vril, the term applied to the life force in Bulwer-Lytton's novel *The Forgotten Race* (1871)

bowfin mudfish found in the Great Lakes and the Mississippi Valley AMERICAN

boxty traditional dish, popular in County Cavan of equal quantities of grated raw potatoes and cooked potatoes stirred into hot milk IRISH

boyaux intestines of slaughtered animals FRENCH

boysenberry hybrid of raspberry, strawberry, loganberry and dewberry

bozbash country soup made from boiled mutton RUSSIAN

Bra partly-skimmed, rennetted, hard, white cow's milk cheese with a sharp, slightly salty flavour ITALIAN

braadhaantje spring chicken DUTCH

braadworst frying sausage DUTCH

braam blackberry DUTCH

brabançonne, à la	garnish of pastry tarts filled with puréed sprouts or endives covered with sauce mornay, served with potato croquettes FRENCH
brace, alla	on charcoal ITALIAN
Brachse	bream GERMAN
braciola	escalope ITALIAN
braciola di maiale	pork chop ITALIAN
bracioletta	small slice of meat ITALIAN
braciolette	thin slices of veal or beef covered with a slice of ham, topped with a mixture of grated Parmesan, pine nuts, sultanas and parsley, rolled up and skewered ITALIAN
bracken	genus of fern found almost all over the world; the unopened leaves are edible
bräckkorv	smoked pork sausage SWEDISH
bräckt	sautéed, fried SWEDISH
braendende kaerlighed	creamed potatoes covered with cubes of fried green bacon DANISH
bragance, à la	garnish of tomatoes stuffed with sauce béarnaise and served with potato croquettes; beef consommé garnished with sago balls, cucumber balls and royale garnish julienne FRENCH
brain	various animal brains are sold as offal and cooked in a number of ways
braisé	braised FRENCH
braising	slow method of cooking cuts of meat, poultry and game that are too tough to roast
bramborák	potato cakes made from raw potato CZECH
bramborová kaše	mashed potato CZECH
bramborové šišky	small flour and potato dumplings CZECH
bramborové škubánky	potato pudding CZECH
bramborové knedlíky	potato dumplings CZECH
bramborové omelety se spenátem	potato omelettes with spinach CZECH
bramborové placky	potato pancake CZECH
brambory	potato CZECH
bran	the outer layer of cereal grains, usually wheat or oats
brancas	beef consommé garnished with chiffonade of lettuce and sorrel, cooked vermicelli and julienne of fried mushrooms FRENCH
branche	leaf FRENCH
brancino	perch-like fish found in the Adriatic, often eaten in Venice ITALIAN

brandade de morue   salt cod flavoured with garlic FRENCH

Brandkrapferlsuppe   traditional soup of beef broth with fried profiteroles AUSTRIAN

brandy   spirit distilled from wine; a variety of fruit liqueurs distilled from fruit juice

brandy butter   hard sauce of softened butter, caster sugar and brandy

brandy snap   cylindrical crisp biscuit filled with whipped or chantilly cream

brantôme   sauce for fish of beaten cream, white wine, oyster juice and crayfish butter FRENCH

branzino   bass ITALIAN

bras   rice (uncooked) BM

brasa, na   charcoal-grilled PORTUGUESE

brasato   braised ITALIAN

brasede kartofler   sliced, sautéed potatoes DANISH

brasem   bream DUTCH

bräserad   braised SWEDISH

Bratapfel   baked apple GERMAN

braten   roast GERMAN

Bratfisch   fried fish GERMAN

Brathähnchen   roast chicken GERMAN

Bratheringe   soused herrings dipped in flour and fried in oil GERMAN

Bratkartoffel   fried potato GERMAN

Bratklops   rissole, usually served with sauerkraut GERMAN

Bratwürst   pale-coloured sausage made of finely minced pork or veal GERMAN

braune Suppe mit Leberpurée   brown soup of puréed cooked liver GERMAN

Braunkohl   kale or broccoli GERMAN

Braunschweiger Kuchen   rice, fruit and almond cake GERMAN

brawn   boned meat from pig's head set in moulds to form a jelly, and eaten cold

brazil nut   large oval nut eaten raw, used in sweet making, or in savoury dishes

bread   cereal-based food made mostly from wheat flour combined with yeast, salt and liquid, it is found in variety of forms all over the world

bread and butter pudding   hot pudding made with layers of stale bread and butter mixed with dried fruit and sugar, covered in custard and baked

bread pudding	pudding made from stale white bread soaked in milk, mixed with dried fruit and candied peel, suet, sugar, egg, mixed spice and baked
bread sauce	sauce of breadcrumbs and milk flavoured with onion, cloves, bay and pepper, traditionally served with roast poultry
breadcrumbs	available both fresh or dried, white or brown and give a crunchy topping or coating to sweet and savoury dishes
breadfruit	round football-sized tropical tree fruit eaten as a vegetable in South East Asia
breakfast biscuit	crisp, rusk-like biscuit
breakfast cereals	most are based on maize, rice, wheat and oats and are modified to make them ready to eat
bream	round red-backed, silver-bellied fish
brebán	garnish for meat of puréed broad beans on artichoke bottoms or cauliflower with sauce hollandaise and potatoes FRENCH
brebis	ewe FRENCH
Brei	porridge, mash, purée GERMAN
bréjauda	traditional soup from Limousin, of stock, sliced cabbage and diced bacon FRENCH
brekkbønne	French bean NORWEGIAN
brème	bream FRENCH
Brennender Pudding	pudding steamed in ring mould, served hot with flambéd sugar cubes soaked in brandy GERMAN
bresanne	sauce of sauce espagnole, Madeira and orange juice, and puréed chicken livers FRENCH
bresaola	Lombardy speciality of strips of mature, air-dried beef marinated in olive oil, lemon juice, and black pepper ITALIAN
bresolles	finely chopped ham with chopped onion, mushrooms, garlic, seasoning and nutmeg, probably invented by the Marquis de Bresolles' chef FRENCH
brestois	cake from Brest, cooked in brioche moulds and slow baked FRENCH
breton	a cake (which does not come from Brittany) made by placing different cakes, iced in different colours, on top of one another and decorating the structure with almond paste FRENCH
breton far	commercially-made cream flan from Brittany FRENCH

bretonne — sauce of onion, butter, white wine, espagnole sauce, tomato sauce and herbs FRENCH

bretonne, à la — dish garnished with haricot beans or bean purée; eggs or fish coated with bretonne sauce FRENCH

bretonneau — old Norman name for turbot FRENCH

brewing — the process of fermenting of grains to produce alcohol

brewis — 'teakettle' broth, made from oat-husks boiled with fat bacon WELSH

Brezel — salted, knot-shaped roll (US: pretzel) GERMAN

brézolles — slices of veal from the inside part of the leg FRENCH

briand — chicken consommé with diced chicken, ham and veal FRENCH

brick — sweet, medium-firm, rennetted cow's milk cheese with many holes; one of few cheeses originating from the States; particularly popular in Wisconsin AMERICAN

bricquebec — cow's milk cheese from Normandy FRENCH

brider — to truss FRENCH

bridge roll — small, slim roll made from an egg-enriched dough

brie — soft-textured cow's milk farm cheese FRENCH

Bries, Brieschen, Briesel — sweetbreads GERMAN

Briesuppe — soup of stock, calves' sweetbreads, onions, carrots and a shredded cabbage garnished with asparagus tips and diced fried bread AUSTRIAN

Brighton rock — small fruit cake with ground almonds and rosewater ENGLISH

brill — good-flavoured flat sea fish resembling turbot

brilloli — sweet porridge made from chestnut flour CORSICAN

brine — salt and water solution in which food is preserved

bringebĺr — raspberry NORWEGIAN

bringukollar — breast of lamb spiced and soured with pickling brine ICELANDIC

brinometer — instrument to measure the saturation of brine

brînză — cheese ROMANIAN

brioche — enriched yeast dough baked in the shape of a cottage loaf, usually eaten warm for breakfast or as dessert FRENCH

brioli — chestnut meal prepared as polenta CORSICAN

brionne — alternative name for chayote FRENCH

brisket — one of the less tender, fatty cuts of beef, suitable for braising, stewing or pot-roasting

brisler	sweetbreads DANISH
brisling	young herring DANISH, NORWEGIAN
bristol	garnish of small croquettes of rice, creamed flageolet beans and pommes noisettes FRENCH
brit, bret	a small turbot (US: a small herring) ENGLISH
britannia	beef consommé, thickened with tapioca and garnished with crayfish royale and julienne of truffles FRENCH
brizol	grilled beefsteak POLISH
broa	thick maize-meal cracker; type of gingerbread PORTUGUESE
broad bean	should be picked and cooked whilst young and tender
broas	small Madeira cakes, popular in the 19th century British
broccio(u)	goat's milk or soured ewe's milk cream cheese CORSICAN
broccoli	green vegetable with purple, white or green shoots; calabrese produces a single large, closed head; white flowering broccoli is also known as Chinese broccoli, Chinese kale, gai lan, kaai laan, tsoi kailan
broche	spit FRENCH
brochet	pike FRENCH
brocheta	skewer SPANISH
brochette	meat or fish cooked on a skewer or spit FRENCH
brocoletto	*see* choy sum, flowering pak choi, flowering white cabbage, hong tsoi sum, hon tsai tai kozaitai, pak tsoi sum, choy sum, rape
brócolos	broccoli PORTUGUESE
bröd	bread SWEDISH
brød	bread DANISH, NORWEGIAN
bröd och smör	bread and butter
brodet	fish stew YUGOSLAVIAN
brodetto	fish soup with onions and tomato pulp ITALIAN
brodo	bouillon, broth or soup ITALIAN
broglie	demi-glace reduced with mushroom stock, butter and Madeira, garnished with finely chopped ham FRENCH
broil	to grill AMERICAN
broiler	a grill; a young chicken AMERICAN
brokkoli	broccoli HUNGARIAN
brombaer	blackberry DANISH

Brombeere	blackberry GERMAN
brønnkarse	watercress NORWEGIAN
brood	bread DUTCH
broodje	bread roll DUTCH
broodje halfom	buttered roll with liver and salted beef DUTCH
broodje kaas	buttered roll with cheese DUTCH
broodmaaltijd	bread served with cold meat, egg, cheese, jam or other garnishes DUTCH
broodpudding	kind of bread pudding with eggs, cinnamon and rum flavourings DUTCH
brooklime	edible veronica which grows in bogs, a substitute for watercress; known in Scotland as water pimpernel
broom	shrub of the pea family; the buds were preserved in vinegar in mediaeval England and used as capers ENGLISH
broonie	gingerbread made with oatmeal ORKNEY ISLANDS
brose	resembling gruel, boiling water is poured over oatmeal or barley with a little added salt SCOTTISH
broskev	peach CZECH
bröst	breast SWEDISH
Brot	bread GERMAN
brotchán	originally porridge; now broth or soup IRISH
Brötchen	roll GERMAN
broth	liquid produced after boiling meat or fish in water for a long time
brótola de fango	grey fish with reddish fins, found in Spanish waters SPANISH
brouillé	scrambled FRENCH
brousses	ewe's milk cheese from Provence FRENCH
broutes	Béarnais Lenten dish of old cabbage roots or stumps cooked in salted water and seasoned with oil and vinegar FRENCH
brown betty	pudding of layers of apples, breadcrumbs, butter, brown sugar, lemon juice, peel and cinnamon baked until golden brown AMERICAN, ENGLISH
brown sauce	roux cooked until brown, it ranges from simple gravy to sauce espagnole
brown trout	by far the best freshwater trout
brownie	a rich chocolate cookie (biscuit) AMERICAN
browning	giving an already cooked dish a golden colour by placing it under a hot grill or flaming it with a blowlamp

browning dish	special microwave dish to sear and brown food
browning element	built-in browning element in a microwave oven
browning, gravy	dark liquid used to colour gravy, soups and stews
broye	white (uncooked) or roasted maize flour cooked with vegetable stock until thick, cooled, sliced and fried FRENCH
bruciate briache	'burning drunkards'; baked peeled chestnuts sprinkled with sugar, soaked in hot rum and ignited ITALIAN
Bruckfleisch	stewed beef offal with root vegetables GERMAN
brugnon	a cross between a plum and a peach FRENCH
Brühe	broth; consommé GERMAN
bruine bonen (mit spek)	kidney beans (with bacon) DUTCH
brukiew	turnips POLISH
brukselka	Brussels sprouts POLISH
brûlée	dish with crisp topping of caramelised sugar FRENCH
brun, brune	brown FRENCH
brun kage	brown, spicy biscuit (US: cookie) DANISH
brun lapskaus	brown beef stew NORWEGIAN
brun løksaus	brown onion sauce NORWEGIAN
bruna bönor	baked beans SWEDISH
brunch	meal combining breakfast and lunch
brunede kartofler	boiled, caramelised potatoes DANISH
brunet smør	browned butter sauce DANISH
Brunnenkresse	watercress GERMAN
brunoise	finely diced or shredded mixed vegetables used as the basis for soup, sauce or a garnish FRENCH
brunswick stew	stew of jointed squirrels with corn on the cob, lima beans, potatoes and tomatoes
bruschetta	baked slices of white bread rubbed with garlic; olive oil is poured over before serving ITALIAN
Brüsseler Endivie	chicory (US: endive) GERMAN
Brussels lof	chicory (US: endive) DUTCH
Brussels sprout	small member of the cabbage family about the size of a walnut; popular winter vegetable
Brust	breast GERMAN
Bruststück	brisket GERMAN
brut	unsweetened; describes champagne or dry wine FRENCH

bruxelloise, à la	sauce for asparagus made from melted butter, salt, pepper, lemon juice and sieved hard boiled eggs; garnish of Brussels sprouts, pommes fondantes and clear veal gravy or thin demi-glace FRENCH
brylé pudding	crème caramel SWEDISH
bryndza	rennetted ewe's milk cheese HUNGARIAN
brynt	browned SWEDISH
brynza	ewe's milk cheese CZECH
brysselkål	Brussels sprout SWEDISH
brysselkäx	vanilla biscuits SWEDISH
brzlík	sweetbreads CZECH
brzoskwinie	peaches POLISH
BSE	bovine spongiform encephalopathy, a disease of animals which can infect humans
buah kras	roasted candle nut seeds
bubble and squeak	cold boiled beef mixed with cold cooked potatoes and chopped cabbage or other greens and fried; the meat can be omitted
buberts	traditional pudding flavoured with vanilla, chopped nuts and lemon peel LATVIAN
bublanina	fruit sponge CZECH
bublichki	sweet bread ring sprinkled with poppy seeds RUSSIAN
bucarde	cockle FRENCH
bucatini	a thin macaroni ITALIAN
buccin	whelk FRENCH
bûche de chévre	soft goat's milk cheese FRENCH
bûche de Noël	type of Swiss roll known as a Yule log FRENCH
Buchteln	yeast bun with jam inside AUSTRIAN
buchty	yeast bun CZECH
buck	male roe and fallow deer, reindeer, chamois, antelope, hare and rabbit
buck rarebit	*see* Welsh rarebit
Buck's fizz	cocktail made from two parts champagne and one part orange juice
buckling	smoked whole herring
Bückling	bloater GERMAN
Bücklinge	smoked herring fillets baked with eggs and butter AUSTRIAN
buckwheat	triangular grain of a fruit related to rhubarb, used to make gluten-free flour
budding	pudding DANISH

budgerigar	a small, green Australian parrot *Melopsittacus undulatus* from native Australian *budgeri* good (to eat) gar cockatoo
budín	blancmange, custard SPANISH
budino	pudding, usually cooked, often containing cheese, fruit or nuts; blancmange, custard ITALIAN
budyń	steamed or boiled sweet or savoury pudding POLISH
bue	beef ITALIAN
buey	OX SPANISH
buffalo	Cape buffalo, African cattle Synercus caffer; US name for bison
buffalo berry	red or yellow acidic berries with a pleasant flavour AMERICAN
buffalo currant	cultivated variety of American currant with a distinctive smell, mostly used in pies and jams AMERICAN
buffalo fish	freshwater fish, plentiful in the Mississippi Valley and the Great Lakes AMERICAN
buffel-headed duck	butterback duck, which can be cooked as wild duck NORTH AMERICAN
buffet	meal in which guests help themselves from a selection of cold dishes
buřské orísky	peanuts CZECH
buggyantott	poached HUNGARIAN
bugnes	fritter of dough rolled and fried in oil FRENCH
buhara pilâvi	speciality dish of baked rice with pistachio nuts, currants, chopped chicken livers and grated carrots TURKISH
buisson, en	various foods, particularly shellfish, arranged to resemble a bush FRENCH
bujón	bouillon CZECH
bukiet z jarzyn	mixed vegetables POLISH
bukta	bun HUNGARIAN
Bulette	meat- or fishball GERMAN
bulgar	whole wheat grains, steamed, spread out to dry, and broken into pieces; cracked wheat TURKISH
bulgare	garnish of mayonnaise mixed with tomato sauce with cooked diced celery hearts FRENCH
bulion z diablotką	consommé with meat fillet POLISH
buljong	clear soup, bouillon or consommé NORWEGIAN
buljons ar frikadelém	clear soup with quenelles LATVIAN
bulk cheese	slang name for Canadian cheddar CANADIAN

bulki	rolls POLISH
bullace	wild plum tree; the fruit is small, round, green in colour and rather sour
bully beef	salted, spiced beef ENGLISH
bulrush	aquatic plant; the leaves and young shoots can be used in salad, and the starchy roots are also edible
bulvių desros	potato sausage LITHUANIAN
bulvė	potato LITHUANIAN
bun	small, sweet cake made from a mixture containing yeast
bundeva	pumpkin SERBO-CROAT
Bündnerfleisch	cured, dried beef served in very thin slices GERMAN, SWISS
Bündnerwürst	sausage of lean minced pork, diced bacon, cloves, salt and pepper SWISS
Bunter Hans	large, light, breadcrumb dumpling, poached in water and served with vegetables or stewed dried fruits GERMAN
buñuelo	doughnut; fritter SPANISH
buñuelos	ham, prawns, mussels, chicken, cheese and potatoes dipped into fritter batter and fried in oil SPANISH
buraczki	beetroot POLISH
buraki	beetroot POLISH
burbot	European river fish; the only fresh water member of the cod family
burdock	wild perennial plant with burrs; the young shoots and roots are used like salsify; also known as gobo
burfi	fudge-like Indian sweet INDIAN
burger	short for hamburger; now a suffix for any amorphous foodstuff in an often tasteless bread roll (cheeseburger, chickenburger etc)
burghul	cracked wheat
burgonya	potatoes HUNGARIAN
burgonya paradi cscommal	dish made from potatoes and tomatoes, traditionally eaten on the great Hungarian holiday, St Stephen's day (16 August) HUNGARIAN
burgonya saláta	potato salad HUNGARIAN
burgonyafött	boiled potatoes HUNGARIAN
burgonyahasáb	chips HUNGARIAN
burgonyakrémleves	cream of potato soup HUNGARIAN
burgonyasült	baked potatoes HUNGARIAN

burgoo	Kentucky stew of vegetables and squirrel brains, perhaps causing CJD in its eaters
burgos	popular soft ewe's milk cheese SPANISH
Burgundy	region of France famous for its wines
burma bean	variety of lima bean
Burmeister	trade name of a soft, ripened cheese from Wisconsin AMERICAN
burnet	herb with a slightly nutty flavour with a hint of cucumber
burrida	fish casserole, strongly flavoured with spices and herbs ITALIAN
burridà, la	cold dogfish soup SARDINIAN
burrini	cheese with an outer layer of butter ITALIAN
burrito	wheat flour flat bread wrapped around a filling of shredded meat
burro	butter ITALIAN
busecca	thick tripe and vegetable soup ITALIAN
bustard	delicious bird, now extinct in Britain
buster	the name, especially in New Orleans, for crab at the stage between hard and soft shell; cleaned, dipped in batter, cooked whole in butter, and often served with sauce béarnaise, they are considered a delicacy AMERICAN
butcher's broom	*Ruscus* the only monocotyledonous lily, whose bitter roots are used to make the aperitif petit-houx, and whose young shoots are eaten in France as pragon
butifarra	sausage of minced pork mixed with white wine, cloves, nutmeg, salt and pepper SPANISH
butt	old English and current American cut of pork, part of the shoulder and neck ENGLISH, AMERICAN
Butt(e)	brill GERMAN
butter	edible fatty yellow-white solid made by churning cream
butter bean	large flat, oval dried bean with a floury texture
butter cream icing	soft, creamy cake icing made with softened butter and icing sugar
butter, fruit	soft butter-like preserve, used like jam
Butterkäse	soft cheese shaped as a loaf AUSTRIAN
Butterknöpfe	garnish for soup made of butter creamed with egg, flour salt and nutmeg – buttons of the batter are boiled in the soup for about 10 minutes GERMAN

buttermilk	sour liquid left after cream has been churned to butter
Butternockerlsuppe	soup of rich beef broth with small dumplings AUSTRIAN
butternut	mild-flavoured nut similar to walnut
butternut squash	North American club-shaped winter squash with smooth, pale yellow skin and deep yellow flesh AMERICAN
butterscotch	hard toffee made with butter, sugar and water
buttiri	Calabrian buffalo or cow's milk cheese with an 'egg' of butter in the middle ITALIAN
button mushroom	small mushroom before the gills have opened
button onion	small onions picked at an early stage
búza	wheat HUNGARIAN
by-am	spinach BM
byron	sauce of red wine thickened with arrowroot and butter, garnished with finely sliced truffles FRENCH

C

caballa	fish of the mackerel family SPANISH
cabanossi	thin, spicy sausage ITALIAN
cabbage	vegetable of the brassica family which is nutritious raw but quickly loses nutrients when cooked; it may be pickled
cabbage palm	the terminal of some species of edible palm
cabbage, red and white	firm and round with shiny leaves
cabbage, Savoy	dark green cabbage with crinkly leaves
cabbie-claw	fish dish made from very fresh codling SHETLAND ISLANDS
cabécou	goat's milk cheese FRENCH
cabello de ángel	'angel's hair'; jam made from the sidra gourd, which looks like fine strands of golden hair when cooked SPANISH
cabeza de ternera	calf's head SPANISH
cabidela	chicken cooked in a rich sauce PORTUGUESE
cabillaud	fresh cod FRENCH
cabinet pudding	simple moulded pudding made from bread and butter or sponge cake and glacé cherries ENGLISH
cabinet, pouding de	pudding of sponge fingers soaked in kirsch, chopped crystallised fruits and raisins, layered in a mould, filled with vanilla-flavoured custard and baked FRENCH
caboc	very rich, soft, double cream cheese from the Highlands SCOTTISH
cabra	female goat PORTUGUESE
cabra	goat SPANISH
cabrales	strong, semi-hard, blue-veined cheese, traditionally made from goat's milk SPANISH
cabreiro	cheese made from a mixture of ewe's milk and goat's milk PORTUGUESE
cabrilla	collective name for a number of edible fish of the sea-perch family found in the Mediterranean
cabrion	goat's milk cheese from Burgundy, soaked in eau de vie de marc and ripened in the husks of pressed grapes FRENCH
cabrito	kid PORTUGUESE, SPANISH
caça	game PORTUGUESE

caçador	simmered in white wine with carrots, onions, herbs and sometimes tomatoes PORTUGUESE
cacahuete	peanut SPANISH
cacalaousada, la	sauce for snails made from minced ham, chopped herbs and milk FRENCH
cacalaus	cooked snails served with aïoli sauce or fresh tomato sauce FRENCH
cacao	COCOA FRENCH
cacciagione	game ITALIAN
cacciatora, alla	'hunter style'; a term generally used for game or poultry ITALIAN
cacciatori	small salami ITALIAN
caccio cavallo	mild semi-hard skimmed cow's milk cheese ITALIAN
cacciucco	spicy fish soup, usually with onions, green pepper, garlic and red wine ITALIAN
cacciucco livornese	leghorn stew, made with coarse fish, octopus, squid, crab and small lobster ITALIAN
cacen-gri	griddle scones, served hot with butter WELSH
cachat	ewe's or goats milk cheese matured with wine vinegar and pressed FRENCH
cachelada	whole chorizo sausage boiled with quartered potatoes SPANISH
cachelos	a dish of meat and vegetables cooked together but served in separate dishes SPANISH
cachelos	diced potatoes boiled with cabbage, paprika, garlic, bacon and sausage SPANISH
cachorro	hot dog PORTUGUESE
cachucho	small sea-bream PORTUGUESE
cacio a cavallo	firm, slightly sweet, cow's or sheep's milk cheese ITALIAN
caciotta, caciotto, cacio fiore	buttery semi-hard cheese made in small cylindrical shapes ITALIAN
Caerphilly	soft, mild, creamy white cheese, eaten in its 'green' state when only ten days old WELSH
caesar salad	salad of cos lettuce, croutons, anchovies, Parmesan cheese and raw egg, tossed with a dressing AMERICAN
café au lait	hot black coffee mixed with scalded milk FRENCH
café da manhã	breakfast PORTUGUESE
café glacé	coffee-flavoured ice-cream dessert FRENCH
café liègeois	sundae of vanilla or coffee ice cream mixed with sweet, strong black coffee until thick and creamy and topped with whipped cream BELGIAN

caffè latte   strong espresso coffee mixed with hot milk ITALIAN

caffeine   stimulant with diuretic properties present in coffee, tea and cola nuts

caille   quail FRENCH

caillebotte   the name in parts of France for curds when eaten fresh FRENCH

cailletot   the name in Normandy for young turbot FRENCH

cáis   cheese IRISH

caisse   small earthenware, china, silver or paper container for hors d'œuvres FRENCH

caju   cashew nut INDIAN, PORTUGUESE

cajun   a style of cooking popular in southern States with crayfish as a popular ingredient; famous dishes include gumbo and jambalaya (from Acadian) AMERICAN

cake   various sweet, baked items made from flour, eggs, sugar and fat, served as a dessert or at tea-time

calabacín   vegetable marrow; courgette SPANISH

calabacines   small marrows SPANISH

calabaza   pumpkin SPANISH

calabrese   green or purple sprouting broccoli, which grows during late summer and autumn

calaloo   see amaranth, bayam, Chinese spinach

calamar   squid PORTUGUESE, SPANISH

calamares   small squid or inkfish SPANISH

calamares a la romana   squid fried in batter SPANISH

calamaretti   small calamary eaten with scampi ITALIAN

calamaretto   young squid ITALIAN

calamari   squid or inkfish; rings are fried in oil or included in soup ITALIAN

calamaro   squid ITALIAN

calamaroni   type of inkfish used generally for making soups ITALIAN

calamary   squid, found in the Mediterranean and Spanish waters

calamint   small herb with blue thyme-like flowers, it smells similar to mint

calamus   marsh plant used to flavour liqueurs

calappa   crustacean similar to crab, also called the box crab

calas   traditional rice fritter from New Orleans AMERICAN

calcionetta   dessert-like sweet fried ravioli ITALIAN

calcium	naturally-occurring mineral, important to maintain strong bones and teeth
caldeirada	fish stew of octopus, small squid, prawns, shrimps and lobster PORTUGUESE
caldeirada	fish stewed with potatoes, onions, tomatoes, pimentos, spices, wine and olive-oil PORTUGUESE
calderada	fish soup similar to bouillabaisse SPANISH
caldereta	general term for a fish or meat stew SPANISH
caldereta da cabrito	kid stew SPANISH
caldillo de congrio	conger-eel soup with tomatoes and potatoes SPANISH
caldo	broth PORTUGUESE, SPANISH
caldo	hot ITALIAN
caldo	clear soup; consommé PORTUGUESE, SPANISH
caldo verde	vegetable soup made with olive oil, potatoes and finely shredded dark green cabbage PORTUGUESE
calf	young bovine animal; a cow in its first year of life
calf's foot jelly	a calf's foot is boiled to make stock; it is made into jelly on the following day, and fed to the sick
California quail	game bird of the American partridge family
calipash	corruption of carapace, the shell of a turtle; in culinary terms the gelatinous green fat attached to the upper shell
callaloo, calaloo, calalou, callilu	the edible leaves various plants used as vegetables or for soup making CARIBBEAN
callos	tripe SPANISH
calorie	scientific term for the measurement of the energy value of food
călugăresc	'monk'; name often given to large vegetable stews ROMANIAN
calvados	apple brandy from orchards of Normandy, which may be served as a liqueur apéritif FRENCH
calville	apple with thin golden yellow skin BELGIAN
calzone	filled and folded over pizza, never containing tomatoes; pizza dough envelope baked with ham, cheese, herbs ITALIAN
camarão	shrimp – eaten plain, boiled or steamed PORTUGUESE
camargue	ewe's milk cheese from Provence FRENCH
camarões	shrimps PORTUGUESE
camarón	shrimp SPANISH
cambacérès	fish garnish of white wine sauce made with crayfish stock, crayfish tails, mushrooms and truffles FRENCH

Cambazola   full-fat cheese with blue mould and a creamy texture
              GERMAN

Cambridge sauce   English substitute for mayonnaise; a cold sauce for
cold meat or fish dishes

Cambridge sausage   lean sausage flavoured with herbs and spices

cambuquira   tender shoots of pumpkin stewed with meat
              PORTUGUESE

camel   often eaten in desert areas or used for its milk

Camembert   soft, cow's milk cheese inoculated with white
mould, and with a pungent flavour
              FRENCH, POLISH, SWEDISH

camerani   garnish of small tartlets stuffed with goose liver
purée and slices of ox tongue and macaroni; beef
consommé garnished with diced carrots, leeks,
celery and pasta, served with grated Parmesan
              FRENCH

camomile   aromatic, bitter-scented, daisy-like plant used to
make tea

camosun   semi-soft cheese, developed as a means of using up
surplus cow's milk AMERICAN

campagnola   with vegetables, especially onions and tomatoes
              ITALIAN

Campden tablets   sodium metabisulphite CANADIAN

cheddar   made since the first cheese factory opened in 1864,
from unpastuerised cow's milk CANADIAN

Canadian colby   quickly ripening cheese, with a looser texture and a
softer paste than cheddar; sometimes called stirred
curd CANADIAN

Canadian partridge   game bird inhabiting the wooded parts of south
eastern Canada; also known as spruce partridge
              CANADIAN

canapé   small piece of food served hot or cold as an
appetiser, usually with drinks FRENCH

canapé   small open sandwich PORTUGUESE

canard   duck FRENCH

canard sauvage   mallard; wild duck FRENCH

canard siffleur   male widgeon FRENCH

cancalaise, à la   garnish for fish, of poached oysters and shelled
shrimps mixed with sauce Normande; fish soup
garnished with oysters, whiting, quenelles and strips
of sole FRENCH

cancoillote	very strongly-flavoured skimmed, rennetted cow's milk cheese, melted and mixed with butter and white wine before serving FRENCH
candied peel	the outer coating, usually of a citrus fruit, cooked slowly in sugar syrup until crystallised
candle fish	fish, resembling an oily smelt, found in the northern Pacific
candle nut	round, cream-coloured nut, mildly poisonous when eaten raw
candy	sweet made from crystallised sugar
candying	method of impregnating pieces of fruit or peel with sugar to preserve them
cane ribbon syrup	syrup made from cane sugar, used in the southern States AMERICAN
canederli	dumplings made from ham, sausage and breadcrumbs ITALIAN
canela	cinnamon PORTUGUESE, SPANISH
canella	a tree; a digestif, aromatic condiment is made from the inner peel WEST INDIAN
canelle knife	tool used to crimp the surface of fruit and vegetables for decorative effect
canelones	type of cannelloni SPANISH
canestrato	cheese made from ewe's milk or a mixture of ewe's and goats milk SICILIAN
caneton	duckling FRENCH
cangrejo	small sea and estuary crabs, also known as centolla SPANISH
cangrejo de mar	crab SPANISH
cangrejo de río	crayfish SPANISH
canja	chicken and rice soup PORTUGUESE
canja com arroz	chicken soup with rice, onions, tomatoes and root vegetables PORTUGUESE
canjica	dessert of peanuts and sweet-corn cooked in milk with cloves and cinnamon and served in fresh coconut milk PORTUGUESE
canneler	to flute the edges of pastry and cakes FRENCH
cannella	cinnamon ITALIAN
cannelle	cinnamon FRENCH
cannellino bean	creamy-white dried kidney bean ITALIAN
cannelloni	large thin squares of pasta, rolled and stuffed with a variety fillings; tubular dough stuffed with meat,

	cheese or vegetables, covered with white sauce and baked ITALIAN
canning	means of preserving food by sealing in a tinned iron container while hot
cannocchie	flat-tailed Adriatic and Mediterranean crustacean of the squill family, also called pannocchie
cannòli	fried pastry tube filled with mixture of sugar, ricotta, chocolate, candied peel and pistachio nuts SICILIAN
cannolo	rolled pastry filled with sweet, white cheese ITALIAN
canola oil	colourless and odourless oil extracted from oil seed
cantal	hard, strong French cheese, which has been made in the Auvergne for more than 2,000 years FRENCH
cantaloup	a muskmelon *Cucumis melo cantalupensis*, first cultivated in a former papal villa at Cantaluppi, near Rome, in the 18th century. ITALIAN
cantarela	chanterelle mushroom SPANISH
cantelo	bread baked in a ring shape; a speciality for weddings SPANISH
Canterbury pudding	plain baked sponge pudding served with hot wine sauce ENGLISH
canvasback duck	possibly the most highly prized North American wild duck, it has a chestnut head and much lighter coloured back
capa santa	alternative name for scallops ITALIAN
capão, capãœo	capon PORTUGUESE
caparozzolo	name in Venice for sea truffle ITALIAN
cape gooseberry	*see* physalis
capelin	small fish of the smelt family; prepared as whiting
capendu	variety of red apple with a very short stalk FRENCH
caper	pickled flower-bud of a low-growing deciduous native southern European shrub
capercaillie	game bird with a distinctive flavour, it is the largest member of the grouse family
capillaire	popular 19th-century infusion of maidenhair fern syrup and orange-flower water, used as flavouring for cocktails ENGLISH
capilotade	ragoût of several different kinds of reheated poultry FRENCH
capitaine	saltwater fish similar to carp FRENCH
capitone	large eel ITALIAN
capocollo	cured shoulder of ham from Parma ITALIAN
capocollo	smoked salt pork ITALIAN

capon	castrated cockerel, specially fed until it is killed between the ages six and nine months
caponata	hors d'œuvre of fried eggplants mixed with a sauce made with capers, olives, celery and anchovies, garnished with tuna fish and spiny lobster SICILIAN
caponata	aubergine, green pepper, tomato, vegetable, marrow, garlic, oil and herbs ITALIAN
caponi	red gurnard GREEK
cappelletti	'little hats'; type of small ravioli filled with meat, herbs, cheese and eggs ITALIAN
cappero	caper ITALIAN
cappon magro	large Genoese fish and vegetable salad served on a base of ships' biscuits or stale bread soaked in olive oil and wine vinegar; pyramid of cooked vegetables and fish salad ITALIAN
cappone	capon ITALIAN
cappuccino	espresso coffee topped with frothed milk ITALIAN
câpres	capers FRENCH
capretto	kid ITALIAN
capricet des dieux	post-war cheese, rich, creamy and delicately flavoured, with a soft rind FRENCH
caprino	soft goat's cheese ITALIAN
capriole	capers ITALIAN
capriolo	roebuck ITALIAN
capsicum	family name for a variety of peppers such as the chilli and sweet pepper
capsuni	strawberries ROMANIAN
capucijners	dried brown peas DUTCH
capucin	variety of caper; name for hare given by French sportsmen FRENCH
capucine, à la	chicken consommé garnished with shredded spinach and lettuce chiffonade, sometimes served with chicken purée-filled profiteroles; garnish of cabbage leaves or mushrooms stuffed with forcemeat FRENCH
caqui	persimmon PORTUGUESE
caracóis	snails PORTUGUESE
caracol	edible sea or land snail SPANISH
caracol	snail; spiral-shaped bun filled with currants PORTUGUESE, SPANISH
carageen, carrageen, carragheen	Irish Moss; an edible, red seaweed, *Chondrus crispus*, found on rocky shores of North America and Northern Europe, used to make a

	beverage, medicine and jelly; any product of this seaweed (the name comes from Carragheen, near Waterford, Ireland, where it is plentiful)
carambola	fruit of a tree from Indonesia and Malaysia; more commonly called a star fruit
caramel, burnt sugar	sugar syrup heated very slowly until it becomes a golden colour, which sets hard on cooling
caramel, toffee	sweet made like toffee but not boiled to such high temperatures
caramellato	caramelised ITALIAN
caramel pudding	caramel mould DUTCH
caramelva	caramel custard DUTCH
caramote	large prawn ITALIAN
caranguejo	small crab PORTUGUESE
carapau	horse mackerel PORTUGUESE
carasau	traditional unleavened bread SARDINIAN
carassin	freshwater fish of carp family FRENCH
caraway	small brown liquorice-flavoured seeds with tapering end, used as a spice
carbohydrate	exist in food as sugars, starches and cellulose, and provide most of the energy in human diet
carbon dioxide	gas used for carbonating drinks
carbonada criolla	baked pumpkin stuffed with diced beef SPANISH
carbonade, carbonnade	rich stew or braise of meat which includes beer FRENCH
carbonara	pasta with smoked ham, cheese, eggs and olive oil ITALIAN
carbonata	grilled pork chop; beef stew in red wine ITALIAN
carciofino	small artichoke ITALIAN
carciofo	artichoke ITALIAN
cardamine	plant of American origin, with violet flower spikes, similar watercress, but not as peppery
cardamom	green or black, whole or ground, it has a strong, bitter-sweet, slightly lemony flavour and should be used sparingly
cardiga	mild, hard, slightly oily cheese PORTUGUESE
cardinal	dish with scarlet effect, perhaps dusted with paprika or cayenne; iced dessert made with red fruits or served with red fruit sauce FRENCH
cardinal fish	red fish found off the European coasts, cooked as mullet

cardinaliser   to turn crustacea red by plunging in to boiling court bouillon FRENCH

cardo   cardoon ITALIAN

cardon   cardoon FRENCH

cardoon   edible thistle slightly resembling globe artichoke in taste and appearance

Carême   chicken and veal consommé double garnished with carrots, turnips, lettuce chiffonade and asparagus tips; fish garnish of quenelles fish, truffles, cream sauce and fleurons; garnish of large pitted olives stuffed with ham, forcemeat, Madeira sauce and potato croquettes – named after Antonin Carême, master chef FRENCH

caribou   large antlered animal of the reindeer family

caricolles   sea-snail BELGIAN

caril   curry PORTUGUESE

caringue   fish similar to, and cooked as, saurel FRENCH

Carlsbad plum   crystallised plum, a speciality of Carlsbad

carlin(g)s   peas cooked in butter, as eaten on Carling Sunday (fifth in Lent)

carmélite, à la   compound sauce consisting of sauce bourgignonne with juliennes of ham and glazed button mushrooms; slightly thickened fish consommé garnished with rice and fish forcemeat balls FRENCH

carmen   beef consommé with fumet of tomatoes and sweet peppers, garnished with rice and chervil FRENCH

carmine   carnation-red food colouring derived from cochineal

carmoisine   red food colouring (E122) used to colour jams and preserves

carnatz   equal quantities of seasoned pork and beef, shaped into croquettes, coated in breadcrumbs and fried
ROMANIAN

carne   meat ITALIAN, SPANISH, PORTUGUESE

carne de sol   salted, sun-dried meat PORTUGUESE

carneiro   mutton PORTUGUESE

carnero   mutton SPANISH

carnes frias   cold meat PORTUGUESE

carob   sugary pulp from the dark brown bean of the carob tree, also called locust bean, used as a substitute for chocolate

caroline   small choux pastry stuffed with meat pâté purée with chaud-froid FRENCH

carosella   local name in Naples for a species of fennel ITALIAN

carota	carrot ITALIAN
carotene	yellow-orange pigment present in yellow and green vegetables – derivatives are used as colouring in margarine and soft drinks
carotte	carrot FRENCH
carottes vichy	steamed carrots FRENCH
carp	several varieties of freshwater fish
carpa	carp ITALIAN, SPANISH
carpaccio	thin slices of raw meat ITALIAN
carpe	carp FRENCH
carpetshell	clam found off the coasts of Kerry and Cork, similar to a cockle but with a smooth surface
carpillon	small carp found in the Rhône, Saône and other rivers FRENCH
carrageen	dark purple or green seaweed which may be cooked and eaten as a vegetable, dried and bleached, used as a substitute for gelatine, or as a thickening agent
carré	best end of neck cutlets of pork, lamb and veal, from between the neck and saddle FRENCH
carré affiné	fermented ancient imperial cheese FRENCH
carré de bonneville	cow's milk cheese from Normandy. FRENCH
carré de l'est	mild, soft, pasteurised cow's milk cheese FRENCH
carrelet	flounder, plaice or sand dab FRENCH
carrot	probably the most familiar root vegetable, it is available all year in a variety of shapes, sizes and shades of orange
carrowgarry	full cream cow's milk cheese with a texture similar to Port-Salut IRISH
cartoccio	fish baked in tightly folded oiled paper to keep the juices in ITALIAN
caruru	green amaranth; minced herbs stewed in oil and spices PORTUGUESE
carving	cutting a joint of cooked meat or poultry into slices or portions for serving
casalinga	home-made ITALIAN
casanova garnish	garnish for fish of oyster, mussels, truffles and white wine sauce FRENCH
cascavaddu	cheese similar to cacio-cavallo SICILIAN
cascaval	ewe's milk plastic-curd cheese BALKAN
casero	home-made SPANISH
cashel blue	sharp, semi-soft blue cheese made from unpasteurised cow's milk IRISH

cashew nut   whitish, kidney-shaped tropical tree nut with a delicate sweet flavour

casigiolu   cow's milk plastic-curd cheese, also known as panedda SARDINIAN

casoeula   pork and vegetable stew ITALIAN

cassareep   syrupy substance used in a stew CARIBBEAN

cassata   frozen ice cream dessert shaped around a bombe mixture of chopped nuts, candied fruit and peel

ITALIAN

cassata alla Siciliana   layers of sponge cake soaked in liqueur, sandwiched together with ricotta cheese and topped with crystallised fruit and chocolate SICILIAN

cassava   long, brown-skinned tuber with white starchy flesh, shaped like a large carrot; cassava

casse museau landais   'jaw-breaker'; a very hard cake FRENCH

casserole   ovenproof dish with tightly fitted lid used for slow cooking; to cook slowly in the oven; a dish cooked by this method

casseruola   casserole ITALIAN

cassette   fermented cow's milk cheese shaped int balls wrapped in walnut leaves or pressed into osier baskets BELGIAN

cassia   the inner bark of a type of cinnamon tree, which it resembles in flavour

cassis   blackcurrant-flavoured liqueur from Dijon FRENCH

cassolette   heatproof dish which holds one portion of a savoury mixture, served as an hors d'oeuvre, entrée or after-dinner savoury FRENCH

cassonade   brown sugar FRENCH

cassoulet   haricot bean stew made from pork, lamb and goose, traditionally made in an earthenware dish known as a cassole FRENCH

cassoulet toulousain   butter-bean stew with goose, mutton, pork or sometimes sausage FRENCH

castagnacci   chestnut flour fritters CORSICAN

castagnaccio   chestnut cake with pine kernels, raisins and nuts ITALIAN

castagne   chestnut ITALIAN

castagnole Romagna   small fritters like very light doughnuts, traditionally eaten in Rome ITALIAN

castaña   chestnut SPANISH

castanha   chestnut PORTUGUESE

castañola	sea perch SPANISH
castellane	garnish of cooked tomatoes, small potato croquettes and onion rings FRENCH
castellane, consommé	meat soup flavoured with snipe fumet FRENCH
castello	sharp tasting cream cheese DANISH
castelmagno	blue mould cheese, similar to gorgonzola ITALIAN
castelo branco	semi-soft fermented ewe's milk cheese PORTUGUESE
castelo de vide	farmhouse-made variety of serra cheese ITALIAN
castiglione, à la	garnish of large mushrooms stuffed with cooked rice, aubergine and slices of poached beef marrow FRENCH
castle pudding	rich sponge pudding, baked or steamed in dariole moulds and served with jam ENGLISH
catalana	with onions, parsley, tomatoes and herbs SPANISH
catalane, à la	dish garnished Spanish-style, usually with aubergine, rice, tomatoes, olives or artichokes FRENCH
cataplana	steamed in a copper pan shaped like a big nutshell PORTUGUESE
catfish	sea fish with long whiskers reminiscent of a cat
catmint	aromatic herb, loved by cats
catsup	tomato catsup; sweet tomato sauce made with tomatoes, onions, pepper, sugar and vinegar (ketchup)
cauchoise	beef consommé with diced cooked lamb, bacon and braised vegetables FRENCH
caudle, caudel	very old English dish of hot spiced oatmeal with brandy, ale or sherry ENGLISH
caul	thin lace-like membrane covering the lower portion of an animal's intestine, used in sausage making
cauliflower	brassica with a compact, white flower head surrounded by green leaves
cauliflower cheese	lightly cooked cauliflower florets with cheese sauce, browned under the grill
cavaillon melon	melon from the district of Cavaillon FRENCH
cavala	mackerel PORTUGUESE
cavallo nero	black cabbage ITALIAN
caveach	fish preserved by pickling in vinegar
caviale	caviar ITALIAN
caviar	salted sturgeon roe; there are several kinds, of varying price, beluga being the most expensive, sevruga half the price; the roe from other fish, such as the lumpfish, is sold as mock caviar

cavolfiore	cauliflower ITALIAN
cavoli	cabbage ITALIAN
cavolino di Bruxelles	Brussels sprout ITALIAN
cavolo	cabbage ITALIAN
cavour	garnish of semolina croquettes and timbale of lasagne and ravioli; garnish of round polenta cakes mixed with Parmesan cheese and mushrooms stuffed with chicken livers; chicken soup with green peas, elbow macaroni and garnished with batter poured through a colander into hot fat FRENCH
cavourma	spinach fried with onion and pieces of mutton, garnished with a poached egg TURKISH
cawl	a Welsh stew of meat and vegetables (including leeks) served with fresh bread and cheese
cayenne	spice prepared from the smallest, hottest red chilli, which is sweet, pungent and very hot
cayettes	flat sausage made from minced pork, herbs and chopped blette, shaped like a large rissole and baked in the oven FRENCH
caza	game SPANISH
cazadora	with mushrooms, spring onions and herbs in wine SPANISH
cazuela a la catalana	minced beef browned in an earthenware dish, carrots, tomatoes and onions are added and the dish is cooked on a low flame SPANISH
cazuela de cordero	lamb stew with vegetables SPANISH
cazzoeula	casserole of pork, celery, onions, cabbage and spices ITALIAN
cebola	onion PORTUGUESE
cebolada	fried onion garnish PORTUGUESE
cebolha	onion PORTUGUESE
cebolla	onion SPANISH
cebolleta	chive SPANISH
cebrero	fine textured mushroom-shaped cheese with pale yellow rind and very faint blue veining SPANISH
cebula	onion POLISH
cebulka	shallot POLISH
cebulka marynowana	pickled onion POLISH
cece	chick-pea ITALIAN
cefalo o muggine	grey mullet, cleaned, brushed with oil and roasted on a bed of wild fennel branches – served with flaming brandy poured over it ITALIAN

cékla	beetroot HUNGARIAN
celer	celery CZECH
céleri	celery FRENCH
celeriac	large, knobbly swollen root with pronounced celery taste
céleri-rave	celeriac FRENCH
celerový salát	celeriac salad CZECH
celery	two types are available, self-blanching with clean, green or golden stalks and main crop, often dirty as it is covered with earth to keep the stalks white
celery cabbage	*see* bok choy, Chinese leaves, headless Chinese cabbage michihili, pe-tsai, wong bok
celery salt	flavouring combining ground celery seeds with salt
celery seed	spice obtained from a different variety of celery than that used in cooking, but with a similar taste
célestine	chicken soup garnished with chopped pancake stuffed with chicken forcemeat and chervil FRENCH
celsius	(centigrade) scale for measuring temperature; the freezing point of water is 0°C and the boiling point is 100°C
cena	dinner, supper ITALIAN, SPANISH
cenci	fried pastry resembling a lover's knot, usually served with dessert ITALIAN
cendré de la brie	cow's milk cheese from the Ile-de-France FRENCH
cenoura	carrot PORTUGUESE
center cut	a thickened end of tenderloin AMERICAN
centolla	spider-crab SPANISH
cep	large, wild edible mushroom
cèpe	boletus; particular member of boletus family FRENCH
cephalopods	group belonging to the mollusc family but with no external shell, such as squid, octopus and cuttlefish
cerceta	teal SPANISH
cerdeña	sardine SPANISH
cerdo	pork SPANISH
cereal	farinaceous food such as oats, rice, wheat, barley, rye, millet and buckwheat
céréales	cereals FRENCH
cereja	cherry PORTUGUESE
cerejas	cherries PORTUGUESE
cereza	cherry SPANISH
cerf	red deer FRENCH
cerfeuil	sweet cicely and chervil FRENCH

cerfeuil tubéreaux	turnip rooted chervil FRENCH
cerfoglio	chervil ITALIAN
cerise	cherry FRENCH
cerneaux au verjus	hors d'oeuvre of sliced peeled green walnuts, covered with grape juice and seasoned with pepper and shallot FRENCH
čermýkuba	barley porridge simmered with caraway seeds, miled with mushrooms and herbs when cool CZECH
čerstvý	fresh CZECH
certosina	creamy white cow's milk cheese ITALIAN
cervelas	short, fat, pork sausage, often flavoured with garlic FRENCH
Cervelatwürst	large smoked sausage made from pork and beef GERMAN
cervella	brains ITALIAN
cervellata	pork sausage flavoured with spices, Parmesan cheese and saffron ITALIAN
cervelles	brains FRENCH
červená řepa	beetroot CZECH
červené zeli	cabbage with onion, caraway CZECH seeds, with soured cream stirred in just before serving
červený rybix	redcurrants CZECH
cervo	deer ITALIAN
česnečka	garlic soup CZECH
česnek	garlic CZECH
cestinhos de verduras	'vegetable baskets' of buttered peas, carrots, turnips and beets cooked in pastry case PORTUGUESE
cetrioli, cetriolo	cucumber ITALIAN
cetriolino	gherkin ITALIAN
ćevapcići	minced pork, beef, garlic and seasoning formed into short fingers and grilled over charcoal YUGOSLAVIAN
čevabčiči	minced meat grilled in rolled pieces, served with minced raw onion CZECH
ceviche	fish marinated in lime or lemon juice flavoured with onion and garlic, served with tomato, pepper and sweetcorn SOUTH AMERICAN
ceviche	fish marinated in lemon and lime juice SPANISH
Ceylon	fairly hot curry, usually with coconut and chilli INDIAN
Ceylon spinach	see basella, Malabar spinach, Indian spinach
chłodnik	chilled cream of beetroot soup with vegetables POLISH

chaat	fruit salad INDIAN
chabichou	small, soft goat's milk cheese from Poitou FRENCH
Chablis	light, very dry, white Burgundy wine FRENCH
chaboisseau	ugly fish with a large head found in the Mediterranean FRENCH
chabot	chub, freshwater fish of the carp family; freshwater fish of the *Cottus* family with a delicate flavour FRENCH
chabris	goat's milk cheese of the camembert type FRENCH
chacklowrie	cooked cabbage mashed with pearl barley broth SCOTTISH
chacumber	salad INDIAN
chafing dish	heatproof dish, usually positioned over a small burner, used at the table to cook food or to keep it warm
chakhokhbili	stew of jointed chicken of lamb with tomatoes, onions and seasoning RUSSIAN
chalber bälleli	meatballs of minced pork and veal with light cream, egg whites and seasoning AMERICAN
challah	traditional twisted white Sabbath loaf JEWISH
chalote	shallot SPANISH
chalotteløg	shallot DANISH
chalwa	sugary loaf made with honey and often pistachio nuts; halvah POLISH
chamberlain tartelette	puff pastry tart filled with chopped breadcrumbs, sugar, cinnamon, lemon zest and rum, covered with hard icing FRENCH
chambertin sauce	wine sauce using Chambertin, a dry red burgundy FRENCH
chambéry	salad of tomatoes filled with diced lobster, salmon, artichoke bottoms, gherkins and shredded lettuce bound with mayonnaise; omelette mixed with cooked leeks, bacon, potatoes and cheese; method of serving potatoes FRENCH
chambord	sauce of fish stock with mirepoix, red wine and anchovy essence; garnish for fish of fish quenelles, mushrooms, soft roes, shrimps, large rounds of truffles and fleurons with sauce chambord FRENCH
Chambourcy	make of yoghurt
chambré	at room temperature FRENCH
chamomille	herb which can be used as a tea FRENCH

champ	traditional potato dish of hot mashed potato with spring onions, placed in a deep dish with a well in the centre into which melted butter is poured IRISH
champagne	sparkling wine produced within the boundaries of the ancient region of Champagne FRENCH
champenois	cow's milk cheese from the Champagne region FRENCH
champignon	button mushroom FRENCH
champignon	mushroom DUTCH
champigny	puff pastry case filled with apricot jam, kirsch and apricot kernels FRENCH
champinjon	mushroom SWEDISH
champiñón	mushroom SPANISH
champoléon	hard skimmed cow's milk cheese of the Cancoillote type, also known as queyras FRENCH
chana	chick peas INDIAN
chana masala	dry chick pea curry INDIAN
chanahki	stew made with cubed lamb, sliced potatoes, onion, green beans, tomatoes and chopped aubergine GEORGIAN
chancho adobado	pork braised with sweet potatoes, orange and lemon juice SPANISH
chanfaina	a famous stew made from the offal, feet and head of a young goat, with artichokes, chard lettuce and peas SPANISH
chanfaina	goat's liver and kidney stew served in a thick sauce SPANISH
channel cat	highly prized fish of the lower Mississippi Valley AMERICAN
chanquetes	small fish, similar to whitebait, found off the coast of Spain SPANISH
chantelle	trade name for a semi-soft, mature cheese from Illinois AMERICAN
chanterelle	small, yellow, delicately-flavoured edible mushroom FRENCH
chantilly cream	sweetened whipped cream, sometimes flavoured with vanilla or brandy FRENCH
chantilly sauce	mayonnaise sauce with lemon juice and cream; béchamel sauce mixed with whipped cream; sauce allemande with whipped cream added just before serving FRENCH
chantilly, à la	method of serving chicken FRENCH

chaource	cow's milk cheese from the Champagne region FRENCH
chapatti	unleavened bread or pancake used to scoop up food INDIAN
chapeler	to make breadcrumbs from bread dried in the oven FRENCH
chapon	pinkish-red Mediterranean fish, used in bouillabaise; bread rubbed with garlic and seasoned with olive oil and vinegar FRENCH
char	freshwater fish, a member of the salmon family
charbonnade	charcoal-grilled meat FRENCH
charbonnier	coalfish FRENCH
charcoal	black porous residue of partially burnt organic matter, which gives a steady heat when used for cooking
charcuterie	traditionally cooked pork products, such as ham, sausages and patés; now includes other meats FRENCH
charcutière, sauce	finely-chopped onion softened in butter, added to demi-glace consommé, white wine or stock; gherkins are added before serving with grilled meat FRENCH
chard	annual vegetable with spinach-like leaves and broad white mid-ribs
Chardonnay	a variety of grape
chard, Swiss	a variety of beet, *Beta vulgaris cicla*, whose thick stalks and succulent leaves resemble spinach; also known as chard, leaf beet and seakale beet
Charles Hiedsieck	a champagne
charlotte	hot or cold moulded dessert FRENCH
charlotte Russe	chilled dessert lined with sponge fingers soaked in liqueur, filled with Bavarian or Chantilly cream FRENCH
Charnwood	a smoked Cheddar cheese ENGLISH
charollais	a breed of cattle noted for the quality and leanness of its meat FRENCH
charollaise	garnish of cooked cauliflower sprigs filled with mashed turnips; clear oxtail soup garnished with small pieces of braised oxtail, julienne of carrot and onion and small cabbage leaves balls stuffed with minced meat FRENCH
charolles	goat's milk cheese from Mâconnais FRENCH

charoset traditionally eaten at Passover to symbolise the clay from which Israelites made bricks during Egyptian slavery, it is made from finely chopped apples, nuts and raisins, mixed with cinnamon and red wine JEWISH

charqui jerky; sun-dried strips of beef SPANISH-AMERICAN

Chartreuse herb-flavoured, brandy-based liqueur; vegetables, especially braised cabbage, arranged in layers in a mould and served with meat or game FRENCH

chasnidarth sweet and sour sauce INDIAN

chasse venison FRENCH

chasse royale various types of game arranged in a pyramid on a large dish FRENCH

chasseur 'hunter'; dish cooked with mushrooms or served with mushroom sauce; before their cultivation mushrooms were hunted by dogs FRENCH

chasseur, à la garnish of mushrooms sautéed with shallots and moistened with white wine; sauce of white wine, mushrooms and shallots; meat or game cooked with shallots, mushrooms, strongly flavoured with tomato; game soup garnished with mushrooms cooked in Madeira and served with small profiteroles filled with game FRENCH

château thick slice of sirloin steak or a slice from a rib of beef; method of preparing potatoes FRENCH

château salad salad of cooked frogs' legs, shredded lettuce and watercress, dressed with vinaigrette or mayonnaise FRENCH-CANADIAN

châteaubriand large, thick steak cut from fillet of beef, large enough to serve two people, traditionally grilled and served with maÊtre d'hotel butter or béarnaise sauce FRENCH

châteaubriand, sauce the true accompaniment for châteaubriand of white wine, demi-glace, shallots, tarragon, cayenne pepper and lemon juice FRENCH

châtelain garnish of pommes château, braised celery, cooked artichoke bottoms and grilled tomatoes; artichoke bottoms stuffed with onion purée, chestnuts and pommes à la Parisienne; omelette filling of mashed chestnuts mixed with gravy; dressing of mayonnaise and whipped cream; chicken soup garnished with artichokes, onions and quenelles of chicken and chestnuts FRENCH

chatouillard	potatoes cut into long ribbons and deep fried; nickname given to an expert fryer FRENCH
chatti, chatty	round-bottomed earthenware cooking pot INDIAN
chauchat	garnish for fish of sliced boiled potatoes, arranged as a border around the fish, which is covered in sauce mornay FRENCH
chaud	warm, hot FRENCH
chaudeau	sweet sauce POLISH
chaudée	high quality apple tart FRENCH
chaudfroid	cold dish of cooked fish, meat, poultry or game coated in thick, white béchamel-based or brown sauce FRENCH
chaudrée	fish soup of court-bouillon, herbs, seasoning, white wine, conger eel, whiting, sole, plaice and other fish FRENCH
chaudron	small copper cauldron for cooking preserved goose and pork FRENCH
chausson	turnover, usually made with puff pastry and often filled with cooked apples, other fruit or savoury fillings FRENCH
chausson au pomme	apple dumpling (US: turnover) FRENCH
chaval, chawal	rice INDIAN
chavender	*see* chub
chavignol	soft goat's milk cheese from Sancerre FRENCH
chayote	pear-shaped squash with smooth or ridged dark green skin FRENCH
chebureki	pastry turnover filled with chopped lamb, onion and rice RUSSIAN
checky pig	curious pasty resembling a little flat pig, filled with minced meat, onion and herbs (originally made in Leicestershire)
chécy	cow's milk cheese from Orléans FRENCH
cheddar	name first given to a cheese made in the Cheddar region of England, but now given to any cheese that undergoes the 'cheddaring' process
chee-koo	sweet fruit with black pips that looks like a potato BM
cheese	solid derivative of milk, the curds are separated from the whey, rennet is added, the whey is drained off and the cheese is allowed to ripen
cheese, fruit	type of jam or jelly preserve of boiled fruit with sugar set in a mould, where it attains a cheese-like consistency

cheeseburger	hamburger containing, or topped with, a slice of cheese
cheesecake	wide variety of flan-like recipes which include soft cheese in the filling
Chelsea bun	small, sweet, yeast cake filled with a mixture of dried fruit, candied peel and brown sugar ENGLISH
Cheltenham pudding	baked suet pudding with dried fruit and preserved ginger ENGLISH
chemisier	to coat food; to line a mould with a thin layer of aspic jelly FRENCH
chen-daw-wan	mushroom BM
chenelle di semolino	small semolina dumplings used to garnish soups ITALIAN
Chenin blanc	variety of grape
Cherbourg	beef soup with Madeira, garnished with mushroom, truffles, poached egg and ham quenelles FRENCH
cherne	black grouper PORTUGUESE
cherry	small, round fruit with a central stone, which varies in colour from white through red to almost black
Cherry Hill	a commercial brand of cheddar CANADIAN
cherry plum	alternative name for myrobalan, a juicy fruit about the size of a cherry
chervèni yaytsà	eggs traditionally painted red as part of Easter celebrations BULGARIAN
chervil	green, leafy herb with a sweet delicate flavour that has a hint of aniseed
Cheshire cat	old cheese measure
Cheshire cheese	said to be the oldest English cheese, it is a hard cheese with a crumbly texture and mild, mellow flavour
chesnok	garlic RUSSIAN
chester français	Cheshire-type cheese from Castres FRENCH
Chester pudding	pudding made from custard mixed with chopped almonds and lemon juice baked in a thin pastry case
chestnut	fruit of the sweet chestnut tree, sold in their skins; they may be dried, cooked, and canned or as a purée
chevaler	symmetrical arrangement of different combinations of a dish by placing them one on another FRENCH
chevalet	slice of bread trimmed and covered with wafer-thin slices of butter or fat pork to which raw chicken breasts are added and baked FRENCH
cheveux d'ange	very fine vermicelli; carrot jam; plain soup garnished with very fine vermicelli FRENCH

Cheviot cheese	type of cheddar cheese flavoured with chopped chives ENGLISH
chèvre	goat; various types of cheese made from goat's milk FRENCH
chevreau	kid FRENCH
chevreuil	roe deer FRENCH
chevreuse	garnish of artichoke bottoms filled with mushroom purée and slices of truffle; purée of turnip-rooted chervil FRENCH
chevrier	type of haricot bean which stays green
chevrotins	small goat's milk cheeses from Auvergne and Savoie FRENCH
chevrotton de Mâcon	goat's milk cheese from Mâcon FRENCH
Chianti	light, fairly dry, red wine; also a good quality white wine ITALIAN
Chiavari	soured cow's milk cheese ITALIAN
chibarzu	large cottage loaf made with wheat flour, salt and yeast SARDINIAN
chícharos	sweet cakes made with dried peas, flour, sugar, butter, lemon zest and juice SPANISH
Chichester pudding	custard pudding stiffened with breadcrumbs; egg whites are folded in and it is baked until set and brown
chickpea	round beige-coloured pulse, the basis of dishes such as hummus; they can be ground into flour.
chicken	domestic fowl, classified as poultry and bred for meat and eggs
chicken brick	unglazed earthenware cooking utensil in which a whole chicken is cooked at high temperature without fat or liquid
chicken corn soup	substantial stew-like soup, traditional in Philadelphia AMERICAN
chicken cream	19th-century dish which uses only the breast and thighs of the bird, minced in a cream sauce and steamed in moulds
chicken kiev	boned, flattened chicken breast, wrapped around a mixture of butter and chives, dipped in breadcrumbs and fried
chicken liver	edible, but should be washed and trimmed before being lightly cooked
chicken salad dressing	mayonnaise dressing with rich chicken broth, thick cream and melted butter AMERICAN

chicken stock cube commercially produced cube containing chicken fat and meat, vegetable oil, onion powder, meat extract, herb and spices, used for enriching soups, stews and casseroles

chicken turbot small or baby turbot

chicksaw plum plum; also called mountain cherry AMERICAN

chicorée chicory FRENCH, GERMAN

chicorée frisée curly-leafed endive FRENCH

chicória chicory PORTUGUESE

chicory in Britain, a spear-shaped vegetable with tightly packed fleshy leaves; in France and the USA what we know as the endive is called chicory; in Italy a variety of red chicory is known as radicchio

chicory gourilos stumps of chicory and endive served as vegetable or hors d'œuvre in France FRENCH

chiffonnade coarsely-shredded lettuce, spinach or other salad vegetable used as garnish for soups or cold hors d'œuvres FRENCH

chiftele meatballs ROMANIAN

chikhirtma soup of mutton, onion and saffron RUSSIAN

chile chilli pepper SPANISH

chiles en nogada green peppers stuffed with whipped cream and nut sauce SPANISH

chilled food foods which should be kept at a low temperature, usually in a refrigerator, but without freezing so as to prevent micro-organisms developing

chilli chillies vary in their hotness and flavour; used for flavouring – see Scoville

chilli con carne speciality dish containing either cubed or minced beef and chilli peppers, and spices such as cumin, cinnamon and onion and tomatoes MEXICAN

chilling cooling food quickly by refrigerating or by surrounding with ice

chilli pepper small, potent, hot peppers that vary greatly in size, shape, colour and strength

chilli powder hot spice of pure ground chilli peppers

chilli sauce sauces made with chillis including *BBQ Sauce from Hell* ('Beyond HOT'), *Ass-kicking Salsa* ('Kick Yo' Ass Hot!'), *Hog's Breath* ('better than no breath at all'), *Death*, and *Beyond Death*

chimaja wild cherry root used in a large number of Mexican dishes MEXICAN

chimichurri	hot parsley sauce SPANISH
China chilo	old English dish made of minced lamb, shredded lettuce and spring onions, butter and green peas, simmered, and with diced cucumber added before serving on a clear white and green dish
chincard	elongated fish of the same family as saurel FRENCH
chine	joints of meat severed from the spine by sawing through the ribs
chine bone	joint of meat, usually pork; part of the backbone of the animal
Chinese broccoli	*see* white flowering broccoli, Chinese kale, gai lan, kailan, kaai laan tsoi CHINESE
Chinese cabbage	type of cabbage with white ribs and elongated leaves, rather like a cos lettuce ASIAN
Chinese celery cabbage	*see*, Chinese mustard (greens), Chinese mustard cabbage, Chinese white cabbage, chingensai, gai choy, green in snow, Indian mustard (greens), kai tsoi, leaf mustard, mustard cabbage, taisin CHINESE
chive	long, thin, dark green stem, similar to common chive, but flat rather than hollow, with strong onion-garlic flavour, also known as Chinese leek, garlic chive CHINESE
Chinese date	tropical tree fruit with scratch-like marks and long pointed seeds, tasting a little like dried date CHINESE
Chinese five spice	equal parts of star anise, cassia, cloves, fennel seed and Chinese pepper CHINESE
Chinese flowering cabbage	cabbage with smooth, dark green leaves and firm white stems CHINESE
Chinese kale	*see* white flowering broccoli, Chinese broccoli, gai lan, kailan, kaai laan tsoi CHINESE
Chinese keys	reddish-brown root vegetable, a member of the ginger family that looks rather like a bunch of oddly shaped keys CHINESE
Chinese lantern	member of the same family as the Cape gooseberries, grown more for its decorative papery husks than its berries CHINESE
Chinese leaves	light green leafy vegetable, also known as bok choy, celery cabbage, headless Chinese cabbage, michihili, pe-tsai, wong bok
Chinese leek	*see* Chinese chive, garlic chive
Chinese mustard cabbage	*see* Chinese celery cabbage, Chinese mustard (greens), Chinese white cabbage, chingensai, gai

choy, green in snow, Indian mustard (greens), kai tsoi, leaf mustard, mustard cabbage, pak choi, taisin CHINESE

Chinese mustard (greens) *see* Chinese celery cabbage, Chinese mustard cabbage, Chinese white cabbage, chingensai, gai choy, green in snow, Indian mustard (greens), kai tsoi, leaf mustard, mustard cabbage, taisin

Chinese spinach *see* amaranth, bayam, calaloo

Chinese water spinach small-leafed, dark green vegetable, faintly resembling spinach but with firmer stems that stay firm when cooked CHINESE

Chinese white cabbage *see* Chinese celery cabbage, Chinese mustard (greens), Chinese mustard cabbage, chingensai, gai choy, green in snow, Indian mustard (greens), kai tsoi, leaf mustard, mustard cabbage, taisin

chingensai *see* Chinese celery cabbage, Chinese mustard (greens), Chinese mustard cabbage, Chinese white cabbage, gai choy, green in snow, Indian mustard (greens), kai tsoi, leaf mustard, mustard cabbage, taisin

chingree, chingri prawns INDIAN

chino conical strainer or colander used with small wooden paddle SPANISH

chinois small Chinese oranges, crystallized or preserved in brandy; conical strainer with fine mesh FRENCH

Chinook salmon *see* quinnat salmon

chiodi di garofano cloves ITALIAN

chiorro Basque national dish of onions, garlic, tomatoes, red wine and other seasonings poured over fish fillets cooked in lemon juice, served on a crouton of fried bread SPANISH

chiozzo gudgeon ITALIAN

chipirones small inkfish (squid) SPANISH

chipolata small pork sausage used to garnish meat dishes and served with roast poultry, or served on sticks as savoury snacks

chipped beef finely sliced, air-dried beef (English: dried beef) AMERICAN

chips colloquial word for fingers of fried potatoes ENGLISH

chiqueter to mark out with a knife the small round top of a vol au vent case or the edge of a tart or flan FRENCH

chirongi nut small, round musky-flavoured nut used in Hyderabadi cooking INDIAN

chispalhada	pig's trotters stewed with navy beans, cabbage, bacon and blood sausage PORTUGUESE
chispe	pig's trotter PORTUGUESE
chispe e feijão branco	soaked dried white beans, cooked slowly with pig's trotters, pieces of pork, garlic and carrots, flavoured with parsley and aniseed PORTUGUESE
chitarra, alla	long thin pasta cut on a board with wire strings ITALIAN
chitterlings	small intestines of a pig
chive	common herb with long, narrow, tubular stems and a purple flower
chivry, sauce	classical sauce served with poultry, eggs or fish, made from velouté, stock and white wine, flavoured with shallots, tarragon, chervil, chives and burnet FRENCH
chlazeno	chilled CZECH
chleb	bread POLISH
chléb	bread CZECH
chléb bíly	white bread CZECH
chléb celozrnny	wholemeal bread CZECH
chléb černy	black bread CZECH
chlebíček	open sandwich CZECH
chlodnik	cold herb soup made with red beetroot, beetroot top, sorrel, chives, dill and the juice of pickled cucumbers POLISH
chlupaté knedlíky se zelím	Bohemian potato dumplings made with raw grated potato, flour and eggs, with cabbage CZECH
chobotnice	octopus CZECH
chocola(de)	chocolate DUTCH
chocolat	chocolate FRENCH
chocolate	derived from the bean of the cacao tree, made into a deliciously rich, smooth, sweet and irresistible confection
chocos	inkfish or cuttlefish PORTUGUESE, SPANISH
chocos com tinta	cuttlefish cooked in its own ink PORTUGUESE
chod	course; dish CZECH
chod hlavní	main course; dish CZECH
choisy	garnish of braised lettuce and pommes château; omelette filling of braised lettuce with cream sauce FRENCH
choklad	chocolate SWEDISH
choke	the edible capitulum of the globe artichoke

choko	pale green fruit of a climbing vine
cholent	Sabbath dish of beef casserole with haricot beans, onion, potatoes and large dumpling JEWISH
cholesterol	fatty substance in the cells of all animals which transports fatty acids around the body in the blood
choo-ka	vinegar BM
chop	slice of meat, usually mutton, lamb, pork or veal, which generally includes a rib but may be cut from the chump or tail end of the loin; chump chop; neck chops are known as cutlets
chopa	kind of sea bream SPANISH
chop potato pudding	potatoes, flour and suet steamed and served with meat and gravy CORNISH
chop suey	originated in the USA as a way of using leftovers; strips of chicken, beef or pork are cooked with onions and vegetables, chicken stock and soy sauce are added, and the dish is served with sliced omelette on top PSEUDO CHINESE
chop suey greens,	*see* chrysanthemum greens, Japanese greens and shunguki
chopa blanca	common rudderfish, found in the Gulf of Florida AMERICAN
chopping	cutting food into small pieces without damaging the tissue
chorbà	soup BULGARIAN
chorichori	marinated and cooked in tomatoes, onions, herbs and cream INDIAN
chorizo	sausage containing pork and pimiento SPANISH
chorizo	pork sausage, highly seasoned with garlic and paprika SPANISH
chorlito	plover SPANISH
choron	garnish of artichoke bottoms, green peas, pommes noisettes and béarnaise sauce blended with tomato purée FRENCH
chou	cabbage FRENCH
chou caraïbe	the root of *Arum esculentum* prepared like a swede FRENCH
chou rouge	red cabbage FRENCH
choucroute	sauerkraut FRENCH
choucroute garnie	sauerkraut, garnished with ham, bacon and sausage FRENCH

chouée	green cabbage boiled in salt water, drained, pressed and a large amount of butter added FRENCH
chou-fleur	cauliflower FRENCH
chou-rave	kolhrabi FRENCH
chouriça, chouriço	smoked pork sausage flavoured with paprika PORTUGUESE
chouriço	smoked, pickled pork sausage flavoured with garlic and paprika PORTUGUESE
choux	pastry used for eclairs and profiteroles, filled with sweet or savoury fillings; cabbage FRENCH
choux de bruxelles	Brussels sprouts FRENCH
chow chow	pickle of mixed vegetables CHINESE
chow mein	meat, vegetables and noodles CHINESE
chowder	stew-like soup, usually containing shellfish AMERICAN
choy sum	see brocoletto, flowering pak choi, flowering white cabbage, hong tsoi sum, hon tsai tai, kozaitai , pak tsoi sum, rape
chrane	preserve of cooked beetroot mixed with grated horseradish covered with malt vinegar and sweetened with sugar JEWISH
chremslach	Passover dish of pancakes sprinkled with almonds and filled with preserved fruits, chopped nuts and honey JEWISH
chrest	asparagus CZECH
Christmas cake	large, rich fruit cake flavoured with spices and brandy, covered with marzipan and decorated with royal icing
Christmas orange	mandarin, naatje, satsuma, tangerine, etc.
Christmas pudding	steamed pudding, made from a rich mixture of dried fruit, candied peel, nuts, suet, breadcrumbs, eggs, flour, sugar and spices
Christópsomo	a Christmas bread decorated with a cross of dough and chopped nuts GREEK
chrust czyli faworki	thin sweet biscuit, fried until crisp and brown and eaten hot or cold POLISH
chrysanthemum	plant often used as decoration for food
chrysanthemum greens	green vegetable, Chrysanthemum coronarium, a member of the daisy family; also known as chop suey greens, Japanese greens and shunguki
chrzan	horseradish POLISH
chrzan z octem	horseradish sauce made with wine vinegar, sugar and salt, but without sour cream POLISH

chub	freshwater fish of the carp family, with little flavour and lots of bones; chavender
chuchel	thick batter cooked in frying pan, served with fruit sauce or syrup SWISS
chuchu	type of marrow PORTUGUESE
chuck	one of the cheapest cuts of beef from the neck ribs
chudleigh	a Devonshire plain yeast bun, split and served with clotted cream and strawberry or raspberry jam ENGLISH
chufa	small, wrinkled, brown tuber with white, crisp flesh and a sweet, nutty flavour EUROPEAN
chukander	beetroot INDIAN
chuleta	cutlet or chop SPANISH
chump	rear end of loin of lamb, mutton or pork
chupe de mariscos	scallops with a creamy sauce and gratinéed with cheese SPANISH
churrasco	charcoal-grilled meat served with hot pepper sauce PORTUGUESE
churro	sugared tubular fritter SPANISH
churros	popular breakfast dish rather like a doughnut made in long spirals, coated with sugar and broken into lengths for serving SPANISH
chutney	thick, piquant purée of fruit and/or vegetables, usually served as a condiment
ciambella	ring-shaped bun ITALIAN
ciastka	cakes or pastries POLISH
ciastka kruche	biscuits POLISH
ciastko	cake POLISH
ciasto	dough or pastry POLISH
cibol	onion WELSH
ciboulette	chives FRENCH
cibule	onion CZECH
cicala di maro	squill-fish ITALIAN
cicoria	chicory; endive ITALIAN
cider	alcoholic drink made from fermented apple juice
cieście	pastry; pasty POLISH
cielęcina	veal POLISH
cietrzew	blackcock POLISH
cigala	Dublin bay prawn SPANISH
cigányrostélyos	steak with brown sauce and braised vegetables HUNGARIAN

ciger	liver TURKISH
cikorka	chicory CZECH
cilantro	coriander SPANISH
ciliegia	cherry ITALIAN
cima	stuffed cold veal ITALIAN
cincho	hard ewe's milk cheese from central Spain SPANISH
cinghiale	wild boar ITALIAN
cinnamon	inner bark of an evergreen tree grown mostly in Sri Lanka, a popular spice with a sweet, pungent flavour
cioccolata	chocolate ITALIAN
cioppino	speciality of San Francisco, a dish of fish and shellfish in a rich sauce, cooked over a charcoal brazier AMERICAN
ciorbă	meat or fish soup RUMANIA
cipolla	onion ITALIAN
cipolla	onion ITALIAN
cipollina	chive, pearl onion ITALIAN
cîrnat	sausage RUMANIA
ciruela	plum SPANISH
cisco	prized white fish from the Great Lakes AMERICAN
ciseler	to make light incisions on the back of fish to reduce cooking time FRENCH
ciste	lamb or pork chops, kidneys, onions, carrot and seasoning are simmered, ciste paste is made from flour and suet to the size of the pan and placed on top of the stew; the whole is then cooked for an hour or so IRISH
cîteaux	cow's milk cheese from Burgundy FRENCH
citrange	hybrid of the sweet orange and the trifoliate orange; more acid than the common orange AMERICAN
citric acid	mild acid that occurs naturally in citrus fruits
citroen	lemon DUTCH
citrom	lemon HUNGARIAN
citron	fruit resembling lemon, but larger, longer and greener – the flesh is too sour to eat raw
citron	lemon DANISH, SWEDISH
citronella	tropical perennial grass with strong lemony smell; the leaves are used sparingly for seasoning and in salad
citrouillat	pumpkin pie FRENCH
citrus fruit	generic name for fruits that grow on trees and shrubs

	in warm or tropical climates, including lemons, limes, oranges and grapefruit; all are slightly acid, and high in pectin and vitamin C
city chicken	veal and pork cubes threaded onto skewers, coated in breadcrumbs, fried then braised in stock AMERICAN
ciuperci	mushrooms ROMANIAN
ciuppin	thick fish soup ITALIAN
civet	applied particularly to game stew cooked with red wine and garnished with small onions, lardons and mushrooms FRENCH
civet de lapin	jugged rabbit FRENCH
civet de lièvre	jugged hare FRENCH
cizze con formaggio	cheese-filled pastry slices fried in olive oil ITALIAN
CJD	Creuzfeldt-Jakob disease, a human form of BSE, transmitted by eating infected parts of animals
clabbered milk	naturally-soured thick, curdy milk
clafoutis	dessert of fresh fruit baked in batter FRENCH
claire	sea enclosures in the Marennes region, where oysters are left to go green and acquire a more delicate flavour FRENCH
clam	bivalve shellfish of the mollusc family, found on both coasts of the Atlantic ocean
Clamart, à la	garnish of tartlets of artichoke bottoms filled with pois à la Française or purée of green peas and new potatoes cooked in butter FRENCH
clapshot	boiled potatoes and turnips mashed with chives, bacon fat, salt and pepper ORKNEY ISLANDS
clara de huevo	egg white SPANISH
claraire	clavaria; usually eaten sautéed in oil or butter FRENCH
claret	the English name for red wine from the Bordeaux region FRENCH
clarifying	clearing or purifying; the release of fat from water or meat juices so it may be used for frying or pastry-making
clary	bitter herb of the sage family which smells a little like grapefruit
clavaria	spindle-shaped, capless fungi, which is tough to eat
clayere	enclosure or bed where oysters are fattened FRENCH
clayon	small wire trays used by pastry cooks FRENCH
clementine	hybrid citrus fruit developed from the tangerine and the Seville orange

clermont garnish of fragments of chestnut mixed with sauce soubise poached in moulds, served with rings of fried onion; garnish of stuffed braised cabbage balls cooked with salt pork, boiled potatoes and demi-glace FRENCH

Clifton puffs small cake from Clifton near Bristol; similar to Banbury cake, but ground rice and ground almonds are added to the pastry

clisse little tray of wicker or rushes used to drain cheeses
FRENCH

clod hanging folds of the neck of ox; used for soups and stews

clonevan full cream milk cheese IRISH

clotted cream traditional Devonshire thick cream

clotting thickening cream by gentle heating

clou de girofle clove FRENCH

cloudberry delicate, very sweet, soft berry, slightly resembling raspberry

clouter to stud pieces of meat, poultry or game with small pieces of another substance such as truffle, ham or gherkin FRENCH

clove pungent nail-shaped spice, available whole or ground

clovisse Provençal name for thick-shelled clam FRENCH

club sandwich double decker sandwich of fresh toast spread with mayonnaise, lettuce, tomato, turkey and bacon
AMERICAN

club steak equivalent to entrecôte AMERICAN

cluny, omelette omelette with hot game purée folded in FRENCH

clupeidae important fish family of saltwater and freshwater fish, which includes herring, anchovy and sardine

cnicaut edible wild cardoon FRENCH

coalfish seafish related to cod and pollack

coating flour, batter, egg and breadcrumb covering applied to food before frying; covering sweet items or cakes with chocolate or icing

cob *see* corn

cobbler sweetened, cooling mixture of fruit and wine or liqueur; meat or fruit dish with topping of round scones ENGLISH

cobnut a type of hazelnut ENGLISH

coburg cakes small sponge cakes, usually flavoured with spices and containing syrup

coca	leaves, traditionally chewed in the Andes and Amazon basin
cocada	coconut macaroon PORTUGUESE
cochifrito (de cordero)	lamb (or kid) and paprika stew with onions, garlic, lemon juice and herbs SPANISH
cochineal	red colouring obtained from the female of small species of native Mexican beetle, which is dried and ground to produce the pigment
cochinillo asado del mesón del segoviano	roast or suckling pig served in Madrid SPANISH
cochlearia	a kind of wild horseradish with a four-petalled flower; the leaves were eaten as salad in France and Ireland
cochon	pig FRENCH
cochon de lait	suck(l)ing pig FRENCH
cocido	cooked; boiled; stew of beef with ham, fowl, chick peas, potatoes and vegetables SPANISH
cock	male bird of any genus or species; male fowl
cock's comb	the fleshy red crest on the head of poultry
cock's kidneys	the testicles of male fowl
cock-a-leekie	thick soup containing chicken, leeks and barley SCOTTISH
čočka	lentils CZECH
cockle	variety of small bivalve mollusc shellfish found around the coast of Britain and elsewhere
čočkový salát	lentil salad CZECH
čočková polévka	lentil soup CZECH
čockoláda	chocolate CZECH
čockoláda mléčná	milk chocolate bar CZECH
čockoláda na veření	cooking chocolate CZECH
čockoláda oříšková	chocolate bar with hazelnuts CZECH
cocktail	short or long alcoholic drink with a variety of ingredients, well-mixed so that no one flavour predominates; cold hors d'œuvre containing a number of ingredients
coco	coconut PORTUGUESE
coco bean	variety of French bean, increasingly popular for its flavour and decorative appearance
cocoa	pulverised seeds of the cacao tree
cocomero	water melon ITALIAN
coconut	fruit of coconut palm, generally harvested young and green; the watery juice is a refreshing drink; coconut

	milk is obtained from the mature, hard, hairy, brown-shelled fruit; coconut flesh is available flaked, shredded, and dried
coconut ice	desiccated coconut mixed into boiled sugar and milk, set in a tin and cut into bars
coconut milk	liquid pressed from coconut flesh
cocotte	lidded pot also known as a casserole; dish cooked in an individual ramekin FRENCH
cocozelle	vegetable marrow ITALIAN
cod	large, round sea fish found in the cold North Atlantic
cod liver oil	oil extracted from fresh cod liver by heating, cooling and processing
cod's roe	available fresh, canned or smoked, it may form a basis of taramasalata
coda di bue	oxtail ITALIAN
cod-burbot	freshwater fish of cod family
coddling	eggs placed in a pan of boiling water, removed from the heat and left to stand for 8–10 minutes, when they will be soft boiled
codorniz	quail PORTUGUESE, SPANISH
coelho	rabbit PORTUGUESE
coentro	coriander PORTUGUESE
coeur à la crème	soured-milk cheese made in special heart-shaped moulds FRENCH
coeur de palmier	palm hearts FRENCH
coffee	popular beverage all over the world, coffee is derived from the berries of the tropical coffee tree
coffee essence	bottled coffee concentrate used to flavour sweet and savoury dishes
coffin	thick dough shaped into a pie dish – acts as a casserole for meat and as a means of storage
cognac	fine brandy made from grapes of a specific region of France FRENCH
cogumelo	mushroom PORTUGUESE
coing	quince FRENCH
Cointreau	orange-flavoured liqueur FRENCH
col	cabbage SPANISH
col de Bruselas	Brussels sprout SPANISH
cola	tropical tree; the nuts contain caffeine AFRICAN
colache	vegetable dish made with onion, garlic, courgettes, tomatoes, sweet corn and green beans, fried in bacon fat MEXICAN

colander	perforated draining basket, larger than a sieve
colazione	lunch ITALIAN
colbert, à	name for a number of dishes; sole colbert is coated in egg and breadcrumbs and fried; consommé à la colbert is garnished with small poached eggs; colbert butter is flavoured with tarragon; colbert sauce is flavoured with lemon, parsley, Madeira and spices FRENCH
colby	mild deep yellow semi-hard cheese with dark brown rind AMERICAN
colcannon	potato, cabbage and other vegetables flavoured with herbs IRISH
Colchester natives	particularly fine oysters cultivated at Colchester (Essex)
cold cuts	cold slices of meat and ham AMERICAN
cold pack cheese	a commercial cheese spread AMERICAN
cole	see rape
coleslaw	salad of finely shredded white cabbage dressed with mayonnaise and possibly grated carrot, chopped apple, onion, nuts or dried fruit
coley	member of the cod family, a large, round sea fish with bluish-black skin
coliflor	cauliflower SPANISH
colin	hake FRENCH
colin, colin-loui	American and Canadian names for bobwhite, a member of the quail family
collar	neck cut of pork, usually cured
collared	various cabbages of the kale type; pickled or salted meat, seasoned, rolled and boiled and served cold
college pudding	suet pudding flavoured with dried fruits and spices
coller	adding dissolved gelatine to a food preparation to make it stiffer
collier's foot	pasty popular in northern England, filled with onion, cheese and slices of bacon
collioure	sauce of mayonnaise, anchovy fillets, parsley and garlic FRENCH
collop	from escalope; a small, boneless piece of meat or a dish of finely minced meat ENGLISH, SCOTTISH
colmenillas	morels SPANISH
colocassi	large, rough-skinned vegetable that looks similar to parsnip, but used as potato

colombine	croquette with outer layer of cooked semolina mixed with Parmesan; chicken soup garnished with carrots, turnips, pigeon breast and poached pigeon eggs FRENCH
colonne	utensil to core fruit FRENCH
colorau	paprika PORTUGUESE
colouring	edible food colourings or dyes added to food to enhance the appearance of a dish, common in processed foods which lose much of their natural colour
Colston Bassett	mellow and deep flavoured creamy Stilton-type cheese made at Colston Bassett in Nottinghamshire from pasteurised milk
Colwick cheese	cow's milk cheese usually sold unsalted as a dessert
colza	*see* rape
comb	leg HUNGARIAN
comb bárány	leg of lamb HUNGARIAN
comber	rack of meat containing a kidney; taken partly from the loin and partly from the rib POLISH
comber barani	saddle of mutton POLISH
comber sarni	loin of venison POLISH
combination oven	oven which can be used as a microwave oven, a conventional oven, or both at the same time
comfrey	herb of the borage family
comida	meal SPANISH
cominho	caraway seed PORTUGUESE
commande, sur	menu term indicating that the food will be cooked to order and could therefore take some time FRENCH
comme	as, like FRENCH
commis	assistant chef FRENCH
commodore	fish garnish; croquettes of crayfish or lobster tails, fish quenelles and mussels and a sauce Normande; fish soup garnished with clams and diced tomatoes FRENCH
composite	member of a large plant family including sunflowers, lettuce, chicory, salsify, and many others
composta	stewed fruit ITALIAN
compota	compote, stewed fruit PORTUGUESE, SPANISH
compote	fresh or dried fruit stewed in sugar syrup, game bird stew, cooked until the meat is very tender FRENCH, ENGLISH

compotier	large shallow dish, usually made of glass, on a raised base FRENCH
Comté	hard cow's milk cheese from the Franche-Comté country FRENCH
concasser	chopped food FRENCH
conch	large edible mollusc found in warm waters
conchiglia	shell, particularly with reference to small shellfish ITALIAN
concombre	cucumber FRENCH
condé	thick moulded rice pudding served with stewed fruit; pastry coated with almond-flavoured royal icing; savoury dishes containing purée of red kidney beans FRENCH
condensed milk	canned milk, usually sweetened
condiment	sauces, pickles and relishes, salt, pepper and mustard, served at table as an accompaniment to food
conejo	rabbit SPANISH
confectioners' custard	rich, thick, creamy custard mixture, usually flavoured with vanilla
confettura	jam ITALIAN
confit	preserve, usually of duck, goose or pork, sealed in its own fat and cooked for a long time FRENCH
confitura	jam SPANISH
confiture	jam FRENCH
congélateur	deep-freeze, freezer FRENCH
conger eel	large saltwater fish, sometimes reaching eight feet in length
congress tart	small pastry tart spread with jam and filled with a mixture of ground almonds, sugar and egg
congrio	conger eel SPANISH
congro	conger eel PORTUGUESE
coniglio	rabbit ITALIAN
conserve	whole or chopped fruits suspended in thick syrup
consistency	the texture of a mixture; firm, stiff, dropping or soft
consolante	alcoholic drink given to chefs while they are working FRENCH
consomé al jerez	chicken broth with sherry SPANISH
consommation	general word for drinks FRENCH
consommé	concentrated and clarified soup or stock FRENCH

consommé all' uovo beef broth heated to just under boiling point and poured over a beaten egg mixed with lemon juice ITALIAN

conta bill PORTUGUESE

contact grill a pair of hinged non-stick heated plates between which any flat food can be cooked on both sides simultaneously

conti garnish of rectangles of bacon cooked with lentils, sieved before serving; lentil soup mixed with butter and garnished with chervil and croutôns FRENCH

contiser fillets of game, poultry or sole studded with truffles soaked in egg white FRENCH

contorno garnish ITALIAN

contre-filet steak cut from the top of the sirloin FRENCH

conversation puff pastry tart filled with a mixture of rum and almonds FRENCH

cookie American sweet biscuits; in Britain, soft-textured biscuit such as a brownie; in Scotland, glazed bread roll made from a yeast dough with dried fruit AMERICAN, BRITISH

coon cheddar cheese cured by a patented method AMERICAN

coot small bird not much valued as food today

copa nuria egg yolk and egg white, whipped and served with jam SPANISH

copate small wafer-like cakes containing honey and nuts, a speciality of Sienna ITALIAN

copeaux small cakes; petits fours FRENCH

coppa usually smoked raw ham cut from the shoulder, more fatty than prosciutto ITALIAN

copper red-coloured metal, an excellent conductor of heat, a popular metal for kitchen utensils

copra coconut INDIAN

coprin chevelu shaggy cap mushroom FRENCH

coq male chicken FRENCH

coq au vin chicken cooked in red wine flavoured with brandy, onion, carrot, garlic, and herbs served with button onions and mushrooms and garnished with croutôns FRENCH

coq de bruyère woodcock FRENCH

coq solidex transparent egg poacher with a clip-on lid FRENCH

coque cockle FRENCH

coque du Lot   Easter cake, a speciality of the Lot region FRENCH

coquelicot   poppy FRENCH

coques à petits fours   almond balls served as petits fours FRENCH

coquillage   shellfish FRENCH

coquille, en   dishes, usually shellfish, served in a shell or made to resemble a shell FRENCH

coquilles Saint Jacques   scallops FRENCH

coquinas   small brightly-coloured clams from the Gulf of Florida

coração   heart PORTUGUESE

coral   the ovaries of hen lobsters, the basis of most lobster sauces

corazón de alcahofa   artichoke heart SPANISH

corazonada   heart stewed in sauce SPANISH

čorba   thick soup SERBO-CROAT

corbeille   basket FRENCH

corbeille de fruits   basket of assorted fruits FRENCH

corda   lamb tripes roasted or braised in tomato sauce with peas ITALIAN

cordée   soggy pastry, a result of too much water being added FRENCH

cordeiro   lamb PORTUGUESE

cordero   lamb SPANISH

cordial   originally a spirit sweetened and infused with fruit to add flavour or scent; today a sweet or concentrated fruit drink

cordon bleu   veal scallop stuffed with ham and cheese DUTCH

cordula   sheep's gut rubbed with herbs and oil and roasted on a spit SARDINIAN

core   removal of the hard, indigestible centre of certain foods; removal of the centre of kidneys

coriander   herb grown both for its leaves and seeds

coriandro   coriander ITALIAN

cormorant   sea bird which feeds entirely on fish; young birds are suitable for eating

corn   in England refers to maize or sweetcorn; in Scotland sometimes denotes oats; in America mostly refers to maize

corn on the cob   a cob of maize, boiled or roasted with the kernels attached, served as a vegetable, often with butter

corn salad   *see* lamb's lettuce

corn syrup	manufactured from cornflour by treatment with acid; a sweetening agent, not as sweet as cane sugar
corncrake	small migratory bird, becoming very rare
corned beef	salt beef
cornelian cherry	edible fruit of a deciduous shrub or tree
cornet	hollow, conical wafer biscuit used to hold scoops of ice cream
cornetti	string beans; crescent rolls ITALIAN
cornflour	finely ground corn kernels, mainly used as thickening agent
cornhusker	cow's milk cheese AMERICAN
cornichon	small gherkin (US: pickle) FRENCH, GERMAN
Cornish burnt cream	alternate layers of baked custard and clotted cream in a pie dish, covered with thinly sliced citron, sprinkled with sugar and lightly browned
Cornish fairings	traditional Cornish biscuits
Cornish pasty	traditional Cornish pastry turnover with a variety of possible fillings, particularly meat and vegetables
Cornish splits	traditional Cornish rolls served hot with jam, cream or treacle
Cornish squab cake	mashed potatoes seasoned with salt and pepper, spread over a thick pastry crust and covered with strips of pickled pork
cornmeal	yellow or white coarse or finely ground corn grain
corn pone	corn bread, especially a plain type made with water SOUTHERN US
coronation chicken	diced, cooked chicken in curry-flavoured mayonnaise, with tomato, wine, onion, lemon, bay and apricot, lightened with whipped cream and served cold
cortadillo	small pancake with lemon SPANISH
corvina	croaker – a type of fish PORTUGUESE
corzo	deer SPANISH
cos lettuce	lettuce with long crisp leaves, but no heart
cosce di rana	frog's legs ITALIAN
coscia	leg, thigh ITALIAN
cosciotto	leg ITALIAN
cosford	hazelnut of good quality and size
costard	English variety of apple
costata	beef steak or chop; entrecôte ITALIAN
costeletta	chop; cutlet PORTUGUESE

costilla chop SPANISH

costmary herb with overpowering minty scent and bitter flavour, once used in beer-making

costoletta cutlet; chop ITALIAN

cotechino pork sausage flavoured with wine, garlic and spices served hot in slices ITALIAN

côtelette cutlet FRENCH

côtelettes de poisson thick cutlets cut across a large fish such as cod or salmon SPANISH

côtelettes de volaille chicken cutlets FRENCH

cotenna pork rind ITALIAN

côtes de boeuf rib of beef, including the muscles covering the ribs and backbone FRENCH

côtes découvertes middle neck cutlets of lamb FRENCH

Cotherstone cheese yellow, crumbly, unpasteurised double cream cow's milk cheese, with a soft crust and mild, slightly sharp flavour; a blue variety is available ENGLISH

cotignac old French sweetmeat for which Orléans was famous FRENCH

cotogna quince ITALIAN

côtoyer to turn a joint when cooking so that all sides get maximum heat FRENCH

cotriade fish soup from Breton similar to bouillabaisse, but using Atlantic fish; the liquid is served on slices of bread and the meat and fish are served separately FRENCH

cotronese ewe's and goat's milk cheese of the percorino type ITALIAN

Cotswold cheese type of Double Gloucester cheese flavoured with chives and chopped onion ENGLISH

cottage cheese soft skimmed milk cheese which is heated and then soured

cottage pie homely dish, similar to shepherds pie, usually made with leftover cooked meat

Cottenham rare, double-cream, semi-hard, blue-veined cheese

cotto cooked ITALIAN

coucher to make pâté, stuffing or purée or other preparation into a round shape on a baking sheet FRENCH

coucouzelle a variety of courgette, picked when quite small and known as zucchetti or zucchini in Italy FRENCH

couennes de porc fresh pork rinds often added to stews to enrich and add gelatinous quality to the gravy FRENCH

coulibiac	fish pie made from layers of sturgeon or salmon, mushrooms, buckwheat and hard-boiled eggs wrapped in brioche or puff pastry RUSSIAN
coulis	originally meat juices, it came to mean various sauces, especially rich gravy; thickened soup, of puréed meat, poultry or fish; thin purée of cooked vegetables, especially tomatoes; purée of fruit served as sauce with desserts
coulommiers	soft, creamy, cow's milk cheese similar to Brie
country captain	curried chicken with raisins and apples ANGLO-INDIAN
country spoon bread	cornmeal bread from the southern States AMERICAN
country-style	simple home cooking
coupe	glass or stainless steel cup or goblet in which cold desserts are served; dessert served in a glass FRENCH
courges	vegetable marrow, squash or pumpkin FRENCH
courgette	member of the squash family; a variety of baby marrow cut before it is fully developed
couronne	crown of meat FRENCH
court bouillon	any seasoned liquid in which meat, poultry, fish or vegetables are poached to give flavour
couscous	grains of semolina formed into tiny pellets coated with fine wheat flour, usually steamed and served as accompaniment NORTH AFRICAN
cousinette	soup of finely chopped spinach, sorrel, lettuce and green herbs FRENCH
coûte au pot	pot au feu is allowed to get cold and the fat removed, squares of toast are put on the bottom of a casserole, the stew is spooned over and reheated FRENCH
couve	cabbage PORTUGUESE
couve tronchuda	cabbage with white midribs which are cooked like sea-kale PORTUGUESE
couve-de-Bruxelas	Brussels sprouts PORTUGUESE
couve-flor	cauliflower PORTUGUESE
Coventry godcakes	triangular cakes of puff pastry filled with mincemeat, traditionally given to godchildren by their godparents
cow	female ox
cow parsnip	a weed; the leaves have a faint flavour of asparagus and can be cooked as spinach
cow pea	herb more closely related to the bean than the pea; the dried peas can be black or white

cowberry	member of the cranberry family with quite large, dark red, very tart berries
cowl	stew WELSH
cowslip	sweetly scented spring flower sometimes eaten with fresh cream or crystallized in sugar, but chiefly used to make wine, vinegar, mead or syrup
cozido	any boiled dish PORTUGUESE
cozonac	elaborate traditional raisin bread RUMANIA
cozza	mussel ITALIAN
cozze pelose	mussels with a shell covered in hair ITALIAN
crab	a decapod crustacean with a wide flat body encased in a hard shell
crab apple	probably the original wild apple, with small, very sour fruits with shiny red or yellow skin and firm flesh
crabe	crab FRENCH
cracked wheat	crushed, whole, uncooked grains of wheat
cracker	plain or salted hard biscuit suitable for eating with cheese
crackling	crisp skin on joint of roast pork
cracknel	type of biscuit made of paste which is boiled before being baked, causing it to puff up
cramique	brioche with raisins BELGIAN
cranberry	hard, sharp-tasting fruit, similar to bilberry
crap	carp ROMANIAN
crapaudine	piquante sauce with mushrooms and a little mustard diluted in tarragon vinegar; method of preparing and cooking certain birds, particularly pigeon, split horizontally, opened, flattened slightly, spread with melted butter and grilled on both sides until cooked FRENCH
crappie	freshwater fish from the Mississippi Valley
crappit heids	stuffed heads of haddock SCOTTISH
craquelin	dry biscuit, sprinkled with vanilla sugar when cooked FRENCH
craquelots	a herring which is only half smoked FRENCH
crauti	sauerkraut ITALIAN
crawfish	rock lobsters, known in France as langouste, they are large clawless crustaceans found in most temperate coastal waters; most of the meat is in the tail
crayfish	freshwater crustacean like a miniature lobster

cream	larger, lighter fat particles of whole cow's milk, skimmed off the top
cream bun	choux pastry with a filling of whipped cream or confectioners' custard
cream cheese	cheese made from full cream milk and single or double cream, prepared like cottage cheese
cream crackers	plain flat biscuits usually eaten with cheese
cream dessert	whole cream is the main ingredient; custard; a combination of cream and custard; fruit; fruit purée and cream and sometimes custard
cream horn	cone-shaped puff pastry confection, usually filled with jam and whipped cream
cream of tartar	raising agent, a component of baking powder
cream tea	afternoon tea including bread or scones served with clotted cream and jam
creaming	beating together fat and sugar until like whipped cream in texture and colour
crécy	dish made or garnished with carrots FRENCH
crédioux	creamy processed cheese shaped as round log or small cake and coated with walnuts FRENCH
creier de vițel pane	pancakes filled with mashed calves' brains, onions, parsley and eggs, rolled up, coated in breadcrumbs and fried ROMANIAN
crema	cornflour pudding sometimes flavoured with orange or tangerine peel and vanilla essence GREEK
crema	cream, custard ITALIAN
crema	cream or mousse; soup SPANISH
creme	cream PORTUGUESE
crème	cream FRENCH
crème à l'anglaise	custard cream FRENCH
crème au beurre	butter cream icing made with butter, sugar, egg yolk, used to fill or coat sponge cakes FRENCH
crème brûlée	rich cream vanilla dessert topped with a crunchy layer of caramelised sugar FRENCH
crème caramel	a pudding made from an egg custard mixture in a mould lined with caramelised water and sugar, which is baked in a bain-marie FRENCH
crème de cacao	very sweet cocoa-flavoured liqueur from the West Indies FRENCH
crème de menthe	peppermint-flavoured liqueur FRENCH
crème des vosges	small, fresh cream cheese from Alsace FRENCH

crème fraiche	cream in which the lactic acids have been allowed to work so that it thickens and has a distinctive flavour FRENCH
crème frite	dessert of crème pâtissière, cooled and cut into squares or rounds, coated in breadcrumbs, fried and served with sugar and apricot sauce FRENCH
crème pâtissière	custard lightened with whipped egg whites, used to fill éclairs and other cakes FRENCH
crème renversée	like crème caramel but turned out upside-down when cold FRENCH
crème royale	vanilla-flavoured custard pudding baked in butter lined moulds in a bain-marie, turned out and eaten when cold FRENCH
crème sauce	sauce of reduced béchamel, fresh cream and butter FRENCH
cremeboller	chocolate pastry buns DANISH
crémets	cow's milk cheeses from Anjou FRENCH
crémets d'Angers	cream cheeses to which fresh whipped cream and stiffly beaten eggs are added, served in a deep dish covered with fresh cream FRENCH
crémets nantais	small, fresh cream cheeses from the lower Loire Valley FRENCH
cremini	generic term for various small, soft, factory-made cheeses ITALIAN
cremino	soft cheese; type of ice-cream bar ITALIAN
crempog	Welsh pancake WELSH
creole	style of cooking that combines the characteristics of West Indian, French, African and Spanish cooking
creole cheese	rich, unripened cream cheese from Louisiana
creole coush-coush	bread made with cornmeal, baked in a pot on the stove until a crust forms, served with milk and sugar or cane ribbon syrup and crisply fried bacon
creole sauce	sauce of chopped onions, mushrooms, green peppers, red peppers and seasoning in sauce espagnole
créole, à la	créole style; dish inspired by West Indian style of cooking, usually including rice, red peppers and tomatoes, or orange, pineapple and rum FRENCH
crêpe	thin pancake, served plain or with savoury or sweet filling FRENCH
crêpe suzette	orange-flavoured pancake, reheated in butter, orange juice, sugar, orange liqueur and lemon juice, flambéed with orange liqueur just before serving FRENCH

crêpes de pommes de terre   potato pancakes FRENCH

crépinette   small, flat sausage made from sausagemeat flavoured with parsley and wrapped in pig's caul

FRENCH

crescenza   soft, creamy, slighty sweet cheese of the stracchino family ITALIAN

crescione   cress; small crescent-shaped pasta for garnishing soup ITALIAN

crescioni   dish containing spinach and shallots ITALIAN

crespolini   special pancakes filled with cooked spinach, cream cheese, parsley, raisins and currants, Parmesan and chicken livers ITALIAN

cress   salad plant, with two small, dark green leaves harvested and eaten as a seedling with two small, dark green leaves

cresson alénois   cress or garden cress FRENCH

crête de coq   cock's comb FRENCH

creux   hollow FRENCH

crever   to overcook rice to the bursting point FRENCH

crevette, crevettes grises   shrimp FRENCH

crevettes roses   prawns or larger shrimps which turn pink when cooked FRENCH

crevettes, sauce   sauce of fish velouté with shrimp coulis FRENCH

criação   fowl PORTUGUESE

criadillas de toro   glands of bull SPANISH

crimping   pinching the edges of a pie, tart or shortbread by pressing at regular intervals to give a fluted effect

crinkleroot   toothwort with very succulent roots AMERICAN

crispbread   dough made from crushed whole grain, such as rye or wheat, made into thin, crisp biscuits

crispelle   small rounds of pizza dough or salted bread, fried on both sides in very hot oil ITALIAN

croaker   small fish found along the eastern seaboard AMERICAN

crocchetta   potato or rice croquette ITALIAN

croissant   crescent-shaped roll made from special leavened dough, folded and rolled with butter to produce rich, flaky pastry FRENCH, PORTUGUESE

cromesqui, kromesky   croquettes; finely diced meats, fish, poultry or game, sometimes with mushrooms or truffles, bound with thick sauce; in Poland they are wrapped in a thin pancake and fried; in Russia in caul; in France they are dipped in batter and fried FRENCH, POLISH, RUSSIAN

crooner	fish of the gurnard family; *see* sea hen
crop	the gullet of birds
cropadeu	oatmeal and water made into a dumpling in the middle of which is put a haddock's liver SCOTTISH
croquant	small boat-shaped pastry resembling meringue with an almond flavour – it crunches when bitten FRENCH
croquante	elaborate centrepiece; a mould with trellised bands of marzipan set on a pastry base, filled with small rounds of puff pastry with a cherry in the middle of each; a sweet shaped like a basket, made of marzipan and filled with ice cream FRENCH
croque au sel, à la	food usually eaten raw with no other seasoning but salt FRENCH
croquembouche	large pyramid-shaped 'cake', usually small choux buns filled with cream, dipped in sugar syrup and stuck together FRENCH
croque-monsieur	hot sandwich of Gruyère cheese and ham between two crustless slices of bread; if topped with a poached egg it is called a croque-madame FRENCH
croquet	almond biscuits, a speciality of Bordeaux FRENCH
croqueta	croquette SPANISH
croquette	cooked mixture of meat, fish, poultry or vegetables, particularly potatoes, bound with egg, made into little rolls, coated in breadcrumbs and fried
croquignolles-parisiennes	Parisian pastry flavoured with a liqueur; small, crunchy, sweet, fried cakes, a speciality of New Orleans FRENCH
crosnes	*see* Chinese artichoke, Japanese artichoke
crosses	knuckle or butt-end of shin of beef or veal FRENCH
crostaceo	shellfish ITALIAN
crostata	pie; flan ITALIAN
crostini	croûtons made from slices of bread covered with cheese and baked ITALIAN
crostini	small pieces of toast, croutons ITALIAN
croubins	dish of pigs' trotters IRISH
croustade	fried bread, pastry or potato case, usually small, used to hold savoury or sweet filling FRENCH
croûte	fried or toasted bread on which game and other main dishes are served; small pastry cases such as vol au vents FRENCH

croûte, en   game, entrées and savouries served on shaped fried bread or pastry; dish of meat, poultry or pâté cooked inside a pastry case FRENCH

croûtons   small pieces of fried bread served as accompaniment to soups and salads, or as a garnish

crow   large blue-black bird, edible when very young

crowberry   heath-like wild plant yielding black berries

crowdie   cheese made from soured milk; oatmeal gruel SCOTTISH

crown of lamb or pork   crown of lamb consists of two best end necks joined together and curved round; crown of pork is similar, but consists of two fore loins

cru   raw, uncooked FRENCH, PORTUGUESE

cru   a vineyard, group of vineyards, or wine-growing region FRENCH

cruchade   porridge similar to polenta; made with maize and milk or water FRENCH

crucian   European cyprinid fish, *Carassius carassius*

cruciferae   family of plants with cross-shaped flowers, including brassicas, cress, mustard and rape

crudités   raw vegetables including carrots, cauliflower, celery and peppers, usually cut into sticks and served with dips FRENCH

crudo   raw ITALIAN, SPANISH

cruibeen   pig's trotter IRISH

cruller   bun rather like a doughnut AMERICAN

crumble   rubbed-in plain cake mixture used instead of pastry as a topping for a fruit pie

crumpet   small, round yeast cake baked on a griddle in a special metal ring

crushing   breaking down food into smaller pieces to release the flavour or to make crumble-like texture

crust   crisp outer part of loaf or pie; deposit of organic salts which wines throw off as they age

crustacé   shellfish FRENCH

crustacean   shellfish with a hard exoskeleton; all are sea fish except crayfish

crystallising   coating with sugar

crystallised fruits   small fruits and segments of larger ones soaked in thick syrup and then drained; crystallization takes place during the draining period

csabai szarvascomb venison stuffed with spicy csabai sausage served in paprika sauce HUNGARIAN

császármorszsa 'Emperor's delight'; fluffy Viennese scrambled pancake HUNGARIAN

császárszalonna bacon HUNGARIAN

cseresznye cherries HUNGARIAN

csereszynepaprika chilli HUNGARIAN

csiga snail HUNGARIAN

csikós tokány strips or chunks of beef braised in a mixture of bacon, onion rings, sour cream and tomato concentrate HUNGARIAN

csiperke gomba champignon mushrooms HUNGARIAN

csipetke small flour dumplings, an important feature of Hungarian soups and stews HUNGARIAN

csipetke tiny dumplings HUNGARIAN

csipkebogyó hip HUNGARIAN

csípös hot HUNGARIAN

csirke chicken HUNGARIAN

csirke paprikàs chicken paprika HUNGARIAN

csokoládé chocolate HUNGARIAN

csokoládéfánk chocolate doughnut HUNGARIAN

csont bone HUNGARIAN

csontleves bone consommé HUNGARIAN

csontvelö bone marrow HUNGARIAN

csuka pike HUNGARIAN

csuka tejfölben sütve fried pike served with sour cream HUNGARIAN

csülök pigs' trotters HUNGARIAN

csurgatott tészta egg dumplings HUNGARIAN

csúsztatott palacsinta multi-layer pancake HUNGARIAN

cuajada junket; cottage cheese SPANISH

cuauhtemoc cooked, dried black beans puréed, fried with tomato, onion and garlic, topped with an egg and baked in the oven MEXICAN

cubeb pepper with pungent, spicy flavour similar to camphor INDONESIAN

cucumber long green vegetable with slightly bitter but mild and refreshing flavour; there are smooth-skinned greenhouse and ridged cucumbers. Dr Johnson: 'A cucumber should be well sliced and dressed with pepper and vinegar, and then thrown out, as good for nothing.' *Tour to the Hebrides* (1785); *see* sea cucumber

cuddy	*see* piltocks, saithe
čufty	meatballs CZECH
cuillère à bouche	flat tablespoon of dry ingredients FRENCH
cuire à blanc	to bake blind; white offal, such as brains, cooked in court bouillon FRENCH
cuire bleu	steaks and chops cooked very rare FRENCH
cuisse	the thigh of certain animals and birds, usually chicken or frog FRENCH
cuisse	leg FRENCH
cuisse de grenouilles	frogs' legs FRENCH
cuisson	the adverb 'cooking'; liquid used in cooking FRENCH
cuissot	haunch FRENCH
cuit	cooked FRENCH
cukier	sugar POLISH
cukier	sugar POLISH
cukierki	sweets POLISH
cukkini	courgette HUNGARIAN
cukor	sugar HUNGARIAN
cukorrépa	beets HUNGARIAN
culatello	smoked raw ham made from lean pork cut from the rump ITALIAN
culatello di zibella	type of ham, a speciality of Parma; in winter it is steeped in white wine before cutting ITALIAN
cullen skink	Aberdonian stew or soup made from smoked haddock, potatoes and onions SCOTTISH
culotte	rump FRENCH
culotte de boeuf	joint of beef, the end of the loin towards the hipbone, used for braising and poaching FRENCH
Cumberland sauce	sauce made from redcurrant jelly, orange, lemon and port, served with ham, venison and lamb
Cumberland sausage	pork sausage flavoured with black pepper and herbs formed into one continuous coil, rather than linked
cumin	strong, slightly bitter flavoured spice from the seeds of a plant related to parsley
cumquat	small, orange-coloured citrus fruit
cunner	small fish found in the Atlantic
cuore	heart ITALIAN
cup	drink made from claret or light white wine diluted with ice or soda water and flavoured with herbs and fruit

cup measure	used for measuring ingredients in cooking – approximately 150g of plain flour
cupate	honey cakes from Tuscany ITALIAN
curaćao	generic term for orange-flavoured liqueur
curanto	seafood, vegetables and suckling pig SPANISH
curau	mashed sweet-corn PORTUGUESE
curd	the centre of a cauliflower – the tree
curds	milk protein and fat, the part of milk which coagulates during fermentation; creamy fruit preserve made with sugar, eggs and butter
curé	cow's milk cheese from Brittany FRENCH
curing	fish, meat or poultry preserved by salting, drying or smoking
curlew	migratory bird of the snipe, sandpiper and plover family
curnieura	local name in Liguria for marjoram ITALIAN
currants	small, round berries of shrubs native to northern Europe, North Africa and Siberia, used in preserves, syrups and pudding; blackcurrants are rich with a slightly sour flavour; redcurrants are sweeter than blackcurrants; white currants are similar to redcurrants, but less commonly used
currany 'obbin	Cornish cake lavishly strewn with currants and raisins
curry	various Indian and Far Eastern savoury dishes, flavoured with varying amounts
curry leaf	similar in appearance to the bay leaf, when used in cooking it imparts a strong curry flavour
curry paste	ready-made paste of dried herbs, fresh chillies, onion, ginger and oil for using in curries
curry plant	attractive plant with strong curry aroma; although not used in Indian curries it can be used in soups and stews
curry powder	ready-made mixture of ground spices, available in a variety of mixes and strengths
curuba	type of elongated passion fruit but slightly more sour
cuscusu trapanese	similar to Arabian couscous; fish soup served with COUSCOUS SICILIAN
cushat	*see* wood pigeon
cushion	cut of meat nearest to the udder in lamb or beef
cusk	*see* torsk

cussy, à la	garnish of large grilled mushrooms stuffed with chestnut purée and whole truffles, cooked in Madeira sauce; sauce of demi-glace mixed with poultry jelly and flavoured with Madeira; game soup garnished with cubes of chestnut, partridge Royale, partridge quenelles and truffles FRENCH
custard	sweet mixture made from egg and milk, used as sauce or cold dessert
custard apple	a group of tropical fruits known as annona fruit; most look similar to apples with green, purple-green, or yellow-brown scaly skin; the edible flesh is custard-like
custard cream	a biscuit or similar confection filled with custard cream
custard marrow	flat pale green, scallop-edged white or yellow squash, which can be sliced and cooked or stuffed and baked
custard powder	powder used to produce an approximation to real custard
custard saus	custard served as a dessert or as a filling for pancakes DUTCH
cut	see joint
cutlet	chop cut from the best end of lamb, veal or pork
cutlet bat	heavy, flat metal bat for flattening escalopes, steaks or cutlets, to tenderise meat
cutting in	to combine one ingredient with others, using a knife in a repeated downward cutting motion
cuttlefish	small cephalopod with soft bag-like body, eight arms and two tentacles
cuvée	vat, or contents of a vat FRENCH
cwikła	beetroot and horseradish sauce, eaten with boiled beef and other meat POLISH
cyclamate	artificial sweetener which is prohibited as an additive, as research has linked it to bladder cancer
cykoria	endive POLISH
cynaderki	kidneys POLISH
cynamon	cinnamon POLISH
cyrano	duck consommé with small duck quenelles covered with sauce suprême and grated cheese FRENCH
cytryna	lemon POLISH
czarevitch	game soup garnished with strips of truffle and hazel grouse quenelles and flavoured with sherry FRENCH

czarina	beef soup flavoured with fennel, garnished with diced cooked vesiga FRENCH
czarna rzepa	black radish POLISH
czarne porzeczki	blackcurrants POLISH
czekolada	chocolate POLISH
czekoladki	chocolate biscuits POLISH
czereśnie	cherries POLISH
czernina	soup of duck blood, broth and vinegar POLISH
czosnek	garlic POLISH
czyściec bulwiasty	Jerusalem artichokes POLISH

D

dab	small, flat sea fish of the plaice family
dace	small, freshwater fish of the carp family
daddel	date NORWEGIAN
daddelblomme	persimmon DANISH
dadel	date DUTCH
dadler	dates DANISH
dagens meny	set menu NORWEGIAN
dagens middag	set menu DANISH
dagens rätt	dish of the day SWEDISH
dagens ret	day's special DANISH
dagens rett	day's special NORWEGIAN
dag-ing	meat BM
dag-ing an-na lem-boo	veal BM
dag-ing ba-bee	bacon, ham or pork BM
dag-ing kam-bing	mutton BM
dag-ing lem-boo	beef BM
dagschotel	day's special DUTCH
daguet	young stag – from the word dague, meaning dagger, and referring to the shape of the horns FRENCH
dahi	yoghurt INDIAN
dahi wada	cooked in a savoury yoghurt sauce INDIAN
dahorp	traditional mutton stew; the meat is boiled with onions and herbs and removed from the stock which is then used to cook rice and green peppers which are then combined with the mutton YUGOSLAVIAN
daikon	variety of radish JAPANESE
daim	fallow deer FRENCH
daiquiri	originally a Cuban cocktail of rum mixed with fresh lime, today it may be flavoured with fruit syrup; frozen daiquiri is made with crushed ice
daisies	type of American cheddar cheese AMERICAN
daktyla	long loaf made in several sections, the top sections usually sprinkled with sesame seeds GREEK
daktyle	dates POLISH
dal	collective name for a variety of lentils, peas and other pulses used in Indian cuisine INDIAN

dalayrac chicken soup thickened with tapioca and garnished with juliennes of chicken, mushrooms and truffles
FRENCH

dalle small slice or escalope of fish, usually cut from salmon, hake or tuna FRENCH

damascenes Shropshire damsons, inferior to common damson, with smaller, rounder fruit

damasco apricot PORTUGUESE, SPANISH

dame-blanche cold dessert; kind of plombières ice cream FRENCH

damper unleavened bread made from a simple dough

dampet steamed DANISH

Dampfnudeln yeast pastry shaped into small balls before baking, served hot with stewed fruit or jam or vanilla sauce
GERMAN

damson said to be derived from the Damascus plum tree, the fruit resembles a small, round, bitter plum with deep blue greenish flesh

danablue blue cheese DANISH

danbo hard, oblong yellow cheese with shiny-rimmed holes and a mild flavour DANISH

dandelion the yellow flowers may be used to make wine; the leaves may be eaten raw in salads or boiled as a vegetable

dangleberry original name for tangleberry

danie meal POLISH

Danish blue cheese whitish, soft, pasteurised cow's milk cheese with blue mould veining and sharp, salty taste

Danish open sandwich thin slice of bread with various toppings DANISH

Danish pastry sweet light pastry with various fillings DANISH

danoise wild duck consommé flavoured with Marsala and garnished with quenelles of game and diced mushrooms FRENCH

Danone make of yoghurt

dansk armbaand 'Danish bracelets'; bacon and tomato patties DANISH

dara semolina HUNGARIAN

darab piece HUNGARIAN

daragaluska semolina dumplings HUNGARIAN

darált minced HUNGARIAN

darazsfeszek biscuits, known as 'wasp's nests' HUNGARIAN

dalchini cinnamon INDIAN

darblay potato soup with finely chopped vegetables FRENCH

dariole	small, narrow mould with sloping sides FRENCH
darne	thick slice of raw fish, on the bone or filleted, usually cut from salmon, hake or tuna FRENCH
dartois	garnish for sliced meat made from two strips of puff pastry sandwiched together with sweet or savoury filling FRENCH
Darwen salmon	local name in Darwen, near Blackburn, for dogfish
dasheen	root vegetable similar to potato, with dark, bark-like skin WEST INDIAN
dashi	stock of dried fish, seaweed and various flavourings JAPANESE
date	fruit of the date palm with firm sweet flesh
date marking	most pre-packed food is marked with a 'use-by' date; food with a life of six weeks to three months has a 'best-before' date
date, dried	available whole, with or without stones, or as pressed blocks; chopped dates are available for baking
dátil	date SPANISH
datle	dates CZECH
datolya	dates HUNGARIAN
datte	date FRENCH
Dattel	date GERMAN
datteri di mare	'sea date'; small shellfish similar to mussels with a very hard shell, found off the Italian coast ITALIAN
dattero	date ITALIAN
daube	meat or vegetables braised in stock, often with wine and herbs FRENCH
daubière	cooking pot for cooking daubes FRENCH
daudet	chicken consommé garnished with juliennes of celeriac, lobster quenelles, cubes of ham and chicken royale FRENCH
daumont, à la	fish garnish of large cooked mushroom head, sauce nantua, fish quenelles and soft roes rolled in breadcrumbs and fried; hollandaise sauce flavoured with oyster liquid and lemon juice, garnished with chopped mushrooms, truffles and oysters; beef soup garnished with strips of mushrooms, ox tongue and rice FRENCH
dauphin	cow's milk cheese from Flanders
dauphine, à la	garnish of pommes dauphines in straw potato nests, demi-glace and Madeira wine; pommes duchesse and choux paste shaped into balls and fried; fillets of

	sole poached in Madeira infused with mushrooms or truffles FRENCH
dauphinois, à la	thinly-sliced potatoes covered with milk or cream, layered with grated cheese and baked FRENCH
daurade	saltwater fish of the sea bream family FRENCH
Daventry	very rich cheese similar to ripe Stilton, dark green in colour
death by chocolate	horrendously rich chocolate dessert
debreceni fatányéros	Debrecen speciality, prepared for large parties, usually containing pork chops, choice fillets and veal, and garnished with lettuce HUNGARIAN
decanting	pouring wine from a bottle into a jug or decanter leaving the lees (sediment) in the bottle
decize	cow's milk cheese not unlike brie FRENCH
découpage	carving FRENCH
deep fry	to cook food by immersing in very hot fat or oil
deer	members of the Cervidae family; antlered, ruminant quadrupeds
déglacer	deglaze FRENCH
deglazing	heating stock, wine or other liquid with meat juices from the pan, to make gravy
dégorger	using salt to draw moisture out of food before cooking; to soak meat, poultry, fish and offal in water to remove impurities FRENCH
dégraisser	to remove fat from soups or stews; to cut excess fat from a joint FRENCH
dehydrated foods	the removal of moisture from food, as a method of preservation; reconstituted by adding liquid
déjeuner	lunch FRENCH
del-ee-ma	pomegranate BM
délice	menu term implying the dish is delectable
delmonico steak	steak cut from the rib of beef AMERICAN
demerara sugar	white cane sugar treated to produce pale brown crystals
demi-deuil, à la	poultry larded under the breast skin with thin slices of truffle and poached in cream sauce FRENCH
Demidoff	the name of a renowned Russian gourmet; chicken sautéed or roasted in butter, served with puréed root vegetables, artichoke hearts and onion rings; braised chicken with vegetables; crescent-shaped truffle pieces are added before serving; sterlet poached in wine with fennel, celeriac, and pickled cucumbers, garnished with crayfish tails and truffles RUSSIAN

demi-espagnole	formerly the word for demi-glace FRENCH
demi-glace sauce	rich brown sauce based on espagnole sauce, usually served with red meat or game FRENCH
demi-sel	fresh-cream, mild-flavoured, lightly-salted cheese, which may contain herbs, paprika or pepper
demoiselles de Caen	small lobsters FRENCH
dénerver	to remove tendons from meat, including gristle and membranes FRENCH
denier, en	potato crisps cut in the shape of a coin FRENCH
dent-de-loup	triangles of bread or other food used as a garnish FRENCH
denté	dentex; toothed FRENCH
dente, al	'to the tooth'; firm cooked pasta ITALIAN
dentelle	the name in Brittany for a very thin crêpe with a lacy texture FRENCH
dentex	saltwater fish found in the Atlantic and Mediterranean
dentice	dentex ITALIAN
dépouiller	to add drops of cold water to a sauce while it is being cooked so that the scum will rise to the surface FRENCH
derby	chicken stuffed with rice, goose liver and truffles, cooked in port and rich veal stock, garnished with slices of truffles and foie gras FRENCH
Derby cheese	hard, closed-textured cheese with a mild flavour that develops as it matures; it is at its best at six months old
dérober	to skin shelled broad beans; to peel vegetables FRENCH
desayuno	breakfast SPANISH
deser	dessert POLISH
desiccation	the process of drying or dehydrating food
designer water	bottled water sold at a price for exceeding that of tap water, and sometimes less pure or hygienic
desosser	to bone FRENCH
dessécher	to dry out boiled vegetables on a high heat before sautéing or other preparation FRENCH
dessert	the last course of a formal dinner; any sweet course
dessert wine	sweet wine usually served with dessert at the end of a meal
desserter	dessert DANISH, NORWEGIAN

desiccating   preserving food by removing the moisture

détrempe   mixture of flour and water FRENCH

Deutsches Beefsteak   hamburger, sometimes topped with a fried egg
GERMAN

deveining   removing the vessel that runs down the back of a prawn or shrimp

devil's food   rich chocolate cake

devilling   highly-flavoured paste or mixture of dry condiments, applied to a dish which is grilled or coated in breadcrumbs and fried

devils on horseback   tea-soaked prunes stuffed with salted, fried almonds, wrapped in a rasher of streaky bacon and grilled

Devonshire cream   deep yellow clotted cream from Devon

Devonshire tea   scones, jam and clotted cream served with a pot of tea as a mid-morning or afternoon meal

dewberry   variety of blackberry, with a more delicate flavour

dextrin   white or yellowish powder produced from starch, dissolved in hot water used as a glaze on bread

dezert   dessert CZECH

dhal   lentils cooked with garlic, ginger and seasoning
INDIAN

dhania   finely ground coriander used in curries INDIAN

dhansak   a dish of Persian origins, made with lentils and tomatoes in a hot, sweet sauce INDIAN

dhingri   mushroom INDIAN

diabetic food   specially-prepared food containing reduced amounts of carbohydrate

diable   unglazed earthenware pot shaped like two bowls, one of which is placed upside down on the other, used for cooking chestnuts, potatoes and other vegetables FRENCH

diable de mer   devil fish FRENCH

diable, à la   devilled or highly spiced food FRENCH

diablotins   garnish for clear soup of round slices of French bread covered with thick béchamel sauce with Parmesan and cayenne; hot puff pastry hors d'œuvres filled with Parmesan and cayenne, shaped into balls, poached, and browned under the grill; commercially-made French chocolates wrapped in tinfoil; 19th-century pastry fritter FRENCH

diablotka   dumpling or meatball served with soup POLISH

diablotki   cheese croûtons POLISH

diætmad	diet food DANISH
diane	partridge soup garnished with truffles, game quenelles and Madeira; sauce poivrade flavoured with game essence and thickened with cream and butter; sautéed steak served with A1 sauce, Worcestershire sauce, cream and butter FRENCH
diastase	class of enzymes which break down sugar into starch
diavola, alla	grilled with a lavish amount of pepper, chilli pepper or pimento ITALIAN
dibs	syrup derived from natural sugars found in raisins, grapes or carob beans, used as a sweetener
dice	to cut into small cubes
dieettiruoka	diet food FINNISH
džem	jam CZECH, POLISH
dieppoise, à la	sea fish garnished with shrimps, mussels and sometimes mushrooms, served with wine sauce FRENCH
diet	the food eaten regularly by a person or group of people, or to a regular pattern of eating; a strict regime of eating, followed, perhaps, for medical reasons
diéta	diet HUNGARIAN
dietmat	diet food SWEDISH
dietní	low calorie CZECH
digester	forerunner of the pressure cooker
digestif	an aid to digestion, usually a drink, taken before or after a meal FRENCH
Dijon mustard	strong French mustard less aromatic than most as it is without the rich combination of herbs FRENCH
dijonnaise	dish prepared with Dijon mustard FRENCH
dild	dill DANISH
dill	feathery-leafed herb plant; the dried seeds are used as a spice
dille	dill DUTCH
dim sum	small savoury or sweet snacks CHINESE
dinde	turkey FRENCH
dindon	turkey FRENCH
dindonneau	young turkey FRENCH
dîner	dinner FRENCH
dinnye	melon HUNGARIAN
dínsztelt	braised HUNGARIAN

dió	walnuts HUNGARIAN
diosmos	mint GREEK
dióspiro	persimmon PORTUGUESE
diostekercs	yeast cake eaten at Christmas HUNGARIAN
dip	soft, well-flavoured mixture, usually accompanied by savoury biscuits, crisps and crudités which are dipped in the mixture and eaten
diples	sweet filo pastries fried in oil and served with syrup, cinnamon and chopped nuts GREEK
diplomate pudding	crystallized fruits placed in the bottom of a mould and filled with layers of sponge fingers soaked in liqueur and bavarois and currants and sultanas FRENCH
diplomate, sauce	sauce normande mixed with lobster coulis and mushroom essence garnished with truffles and lobster meat; garnish of sliced calf's sweetbreads, cocks' combs, cock's kidneys and mushrooms bound with sauce madère FRENCH
dippie	Cornish dish of potatoes and pilchards boiled in thin cream
dippikastike	dip sauce FINNISH
distillation	separating or refining volatile substances by boiling and recondensing
distilled water	water which is virtually free from minerals
disznófej	pig's head HUNGARIAN
disznóhús	pork HUNGARIAN
disznózsír	lard HUNGARIAN
disznózsíron sült	larded roast HUNGARIAN
diverso	varied ITALIAN
divinity fudge	sweetmeat flavoured with vanilla and pecan nuts AMERICAN
divoký kanec	wild boar CZECH
divoký králíc na cesněku	wild rabbit with garlic CZECH
do ztracena	poached CZECH
dobosh torta, dobostorta	thinly-layered sponge cake filled with chocolate butter and egg filling, topped with burnt sugar icing HUNGARIAN
dobrada	tripe PORTUGUESE
dobule	common name for chub FRENCH
doce	sweet; jam PORTUGUESE
doce d'oves	pudding made from egg yolks and sugar PORTUGUESE
dock	sorrel and rhubarb are both members of the large

	dock family
dodine de canard	duck stew with onions, herbs and red wine; galantine of duck FRENCH
doe	female deer
dogfish	name covering a large number of different species of fish of the shark family
dog salmon	not a true salmon; allied to red salmon and quinnat salmon found on the Pacific coast of America
dohi	yoghurt INDIAN
dolce	sweet dishes including cakes, pastries and puddings ITALIAN
dolcelatte	mild, blue, cow's milk cheese ITALIAN
doldurmak	to stuff TURKISH
dollar fish	small sea fish found on the Atlantic coast America
dollma me vaj	speciality of green peppers stuffed with cooked rice, tomato, parsley and lemon juice ALBANIAN
dolmadakia, dolmathakia	very small stuffed vine leaves GREEK
dolmades	stuffed vine leaves, eaten hot or cold GREEK
dolmas	vine, fig, cabbage or other edible leaves stuffed with a savoury mixture, usually lamb TURKISH
domácí	homemade CZECH
domácí šunka	country ham CZECH
domaci beli sir	salted cheese, lightly pickled in brine YUGOSLAVIAN
domácí klobásy	homemade sausages CZECH
domažlické koláče	pie, patterned with stripes of cream cheese, plum cheese and poppy seed filling CZECH
domates	tomato GREEK
dòmàtiz	tomato TURKISH
doner kebab	lamb slices and salad sprinkled with a tahini-based sauce, wrapped in a piece of unleavened bread
donitsi	doughnut FINNISH
doo-koo	sweet fruit, which is yellow when ripe BM
doo-ree-an	very pungent, unpleasant smelling pulp inside a large spiky green fruit BM
doperwt	green pea DUTCH
dopiaza	'do' (two) 'piaza' (onions); a medium hot sweet dish made with, and garnished with, onions INDIAN
dopp i gryten	'dip in the pot'; on Christmas Day seasoned beef stock is added to the skimmed stock in which the ham has been cooked and left on the stove; bits of rye bread are dipped in it ('You'll spoil your

appetite') SWEDISH

doppeltes Lendenstück   thick fillet of beef (US: tenderloin) GERMAN

doppskov   leftover boiled or roasted veal, beef and ham, diced small and sautéed with butter and sliced onions, simmered in a cream sauce with boiled potatoes, and served with a fried egg SWEDISH

dorado   fish, like gilt-poll and sargo, found in Spanish waters

dorado   John Dory SPANISH

dorée   John Dory FRENCH

dorer   to brush pastry or other dish with egg before cooking
FRENCH

doreye au riz   rice tarts BELGIAN

doria   garnish of cucumber cut into pieces the shape and size of olives, cooked slowly in butter; a salad; chicken soup garnished with chicken quenelles, olive-shaped pieces of cucumber and cheese croûtons FRENCH

doria, alla   with cucumbers ITALIAN

Dörrobst   dried fruit GERMAN

Dorsch   cod GERMAN

Dorset knobs   small, round knob-like biscuits common to Dorset

dorsz   cod POLISH

dort   cake CZECH

dort čokolądavý   chocolate cake CZECH

dort punčový   frosted sponge cake sprinkled with rum CZECH

dort z karlovarsk-ych oplateký   'Carlsbad layer cake'; thin wafers sandwiched with walnut and cocoa butter filling, topped with icing CZECH

dory   alternative name for John Dory

dosa   pancake of ground rice and urad dhal, fried on a flat griddle INDIAN

dotterel   fat, delicious bird, a member of the plover family

Dotterkäse   cheese made from skimmed milk and egg-yolks
GERMAN

double d'agneau   cut of lamb peculiar to France, comprising the two hind legs of an animal roasted in one piece FRENCH

Double Gloucester   cow's milk cheese

doubler   to fold in two; to cover pastries which are being cooked with foil or paper, to protect them from too much heat and the danger of burning FRENCH

doucette   alternative name for corn salad FRENCH

dough   thick mixture of uncooked flour and liquid, usually

	combined with other ingredients
dough bird	species of curlew AMERICAN
doughnut	small cake of sweetened dough fried in hot fat and smothered in sugar
douglas	beef consommé garnished with slices of cooked sweetbreads, artichoke bottoms and asparagus tips FRENCH
dourada	guilt-head (fish) PORTUGUESE
doux	sweet, mild FRENCH
douzaine	dozen FRENCH
dove	small member of the pigeon family, which makes an excellent dish
dowitcher	red-breasted or long-billed snipe, prepared as the snipe
doyenné	several varieties of sweet and juicy dessert pear FRENCH
dozelle	small eel-like fish found in the Mediterranean
dršt'ková polévka	tripe soup CZECH
dršt'ky	tripe CZECH
drachena	large pancake spread with brown butter, salt and pepper or sugar RUSSIAN
dragée	fruit or nut coated with hard icing FRENCH
dragon	tarragon DUTCH
dragon marine	weever SPANISH
dragon's eyes	fruit resembling the lychee FAR EASTERN
dragonättika	tarragon vinegar SWEDISH
dragoncelle	tarragon ITALIAN
dragonet	alternative name for corn salad FRENCH
dragonfish	saltwater fish also called weever, found off the European and Mediterranean coasts
dragoni	dragonfish ITALIAN
draining	removing surplus liquid or fat from foods through a sieve, or by placing on absorbent paper
drakena	weever or dragon fish GREEK
Drambuie	whiskey, heather, and honey-flavoured liqueur SCOTTISH
dravle	pudding of curds and cream NORWEGIAN
drawing	removing entrails from poultry or game birds
drawn butter	melted butter, used as a dressing for cooked vegetables
dredging	sprinkling food lightly with flour, sugar or other

	powdered coating
Dresden sauce	cold sauce made with sour cream, mustard and horseradish
dressing	plucking, drawing and trussing poultry and game in preparation for cooking; rearranging crab meat decoratively in the shell; garnishing a dish, or coating a salad
dried beef	finely sliced, air-dried beef (US: chipped beef)
dried fish	method of preserving fish, usually in combination with smoking, dry salting or soaking in brine
dried fruit	method of preservation; water is drawn out, preventing the growth of micro-organisms, leaving the natural sugar to act as a preservative
dried herbs	most herbs are available in the dried form, usually 'rubbed' or chopped into fine pieces; dried herbs are stronger in flavour than fresh herbs
dried meat	seldom used today, moisture is drawn out to prevent the growth of micro-organisms
dried vegetables	pulses are the most frequently dried vegetable; few vegetables are suitable for home drying
drie-in-de-pan	small, fluffy, currant-filled pancake DUTCH
drip pudding	suet pudding boiled in a cloth and then roasted in the fat with the joint
dripping	fat obtained from roasting meat; pieces of fat rendered down
drisheen	blood pudding; *see* packet IRISH
drożdże	yeast POLISH
drożdżowe ciastko	sugared tea cake POLISH
drób	fowl POLISH
drob de miel	calf's stomach filled with lamb's liver, lungs and heart, onions, eggs and herbs, simmered in water or stock ROMANIAN
drop scone	pancake cooked on a griddle or in a heavy pan, also called Scotch pancake SCOTTISH
dropping consistency	the correct texture of a cake or pudding before cooking; the mixture should fall off the spoon within five seconds
drůbež	fowl CZECH
drue	grape NORWEGIAN
druif	grape DUTCH
drumfish	number of fish of the Sciaenidae family; red

drumfish is the best to eat

drumstick lower part of legs of chicken, turkey and other birds; an Indian tree whose flowers, leaves, seed pods and twigs are used as a vegetable

drupe fruit with a single stone

druva grape SWEDISH

dry salting curing food by rubbing salt on to the surface to draw out moisture

drying preserving food by dehydration to prevent deterioration

dušený braised CZECH

dušené stewed CZECH

dušené maso stew CZECH

dušené maso hovezí stewed beef CZECH

dušené maso kuřecí stewed chicken CZECH

dušené maso telecí stewed veal CZECH

duBarry, à la rich cauliflower soup; dishes garnished with cauliflower FRENCH

Dublin Bay prawns small, delicious shellfish, which are not prawns at all but Norway lobsters

Dublin coddle sliced onion, sliced potatoes, and thick rashers of bacon, cooked in layers in a saucepan IRISH

Dublin lawyer live lobster split in two, the flesh cut into chunks and cooked in butter, flambéed in Irish whiskey, and served with a cup of cream IRISH

Dublin rock 19th-century cold sweet of butter or very thick cream beaten with ground almonds, sugar and brandy IRISH

Dubonnet quinine-flavoured aperitif, drunk with ice and lemon or made into a cocktail FRENCH

duchesse à la dish garnished or served with creamed potatoes; tongue and mushrooms in béchamel sauce; various pastries containing an almond mixture FRENCH

duchesse d'angoulême pear which ripens and keeps throughout the winter FRENCH

duck flavoursome bird, delicious roasted and served with its traditional accompaniment of orange sauce

dudi club-shaped gourd, treated like any other summer squash

due pigeon (US: squab) DANISH

dufferin fish soup, slightly curried and garnished with rice, small pieces of sole and curried fish quenelles

dugléré, à la   white fish, poached in white wine and butter with chopped shallots, parsley and seasoning; the stock is reduced and cream, butter, tomatoes and lemon juice are added FRENCH

dügün   feast held on the occasion of a wedding or circumcision TURKISH

dügün eti   mutton stew, flavoured with onions, tomato and lemon juice TURKISH

duif   pigeon DUTCH

Duitse biefstuk   hamburger steak DUTCH

dukátové buchtičky   tiny doughnuts CZECH

dulce   sweet SPANISH

dulce de leche   pudding of egg yolks, sugar, flour, lemon and milk, which is cooled, cut into fingers, rolled in breadcrumbs and fried SPANISH

dulceatza   sweet made from various fruits and rose petals Romanian

dulse   common name for two unrelated edible seaweeds

dum, dum pukht   steamed INDIAN

dumesnil   beef consommé garnished with slices of poached beef marrow, vegetable juliennes and chopped chervil FRENCH

dumpling   ball or outer casing made from sweet or savoury dough

Dundee cake   rich fruit cake decorated with split almonds SCOTTISH

Dunlop cheese   whitish, moist cow's milk cheese SCOTTISH

dur   hard FRENCH

durazno   peach SPANISH

durchgebraten   well-done GERMAN

durian   large Asian fruit tree; the fruits have an unpleasant smell, but taste delicious, and the seeds can be eaten like nuts

duroc   chicken sautéed in butter with mushrooms and herbs garnished with tomatoes and new potatoes FRENCH

durum wheat   A variety of Mediterraneum wheat, *Triticum durum*, with a high gluten content used chiefly for making pastas and procuding semolina

dusená kachna s brušinkami   braised duck with cranberries CZECH

duszone   stewed; braised POLISH

Dutch oven   parabolic reflector stood facing a fire so as to focus the heat on to the material to be cooked

duva	pigeon SWEDISH
duveč	meat casserole with onions, potatoes, rice, tomatoes and green peppers YUGOSLAVIAN
duxelles	shallots and mushrooms, dried and used as flavouring FRENCH
dyes	almost all food colourings are synthetic dyes
dyne	marrow (US: zucchini) CZECH
dynia	pumpkin; edible gourd POLISH
dyrejøtt	deer NORWEGIAN
dyrekølle	venison DANISH
dyresteg	roast venison DANISH
dyrestek	roast venison NORWEGIAN
džem	jam CZECH, POLISH
dziczyzna	game POLISH
dzik	boar POLISH
dzika kaczka pieczona	roast wild duck POLISH
dzikie gęi	wild goose POLISH
džuveč	pork chop, rice and vegetables, baked in the oven CZECH

E

(al) estilo de	in the style of SPANISH
ear	the part of a cereal plant that contains the seeds, grains or kernels
earthnut	*see* truffle
earthenware	simple form of pottery which can be used in the oven
East India mayonnaise	mayonnaise sauce mixed with garlic and good curry powder, served with fish INDIAN
Easter biscuits	small, soft dough biscuits made with fruits and spices
Easter eggs	hollow chocolate egg, which may be of varying sizes, and filled with loose weets
easypeel	mandarin, naatje, satsuma, tangerine, etc.
eau	water FRENCH
eau-de-vie	variety of fruit brandy, drunk as an aperitif or liqueur, or used in cooking FRENCH
ebéd	lunch HUNGARIAN
ebleskiver	a fried cake served hot with sugar, jam or jelly North American
ébouillanter	to scald or blanch FRENCH
écailler	to scale a fish before cooking FRENCH
écalure	the outer peel, skin, or shell of fruit, nuts and vegetables FRENCH
écarlate, à l'	pork or beef pickled in brine to which saltpetre is added to give the meat a reddish tinge, and then boiled FRENCH
Eccles cake	small pastry filled with dried fruit, melted butter and sugar – derived from Eccles, Lancashire
ecet	vinegar HUNGARIAN
ecetes torma	horseradish sauce HUNGARIAN
échalote	shallot FRENCH
échaude	a pastry poached in water, before being cooked in the oven FRENCH
échine de porc	chine or spare ribs of pork, usually cooked as a loin FRENCH
éclair	small, finger-shaped choux pastry filled with whipped cream FRENCH

écorce	outer skin or rind of fruit such as lemon or orange, and bark such as cinnamon FRENCH
écossaise à l'	mutton broth with pearl barley, carrot, celery and leek FRENCH
écosser	to pod peas and beans FRENCH
écraser	to flatten, pound or crush aromatic fruits or seeds; to make oven dry bread into breadcrumbs by the same method FRENCH
écremer	to skim cream from milk FRENCH
écrevisses	freshwater crayfish FRENCH
écuelle	deep dish used for serving vegetables FRENCH
écume	scum on stock or jam FRENCH
écureuil	squirrel; cooked as rabbit FRENCH
Edam cheese	ball-shaped cheese with a red wax coating DUTCH
edamer	cheese, a copy of Dutch Edam AUSTRIAN
edamski ser	imitation Edam cheese POLISH
eddik	vinegar NORWEGIAN
eddike	vinegar DANISH
eddoe	small, tropical root vegetable with a small, central bulb and tuberous growths, prepared and eaten as potatoes
Edelpilzkäse	full fat soft cheese with slight blue veining and a sharp, slightly mouldy flavour AUSTRIAN
édes	sweet HUNGARIAN
édeskömény	caraway HUNGARIAN
édességek	desserts HUNGARIAN
Edinburgh fog	pudding made from stiffly whipped cream, vanilla sugar, crushed ratafia biscuits and chopped almonds SCOTTISH
Edinburgh gingerbread	gingerbread with nuts added SCOTTISH
Edinburgh rock	sweetmeat made from crushed lump sugar, cream of tartar, water, colouring and flavouring SCOTTISH
Edirne	soft white ewe's milk cheese TURKISH
ee-kan	fish BM
eel	long, snake-like fish with shiny, dark green to black skin and dense fatty flesh; the flavour is usually enhanced by strong flavoured sauces; the conger eel is a sea fish
eelachie	cardamom INDIAN
eel pout	freshwater fish of the cod family, prepared and cooked in the same way as eel

eend	duck DUTCH
ee-tay	duck BM
effeuiller	to strip leaves or petals from a plant such as globe artichoke or herbs FRENCH
efterrätt	dessert SWEDISH
egg	rich in protein, the essential ingredient of many cakes, sauces and puddings, and ba breakfast favourite
egg	egg NORWEGIAN
egg harp	frame of thin wires for slicing hard-boiled eggs
egg noodle	type of pasta made with wheat flour, egg and water
egg og bacon	eggs and bacon NORWEGIAN
eggerøre	scrambled eggs NORWEGIAN
eggplant	aubergine
eggs Benedict	poached egg, a slice of ham and hollandaise sauce on an English muffin
eggs Florentine	two poached eggs in a nest of cooked spinach, topped with mornay sauce
églefin	fresh haddock FRENCH
Egli	perch GERMAN
égouttoir	wide-mouthed earthenware jug with a drainer for cheese curds on top FRENCH
égrapper	to remove grapes or berries from their stalks FRENCH
egrefin	eglefin; fresh haddock FRENCH
égrener	to detach corn or other grain from the stalk FRENCH
egres	gooseberries HUNGARIAN
égruger	to grind or pulverise in a mortar or mill FRENCH
egy tábla csokoládé	chocolate bar HUNGARIAN
Egyptian onion	tree onion
egytálétel	one-course meal HUNGARIAN
éhes	hungry HUNGARIAN
Ei	egg GERMAN
ei	egg DUTCH
eider duck	bird chiefly prized for its down; the flesh is not very good eating, but the eggs are regarded as a delicacy
Eierapfel	aubergine GERMAN
Eierauflauf	egg soufflé GERMAN
Eierkuchen	pancake GERMAN
eierkuckas	pancake made from batter mixed with cream and redcurrant jelly AUSTRIAN
eierpannekoek egg	pancake DUTCH

Eierschwamm(erl)	chanterelle mushroom GERMAN
einbren	Yiddish word for flour or matzo used as a thickening JEWISH
eingemacht	preserved (of fruit or vegetables) GERMAN
einkorn	coarse grain wheat, cultivated in poor soils in Spain, Italy, Switzerland and south Germany
einlauf	soup garnish of batter poured slowly over the back of a spoon into boiling soup, covered and cooked for three minutes GERMAN, JEWISH
Eintopf	stew, usually of meat and vegetables GERMAN
eiró	eel PORTUGUESE
eiroses fritas	fried eel PORTUGUESE
Eis	ice; ice-cream GERMAN
Eis bombe	ice-cream dessert GERMAN
Eis krem	ice-cream GERMAN
Eisbein	boiled, pickled shank of pork, served with pease pudding, boiled potatoes and sauerkraut GERMAN
eklerka	chocolate cake with whipped-cream filling POLISH
ekshili tchorba	mutton soup TURKISH
ekuri	spicy scrambled eggs INDIAN
elbo	cheese of the samsoe variety DANISH
elderberry	fruit of the elder, small, round, shiny, almost black berries with a rather bitter flavour, used to make wine and preserves
elderflower	flowers of the elder can be used in several ways to add a sweet, fragrant flavour
elecampane	wild plant with yellow blossoms rather like small sunflowers from which a sugar product called laevulose is commercially extracted
electric cooker	slow cooker or crockpot which cooks dishes at a very slow even rate
electric deep fat fryer	the safest method of deep fat frying, it is thermostatically controlled, reducing the risk of the fat catching fire
élesztö	yeast HUNGARIAN
elgbiff	elk NORWEGIAN
elgstek	roast elk NORWEGIAN
elk	the largest member of the deer family (US: moose)
ellies	olives GREEK
elöételek	appetisers; starters HUNGARIAN
elver	the young of the European eel

elzekaria peasant soup made from sliced onion fried in pork or goose fat, white cabbage, haricots beans, garlic or cloves BASQUE

emballer to wrap a joint of meat, game or poultry or pudding in cloth, pork fat or pig's caul FRENCH

embuchado stuffed with meat SPANISH

embuchado de lomo ham made from cured loin of pork, enclosed in skin like a long straight sausage SPANISH

embutido spicy sausage SPANISH

Ementáli semi-hard, robust Swiss cheese with holesHungarian

ementalski ser a Swiss cheese POLISH

émincé vegetables, fruit or meat cut into thin slices, or shredded FRENCH

Emmentaler(käse) semi-hard, robust Swiss cheese with holes GERMAN

Emmenthal a Swiss cheese made from unpasteurised cow's milk, with a mild, slightly nutty flavour and large 'eyes' Swiss

emmer wheat one of the earliest types of wheat grown in southern Europe

empada small type of pie PORTUGUESE

empadão large type of pie PORTUGUESE

empadinhas pastries filled with chopped fish, olives, game or mushrooms PORTUGUESE

empanada pie or tart with meat or fish filling SPANISH

empanadas de batallon small pastries filled with chopped ham, chorizo or shellfish and red peppers, slightly flavoured with onion, deep fried and served hot SPANISH

empanadilla small patty stuffed with seasoned meat or fish SPANISH

empanado breaded SPANISH

emperador swordfish SPANISH

empereur swordfish FRENCH

empotage the ingredients for a braise FRENCH

emulsion mixing two liquids which are mutually insoluble by vigorous beating or shaking

enbär juniper berry SWEDISH

enchaud de porc à la périgourdine a method of cooking loin of pork from the Périgourd, boned, studded with truffle and garlic, rolled and tied with string, roasted until golden, then stock is added and it is covered and cooked for a further two hours FRENCH

enchidos	assorted pork products made into sausages PORTUGUESE
enchilada	maize flour pancake stuffed and served with vegetable garnish and sauce SPANISH
enchiladas	softened corn tortillas, rolled and stuffed with cheese, chicken, meat or beans; they may be topped with cheese or a hot sauce MEXICAN
encornet	sleeve-fish, a variety of calamary FRENCH
encurtido	pickle SPANISH
endaubage	supplementary ingredients used in a daub; slang for bully or corned beef FRENCH
endibia	chicory SPANISH
endiv	chicory SWEDISH
endiva	endive ITALIAN
endive	plant of Eastern origin, an excellent salad ingredient, but it may also be braised and served as a vegetable
endive gourilos	stumps of curly endive blanched in salted water containing vinegar, drained, battered and fried in butter
endívia	chicory PORTUGUESE
endívia saláta	endive HUNGARIAN
Endivie	endive GERMAN
endorphins	natural pain-killers released by eating hot spices, thus giving the eater a 'high'
eneldo	dill SPANISH
engelsk bof	steak and onions DANISH
Engelwurz	angelica GERMAN
English muffin	round, flat, unsweetened bun served split and toasted
English wheat	variety of wheat, not cultivated in the British Isles, but in the Mediterranean region
enguia	eel PORTUGUESE
enkephalos	brains GREEK
Eno's fruit salts	an old indigestion remedy
enoyauteur	implement for cracking nuts or fruit stones without crushing them FRENCH
enrichment	certain nutrients lost during processing may be added to commercially-produced foods; the addition of eggs, butter or cream to a dish
enrisrökt	smoked over juniper embers SWEDISH
enrober	to coat one food with another FRENCH
ensalada	salad SPANISH

ensaladilla rusa	diced cold vegetables with mayonnaise SPANISH
ensopado	meat or fish casserole served on slices of bread PORTUGUESE
Ente	duck GERMAN
entrada	pot roast of meat and vegetables cooked slowly with only a little liquid GREEK
entrecote	sirloin steak, rib-eye steak SWEDISH
entrecôte	steak cut from the middle part of a sirloin of beef; in France, it is steak taken from between two ribs FRENCH
entrecuisse	the second joint or thick thigh of poultry or winged game FRENCH
entrée	a dressed savoury dish, these days forming the main course of a meal; originally it was the course that followed the fish course and preceded the roast FRENCH
entrelarder	'interlarded'; cooking meat with alternate layers of pork fat; 'streaky'; meat with natural streaks of fat FRENCH
entremés	appetizer, hors d'œuvres SPANISH
entremeses	hors d'œuvres, usually consisting of sardines, sausage, olives, onions and sweet peppers SPANISH
entremet	originally it meant all dishes served after the main course, today it is the dessert course, which in France is served after the cheese FRENCH
entremettier	vegetable cook FRENCH
enyrer	kidney NORWEGIAN
enzyme	found in all unprocessed foods, they are responsible for the changing condition of food as it breaks down chemically
épaule	shoulder FRENCH
épautre	coarse grain wheat that used to be grown in Provence FRENCH
epazote	strong-flavoured herb grown in America and parts of Europe, used in Mexican cooking and to make a tea
eper	strawberries HUNGARIAN
epergne	centrepiece for a dining table with little bowls attached to an ornamental stem, used today for raw hors d'œuvres FRENCH
éperlans	smelts FRENCH
éperons Bachiques	'spurs of Bacchus'; highly spiced hors d'oeuvres, implying that they cause thirst FRENCH

épicé	hot, peppered FRENCH
épices	spices FRENCH
épigramme	lamb cutlet consisting of the 'eye' or best part of the end of neck or breast of lamb cutlet FRENCH
épinard	spinach FRENCH
épine d'Espagne	azarole FRENCH
épine d'hiver	a good quality, fragrant winter pear FRENCH
épine-vinette	barberry FRENCH
eple	apple NORWEGIAN
épluchage	removal of the skin of fruit or vegetable FRENCH
époisses	cow's milk cheese with a scored orange crust, sometimes wrapped in vine leaves FRENCH
éponger	to dry parboiled vegetables on paper or cloth to absorb the moisture; to drain fried food in the same way FRENCH
équille	sand eel FRENCH
érable, tarte l'	tart from the Province of Quebec; a pastry case with cream and maple syrup filling CANADIAN
Erbse	pea GERMAN
erce	cow's milk cheese FRENCH
Erdapfel	south German for potato GERMAN
Erdbeer	strawberry GERMAN
erdei szalonka	woodcock HUNGARIAN
erdélyi r akottkáposzta	layers of cabbage, rice and minced, spiced pork, covered with sour cream and baked in the oven HUNGARIAN
erdélyi tokány	beef, bacon fat and onion stew from Transylvania HUNGARIAN
Erdnuß	peanut GERMAN
Eremite	trade name of a blue cheese made in Canada
erizo de mar	sea urchin SPANISH
Ermite	old boar FRENCH
eröleves	consommé HUNGARIAN
erös	hot HUNGARIAN
Errötende Jungfrau	raspberries with cream GERMAN
ersatz	an artificial or substitute product, thought of as a poor imitation, as in ersatz coffee (= roasted acorns)
ert	pea NORWEGIAN
ertesuppe	pea soup NORWEGIAN
erve doce	herb used in southern Portugal, with a flavour of wild sweet marjoram PORTUGUESE

ervilha	green pea PORTUGUESE
ervy	soft cows milk cheese similar to camembert FRENCH
erwt	pea DUTCH
erwtensoep met kluif	pea soup with diced, smoked sausages, pork fat, pig's trotter (US: feet) parsley, leeks and celery DUTCH
eryngo	sea-holly, a seaside weed with thistle-blue flowers, greenish-blue leaves and fleshy roots; the roots are candied like angelica and make excellent toffee
érythrin	generic name for several thick freshwater fish with large heads and round jaws
escabeche	sauce of fried onions, garlic, olive oil and vinegar PORTUGUESE
escabeche	whole cooked fish, marinated in a spiced oil and vinegar, served as a cold hors d'œuvres SPANISH
escalfado	poached PORTUGUESE
escalope	thin slice of meat from the top of the leg FRENCH
escarcho	red gurnard SPANISH
escargot	snail FRENCH
escarola	endive or escarole shoulder SPANISH
escarole	a variety of curly-leafed endive
eschalot	the English form of the French word échalote, formerly an alternative word for shallot
escolar	large, rough-scaled, mackerel-like deep-sea fish
escombro	mackerel SPANISH
eskalop schabowy	loin of pork POLISH
espada	scabbard fish PORTUGUESE
espadon	swordfish FRENCH
espagnole sauce	classic brown sauce used as the basis for other sauces, served with red meat and game FRENCH
española	with tomatoes SPANISH
espargo	asparagus PORTUGUESE
esparguetes	spaghetti PORTUGUESE
espárrago	asparagus SPANISH
esparregado	purée of assorted greens in cream PORTUGUESE
especia	spice SPANISH
especialidad de la casa	chef's speciality SPANISH
especiaria	spice PORTUGUESE
espetada	beef marinated in herbs, grilled over an open fire and served on a skewer PORTUGUESE
espeto	spit-roasted PORTUGUESE

espinaca	spinach SPANISH
espinafre	spinach PORTUGUESE
espresso coffee	coffee made by forcing steam through finely ground coffee beans
esqueixada	mixed fish salad SPANISH
esquinado	Provençal name for the spider crab FRENCH
Esrom	semi-hard, pasteurised cow's milk, slab cheese; when young the flavour is mild, and it becomes stronger and spicier as it matures DANISH
essence	concentrated liquid used to add a particular flavour; only small quantities are needed
Essex	a cheese which is no longer made ENGLISH
Essig	vinegar GERMAN
esterházy-rostélyos	steak with vegetables, cream and paprika HUNGARIAN
estofado	braised; casseroled SPANISH
estouffade	meat or vegetables cooked very slowly in very little liquid FRENCH
estragão	tarragon PORTUGUESE
estragon	tarragon FRENCH, DANISH, SWEDISH, NORWEGIAN, POLISH
estragón	tarragon SPANISH
estufado	braised PORTUGUESE
ésturgeon	sturgeon FRENCH
esturion	sturgeon SPANISH
esturjão	sturgeon PORTUGUESE
étain, papier d'	oven foil FRENCH
etana	snail FINNISH
étel	food HUNGARIAN
etikka	white vinegar FINNISH
étkezés	meal HUNGARIAN
étlap	menu HUNGARIAN
étouffée	cooked with little or no liquid in a tightly closed pot FRENCH
étourneau	starling FRENCH
eturuoka	warm first course FINNISH
étuve	semi-hard cheeses made from cow's milk FRENCH
étuvée, à l'	meat, poultry or vegetables stewed with butter or oil, but little or no liquid FRENCH
evaporated milk	sweetened or unsweetened milk from which about 40% of the water has been extracted by evaporation under vacuum

evarglice   cheese, usually eaten with peppery raw vegetables YUGOSLAVIAN

Eve's pudding   slices of apple arranged in an ovenproof dish, flavoured with sugar and lemon zest, over which is poured a sponge cake mixture before baking

éventail   fan FRENCH

Everton toffee   brittle sweet, similar to butterscotch, but containing cream or evaporated milk, from Everton, Nottinghamshire

evora, queijo de   local name for a variety of farmhouse-made serra cheese PORTUGUESE

ewe   old female sheep

ewrt   pea DUTCH

excelsior   very rich, rare French cow's milk cheese; garnish of braised lettuce and pommes fondantes FRENCH

Exeter pudding   sponge and raisin pudding with layers of custard and blackcurrant jam, from Exeter, Devon

exocoetus   sea fish also known as flying-fish

Extraaufschlag   extra charge; supplementary charge GERMAN

extract   concentrated flavouring used in small quantities

eye of the sirloin   term for a joint of sirloin AMERICAN

eye-am   chicken, fowl BM

eye-am blan da   turkey BM

eyeballs   a delicacy, usually removed from the head after cooking, and eaten plain MIDDLE EASTERN

eyebright   European herb used dried to make a medicinal tea

eye-of-the-round   a cut of beef called in England the eye of silverside AMERICAN

eye-ur ba-too   ice BM

eye-ur ma-nis   mineral water BM

eye-yur   water BM

eye-yur an-gur   wine BM

F

faarekød	mutton DANISH
fabada	stew of pork, beans, bacon and sausage SPANISH
fabada asturiana	haricot beans, salt pork and beef and pig's ear stew SPANISH
fácán	pheasant HUNGARIAN
fácán gesztenyével, gombával töltve	pheasant with mushroom and chestnut filling HUNGARIAN
fácánleves	pheasant soup HUNGARIAN
Fadennudeln	vermicelli GERMAN
fadge	local name in Donegal and Derry for pan-fried potato cakes IRISH
fågel	fowl, game bird SWEDISH
fågelbo	heaps of anchovy fillets, raw onion, cooked beetroot and potatoes with a raw egg in the middle SWEDISH
faggot	mixture of pork offal, onion and breadcrumbs, shaped into balls or squares; a small bunch of herbs tied and wrapped in two pieces of celery stick
fagiano	pheasant ITALIAN
fagioli	dried beans ITALIAN
Fagiolini	French or string beans ITALIAN
fagiolino	French bean ITALIAN
fagiolo	haricot bean ITALIAN
fagoue	calf's sweetbread; the pancreas FRENCH
fagylalt	ice-cream HUNGARIAN
fahéj	cinnamon HUNGARIAN
fahrenheit	system of measuring temperature; on this scale the freezing point of water is 32° and the boiling point is 212° FRENCH
faisán	pheasant
faisandage	red meat which is 'high' and has developed a marked, but not unpleasant smell FRENCH
faisão	pheasant PORTUGUESE
fáiscre grotha	early cheese which is no longer made IRISH
faisselle	osier or pottery utensil with holes in it, used to drain moisture from cheeses FRENCH
fajitas	stir-fry beef, one of Mexico's favourite dishes MEXICAN

faki brown lentils GREEK

falafel bulgar wheat and chick peas, flavoured with garlic, coriander and cumin, usually shaped into balls or patties, baked or fried and served with salad or as a pitta bread filling MIDDLE EASTERN

fallfish the name given to chub in the eastern States AMERICAN

falscher Hase 'false hair'; beef and pork meat loaf GERMAN

falszywy losoś veal simmered in stock made from vegetables, veal bones and wine vinegar, served with a cold sauce of mashed hard boiled eggs, olive oil and lemon juice POLISH

falukorv lightly smoked pork sausage SWEDISH

famiglioli edible fungus ITALIAN

fanchette tiny puff pastry tart filled with confectioners' custard and topped with meringue; certain types of petits fours FRENCH

fancy brisket the best cut of salt beef AMERICAN

fangri sea-bream GREEK

fänkål fennel SWEDISH

fänkålsås fennel sauce SWEDISH

fanshell shellfish resembling the scallop found off European and American Atlantic coasts

far porridge made from hard wheat flour; a Breton flan made from crème pâtissière FRENCH

får mutton NORWEGIAN, SWEDISH

far poitevin shredded vegetables combined with a little diced pork fat, cream, raw egg, and chives FRENCH

faraona guinea fowl ITALIAN

farce forcemeat or stuffing FRENCH

farci dish from the south of France, usually cabbage stuffed with sausage meat, cooked in stock; stuffed FRENCH

farcidures a Limousin speciality of small balls of buckwheat flour mixed with sorrel and beetroot, wrapped in cabbage leaves and simmered in cabbage soup FRENCH

farcito stuffed ITALIAN

fårefrikassé mutton or lamb fricassee NORWEGIAN

fårekjøtt mutton NORWEGIAN

fårekød mutton DANISH

fårestek leg of lamb NORWEGIAN

farfalle	pasta shape literally meaning 'butterfly' ITALIAN
farfallini	much smaller version of farfalle used to garnish soups ITALIAN
farfel	speciality dish of stiff noodle-like dough, which is allowed to harden, then grated and used as a garnish for soups JEWISH
farigoule	Provençal name for wild thyme FRENCH
fårikål	mutton or lamb in cabbage stew NORWEGIAN
farin heiras	smoked pork fat rolled in flour and cooked in red wine PORTUGUESE
farina	various fine flours made from wheat, nuts or root vegetables
farina dolce	a fecula made from dried, ground chestnuts ITALIAN
farinaceous foods	foods which consist largely of starch, such as bread, oatmeal, pasta and pulses
farine	flour FRENCH
fårkött	mutton SWEDISH
farl	triangular-shaped oatmeal cake, usually a quarter of a whole round loaf SCOTTISH
farofa	cassava-root meal browned in oil or butter PORTUGUESE
farofias	floating island, a pudding of whipped egg whites poached in milk and served with custard PORTUGUESE
färserade	stuffed SWEDISH
farseret	stuffed DANISH
färsk	fresh, new SWEDISH
färska räkor	unshelled fresh shrimps SWEDISH
färskrökt lax	slightly smoked salmon SWEDISH
farsumagru	rolled beef or veal stuffed with bacon, ham, eggs, cheese, parsley and onions ITALIAN
farsz	stuffing POLISH
fasaani	pheasant FINNISH
Fasan	pheasant GERMAN
fasan	pheasant NORWEGIAN, SWEDISH
fasaner	pheasant DANISH
faschierter Braten	meat loaf served with rice and macaroni GERMAN, AUSTRIAN
faséole	a variety of haricot bean grown in Mediterranean regions
fasírozott	meatball HUNGARIAN

fassoeil al furn a Piedmontese bean dish of red kidney beans, pork and herbs and spices ITALIAN

fasola beans POLISH

fassolada soup of beans, celery, carrots, onions, tomatoes and seasonings GREEK

fassolakia freska green beans GREEK

fassolia haricot beans GREEK

Fastern see fitless cock

fastlagsbulle bun filled with almond paste and cream SWEDISH

fasùl yahniya dried white beans with onion, peppers and tomatoes BULGARIAN

fat rascals tea cake, served hot and spread with butter in Yorkshire

fatias slices PORTUGUESE

fats a small amount of fat in the diet is essential, although in most developed countries people eat too much; they are either of vegetable or animal origin

fattiga riddare French toast SWEDISH

fattigmann fried biscuit flavoured with cardamom seeds NORWEGIAN

fatto in casa home-made ITALIAN

faubonne thick Saint-Germain soup served with a julienne of vegetables; pheasant purée garnished with strips of pheasant and a julienne of truffles FRENCH

fava broad beans PORTUGUESE, ITALIAN

favata casserole of beans, bacon, sausage and seasoning ITALIAN

faverolles name given in the south of France to many kinds of haricot beans FRENCH

favorite garnish of sliced foie gras, truffles and asparagus tips; soup garnished with julienne of artichoke bottoms, mushrooms and small potato balls FRENCH

fawn young roe deer or fallow deer

faworki a light, sugared fritter POLISH

fazant pheasant DUTCH

fazole dry beans CZECH

fazole na kyselo sour beans CZECH

fazolové lusky green beans CZECH

feather fowlie soup of jointed fowl cooked with ham, celery, onion and herbs SCOTTISH

febras do porco pork cooked with pimiento, garlic and cumin seeds in red wine sauce PORTUGUESE

fecula	starchy powders obtained from potatoes, rice, corn and arrowroot
fécule	fecula FRENCH
fedelini	very narrow ribbon-shaped pasta, used mainly in soups ITALIAN
feferonky	pimento CZECH
fegatelli	slices of pig's liver ITALIAN
fegatini	chicken and poultry livers ITALIAN
fegato	liver ITALIAN
fehérhagyma mártás	onion sauce HUNGARIAN
fehérrépa	turnip HUNGARIAN
Feige	fig GERMAN
feijão verde	green bean PORTUGUESE
feijoada	dried beans stewed with pig's head and trotters, bacon, sausages and sometimes vegetables PORTUGUESE
feijoada completa	an elaborate dish of pork and beans popular in Portugal and Brazil PORTUGUESE, BRAZILIAN
fejes saláta	lettuce HUNGARIAN
fejeskáposzta-fözelék	boiled cabbage HUNGARIAN
fekete áfonya	blueberries HUNGARIAN
fekete cseresznye	heart cherry HUNGARIAN
fekete ribizli	blackcurrants HUNGARIAN
fél	half HUNGARIAN
Felchen	whitefish; féra GERMAN
felfújt	soufflé HUNGARIAN
félig átsütve	underdone (rare) HUNGARIAN
felvágott	cold plate of carved meat HUNGARIAN
femöring med ägg	small steak topped with fried egg SWEDISH
fenalår	cured leg of mutton NORWEGIAN
fenalår	salted, wind-dried leg of mutton, usually smoked NORWEGIAN
Fenchel	fennel GERMAN
fenkoli	fennel FINNISH
fennel	there are two types of fennel plant: the feathery leaves of one type are used as a herb, the bulbous roots of the other are eaten as a vegetable and the seeds are used as a spice
fennel flower	another name for black cumin – it bears no resemblance to fennel
fennel pear	pear with a slight taste of aniseed, like fennel FRENCH

fennikel	fennel NORWEGIAN
fenouil	fennel FRENCH
fenouil tubereaux	Florence fennel FRENCH
fenugrec	fenugreek FRENCH
fenugreek	a member of the pea family with long pods containing irregular-shaped brown seeds, used as a spice
fer à glacer	salamander FRENCH
féra	kind of salmon trout found especially in Lake Geneva and other Swiss lakes SWISS
ferchuse	pig's offal fried in pork fat, moistened with red wine and covered with stock to which shallots, garlic and bouquet garni are added FRENCH
ferinana	chestnut porridge with olive oil CORSICAN
fermentation	chemical changes such as the decomposition of carbohydrate, with the production of alcohol and carbon dioxide, caused by fermenting agents
fermière, à la	garnish of carrots, turnips, onions, potatoes and celery; celeriac, braised in butter; small slices of carrot, turnip and shredded leek, simmered in butter and served with veal velouté or white wine sauce FRENCH
ferns	young, half-coiled shoots of various ferns are edible
ferri	on the grill, grilled ITALIAN
fersken	peach NORWEGIAN
ferskt kjøtt og suppe	meat and vegetable soup NORWEGIAN
fesa	round cut taken from leg of veal ITALIAN
fesa col prosciutto	leg of veal larded with ham ITALIAN
féta cheese	crumbly, white ewe's milk cheese, originating from Greece GREEK
fetta	salty white cheese made in Sardinia, closely resembling Greek féta SARDINIAN
fettina	small slice ITALIAN
fettuccine	flat narrow noodles ITALIAN
feuillantine	puff pastry cakes FRENCH
feuille	leaf FRENCH
feuille de dreux	cow's milk cheese made in the Ile-de-France FRENCH
feuilletage	puff pastry FRENCH
feuilleton	thin slices of flattened veal spread with various stuffings in layers to a height of about six inches, wrapped in a pork caul and braised FRENCH

fève	broad bean FRENCH
fiambre	cold cooked ham PORTUGUESE
fiambres	cold meat SPANISH
fiatal liba	grouse HUNGARIAN
fiatole	Mediterranean fish with gold bars and spots on dark grey skin FRENCH
fibre	found only in plant foods, it gives structure to plant cell walls; the health promoting properties of fibre result from its ability to absorb fluids
ficelle, à la	beef bound tightly with string and browned in a hot oven, served in boiling consommé FRENCH
fico	fig ITALIAN
fideo	thin noodle SPANISH
fides	a variety of pasta, used especially in soups GREEK
fidget pie	speciality dish of sliced potatoes and apples, layered with onions and unsmoked diced bacon and topped with pastry WELSH
fiélas	the name in Provence for a conger eel FRENCH
fieldfare	bird about the size of a large thrush
fig	sweet, juicy fruit with tiny edible seeds; there are green, white, purple and black varieties, and they are available fresh or dried
fig, dried	sold loose or in pressed blocks
figado	liver PORTUGUESE
figatelli	pig's liver sausage CORSICAN
figeater	a member of the warbler family considered a great table delicacy; it should be eaten whole
figgie hobbin	suet and lard pastry with raisins added to taste CORNISH
figi	figs POLISH
figos	figs PORTUGUESE
figue	fig FRENCH
fiken	fig NORWEGIAN
fíky	figs CZECH
filbert	oblong hazelnut covered by a tapering leafy husk ENGLISH
Filboid Studge	wishing to marry Duncan Dullamy's daughter Lenore, Mark Spayley renamed Pipenta – Dullamy's non-selling breakfast food – Filboid Studge, and advertised it in the Benetton manner whereupon it became a runaway success and the heiress Lenore beyond the reach of Mark, 'a two-hundred-a-year

poster designer' – 'Saki', *The Chronicles of Clovis* (1911). An attempt to use the catchy name for a real cereal in the 1990s seems to have sunk without trace.

filbunke	junket SWEDISH
filé	fillet CZECH, SWEDISH
filé powder	dried leaves of the sassafras tree, which adds spice to dishes
filee	fillet FINNISH
filet	fillet FRENCH, POLISH
filet mignon	small cut of meat from the small end of the fillet of beef; the undercut of a saddle of lamb or mutton FRENCH
filete	fillet of fish PORTUGUESE
filete	steak SPANISH
filetto	fillet ITALIAN
filhó	fritter PORTUGUESE
fillet	the undercut of a loin of meat; the boned breast of a bird; the boned side of fish
filleted	boned; usually applied to fish
filmjölk	sour milk SWEDISH
filo pastry	pastry made with a high gluten flour, stretched until tissue thin
filtering	straining a liquid through a filter or a cloth
filtre	filter FRENCH
fin	wing-like membranes used by a fish for balance and guidance
fin de siècle	cow's milk cheese from Normandy FRENCH
financière sauce	brown sauce with chicken broth, truffle trimmings and chopped mushrooms FRENCH
financière, à la	meat or poultry in Madeira sauce with mushrooms and truffles; garnish of cocks' combs, cocks' kidneys, truffles, olives and whole or sliced mushrooms FRENCH
findik keuftessi	mutton dumplings TURKISH
finger buffet	pieces eaten with the fingers *cf* fork buffet
fines herbes	herb mixture of finely chopped fresh chives, chervil, parsley and tarragon FRENCH
finikia	popular name for small honey-dipped cakes called melomakarona GREEK
fining	to remove cloudiness and sediment
finker	leftover roast beef eaten cold and served with apple sauce DANISH

finnan haddie	smoked haddock from Findon, Grampian SCOTTISH
finnlendskaia	garnish for soup of pancakes made with sour cream, sliced and placed on small pieces of toast thickly spread with grated cheese FINNISH
finocchio	fennel ITALIAN
finocchiona	sausage flavoured with fennel seeds ITALIAN
finte	a freshwater fish that inhabits the rivers of Europe
fior di latte	cheese similar to Mozzarella, but made from cow's milk ITALIAN
fiore sardo	hard cheese made from ewe's milk ITALIAN
fiorentina	Florentine garnish; spinach is always a main ingredient ITALIAN
fios de ovos	dessert of fine golden strands of beaten egg yolk and melted sugar PORTUGUESE
fiouse	the local name in Lorraine for quiche lorraine FRENCH
firespecier	biscuit similar to shortbread DANISH
Fisch	fish GERMAN
Fischklößchen	fishball GERMAN
Fischmilcher	soft roe, often poached and mashed with mustard and white wine GERMAN
Fischschüssel	casserole of fish and diced bacon GERMAN
fish	an excellent source of protein, low in saturated fat and carbohydrates
fish kettle	long, deep, narrow pan designed for poaching whole fish
fisk	fish DANISH, NORWEGIAN, SWEDISH
fiskebolle	fish ball NORWEGIAN
fiskefilet	fillet of fish, usually plaice DANISH
fiskefrikadelle	fried fishball served hot or cold on smørrebrød DANISH
fiskepudding	fish pudding NORWEGIAN
fiskesuppe	fish soup NORWEGIAN
fissurelle	gastropod mollusc rather like a limpet, which can be cooked as calamary
fistulane	headless mollusc with a tubular shell, prepared like cockle FRENCH
fistuline hépatique	beefsteak fungus (US: liver fungus) FRENCH
fitless cock	corruption of Fastern meaning 'fast eve', it is a Highland dish of oatmeal, suet, onion, salt and pepper, bound with egg, shaped in the form of a fowl and boiled SCOTTISH

five-spice powder   mixture of ground spices used in Chinese cuisine, usually containing star anise, anise pepper, fennel seeds, cloves, and cinnamon or cassia CHINESE

fjaderfa   poultry SWEDISH

fjaerkré   poultry NORWEGIAN

fjerkrae   poultry DANISH

Fladen   pancake GERMAN

fladene   tart of vanilla-flavoured broccio CORSICAN

Flädle, Flädli   thin strips of pancake added to soup GERMAN

flądra   flounder POLISH

flæske   pork DANISH

flæskeæggekage   thick omelette with fried bacon, tomato and chives, served with rye bread DANISH

flæskepannekake   thick oven baked pancake with bacon NORWEGIAN

flæskepølse   pork sandwich spread NORWEGIAN

flæskesteg   roast pork with crackling DANISH

flageolet bean   white or pale-green dried bean with a delicate flavour

flair fat   layer of fat found on the inside of a loin of pork, covering the kidneys

flaish un kais   individual turnovers made with cream cheese pastry, seasoned with curry powder, and filled with a mixture of chicken livers, hard boiled eggs, grated onion, cream and curry powder DUTCH-AMERICAN

flake   to separate cooked fish into individual flakes, or to cut hard foodstuffs into slivers

flaki   tripe with seasoning POLISH

flaki jarskie   'vegetable tripe'; stewed, spiced vegetables POLISH

flamande, à la la   dishes based on the Flemish style of cooking, usually served with a garnish of braised vegetables and bacon or small pork sausages; large cuts of meat coated in demi-glace sauce; asparagus served with melted butter and sieved hard-boiled egg FRENCH

flambé   flavouring a dish with alcohol; the warmed spirit is ignited and poured over the food - the alcohol burns off, but the flavour remains FRENCH

flamberad   flamed SWEDISH

flamberet   flamed DANISH

flambiert   flambé; food set aflame with brandy GERMAN

flamenca, a la   with onions, peas, green peppers, tomatoes and spiced sausage SPANISH

flamiche	a speciality of Burgundy and Picardy – a pie filled with leeks and egg yolks; in other parts of France it is a pastry mixed with egg yolks, yeast, sugar and rum or brandy FRENCH
flamingo	long-legged, rosy-coloured water bird SARDINIA
Flammeri	pudding of rice or semolina served with stewed fruit or vanilla custard GERMAN
flamri	boiled semolina pudding made with white wine and water, baked in a bain-marie and served with raw red fruit purée FRENCH
flamusse	a Burgundian pastry tart with a cheese-flavoured cream filling FRENCH
flan	sweet or savoury deep tart such as quiche; the name for crème caramel in the south of Spain and Andorra
flanchet	flank of beef FRENCH
flangnarde	a vanilla-flavoured pudding from the Auvergne and Limousin regions FRENCH
flank	cut of beef from the flap below the loin and following on from the ribs
flannel cakes	griddle cakes served sweet with butter and maple syrup or savoury topped with chicken or turkey in a creamy sauce AMERICAN
flapjack	biscuit, usually made of fat, sugar, rolled oats and golden syrup
flascher Hase	'false hare'; chopped veal, pork and beef mixed with eggs, onions, capers and lemon juice, shaped like a beef fillet, rolled in breadcrumbs and baked GERMAN
fläsk	pork SWEDISH
flat black pak choi	see flat pak choi, rosette pak choi, taatsoi, tasai
flatbread	type of unleavened bread, made without yeast
flatbrød	thin wafer of rye and sometimes barley NORWEGIAN
flatfish	the zoological order to which plaice, sole, halibut and flounder belongs
flat pak choi	see flat black pak choi, rosette pak choi, taatsoi, tasai
flats	a type of American cheddar AMERICAN
flavourings	flavour enhanced or disguised by adding an ingredient; marinating, cooking in a court bouillon, adding herbs and spices or other flavourings
flead	the inner membrane of a pig's stomach; a thin skin of pure lard, beaten into flour to make lard cakes and pastries
Fleckerln	very small, square noodles GERMAN, AUSTRIAN

Fleisch	meat GERMAN
Fleischkäse	seasoned meat loaf of beef and other minced meats GERMAN
Fleischkloß	meat dumpling GERMAN
Fleischroulade	slice of meat, stuffed, rolled and braised GERMAN
flensjes	thin pancakes DUTCH
flet	flounder FRENCH
flétan	halibut FRENCH
fleuriste	garnish of tomatoes filled with vegetables and pommes château FRENCH
fleuron	small, fancy-shaped pastry used as a garnish
fleury, à la	chicken consommé garnished with chicken quenelles and green peas FRENCH
flip	a drink of beaten egg and milk, wine, spirit or beer
flitch	cured, salted side of pork
floating islands	cold dessert of egg custard, topped with poached meringue
flocon	form of cornflake used as a garnish for soups and for making a kind of porridge FRENCH
fløde	cream DANISH
Flohkrebs	prawns GERMAN
florendine	an 18th-century veal pie ENGLISH
florentine	a thin sweet biscuit made from a mixture of chopped nuts, candied peel, glacé cherries and dried fruit in melted butter, sugar and milk or cream, usually coated with plain chocolate
florentine, à la	eggs or fish served with spinach FRENCH
florian	garnish of braised lettuce, browned button onions and olive-shaped carrots FRENCH
Florida dusky duck	duck common in Florida and the southern states of America AMERICAN
fløte	cream NORWEGIAN
fløteost	type of mysost cheese NORWEGIAN
flounder	flat sea fish resembling plaice
flour	finely ground cereal grains, root vegetables and pulses used to make bread, biscuits, cakes, pastry, pasta and other foods
flouring	to dredge flour over food to dry it or coat it for frying; to dust the inside of a greased cake tin with flour; to sprinkle flour over a pastry board before use

floutes	quenelles of small cork-like shapes of mashed potatoes, flour and nutmeg poached in salted boiling water. FRENCH
flowering pak choi	*see* brocoletto, choy sum, flowering white cabbage, hong tsoi sum, hon tsai tai, kozaitai, pak tsoi sum, purple flowered choy sum, rape
flowering white cabbage	*see* brocoletto, choy sum, flowering pak choi, hong tsoi sum, hon tsai tai, kozaitai, pak tsoi sum, purple flowered choy sum, rape
floyeres	almond stuffed pastry rolls made with filo pastry GREEK
fluffy egg nest	the whole yolk dropped into the whisked white, and baked in the oven
flummery	cold dessert of cereal, set in a mould and turned out
Flunder	smoked plaice and flounder GERMAN
flundra	flounder SWEDISH
fluorine	natural trace element, believed to help prevent tooth decay
Fluss-krebs	crayfish GERMAN
fluting	cut tiny vegetables, fruit, cakes or pastries with a serrated edge
flûte	a long loaf, sold in Paris FRENCH
flûte à potage	long roll for making croûtes to serve with soups and stews FRENCH
flyndre	flounder NORWEGIAN
flyndrefilet	fillet of flounder NORWEGIAN
focaccia	flat bread; sweet ring-shaped cake ITALIAN
foe yong hai	omelette of leeks, onions, and shrimps served in sweet-sour sauce DUTCH
föfogás	main course HUNGARIAN
fofos de bacalhau	small fried balls of puréed salted cod PORTUGUESE
fogas	giant pike or perch HUNGARIAN
foggiano	ewe's milk cheese made in Apulia ITALIAN
fogoly	partridge HUNGARIAN
Fogosch	very delicately-flavoured fish found only in Lake Platen AUSTRIAN
foie	liver FRENCH
foie de cerf	deer liver FRENCH
foie gras	specially fattened, abnormally large liver of a goose or duck fed on maize, served hot or cold or combined with other ingredients to make a paté FRENCH

foie-de-boeuf — fistuline hépatique – beefsteak fungus FRENCH

foin — the choke or feathery part of the globe artichoke; a farmhouse method of boiling ham on a bed of sweet hay, with water to cover FRENCH

fokhagyma — garlic HUNGARIAN

fokhagymás majonézes fejes saláta — lettuce salad with garlic-flavoured mayonnaise HUNGARIAN

fokhagymás mártás — garlic sauce HUNGARIAN

földimogyoró — peanuts HUNGARIAN

folding in — combining whisked or creamed ingredients with others by cutting through and turning the mixture to retains lightness

folhado — sweet puffed pastry delicacy PORTUGUESE

fondant — the basis of a number of sweets, and for icing cakes, made of sugar syrup boiled to 116°C

fondants — small croquettes of vegetable purées mixed with grated cheese and fried FRENCH

fondo di carciofo — artichoke heart ITALIAN

fonds blanc simple — simple white stock of meat, water, salt and various herbs FRENCH

fonds brun — estouffade, a highly seasoned beef broth for soups, casseroles and gravies FRENCH

fonds d'artichauts — artichoke bottoms FRENCH

fonds de cuisine — basic culinary preparations indispensable in large establishments as foundations for the preparation of dishes FRENCH

fonds de poisson — highly seasoned fish stock with the addition of white wine FRENCH

fonds de volaille — chicken stock FRENCH

fonds ou jus de veau brun — veal stock of veal, onions, carrots, bacon and herbs FRENCH

fondue — fondue bourguignonne – a pan of oil is kept hot over a burner on the table, lean pieces of beef are cooked on fondue forks in the oil and eaten with condiments; Swiss fondue – chunks of bread are dipped in a mixture of melted Gruyère cheese, wine and other flavourings; fruit can be dipped in a fondue of melted chocolate and cream FRENCH, SWISS

fondue bourguignonne — bite-sized pieces of meat dipped into boiling oil to cook at the table and eaten with a sauce FRENCH

fondue chinoise — paper-thin slices of beef dipped into boiling bouillon and eaten with a sauce FRENCH

fondue du raisin	mild cheese covered in grape pips; relatively flavourless, it adds colour FRENCH
fonduta	similar to Swiss fondue; made of fontina cheese, egg yolk and truffles ITALIAN
fontainebleau	soft, creamy fresh cow's milk cheese; garnish for tournedos and noisettes of bouchées of pommes duchesse filled with vegetables in cream sauce FRENCH
fontal	even-textured cow's milk cheese with a mild flavour, similar to fontina
fontina	mild flavoured, dark yellow, unpasteurised cow's milk cheese full of holes, from Piedmont, with a slightly rubbery texture ITALIAN
fontine	cow's milk cheese from Franche-Comté FRENCH
food	nourishment needed by living things to sustain life
food poisoning	illness caused by consumption of food contaminated with bacteria, bacterial toxins, or chemicals
food processor	electric appliance to chop, slice, grate, cream, knead and beat
foogath	savoury dish of cooked vegetables INDIAN
fool	cold dessert of puréed fruit and whipped cream or custard
forårsrulle	(Chinese) spring roll; egg roll DANISH
forcemeat	rich, highly flavoured mixture used by itself or as stuffing for various meats
forel	trout RUSSIAN
forell	trout SWEDISH
Forelle	trout GERMAN
for-eller mellomrett	hors d'œuvres NORWEGIAN
forelli	trout FINNISH
forestière, à la	meat or poultry dish with mushrooms, ham or bacon and fried potatoes FRENCH
Forfar bridies	a kind of Cornish pasty made with strips of rump steak, with a hole cut in the top to let the steam out. SCOTTISH
fork buffet	pieces eaten with a fork – cf finger buffet
forkbread	fish belonging to the cod family ENGLISH
forloren hare	meat loaf of pork and veal, served with apple halves filled with redcurrant jelly, potatoes and red cabbage DANISH
forlorne kyllinger	'mock chicken'; veal rolls filled with butter, minced parsley and seasoning, rolled in flour and fried DANISH

formaggini   small cream cheese sometimes eaten with olive oil
ITALIAN

formaggini di Montpellier   soft cheese of curdled cow's milk and white wine with thistle blossoms added ITALIAN

formaggio   cheese ITALIAN

formaggio di Lecco   cow's milk cheese with added goat's milk, made in Lecco, Lombardy ITALIAN

formaldehyde   a gas; in solution with water it can be used as a disinfectant and for sterilisation

formic acid   a strong acid which can be used to disinfect wine barrels; it is too strong for general household use

forno   baked ITALIAN, PORTUGUESE

förrätt   starter; first course SWEDISH

forret   starter; first course DANISH, NORWEGIAN

forró   hot HUNGARIAN

forshmak   minced cold meat or poultry mixed with salt herring, mashed potato, onion, sour cream and breadcrumbs
RUSSIAN

forszmak   veal in tomato sauce POLISH

forte   hot; spicy ITALIAN

fortified wine   wine with extra spirit added during fermentation, thus achieving a higher alcohol content

fött   boiled; stewed HUNGARIAN

fött tojás   boiled egg HUNGARIAN

fouace   an old form of pastry made from fine wheat flour
FRENCH

fouée   circle of uncooked bread dough, covered with cream, butter or olive oil, baked in a very hot oven FRENCH

fouet   whisk FRENCH

fouetté   whipped FRENCH

fougasse   a Provençal bread of fine flour and olive oil flavoured with aniseed FRENCH

four spices   spice mixture of white peppercorns, nutmeg, cloves and ginger

four, au   cooked in the oven FRENCH

four-square breakfast   egg, fried bread, bacon and tomato

fourme d'ambert, fourme de montbrison   firm soft, creamy cheese with rich full-bodied flavour FRENCH

fournitures   salad greens and fresh herbs FRENCH

fowl   edible bird; often applied to older, tougher birds

foyot sauce   béarnaise sauce with meat glaze FRENCH

fözelékek   vegetables HUNGARIAN

fra diavolo   with a spicy tomato sauce ITALIAN

fragole   strawberries ITALIAN

fragole di mare   'sea strawberries'; tiny fish, members of the squid and inkfish family ITALIAN

fraîche   fresh FRENCH

fraise   strawberry FRENCH

fraise de veau   calf's mesentery FRENCH

framboeza   raspberry PORTUGUESE

framboise   raspberry FRENCH

framboos   raspberry DUTCH

frambuesa   raspberry SPANISH

francesa, a la   sautéed in butter SPANISH

francolin   partridge-like bird found in all warm European countries

frangipane   originally an almond cream flavoured with jasmine; today it is an almond flan; a thickening mixture similar to choux pastry, used in stuffings FRENCH

frango   pullet PORTUGUESE

frankfurter   smoked sausage traditionally made with minced pork and salted bacon fat, usually used to make hot dogs GERMAN

Frankfurter Bohnensuppe   soup of kidney beans and vegetables, with sliced frankfurter sausages added GERMAN

franskbröd   white bread SWEDISH, DANISH

frappé   dishes or drinks served iced, frozen of chilled FRENCH

frascati, à la   garnish of thin slices of foie gras, asparagus tips, mushrooms and truffles FRENCH

frasvåffla   warm waffle SWEDISH

frattaglie   giblets ITALIAN

freeze-drying   preserving foodstuff by rapid freezing (with liquid nitrogen at -195.8C) and then vacuum drying

freezing   fresh or cooked foods preserved by storing in a frozen state

fregula   soup with semolina and saffron dumplings ITALIAN

frémissement   simmering FRENCH

French beans, string beans   class of beans usually including kidney beans, snap beans and wax-pod beans, usually grown for the pods, which are picked before the seeds reach maturity

French dressing	salad dressing of olive oil, lemon juice or vinegar and seasoning AMERICAN
French fried onions	deep fried, battered onion rings AMERICAN
French fries	deep fried potato chips – or the uniform extruded potato material AMERICAN
French mustard	mustard usually regarded as particularly fine FRENCH
French toast	slices or fingers of bread dipped in egg and milk mixture and fried FRENCH
fresa	a variety of caciotta cheese, made from cow's milk and sometimes goat's milk SARDINIAN
fresa	strawberry SPANISH
fresco	cool, fresh, uncooked ITALIAN, PORTUGUESE, SPANISH
fresón	large strawberry SPANISH
fressure, issues	pluck FRENCH
frétins	small fry, such as white bait FRENCH
friand	'dainty'; hot hors d'œuvres, often including a sausage roll FRENCH
friandise	delicacy; sweetmeat FRENCH
friar's fish-in-sauce	a 19th-century recipe of trout, carp or perch rubbed with salt and mixed spices and poached in a good, seasoned stock containing a good claret; the fish is removed, the sauce thickened and a few oysters added SCOTTISH
friar's omelette	sweet omelette with cooked, sweetened apple, served cold
fribourg vacherin	type of Gruyère cheese with a high fat content and white curd SWISS
fricadelles	small flat cakes of minced meat with herbs, milk, bread or potato, coated in breadcrumbs and fried FRENCH
fricandeau	long thick piece from top rump of veal, larded and braised or roasted; slices or fillets of sturgeon or fresh tuna braised in fish stock FRENCH
fricandelles	pork balls BELGIAN
fricandó	veal bird – thin slice of meat rolled in bacon and braised SPANISH
fricassé	casserole, usually of lamb or veal in cream sauce PORTUGUESE
fricassée	white stew of chicken, rabbit, veal or vegetables, finished with cream and egg yolks FRENCH
fricassée z dorsza	oven baked cod with mushrooms, cauliflower and French beans POLISH

Fridatten	garnish for soup of pancake cut into match-like strips AUSTRIAN
friesian	a cheese flavoured with cloves and cumin DUTCH
frigideira	sautéed PORTUGUESE
frigolet, farigoule	Provençal name for wild thyme FRENCH
frijol	bean SPANISH
frijole	bean MEXICAN
frijoles refritos	fried mashed beans SPANISH
frikadell	boiled veal meat ball SWEDISH
Frikadeller	small meatballs or burgers made of minced pork, usually served with tomato sauce SWEDISH
German Frikassee	fricassée; stew GERMAN
frinault cendré	a cow's milk cheese coated with wood ash FRENCH
frio	cold PORTUGUESE
frío	cold SPANISH
frisch	fresh GERMAN
Frischkäse	fresh, soft, cream cheese GERMAN
Frischling	young wild boar GERMAN
frisk	fresh DANISH
frissen sültek	made to order HUNGARIAN
frit	fried FRENCH
fritada de peixe	deep-fried fish PORTUGUESE
fritas	fritters SPANISH
friteerattu	deep-fried FINNISH
fritelle	fritters; often squares of fresh uncooked ravioli pasta filled with cheese and ham and fried in oil ITALIAN
friterad	deep-fried SWEDISH
frites, frieten	chips (US: French fries) DUTCH
frito	fry; fried; fritter; PORTUGUESE, SPANISH
fritot	any type of deep fried fritter; small pieces of meat, fish, fruit or vegetable dipped in batter FRENCH
frittata	similar to an omelette but firmer and not folded, with a variety of fillings ITALIAN
frittatine imbolitte	stuffed pancakes with ravioli stuffing, garnished with grated cheese and cooked in a little meat or chicken broth ITALIAN
frittella	fritter; pancake ITALIAN
fritter	a portion of sweet or savoury food coated in batter or breadcrumbs and fried
fritto	deep-fried ITALIAN

fritto misto	variety of small, thin pieces of meat, poultry or vegetables coated with batter or breadcrumbs and fried ITALIAN
fritura	fry SPANISH
friture	fried food of any kind; the oil used for frying; the term for deep-frying FRENCH
frog	only the hind legs of the edible frog are eaten, fried in butter or cut up and stewed in mushroom sauce
froid	cold FRENCH
froise	term found in old English cookery books; the meaning is uncertain, but it appears to mean fried food, sometimes in batter ENGLISH
frokost	lunch DANISH
frokost	breakfast NORWEGIAN
frokost bord	buffet of cold and hot specialities to make your own smorrebrod DANISH
frokost platte	hot and cold specialities to make your own smørrebrød, served on a tray DANISH
frokostbord	buffet of hot and cold specialities to make your own smørrebrød DANISH
frølår	frogs' legs DANISH
fromage	cheese FRENCH
fromage	blancmange, mousse (pudding) DANISH, SWEDISH
fromage à la crème	fresh cream cows milk and cream cheese FRENCH
fromage blanc	very low fat cheese with a light, fresh, clean taste FRENCH
fromage d'Italie	type of brawn made from pig's liver FRENCH
fromage de Bruxelles	soft, fermented, skimmed milk cheese BELGIUM
fromage de monsieur	soft, slightly fermented cow's milk cheese from Normandy FRENCH
fromage de porc	brawn FRENCH
fromage fort	a French cheese paste from Lyons; the cheese is thinly layered in stone pots with salt, herbs or leek juice and cream, filled with white wine and a little brandy, and the pots are sealed and left to ferment for a few weeks FRENCH
fromage frais	similar to fromage blanc, a soft cheese sometimes enriched with cream; fromage frais is served as a dessert flavoured with fruit FRENCH
fromage sec	a dry cow's milk cheese; white cheese is dried in straw baskets, drained well and dusting with pepper FRENCH

fromager to add grated cheese to a sauce or dough; to sprinkle grated cheese over a dish and brown it under the grill FRENCH

fromasj mousse, blancmange NORWEGIAN

froment renflé variety of wheat grown in Mediterranean countries

fromenteau variety of dessert grape FRENCH

fromgey white cow's milk cheese from Lorraine FRENCH

Froschkeulen frogs' legs GERMAN

frosted fruit soft juicy fruit with a crisp, sparkling coating of fine sugar

frosting icing; fruit, flowers and the rims of cocktail glasses decorated with a fine layer of sugar AMERICAN

frothing browning roast meat by dredging with flour and placing in a hot oven until it turns brown

frozen food many uncooked foods or complete meals may be preserved by freezing

Frucht fruit GERMAN

fructose a hexose sugar, the chief sugar found in fruit juices

frugt fruit DANISH

frugtsuppe raspberry and redcurrant soup DANISH

Frühlingssuppe soup with diced spring vegetables GERMAN

Frühstück breakfast GERMAN

Frühstückskäse a soft, whole or partly-skimmed cow's milk cheese GERMAN

Frühstücksspeck smoked bacon GERMAN

fruit the ovary or seed-bearing part of a plant; eaten raw and cooked, all over the world

fruit brandy fruit brandies are distilled from fruit wines from numerous fruits

fruit cake rich moist cake of dried and crystallised fruit, nuts and peel

fruit cap refreshing drink of fruit pieces and fruit juices, lemonade or alcohol

fruit cocktail fruit chunks doused with lemon juice, sprinkled with sugar

fruit confit candied fruit FRENCH

fruit kernel the soft part inside the hard shell of a stone fruit, usually edible though it may be bitter

fruit leather a chewy confectionery made with fruit purée

fruit salad dessert of sliced or diced fresh fruit served in natural juice or syrup

fruit, dried fruit preserved by having its natural water content reduced by drying

fruits de mer assorted crustacea and shellfish served together FRENCH

frukost breakfast SWEDISH

frukostflingor breakfast cereal SWEDISH

frukt fruit NORWEGIAN, SWEDISH

frumenty mediaeval English dish prepared at harvest time; new wheat grains were steeped in water, left on a low fire until soft, drained and boiled with milk to make a porridge, which was then spiced and sweetened ENGLISH

frusen grädde frozen whipped cream SWEDISH

frushie Victorian fruit flan with a trellis of pastry over the fruit ENGLISH

fruta fruit PORTUGUESE, SPANISH

frutta fruit ITALIAN

frutti di mare shellfish ITALIAN

fry young fish no more than a few inches long; the intestines of a lamb or pig

frying cooking food in hot fat or oil; shallow frying, using a little oil in a frying pan, is used to brown or seal meat and to cook dishes such as bacon and steaks; deep frying is used for cooking fritters, croquettes and similar dishes – the food is immersed completely in hot oil; stir-frying, cooking food very quickly in very hot oil in a wok – a Chinese method of cooking; dry-frying uses no extra oil or fat, and is suitable for cooking fatty foods

frying pan metal utensil for frying

frytki chips POLISH

fubá maize flour PORTUGUESE

fucetola southern Italy name for the figeater ITALIAN

fudge sweet made from sugar, butter and milk

füge figs HUNGARIAN

fuggan traditional Cornish oval-shaped cake; a cross is marked on top with a knife

fugl fowl NORWEGIAN

ful medames a rounded oval-shaped brown bean FRENCH

Füllung stuffing, filling, forcemeat GERMAN

fulmar Arctic petrel, an oceanic bird similar in size and colour to a herring gull

fumado	smoked PORTUGUESE
fumé	smoked FRENCH
fumet	liquid to give flavour and body to soups and sauces; meat, fish or vegetables are cooked in stock which is reduced until it reaches a syrupy consistency FRENCH
funcho	fennel PORTUGUESE
funghi	mushrooms ITALIAN
fungus	type of plant without chlorophyll or leaves, reproducing by mycelium or spores, that lives off other living, dead or decaying matter; includes mushrooms and toadstools, some edible, some poisonous
furcula	wishbone; merrythought
fürj	quail HUNGARIAN
Fürstpücklereis (bombe)	chocolate, strawberry and vanilla ice-cream dessert GERMAN
fun size	marketspeak for an undersized fruit, etc
fusilli, helix	thin spiral-shaped pasta formed into a twist like a corkscrew ITALIAN
füstölt	smoked HUNGARIAN
füszer	spice HUNGARIAN
füszerkeverék	mixed herbs HUNGARIAN
fyld	stuffing; forcemeat DANISH
fyldt	stuffed, filled SWEDISH
fyldt hvidkål	cabbage stuffed with minced veal and pork DANISH
fyll	stuffing, forcemeat NORWEGIAN
fylt kalhode	braised cabbage stuffed with minced meat NORWEGIAN
fynbo	cheese made on the island of Funen DANISH
fyrstekake	almond flan NORWEGIAN

G

gaar	well done DUTCH
Gabelfrühstück	brunch GERMAN
gachas	an aniseed-flavoured sweet dish from Cádiz SPANISH
gachas manchegas	traditional dish from La Mancha, of pig's cheek cut into small pieces and fried in oil SPANISH
gädda	pike SWEDISH
gäddfärsbullar	pike dumplings SWEDISH
gade	Normandy name for redcurrant FRENCH
gado gado	salad of cooked and raw vegetables INDONESIAN
gadwall	wild duck; not unlike the mallard
gaffelbidder	cured herrings of exceptional quality DANISH
gaffelbitter	'fork bits'; cured herring fillets NORWEGIAN
gai choy	see Chinese celery cabbage, Chinese mustard (greens), Chinese mustard cabbage, Chinese white cabbage, chingensai, green in snow, Indian mustard (greens), kai tsoi, leaf mustard, mustard cabbage, taisin
gai lan	see white flowering broccoli, Chinese broccoli, Chinese kale, kailan, kaai laan tsoi
gajjar	carrot INDIAN
gajjar ka halwa	carrot pudding INDIAN
galactose	a monosaccharide sugar obtained by hydrolysing lactose (milk sugar)
galamb	pigeon HUNGARIAN
galangal	spice plant related to ginger; it is obtained from the rhizome ARABIAN
galantina	pressed meat in gelatine PORTUGUESE
galantina tartufata	truffles in aspic jelly ITALIAN
galantine	white meat, boned, sometimes stuffed, rolled, cooked and pressed into a symmetrical shape
galareta	jelly POLISH
galaretka owocowa	jam POLISH
galaretka z nóżek cięlecych	calf's trotters in gelatine POLISH
galathée	crustacean rather like freshwater crayfish FRENCH
galatoboureko	elaborate vanilla cream or custard pie GREEK
galerts	traditional dish of jellied potted veal LATVIAN
galette	sweet or savoury flat; round cake; biscuit FRENCH

galettes suisses	almond biscuits SWISS
galichons	small, iced almond cakes, a speciality of Aix-en-Provence FRENCH
galicien	very light cake-like dessert FRENCH
galingale	plant with edible tubers which taste a little like a gingery Hamburg parsley root; when cooked the roots are pinkish in colour and smell of roses
galinha	hen PORTUGUESE
galinhola	woodcock PORTUGUESE
galletas	small cakes or biscuits twisted into different shapes SPANISH
Galliano	golden, spicy, herbal liqueur ITALIAN
gallimaufry	mediaeval chicken stew, with bacon, verjuice, ginger, mustard and wine
gallina	hazel grouse SPANISH
gallina	hen ITALIAN, SPANISH
gallina del mar	gurnard SPANISH, MALTESE
gallinaccio	chanterelle mushroom; woodcock ITALIAN
gallinella	water-hen ITALIAN
gallinule	another name for a moorhen, but also the name for another genus of the same family
gallo	cockerel SPANISH
gallo cedrone	grouse ITALIAN
gallo de San Pedro	John Dory SPANISH
gallon	imperial measure for liquids; 8 pints
gallopoulo	turkey GREEK
galo das urzes	grouse PORTUGUESE
galushki	dumplings served with butter or sour cream UKRAINIAN
galuska	dumplings, noodles HUNGARIAN
gamay	variety of grape FRENCH
gamba	prawn SPANISH
gambas con mayonesa	shrimp cocktail SPANISH
gamberetti	prawn; shrimp ITALIAN
gambero	crayfish, crawfish ITALIAN
gambero do mare	lobster ITALIAN
game	wild birds and animals hunted for food, including pigeons, rabbits and quails which are farmed
game chips	wafer-thin slices across potato, fried until golden brown, and served with game and poultry

game crumbs dry breadcrumbs fried in melted butter until golden, drained and served separately with roast game

gammelost the most popular skimmed cow's milk hard cheese, it is made from naturally soured curd NORWEGIAN

gammon originally cured forelimb of a pig; today often from the top of the ham

ganga type of hazel grouse common in the Pyrenees FRENCH

gannet large white seabird with black tipped wings

gans goose DUTCH

Gans goose GERMAN

Gänseklein goose giblets GERMAN

ganso goose PORTUGUESE

gantois Flemish pastries, flavoured with almond and candied orange peel and spread with apricot and greengage jam FLEMISH

gaper a bivalve which lives in sand or mud flats at the mouths of rivers or estuaries, prepared as cockles

gaperon cow's milk cheese from Limagne FRENCH

gar slender sea fish with green bones

ga-ram salt BM

garam masala various mixtures of ground spices used in Indian cooking, which often include black and green cardamom, peppercorns and cumin INDIAN

garbanzo chick pea SPANISH

garbure thick soup from Béarn, made with cabbage and rye bread FRENCH

garden relish relish of tomato, celery, cucumber, green pepper and onion AMERICAN

garfish sea needle or sea eel, a cross between an eel and a mackerel

garganey the summer teal

garibaldi flat sweet biscuit of Italian origin, flavoured with currants and spices ITALIAN

garides, garithes shrimps GREEK

garlic bulb consisting of a cluster of curved cloves around a central stem, used to enhance the flavour of meat, vegetables and salads

garlic butter a savoury butter of crushed garlic, butter, salt and chopped parsley, which may be added to sauces, as a garnish, or to make garlic bread

garlic chive *see* Chinese chive, Chinese leek

garlic salt	ready-made seasoning of pounded, dried garlic mixed with refined salt crystals
garnaal	shrimp; prawn DUTCH
Garnele	shrimp GERMAN
garni	garnished FRENCH
garnish	usually edible decoration, placed on a savoury dish to enhance its appearance
Garnitur	garnish GERMAN
garniture	garnish FRENCH
garofolato	beef stew with cloves ITALIAN
garoupa	large grouper PORTUGUESE
garri	meal produced from the cassava plant
garum	basic condiment used by the Romans made from the entrails of small fish, sun-dried, strained and potted
gås	goose DANISH, NORWEGIAN, SWEDISH
gas mark	another name for Regulo setting; not to be confused with the unit relating a speed to that of sound devised by the Austrian physicist and philosopher Ernst Mach
gåselever	goose liver
gåselever (postej)	goose liver (pâté) NORWEGIAN, DANISH
gåsesteg	roast goose DANISH
gåsesteg med æbler og svesker	roast goose stuffed with apples and prunes DANISH
gåsestek	roast goose NORWEGIAN
gaski marynowane	marinated chanterelle mushrooms POLISH
gaspacho	chilled soup of diced tomatoes, sweet peppers, onions, cucumber and croutons PORTUGUESE
gastronome	garnish of glazed chestnuts, truffles, rognons de coq and morels; demi-glace sauce containing champagne, Madeira and cayenne pepper FRENCH
gastropod	univalve mollusc with a single, coiled shell, such as the snail, winkle and limpet
gâteau	elaborate cakes or desserts made with a sponge, biscuit or pastry base, and containing fruit, jelly or cream FRENCH
gâteau Saint-Honoré	ring of choux pastry piped around the edge of a pâté sucrée base, topped with a crown of choux buns, glazed with caramel, and decorated with whipped cream, cherries, and angelica FRENCH
gaudes	porridge similar to polenta, made from maize flour FRENCH

gaufre	waffle made from batter mixture BELGIAN, FRENCH
gaufrette	small, crisp, sweet wafer FRENCH
gauja	sweet crisp snacks INDIAN
gauloise, à la	garnish served with consommé; garnish for vol-au-vents; chicken consommé; small cakes of pain de gênes mixture FRENCH
gaur	green bean used mainly in India; a source of gum used in ice-creams, processed cheese, salad dressings and canned fruit INDIAN
gautrias	cow's milk made cheese from Mayenne FRENCH
gaves	river trout from Béarn FRENCH
gayette	small, flat sausage, usually made from pig's liver, kidney and lung, flavoured with garlic and parsley FRENCH
gazeux	gassy; fizzy; sparkling FRENCH
gazpacho	seasoned broth of raw onions, garlic, tomatoes, cucumber and green pepper – served cold SPANISH
gešinka	soup of celeriac, carrot, onion and mushroom POLISH
gean	dialect name for wild cherry SCOTTISH
Gebäck	pastry GERMAN
gebacken	baked GERMAN
gebak	pastry, cake DUTCH
gebakken	fried DUTCH
gebie	small crustacean, similar to a shrimp
gebonden soep	cream soup DUTCH
gebraden	roasted DUTCH
gebraten	roasted; fried GERMAN
gedämpft	steamed GERMAN
gedde	pike DANISH
gedroogde pruim	prune DUTCH
gedünstet	braised, steamed GERMAN
geś	goose POLISH
gefillte fish	stuffed fish JEWISH
Geflügel	fowl or poultry GERMAN
Gefrorenes	ice-cream GERMAN
gefüllt	stuffed GERMAN
gegrillt	grilled GERMAN
Gehacktes	minced meat GERMAN
gehakt	minced; minced meat DUTCH
Gehirnwürst	sausage made from pork GERMAN
geitekilling	kid NORWEGIAN

geitost	bitter-sweet, brown, goat's milk cheese NORWEGIAN
gekocht	cooked; boiled GERMAN
gekookt	boiled DUTCH
gekruid	seasoned DUTCH
gekruid ijs	spiced ice cream DUTCH
gelado	ice cream; chilled PORTUGUESE
gelatina	aspic jelly ITALIAN
gelatine	gelling agent, usually sold in powder form to be mixed with water
gelato	ice cream; iced dessert ITALIAN
gelé	jelly, aspic SWEDISH
Gelee	aspic; jelly; jam GERMAN
gelées	jellies FRENCH
geleia	jelly; jam PORTUGUESE
gélinotte des bois	hazel grouse FRENCH
gemarineerd	marinated DUTCH
gember	ginger DUTCH
gemberkoek	gingerbread DUTCH
gemengd	assorted; mixed DUTCH
gemischt	mixed GERMAN
Gemüse	vegetable GERMAN
gendarme	popular colloquial name for a type of herring; small, flat rectangular smoked sausage FRENCH
genévoise, sauce	classical sauce, which includes fish stock FRENCH
gengibre	ginger PORTUGUESE
genièvre	juniper FRENCH
gennemstegt	well-done DANISH
Genoa cake	fruit cake decorated with almonds or brazil nuts
genoese	light sponge cake, a whisked egg mixture enriched with melted butter
genovese, salsa	a Genoese pasta sauce ITALIAN
gentian	yellow flowering plant; the roots make a bitter essence, which is an ingredient of many apéritifs
Georges Sand	fish consommé with fish quenelles, morels, beurre écrevisses and croëtons with carp soft roe FRENCH
georgette	food stuffed with braised crayfish tails FRENCH
gepaneerd	breaded DUTCH
gepocheerd ei	poached egg DUTCH
geranium	popular flowering plant; an infusion of the leaves may be used as flavouring
geraspt	grated DUTCH

geräucherte Bratwürste   smoked sausage GERMAN

gerecht   course; dish DUTCH

Gericht   dish GERMAN

germaine   chicken or meat consommé with chicken quenelles and cubes of green pea royale FRENCH

German pound cake   similar to Genoa cake, containing less fruit and no almonds

German sago   potato flour

German sausage   variety of sausage, salted and spiced, commonly with garlic

Germbutterteig, Germteig   form of puff pastry made with yeast GERMAN

germinal   meat consommé with tarragon FRENCH

germon   bonito; name for small, long finned tuna fish FRENCH

géromé   cow's milk cheese from the valleys of Vosges

FRENCH

gerookt   smoked DUTCH

geroosterd brood   toast DUTCH

geröstet   roasted GERMAN

gerst   barley DUTCH

Gerste   barley GERMAN

gerty meat puddings   Cornish form of haggis

gerty milk   Cornish breakfast dish

gervais   a small, soft, delicately flavoured cream cheese from Normandy FRENCH

gesalzen   salted GERMAN

geschmort   stewed, braised GERMAN

Geschnetzeltes   meat cut into thin, small slices GERMAN

Geschnitzeltes mit Rösti   finely chopped veal in white wine broth SWISS

Geselchtes   cured or smoked pork GERMAN

gesotten   simmered; boiled GERMAN

gespickt   larded GERMAN

gestoofd   braised DUTCH

gesülzt   jellied; in aspic GERMAN

gesztenye   chestnut HUNGARIAN

gesztenyés libamájes pulyka   turkey with goose liver and chestnut stuffing HUNGARIAN

getost   soft, sweet goat's cheese SWEDISH

gevetch-de-peshte   fish and vegetable dish JEWISH

gevogelte   fowl DUTCH

gevuld   stuffed DUTCH

Gewürz   spice GERMAN

gewürzt	spiced, hot GERMAN
gex	blue veined cow's milk cheese FRENCH
gezouten	salted DUTCH
ghagin fin	star or coin shaped pasta MALTESE
ghee	type of clarified butter, with a better flavour than ordinary clarified butter; much used in Indian cookery INDIAN
gherkin	small, dark green cucumber, with a rough skin, which is usually pickled
ghiacciato	iced; chilled ITALIAN
ghiozzo	gudgeon ITALIAN
ghiveci	vegetable casserole ROMANIAN
gianduiotto	chocolate or nougat from Alba or Cremona ITALIAN
giant perch	large variety of perch
gibanica	a pastry YUGOSLAVIAN
gibassier	cake traditionally eaten on Christmas Eve FRENCH
gibelotte	stew of rabbit, bacon, onions and herbs in red or white wine FRENCH
gibier	wild animals and birds hunted for food FRENCH
giblets	edible parts of the entrails of birds, the gizzard, liver, heart and the neck
gicz	leg POLISH
gigot	a cut of lamb or mutton taken from the leg FRENCH
gild	to brush food with egg yolk to turn golden during cooking
gilderne soup	chicken soup served at 25th and 50th wedding anniversaries; the chicken fat floats on the surface to signify further happiness for the couple JEWISH
gill	liquid measurement one quarter of a pint (though in Northern British dialect it may be half a pint); equivalent to 150 ml
gilthead	saltwater fish from the bream family
gilt-poll	saltwater fish
gin	colourless spirit distilled from rye, barley or maize, flavoured with juniper berries; the purest of all spirits
ginanchetti	small, boneless white fish ITALIAN
ginat crab	large variety of the common crab
ginepro	juniper ITALIAN
ginga	prawns INDIAN
ginger	plant grown for the hot, sweetish flavour of its rhizome

ginger ale	soft drink made from carbonated water flavoured with ginger
ginger beer	slightly alcoholic effervescent drink, flavoured with ginger
ginger beer plant	means of producing ginger beer at home by daily division and feeding of the stock, which rapidly takes over the whole house
ginger wine	drink of water, ginger, yeast, lemon, sugar, raisins, pepper and sometimes alcohol
gingerbread	moist brown cake, flavoured with ginger, containing treacle or syrup
ginja	Morello cherry PORTUGUESE
ginkgo nut	the kernel from the ginkgo tree; the fruit is not edible, but the nuts are an important part of Japanese cooking JAPANESE
gioddù	yoghurt SARDINIAN
giouvarlakia	lamb or mutton meatballs, cooked in stock GREEK
Gipfel	crescent-shaped roll GERMAN
girdle	*see* griddle
girella	saltwater fish
girello	round steak from the leg ITALIAN
gitanilla, a la	with garlic SPANISH
gîte à la noix	silverside cut of beef FRENCH
Gittertorte	almond cake or tart with a raspberry topping GERMAN
Gitzi	kid GERMAN
gizzard	part of a bird's digestive system, a muscular organ that acts as a second stomach
gjedde	pike NORWEGIAN
gjillo	cooked in garlic and oil SPANISH
glaçage	glazing or browning in a hot oven, or under a grill; a term used in relation to freezing or icing food
glace	ice cream FRENCH
glacé	iced or glossy FRENCH
glace au four	sponge cake filled with ice cream and covered with meringue (baked Alaska) SWEDISH
glace de viande	meat jelly; reduced brown or white stock FRENCH
glacé fruit	fruit preserved by impregnation with a concentrated sugar syrup
glacé icing	simple glossy icing, made from icing sugar and water
Glamorgan sausage	traditional Welsh sausage, made without meat; but containing Caerphilly cheese, onions, breadcrumbs,

	mustard and seasoning, which is bound with an egg and fried
glarecie	gelatine POLISH
glaserade ägg	eggs in aspic SWEDISH
Glasgow bailies, Glasgow magistrates	method of cooking herrings SCOTTISH
glass	ice cream SWEDISH
glassmestersild	glazed herring NORWEGIAN
glasswort	variety of samphire
Glattbutt	brill GERMAN
glattes Mehl	fine white flour milled from Italian and Hungarian wheat AUSTRIAN
glayva	a whiskey-based liqueur, flavoured with honey and herbs SCOTTISH
glaze	any food which gives a glossy coating to sweet or savoury dishes
glazing	giving sweet or savoury foods a glossy, decorative coating
glessie	old fashioned sweetmeat SCOTTISH
gliny	west of England name for guinea fowl
globe artichoke	the original artichoke; only the young flower bud is eaten
gloebie	pigeon POLISH
głog	hawthorn berry POLISH
glorias	pastry turnover filled with a mixture of cinnamon, icing sugar, flour, sweet potatoes, ground almonds, rum and aniseed SPANISH
glossa	fish resembling flounder GREEK
główka	animal's head POLISH
główka cieleca	calf's head POLISH
Gloucester cheese	Gloucester cheese is from the milk of Gloucester cattle, and Double Gloucester from a mixture of morning and evening milk ENGLISH
Gloucester pudding	steamed suet pudding containing finely chopped raw apple and mixed peel ENGLISH
Gloucester sauce	sauce, mainly used for dressing meat and salads
glucose	sugar found in fruits
glukhar	capercaillie, a bird popular in Russia RUSSIAN
gluten	a protein substance, a constituent of wheat and other cereals, which develops into elastic strands when mixed with water

glux	cow's milk cheese from the Nivernais FRENCH
glycerine	sweet, colourless, oily liquid, a compound of carbon, hydrogen and oxygen, which may be added to royal icing to keep it moist
glyko	jam or fruit preserve GREEK
Gnagi	cured pig's knuckle GERMAN
gnocchetti sardi	pasta made from white flour SARDINIAN
gnocchi	small dumplings cooked in boiling water, served as pasta with a sauce ITALIAN
goździki	cloves POLISH
gołębie pieczone	roast pigeon POLISH
gołąbki	cabbage POLISH
goa bean	green bean, grown in Africa and Asia, with angular pods which are cooked whole
goat	often eaten in the Mediterranean; in Britain they are mostly kept for milk
goat's beard	wild relative of salsify
goat's milk	higher in fat and protein than most cow's milk, with a stronger flavour, it is widely used for making cheese
gobi	cabbage; cauliflower INDIAN
gobo	*see* burdock
goby	family name for a large number of small saltwater and freshwater fish with broad heads and large mouths, highly prized gastronomically in France
gocce d'oro	'drops of gold'; golden plum from the Venice region ITALIAN
godard	garnish for poultry and sweetbreads, named in honour of Eugène Godard, who organised the aerial post during the siege of Paris in 1870–71 FRENCH
godiveau	veal forcemeat used in French garnishes FRENCH
godwit	bird, similar to curlew
goémon	colloquial name for a type of seaweed used for bird's nest soup FRENCH
gofio	a speciality flour of the Canary Islands, made from a variety of toasted cereals SPANISH
gogol-mogol	an egg custard flavoured with vanilla UKRAINIAN
gogoşari	capsicum; sweet pepper ROMANIAN
gogues	bacon and vegetable dish from Anjou FRENCH
goguette	flat, highly-spiced pork sausage FRENCH
goiaba	guava PORTUGUESE

goiabada	guava paste PORTUGUESE
golden buck	savoury dish of cheese, butter, eggs, cream, beer, cayenne pepper and Worcestershire sauce, heated until melted and served on toast ENGLISH
golden cross cheese	white, soft, flaky cheese from East Sussex, made from unpasteurised goat's milk
golden currant	North American currant, which grows on the banks of streams AMERICAN
golden drop	soda bread IRISH
golden plover	small bird of the genus Pluvialis
golden sauce	sweet sauce ENGLISH
golden syrup	light-coloured syrup, produced by further refining a by-product of sugar refining
golden thistle	thistle, native to southern Europe, similar to salsify
golden-eye	duck which breeds in north Europe and Asia
Goldwasser	aniseed flavoured liqueur, containing little gold particles GERMAN
golonka	speciality dish, made from leg of pork POLISH
gomashio	seasoning powder of ground roasted sesame seeds and sea salt, used in Japan instead of salt JAPANESE
gomba	mushrooms HUNGARIAN
gombaleves	mushroom soup HUNGARIAN
gombo	okra PORTUGUESE
gomost	curdled milk, eaten with salt or sugar NORWEGIAN
goober	another name for peanut AMERICAN
good King Henry	common herb of the spinach family ENGLISH
goo-la	sugar BM
goose	originally a game bird, today domesticated, a substitute at Christmas and Easter for roast turkey
gooseberry	summer fruit; there are several varieties – long, round, hairy and smooth
go over	on the turn
go-reng goràce	hot POLISH
gorczyca	Russian mustard POLISH
gordo	fatty; rich SPANISH
gorge	elongated 'throat' sweetbread; neck flap adjoining a pig's front leg FRENCH
gorgonzola	semi-hard, blue-veined sharp-flavoured cow's milk cheese ITALIAN
görögdinnye	water melon HUNGARIAN
gös	pike; perch SWEDISH

gosht	lamb INDIAN
gota	brightly-coloured mixture of spices served at the end of a meal, an aid to digestion INDIAN
göteborgs sallad	a salad from Gothenburg. SWEDISH
Gotham pudding	speciality pudding from Gotham, near Nottingham ENGLISH
gotowane	braised POLISH
Götterspeise	fruit jelly dessert GERMAN
Gouda	wheel-shaped cheese; similar to Edam in taste DUTCH
gouda	imitation Dutch-style cheese POLISH
Goudakaas, Goudse kaas	renowned Dutch cheese, similar to Edam; large, fat and round, it improves in flavour with maturity DUTCH
goudale	garbure, to which red or white wine is added; when the bread and vegetables have been eaten, a glass of wine is added to the liquid remaining in the dish, and then drunk; it is thought to be a safeguard against illness FRENCH
gouère aux pommes	an apple dish from the Berry region FRENCH
gougère	pastry, usually choux pastry (sometimes cheese flavoured) piped in a ring, filled with a savoury mixture FRENCH
gougnette	type of doughnut from the Lot region FRENCH
goujon, en	small fried strips of plaice or sole FRENCH
goujonette	small diagonally cut strip of fish, battered or floured and deep fried FRENCH
goulash	rich beef stew, flavoured with paprika
goumi	berry CHINESE
gourd	member of the squash family; there are over 500 varieties, some of which are edible
gournay	cow's milk cheese from Normandy FRENCH
gouronpoulo	suckling-pig GREEK
govyadina	beef RUSSIAN
graavi (lohi)	salmon, cured with salt, sugar, pepper and dill FINNISH
grädde	cream SWEDISH
gräddfil	sour cream SWEDISH
gräddmjölk	light cream SWEDISH
gräddtårta	sponge layer cake with cream and jam filling SWEDISH

graham flour	unbolted wheat flour ground from whole-wheat grain, developed by the nutritionalist of the same name AMERICAN
grahamkorput	rusks made with graham flour FINNISH
grahamleipä	graham bread FINNISH
graining (n)	another name for dace;
graining (v)	boiling sugar to a point where it forms crystals, or 'grain'
grains	edible seeds of grasses
grains of paradise	grains of a tropical plant, which can be used as a spice WEST AFRICAN
graisse	fat FRENCH
gram flour	fine yellow flour made from ground pulses INDIAN
gramolatas	sherbet of iced fruit syrup FRENCH
grana	local name for Parmesan ITALIAN
granada	pomegranate SPANISH
granadilla	another name for passion fruit
Granat	prawn GERMAN
Granatapfel	pomegranate GERMAN
granátové jablko	pomegranate CZECH
grancevole	common crabs from the Adriatic
granchio	crab ITALIAN
Grand Marnier	orange-flavoured liqueur FRENCH
grand sallett	16th-century salad, also known as salmagundi
grand veneur, sauce	classical sauce, served with venison and game, made from sauce poivrade, venison essence, redcurrant jelly and cream FRENCH
grand-duc	garnish for fish and fowl of asparagus tips and truffles FRENCH
grande	large SPANISH
granita	half-frozen water ice; large crystals give it a coarse texture ITALIAN
granny's leg	spotted dick
granola	breakfast dish similar to muesli, usually including oats, wheat flakes, rye flakes, seeds and nuts
grant loaf	coarse wholemeal bread, made by Doris Grant
grão	chick-pea PORTUGUESE
grape	fruit of the vine, used to make wine, dried to make currants, raisins and sultanas, or may be eaten raw
grapefrugt	grapefruit DANISH

grapefruit	large citrus fruit with thick yellow skins and pink or yellow flesh, which grows in clusters rather like grapes
grapefrukt	grapefruit NORWEGIAN, SWEDISH
grapiaux	large pancakes cooked in pork fat FRENCH
Grappa	brandy-like spirit; made from the remains of grapes that have been pressed to produce wine ITALIAN
gras, au	dish cooked and dressed with a rich gravy or sauce FRENCH
gras-double	tripe FRENCH
grasløk	chives NORWEGIAN
gräslök	chives SWEDISH
grasmere gingerbread	form of gingerbread, similar to parkin named after Grasmere, Cumbria (home of William Wordsworth and of Thomas de Quincy)
grass snake	non-poisonous snake, sometimes eaten in France FRENCH
grasso	rich with fat or oil ITALIAN
gratäng	(au) gratin SWEDISH
grater	implement used to grate foods
grateron	rennet, used in cheese making FRENCH
graticola, alla	grilled ITALIAN
gratiini	gratin FINNISH
gratin	baked casserole DANISH
gratin dauphinois	sliced potatoes, gratinéed in the oven with eggs, cream and cheese FRENCH
gratin de fruit de mer	shellfish in heavy cream sauce and gratinéed FRENCH
gratin forcemeat	forcemeat spread on croëtons and canapés, sometimes used as stuffing FRENCH
gratín, al	gratinéed SPANISH
gratin, au	dish coated with sauce, sprinkled with breadcrumbs or cheese and browned under the grill FRENCH
gratinado	oven-browned PORTUGUESE, SPANISH
gratinata	sprinkled with breadcrumbs and grated cheese ITALIAN
gratinerad	oven-browned SWEDISH
grating	shredding food with a grater
gratiniert	oven-browned; gratinéed GERMAN
gratinoitu	gratinéed FINNISH
grattons, gratterons	melted fat or rind of pork, goose, or turkey FRENCH
grattugiato	grated ITALIAN

Graubrot	brown bread (US: black bread) GERMAN
Graupensuppe	barley soup GERMAN
gravad lax,	fresh salmon, cured with sugar, sea salt, pepper and dill SWEDISH
gravad strömming	marinated Baltic herring SWEDISH
gravel path	biscuit of oatmeal and golden syrup
gravenche	fish of the salmon family, found mainly in Swiss and Bavarian lakes
Graves	wines produced in the Graves region of France
gravet ørret	salt-cured trout flavoured with dill NORWEGIAN
gravieri	a cheese made in Crete GREEK
gravlaks	cured salmon NORWEGIAN
gravlax	raw pickled salmon SWEDISH
gravy	brown sauce, made from the juices obtained from the meat during cooking, which may be thickened, diluted or concentrated and extra flavouring can be added
gravyer	hard ewe's milk cheese TURKISH
grayling	silvery freshwater fish of the salmon family
Great Lake herring	whitefish from the North American Great Lakes AMERICAN
great snipe	the largest snipe found in the British Isles
grecque, à la	dishes of Greek origin, more often describing dishes cooked Mediterranean style, with lemon, olive oil and spices FRENCH
green bacon	cured, unsmoked bacon
green goddess dressing	anchovy-flavoured mayonnaise; thick mayonnaise thinned with soured cream, flavoured with garlic, anchovy, parsley and lemon juice
green ham	cured unsmoked ham
green in snow	*see* Chinese celery cabbage, Chinese mustard (greens), Chinese mustard cabbage, Chinese white cabbage, chingensai, gai choy, Indian mustard (greens), kai tsoi, leaf mustard, mustard cabbage, taisin
green plover	bird of the genus *Vanellus*; the lapwing or peewit
greengage	a distinct group of sweet dessert plums
greenshank	bird, similar to the snipe, but a little larger
gregen	the fat and skin from the neck, thigh, and rear of poultry JEWISH
greippi	grapefruit FINNISH
Greisspudding	pudding SWISS

grejpfrut	grapefruit POLISH
grelhado	grilled PORTUGUESE
grelo	turnip greens SPANISH
grelos	turnip greens PORTUGUESE
gremolata	Milanese name for a prepared mixture of parsley, garlic and lemon peel, always sprinkled on to ossi buchi alla milanese before serving ITALIAN
grenache	variety of grape
grenade	pomegranate FRENCH
grenadier	a river fish with a head shaped like a grenadier's cap FRENCH
grenadine	red syrup from pomegranate juice, used to sweeten and colour cocktails
grenadins	small slices of fillet of veal or turkey, larded with bacon and braised with white wine, onions, carrots and stock FRENCH
grenouille	frog FRENCH
grenu	lumpy FRENCH
gresiller	to shrink by heating FRENCH
gressløk	chive NORWEGIAN
Greyerzer(käse)	Gruyère, a cheese rich in flavour, smooth in texture GERMAN
gribiche, sauce	classical sauce made from pounded yolks of hard-boiled eggs, olive oil, wine vinegar and chopped gherkins, capers, parsley, chervil and tarragon, and a julienne of the whites of the eggs; served with cold fish FRENCH
griby	mushrooms, usually those found in the woods RUSSIAN
griddle	heavy, flat, metal plate for cooking scones and teacakes; also known as girdle
griddle cake	small flat cakes, cooked on a griddle
Griebenwürst	larded frying sausage GERMAN
griesãiai	parsnips LITHUANIAN
griesmeel	semolina DUTCH
Grieß	semolina GERMAN
griet	brill DUTCH
grifole	an edible fungus ITALIAN
grig	small freshwater eel
griglia, alla	from the grill ITALIAN
grignon	dry bread baked very hard; the end crust of a loaf FRENCH

gril	grill CZECH
griljert	breaded NORWEGIAN
grill	to cook food quickly by direct heat
grillad	grilled, broiled SWEDISH
grillade	grilled food FRENCH
grillardin	chef in charge of grilling in a French restaurant FRENCH
grillattu	grilled FINNISH
grille	deep frying basket FRENCH
grillet	grilled NORWEGIAN
grillettes	old name for thin slices of fried pork FRENCH
grillezett	grilled HUNGARIAN
grilli (makkara)	grilled (sausage) FINNISH
grilliert	grilled GERMAN
grilling	food cooked by direct heat, under a grill or over hot coals
grillkorv	grilled sausage SWEDISH
grill-room	wherein grilled steaks and other meats are served
grilovací jehla	skewer CZECH
grilovaný	grilled CZECH
grilovat	to grill CZECH
grilse	young salmon when it first leaves the sea to go upstream
grimaldi	chicken consommé with tomato fumet garnished with julienne of celeriac and tomato royale FRENCH
grimslich	Passover dish of matzo fritters JEWISH
grinding	to reduce hard food to small particles in a food mill or with pestle and mortar
griottes	bitter Morello cherries FRENCH
gris	pork SWEDISH
gris de lille	cow's milk cheese from north east France FRENCH
griskin	spine, chine or backbone of a pig; an inferior loin of pork ENGLISH
grissini	long sticks of hard baked bread ITALIAN
gristle	tough indigestible substance, part of the connective tissue in animals, found in poorly trimmed meat
grits	short for hominy grits
gríz	semolina HUNGARIAN
groats	hulled and crushed grain of oats, wheat and other cereals
grochówka	pea soup POLISH

grød	rice pudding, covered with cinnamon DANISH
grodlår	frog's legs SWEDISH
groente	vegetable DUTCH
grog	drink of spirits, sugar and hot water, served in winter as a warming drink, named after Admiral Vernon (1684–1757) who began the naval rum ration in 1740, known as Old Grog because of his grogram cloak
grøn bønne	French bean (US: green bean) DANISH
grøn salat	lettuce DANISH
grønært	green pea DANISH
grønærtesuppe	pea soup DANISH
grondin	gurnard; gurnet FRENCH
grönkål	kale SWEDISH
grønlangkål	creamed kale DANISH
grønnsak	vegetable NORWEGIAN
grönpeppar	green peppercorn SWEDISH
grønsager	vegetables DANISH
grönsak	vegetable SWEDISH
grönsakssoppa	vegetable soup SWEDISH
grönsallad	lettuce SWEDISH
gros sel	crystalline unrefined sea-salt FRENCH
gros-blanquet	greeny-yellow skinned pear FRENCH
groseille	currant FRENCH
groseille à Maquereau	gooseberry FRENCH
groseille rouge	redcurrant FRENCH
groselha	redcurrant PORTUGUESE
grosella	currant SPANISH
Gröstl	hash made from grated fried potatoes, fried onions and meat, seasoned with caraway seeds AUSTRIAN, GERMAN
groszek	green peas POLISH
gröt	porridge SWEDISH
grøt	porridge; cereal NORWEGIAN
ground cherry	see physalis
ground nut	another name for peanut AMERICAN
ground rice	rice ground to a fine powder
grouper	large family of sea fish from warm waters
grous, groux	Breton name for thick gruel of buckwheat flour and milk or water FRENCH

grouse	a group of gallinaceous game birds of the family Tetraonidae with stocky body and feathered legs and feet
grovbrød	brown bread NORWEGIAN
grovey cake	heavy Cornish cake
groviera	a cheese similar to Gruyère ITALIAN
gruau	husk; very small pasta made of potato flour FRENCH
grue	crane FRENCH
gruel	drink or thin porridge of fine oatmeal or barley meal boiled in water, milk or stock
Gründling	gudgeon GERMAN
grüne Bohne	French bean (US: green bean) GERMAN
Grunkohl	kale GERMAN
grunt	a tropical marine fish, genus *Sciaenidae*, so called because it issues a grunt when caught; *see* sailor's-choice
grus	old hard-pressed, cow's milk cheese IRISH
gruszki	pears POLISH
gruth	modern Irish word for curd; formerly an unpressed cheese IRISH
gruviera	mild cheese with holes ITALIAN
Gruyère	hard, unpasteurised, cow's milk cheese, with a distinctive sweet taste SWISS
gryczanki	buckwheat cakes POLISH
gryderet	stew of meat and vegetables DANISH
grydestegt	braised DANISH
grytstek	pot roast SWEDISH
grzanki	croĕtons; toast POLISH
grzybek Êmietankowy	a rich, sweet pancake mixture POLISH
grzyby	wild mushrooms POLISH
guacamole	purée of ripe avocado, flavoured with tomato, onion and chilli, served as a dip or as a filling for tacos MEXICAN
guanciale	cured cut of bacon from the jaw of a pig ITALIAN
guar	variety of long, thin, green bean, eaten in India and grown as cattle fodder in the American south west; the beans are a source of gum used as a thickening agent INDIAN
guaraná	very sweet tropical fruit PORTUGUESE
guard of honour	roast of two racks of lamb, arranged back to back, fat side out, to form an arch of interlinking bones; the cavity may be filled with stuffing

guards' pudding	steamed suet pudding made with breadcrumbs, brown sugar, eggs and jam, served hot with jam or cream ENGLISH
guarnición	garnish; trimming SPANISH
guarracino	black fish usually used in soups ITALIAN
guastiedda siciliana	hot fresh rolls filled with ricotta and strips of cascavaddu cheese which has been tossed in hot lard SICILIAN
guava	round or pear-shaped tropical fruit with white or pale pink flesh and edible seeds
guayaba	guava SPANISH
guazzetto	meat stew containing garlic, rosemary, pimentos and tomatoes ITALIAN
gudbrandsdalsost	slightly sweet, brown, goat's and cow's milk cheese NORWEGIAN
gudgeon	freshwater fish of the carp family, found in European waters
Güggeli	spring chicken GERMAN
Guglhupf, Gougelhopf	traditional yeast cake AUSTRIAN
guigne	gean, one of two main types of sweet cherry FRENCH
guignette	sandpiper (*see* maubèche), a small wading bird; another name for a mollusc called littorine FRENCH
guillemot	sea bird common to Europe and America; the bird is not eaten - only the eggs
guinda	sour cherry SPANISH
guindilla	chilli; morello cherry SPANISH
guinea fowl	originally a game bird, today farmed and classed as poultry; may be cooked as chicken or pheasant.
guinea pig	once a popular dish in England, today eaten only in South American countries
guisado	stew, usually containing chicken, goose, game or turkey; stewed SPANISH, PORTUGUESE
guisantes	peas SPANISH
guisias	a wild pea, white in colour SPANISH, IBIZAN
gül receli	fresh rose petal jam made TURKISH
gulá vepřový	spicy pork stew CZECH
guláš	goulash; a spicy meat stew CZECH
guláš bramborový	spicy meat stew with potatoes CZECH
guláš hovězí	spicy beef stew CZECH
guláš segedínský	spicy meat stew with sauerkraut and onion CZECH
guláš telecí	spicy veal stew CZECH

guláš z hovězího masa na smetaně beef goulash with cream sauce CZECH

gulab jaman almond balls in syrup INDIAN

gulab tulsi basil INDIAN

gulasch national dish, made from meat or poultry Austrian

gulàsová polévka goulash soup of beef chunks, potatoes, onions, tomatoes and peppers, richly spiced with paprika , caraway seeds and garlic HUNGARIAN

gulasz goulash POLISH

gule ærter med flæsk split pea DANISH

gulerødder carrots DANISH

gulerot carrot NORWEGIAN

gull sea bird of the Laridae family; only the eggs are normally eaten

gulyás 'cow herd'; the national dish, so called because it was invented by wandering cow herds HUNGARY

gulyásleves thick goulash soup, of beef, onion, potatoes, mild paprika, caraway seeds, garlic, vegetables, and tiny dumplings HUNGARIAN

gum sticky substance, obtained from trees and plants, which hardens on exposure to air; may be used to make sweets or as a thickening agent

gumbo okra; soup based on the mucilagenous pods of okra with fish, prawn etc

AFRICAN, LOUISIANA CREOLE, WEST INDIAN

gum tragacanth gum obtained from plants of the genus *Astragalus*, especially *A.gummifer, see* gum

Gundel palacsinta flambéd pancake with nut cream and raisin filling

HUNGARIAN

gundy sweetmeat flavoured with aniseed or cinnamon

SCOTTISH

gurda kidney INDIAN

gurka cucumber; gherkin SWEDISH

Gurke cucumber GERMAN

gurnard small, round sea fish with a large distinctive bony head

gurneau, grondin gurnard FRENCH

gury traditional dish of white cabbage, beetroot and red peppers RUSSIAN

gus goose RUSSIAN

gut to clean the inside of a fish, removing all the entrails

gutui quince ROMANIAN

gwyniad	herring-like fish found in Lake Bala WELSH
gymnètre faux	saltwater fish from the Mediterranean FRENCH
gyömbér	ginger HUNGARIAN
gyöngytyúk	guinea fowl HUNGARIAN
gypsum	common mineral, which may be used to increase acidity in wine
Gyulai kolbász	spicy, slightly hot smoked sausage HUNGARIAN
gyümölcs	fruit HUNGARIAN
gyümölcskenyér	Bishop's bread, a fruit and nut cake HUNGARIAN
gyuvèch	a national dish, also eaten throughout the Balkans, made from beef, veal, lamb or pork BULGARIAN

H

Häagen-Dazs	a brand name for an ice cream invented to be inconfusable with any other
Haagse bluf	whipped egg-whites with redcurrant sauce DUTCH
haantje	cockerel DUTCH
haas	hare DUTCH
habañero	the world's hottest chilli originating f rom Havana, it measures 10 (300,000 units on the Scoville scale) CUBAN
habas	broad beans SPANISH
haberdine, haburden	old English name for salt cod, much of which was exported from Aberdeen, from which the name is a corruption ENGLISH
habichuela verde	French bean (US: green beans) SPANISH
habillage	the dressing of poultry, game or fish FRENCH
hachage	chopped food; the chopping of food FRENCH
haché	minced; chopped FRENCH
hachee	hash of minced meat onions and spices DUTCH
hachis	very finely chopped foods; garnish of chopped parsley, garlic and ham; hash FRENCH
Hachse	knuckle; shank GERMAN
hackad	minced; chopped SWEDISH
Hackbraten	meat loaf of beef and pork GERMAN
Hackfleisch	minced meat GERMAN
haddock	round sea fish, similar to the cod, but smaller and with a dark streak that runs down its back, and two black thumb prints above the gills
Haferbrei	oatmeal, porridge GERMAN
Haferflocken	rolled oats GERMAN
Hagebuten	rose hips, used in Germany for soups GERMAN
hagejordbaer	cultivated strawberries NORWEGIAN
haggamuggie	fish haggis SHETLAND ISLANDS
haggis	national dish, a type of sausage made of oatmeal, suet, onions, herbs and sheeps' offal SCOTTISH
hagyma	onion HUNGARIAN
Hähnchen	spring chicken GERMAN
hákarl	a speciality dish containing smoked shark ICELANDIC

hake	food fish of the genus *Merluccius* (the European hake); North American fish of the genus *Urophycis*; Australian name for *Thyrsites atun*, the barracouta, a large predatory Pacific fish with protruding lower jaw and strong teeth
hake	a wooden frame for drying cheese or fish
hakkebøf	hamburgers DANISH
hakkebøf med løg	hamburger steak with fried onions DANISH
hakket	chopped; minced DANISH
hal	fish HUNGARIAN
halal, hellal	to kill animals following Muslim law; meat killed in this way
hal fatányéros	assorted fish, served with tartare sauce HUNGARIAN
halászlé	fisherman's soup HUNGARIAN
halb	half GERMAN
ha-lee-ah	ginger BM
halételek	fish; sea food HUNGARIAN
halibut	very large, flat fish similar to turbot, considered one of the best flavoured fish
halibut liver oil	very good source of vitamins A and D, it may be taken as a supplement
halicot	former term for very finely chopped FRENCH
hallal	*see* halal
hallal töltött paradicsom	tomato stuffed with fish HUNGARIAN
hälleflundra	halibut SWEDISH
hallon	raspberry SWEDISH
halloumi	semi-hard, mild, salty goat's milk cheese with a slightly rubbery texture GREEK
halorini	ewe's milk cheese GREEK-CYPRIOT
halsaláta szegedi módra	fish salad Szeged-style, made of fish pieces, diced peppers, tomatoes and chives turned in oil, and accompanied by lettuce and hard-boiled eggs HUNGARIAN
hälsokost	organic health food SWEDISH
halstrad	grilled over an open fire SWEDISH
halstrattu	barbecued (fish) FINNISH
halušky	luncheon dish of boiled noodles, onion and mushrooms, with a mixture of eggs and milk poured over and the whole baked CZECH
halv, halvdel	half DANISH
halva	sweetmeat made of crushed sesame seeds or almonds mixed with boiled sugar syrup EASTERN

halvas	Easter cake GREEK
ham	hind leg of a pig cut from the carcass, cured and matured separately
hamantaschen	three-cornered pastry filled with poppy seeds and chopped nuts JEWISH
Hamburg parsley	turnip-rooted parsley, which has a fleshy root which may be cooked like a carrot, and a flavour similar to celeriac
hamburger	minced beefsteak with seasoning and sometimes onion
Hamburger Aalsuppe	eel soup from Hamburg GERMAN
Hamburger Rauchfleisch	smoked brisket of beef, boiled and sliced GERMAN
hamburgerrygg	smoked loin of pork in a sausage shape DANISH
hamburguesa	hamburger SPANISH
hamlet	large sea fish of the grouper family; large black and yellow eel from the West Indies AMERICAN, WEST INDIAN
Hamme	ham GERMAN
Hammel(fleisch)	mutton GERMAN
hampurilainen	hamburger FINNISH
hanche	haunch FRENCH
hand	joint of meat from the forequarter of a pig
hand cheese	sour cow's milk cheese AMERICAN
Handkäse	sour milk cheese with a pungent aroma GERMAN
hangikjöt	smoked leg of lamb ICELANDIC
hanging	meat or game suspended in a cool, dry place, so that air can circulate, to tenderise and allow the flavour to develop
hangop	'hang up': a dessert dish of creamed buttermilk served with brown sugar and cinnamon DUTCH
hanhenmaksa	goose liver FINNISH
hanhenmmaska pasteija	goose liver pâté FINNISH
hanhi	goose FINNISH
hanoi	small pink fish found in Greek waters GREEK
hapan(imelä)	sweet-and-sour FINNISH
hapukapsa salat	a national dish, usually served with meat, of a salad of sauerkraut with apples, onion, sour cream, sugar and salt ESTONIAN
hapupiim	sour milk ESTONIAN
härän(filee)	fillet of beef FINNISH
harcsa	white shad from the Danube and Tisza rivers HUNGARIAN

hard sauce	US version of brandy or rum butter AMERICAN
harðfiskur	traditional fish dish; the fish is cleaned, dried out of doors, and served with butter ICELANDIC
hardgekookt ei	hard boiled egg DUTCH
hårdkogt æg	hard boiled egg DANISH
hard roe	fish eggs in the ovarian membrane
hare and rabbit	two different species; rabbits are available all year and may be wild or farmed; hares are darker with a more gamey flavour and are available late summer to early spring
hareng	herring FRENCH
haresteg	roast hare DANISH
hari chutney	chutney made with green vegetables and herbs INDIAN
haricot	bean FRENCH
haricot bean	generic name for a family of beans; generally used as the name of small, white, oval dried bean; the principle of baked beans
haricots verts	French beans SWEDISH
haring	herring DUTCH
harissa	hot mixture of chilli and other spices, used in Middle Eastern cookery MIDDLE EASTERN
harlequin	chocolate sponge cake with whipped cream CZECH
harnois de gueule	slang expression for food – similar to 'grub' FRENCH
harstek	roast hare SWEDISH
hart	heart DUTCH
Hartkäse	firm cheese, hard enough to be sliced GERMAN
hartshorn	European weed used in salad when young; deer's antlers
harvey sauce	old English bottled relish ENGLISH
harze	cow's milk cheese BELGIAN
Harzer Käse	the German version of harze GERMAN
hasábburgonya	chips HUNGARIAN
Haschee	hash GERMAN
Hase	hare GERMAN
Haselhuhn	hazel grouse GERMAN
Haselnuß	hazelnut GERMAN
Hasenpfeffer	jugged hare GERMAN
hash	diced cooked meat, reheated in highly-flavoured sauce
hasha	equivalent of thyme INDIAN

hash brown	diced boiled potato, mixed with chopped onion, shaped and fried until golden
hasina kebab	marinated meat skewered with sweet peppers, onions and tomatoes and barbecued TURKISH
haslet	old country dish made from pig's fry ENGLISH
hasselbackspotatis	sliced potatoes covered with melted butter and roasted SWEDISH
hasselnød	hazel nut DANISH
hasselnöt	hazelnut SWEDISH
hasselnøtt	hazelnut NORWEGIAN
hasselpähkinä	hazelnut FINNISH
hasty pudding	old pudding of milk, thickened with flour, semolina, tapioca, etc, butter and spices; in US cornmeal mush served with treacle sugar
ha-tee	liver BM
hâtereau	old French word for pork or liver balls; hot hors d'œuvres FRENCH
hátrész	saddle HUNGARIAN
hátszín	sirloin HUNGARIAN
hattelle, hâtelette	old French word for the livers, giblets etc, of small birds, roasted on skewers FRENCH
haudutettu	braised FINNISH
hauki	pike FINNISH
haunch	hind quarters of certain wild mammals, normally deer or venison
Hauptgericht	main course GERMAN
hausgemacht, von Haus	home-made GERMAN
Hausmannskost	plain food GERMAN
Haussulz	brawn, made from a pig's or calf's head AUSTRIAN
hauteluce	goat's milk cheese from Savoy FRENCH
havarti	semi-hard, pasteurised cow's milk cheese, with a full flavour; known as the 'ladies' cheese DANISH
haver	from the Norse word for oats, a northern English name for thin oatcake; loaf ENGLISH
havermoutpap	oatmeal porridge DUTCH
havre	oats NORWEGIAN
havregrød	oatmeal DANISH
havregryn	oats SWEDISH
havregrynsgröt	oatmeal SWEDISH
havskräfta	seawater crayfish; Dublin Bay prawn SWEDISH
hawfinch	seed-eating bird EUROPEAN

hawksbill turtle   a tortoise; only the eggs are eaten AQUATIC

hawthorn   small shrub or tree; the berries are used to make a jelly

Haxe   knuckle, shank GERMAN

hayaca central   maize-flour pancake SPANISH

hay box   airtight box full of hay, used for cooking by retained heat

hazel grouse, hazel hen   game bird from the family Tetrastes bon asia with tender white flesh and an excellent flavour

hazelnoot   hazelnut DUTCH

hazelnut   fruit of the hazel tree, available dried in their shells, shelled whole, plain or roasted, chopped, flaked or ground

hazepeper   spiced hare DUTCH

házias   home-made HUNGARIAN

head   pigs' and sheeps' heads are usually sold whole or split in half; the best brawn is made from boiled pigs' head; head meat can be used in pie fillings

head cheese   brawn AMERICAN

headless Chinese cabbage   *see* bok choy, celery cabbage, Chinese leaves, michihili, pe-tsai, wong bok

heart   classified as offal, it is a very nutritious food

Hecht   pike GERMAN

hedgehog   also known locally as vuzpeg (furze pig) or ajiboar (hedge-boar – Devonshire); small spiny quadruped, traditionally eaten by gypsies who bake it in clay which, when removed, takes the spines with it

Hefekranz   ring-shaped cake GERMAN

Heidelbeere   bilberry (US: blueberry) GERMAN

Heilbutt   halibut GERMAN

heiß   hot; very warm GERMAN

hel fisk i kapprock   stuffed mackerel or trout baked in paper SWEDISH

helado   ice-cream; ice SPANISH

helder, à la   garnish for tournedos FRENCH

heldere soep   consommé; clear soup DUTCH

helgeflundra   halibut SWEDISH

hélianthe   tuberous vegetable FRENCH

helkornbrød   wholemeal bread NORWEGIAN

hellefisk   halibut NORWEGIAN

helleflynder   halibut DANISH

helleflyndre   halibut NORWEGIAN

helstekt	roasted whole NORWEGIAN, SWEDISH
helston pudding	traditional Cornish dish made with raisins, suet, sugar, breadcrumbs and ground rice ENGLISH
helvella	genus of fungus, the false morel EUROPEAN
Helzel	neck of poultry GERMAN
hemlagad	home made SWEDISH
hénon	local name for a cockle from the river Somme FRENCH
Henri IV	garnish for watercress or artichoke of sauce béarnaise mixed with liquid meat glaze; clear, strong beef broth FRENCH
herbatniki	biscuits POLISH
herbes	herbs FRENCH
herbs	group of aromatic plants with distinctive flavours which heighten or improve meat, fish and vegetable dishes
Hering	herring GERMAN
Heringskartoffeln	casserole of layers of herrings and potatoes GERMAN
Heringskönig	John Dory (fish) GERMAN
herkkusieni	button mushroom FINNISH
hermit crab	crustacean with no shell, which can be cooked like a shrimp, grilled or baked
herne	pea FINNISH
herne keitto	thick pea soup with pork FINNISH
heron	river bird, once eaten in a pie
herrgårdsost	popular whole cow's milk cheese SWEDISH
herring	fairly, small, round, oily fish, with creamy coloured flesh and a distinctive flavour
hersenen	brains DUTCH
Herve	soft whole cow's milk cheese BELGIAN
hervido	boiled; Latin-American stew of beef and vegetables SPANISH
Herz	heart GERMAN
hete bliksem	potatoes, bacon, and apples, seasoned with butter, salt and sugar DUTCH
hibachi	'fire bowl'; a small barbecue JAPANESE
hickory nut	various types of walnut grown in America, the best known being the pecan nut AMERICAN
hideg	cold HUNGARIAN
hideg fogas tartármártással	giant pike or perch with tartare sauce HUNGARIAN

hideg gyumolcsleves cold fruit soup HUNGARY

hideg sülthús cold cuts HUNGARIAN

hideg tlöételek cold hors d'œuvres HUNGARIAN

hidegtál cold meals HUNGARIAN

hielo ice SPANISH

hienonnettu mashed; minced FINNISH

hierba herb SPANISH

hierbas finas finely chopped, mixed herbs SPANISH

hígado liver SPANISH

high moisture jack whole cow's milk cheese AMERICAN

highland crowdie farmhouse cheese similar to cottage cheese, but more finely ground SCOTTISH

higo fig SPANISH

hiillostettu barbecued FINNISH

hiivaleipä yeast bread FINNISH

hillo jam FINNISH

hilopites me kima lamb, onion, garlic and tomato GREEK

Himbeere raspberry GERMAN

Himmel und Erde 'heaven and earth'; apple and potato, seasoned and cooked in broth, puréed an d served with black pudding or pork GERMAN

hina goose GREEK

hindbær raspberry DANISH

hindle wakes chicken very old English method of cooking fowl

hing equivalent of asafœtida INDIAN

hinojo fennel SPANISH

hippocras mediaeval drink of wine, heavily sweetened with honey and flavoured with herbs and spices

hirino pork; pig GREEK

Hirn brains GERMAN

Hirsch stag (venison) GERMAN

Hirse millet GERMAN

hirtelen sült sautéed HUNGARIAN

hirven/karistys roast elk served in cream sauce FINNISH

hirvipaisti roast elk FINNISH

hiyar taratorv almonds or pistachio nuts pounded with salt and garlic, mixed with bread to a paste, and mixed with vinegar and lemon juice; the sauce is poured over green salad and sprinkled with olive oil TURKISH

hjemmelaget home made NORWEGIAN, DANISH

hjerte heart DANISH

hjerter i flødesovs	hearts (usually pigs) in cream sauce DANISH
hjortekjøtt	red deer meat NORWEGIAN
hjortron	Arctic cloudberry SWEDISH
hlávkovy salàt	green salad CZECH
hlemyždi	snails CZECH
hocco	turkey-like game bird CENTRAL AMERICAN
hochepot	hot pot containing brisket of beef, pig's trotters and ears, veal, mutton, herbs, cabbage, carrots, onions, leeks, celery, turnip, chipolata sausages and seasoning; the meat is served with a little of the stock and the remainder as soup BELGIAN
hock	white wines from the Rhine Palatinate and other parts of Germany; meat from just above the foot of a pig, bullock or sheep GERMAN
hodgils	border name for oatmeal dumplings SCOTTISH
hodmedod	East Anglian snail
hoffdessert	layers of meringue and whipped cream, topped with chocolate sauce and toasted almonds NORWEGIAN
horčák	bitter CZECH
horčice	mustard CZECH
hog pudding	kind of pork sausage
hogfish	sea fish, with a large, spiny head
hogget	yearling lamb ENGLISH
hohe Rippe	roast ribs of beef GERMAN
hoisin sauce	sweet, reddish brown, spicy sauce made from garlic, soya beans, sugar and spices
hökarpanna	kidney stew with bacon, potatoes and onions SWEDISH
holischkes	stuffed cabbage, traditionally eaten at Succoth and other holidays JEWISH
hollandaise sauce	white sauce thickened with eggs rather than flour FRENCH
hollandaise, à la	method of serving fish poached in court bouillon; consommé seasoned with paprika FRENCH
Hollands	type of gin distilled in Holland, the best known being Schnapps DUTCH
Hollandse biefstuk	loin section of a porterhouse or T-bone steak DUTCH
Hollandse koffietafel	traditional dish of sliced sausages, cold meats, breads, jams, sweet spreads, fruit and coffee DUTCH
Hollandse nieuwe	freshly caught filleted herring DUTCH
Hollandse palingsoep	traditional eel soup DUTCH
holstein	garnish for veal escalope FRENCH

Holsteiner Schnitzel breaded veal cutlet topped with a fried egg and served with vegetables GERMAN

holub pigeon CZECH

Holundersuppe soup of elderberries, apple, lemon, sugar and salt GERMAN

homar lobster POLISH

homard lobster FRENCH

hominy, hominy grits coarsely ground, hulled and split maize

homogenizing commercial processing of milk to break down the fat into particles of uniform size, thus preventing the cream separating out

höna boiling fowl SWEDISH

høne fowl DANISH, NORWEGIAN

honey sweet, syrupy liquid made by bees from the nectar of flowers, a highly nutritious food easily assimilated into the body

honey fungus fleshy edible fungus

honeycomb waxy structure made by bees, in which honey is stored

honeycomb mould light dessert of whisked egg white folded into a fruit jelly

honeydew melon round melon with juicy, pale green flesh

hongo mushroom SPANISH

hongroise, à la meat, poultry, egg or vegetable dishes cooked in paprika sauce FRENCH

Honig honey GERMAN

honing honey DUTCH

honning honey DANISH, NORWEGIAN

höns med ris och curry boiled chicken, curry sauce and rice SWEDISH

hønsebryst chicken breast DANISH

hønsefrikassé chicken fricassée NORWEGIAN

hønsekødsuppe chicken broth DANISH

hong tsoi sum (purple flowered) *see* brocoletto, choy sum, flowering pak choi, flowering white cabbage, hon tsai tai, kozaitai, pak tsoi sum, purple flowered choy sum, rape

hon tsai tai (purple flowered) *see* brocoletto, choy sum, flowering pak choi, flowering white cabbage, hong tsoi sum, kozaitai, pak tsoi sum, purple flowered choy sum, rape

honung honey SWEDISH

hopfensalat salad of young hop buds GERMAN

hops	ripened catkins or flowers of the hop plant, which give beer its distinctive bitter flavour
horehound	perennial herb; from the mint family
hornazo	savoury tart or pasty SPANISH
Hörnchen	crescent-shaped roll GERMAN
horner's cheese	cream cheese from Worcestershire ENGLISH
hornfisk	garfish DANISH
horno	baked SPANISH
hors d'œuvre(s)	any dish served as the first course of the meal; strictly, it is a selection of cold foods served as an appetiser (outside the work(s)) FRENCH
horse	the meat is said to have quite a sweet flavour; it is eaten in some European countries, but not in Britain
horse gram	pulse grown and eaten in southern India INDIAN
horse mackerel	the scad; the mackerel-like *Trachurus trachurus* found in European and Atlantic waters (US: saurel)
horseradish	plant of the mustard family, cultivated for its root; it is grated raw into dressings of cream and vinegar; it has a hot, biting, pungent flavour and is traditionally served with roast beef
horta	green vegetables GREEK
hortaliça	fresh vegetables PORTUGUESE
hortaliza	greens SPANISH
hortelã	mint PORTUGUESE
hortobágyi húsos palacsinta	stuffed pancakes Hortobágyi style; fillet of veal or pork meat and sour cream HUNGARIAN
hortobágyi rostélyos	steak braised with bacon and stock and served with a large semolina dumpling HUNGARIAN
hoşaflar	sherbets, often made with morello cherries TURKISH
hot cross bun	yeast bun, containing currants, chopped peel and spices, traditionally eaten at Easter time, characterised by a cross marked on top
hot dog	long, thin sausage, usually frankfurter, served hot in a soft bread roll, optionally with fried onions, mustard or ketchup
hotch-potch	thick soup or stew of meat and vegetables
hotová jídla	short-order dishes; ready-to-serve dishes CZECH
hot-pot	baked stew or casserole, of meat, fish or vegetables, topped with sliced potatoes or savoury crumble
hotwater pastry	pastry made with hot water, lard, flour and salt, used for traditional English pies ENGLISH
houblon	hop FRENCH

houby	mushrooms CZECH
hough	dish of boiled shin of beef, peppercorns, mace and salt SCOTTISH
houtsnip	woodcock; cheese sandwich on rye bread DUTCH
hovdessert	meringue with whipped cream and chocolate sauce SWEDISH
hovedret	main dish DANISH
hovězi maso	beef stew CZECH
howtowdie	dish of boiled chicken, poached eggs and spinach SCOTTISH
hozzávalók	ingredient HUNGARIAN
hrášek	green peas CZECH
hrách	dry peas CZECH
hrachová polévka s uzenym masem	pea soup with smoked meat CZECH
hranolky	chips (US: French fries) CZECH
hřebíček	cloves CZECH
hroznové víno červené	(red) grapes CZECH
hroznové víno bílé	green grapes CZECH
hruška	pear CZECH
htapodi	octopus GREEK
hubertusleves	hare soup HUNGARIAN
Huchen	huck GERMAN
hucho, huck	fresh water fish of the salmon family ENGLISH
huckleberry	wild berry NORTH AMERICAN
hueso	bone SPANISH
huesos de santo	'Saint's bones'; sweet from Grenada eaten on All Saints' Day SPANISH
huevo	egg SPANISH
huevos de mújol	grey mullet roe SPANISH
huff paste	Scottish and northern England name for a suet crust pastry
Huhn	chicken GERMAN
Hühnchen	chicken GERMAN
hühnerklein	chicken giblet GERMAN
huile	oil FRENCH
huile, à la	dishes served with olive oil or with a dressing made from olive oil FRENCH
huitalacoche	fungus that grows on ears of maize, making the kernels sweet MEXICAN
huitres	oysters FRENCH
huitrier	oyster-catcher bird FRENCH

hulling	removing the calyx from soft fruits, such as strawberries
humbug	hard cushion-shaped boiled sweet, usually flavoured with peppermint
humita	boiled maize with tomatoes, green peppers, onions and cheese SPANISH
hummer	lobster DANISH, SWEDISH, NORWEGIAN
Hummer	lobster GERMAN
hummeri	lobster FINNISH
hummumdusta ka duntee	pestle and mortar INDIAN
hummus	dip of puréed cooked chick pea and olive oil, flavoured with tahini, garlic, and lemon juice MIDDLE EASTERN
humr	lobster CZECH
hunaja	honey FINNISH
hunaja meloni	cantaloupe FINNISH
hundreds and thousands	tiny coloured sugar strands and balls, used as simple decoration for dessert and cakes
Hungarian sweet pepper, Hungarian yellow wax	see banana pepper
hünkâr beğendi	lamb stew GREEK, TURKISH
Huntsman cheese	a processed cheese, comprising two layers of Double Gloucester sandwiching a layer of Stilton ENGLISH
Hunyadi töltött	traditional dish of sirloin steak stuffed with a macaroni mixture, named after Janos Hunyadi, who liberated Hungary from the Turks HUNGARIAN
Hunyadi torta	cake HUNGARIAN
huppe	a kind of lark with a tufted head FRENCH
huppemeau	cow's milk cheese from the Orléanais FRENCH
hure de porc	potted pig's head FRENCH
hurt	local Surrey name for bilberry (also known as hurtleberry) ENGLISH
husa	goose CZECH
husarenfilet	speciality of fillet steak, ham and cucumber Austrian
Husarenfleisch	braised beef, veal and pork fillets, with sweet peppers, onions and sour cream GERMAN
húsételek	meat HUNGARIAN
hush puppies	drop scones, a recipe from the southern States AMERICAN
husí žaludky zadělávané	goose stomach in white sauce CZECH
husí játra	goose liver CZECH

husí játra smaženą   fried goose liver in bread crumbs CZECH

husí krky plněné   stuffed goose neck CZECH

husk   outer casing of a grain of wheat, oats or barley

húsleves májgombóccal   clear chicken soup with chicken liver dumplings, traditionally eaten on St Stephen's Day, 20 August HUNGARIAN

husmanskost   home cooking, plain food SWEDISH

huss   long, pointed sea fish, with light brown skin and a cream belly

hussarde, à la   meat garnish of stuffed tomatoes FRENCH

huszárrostélyos   fried bread HUNGARIAN

hutspot   hodge-podge; hot-pot DUTCH

hutspot met klapstuck   hotch-potch of mashed potatoes, carrots and onions, served with boiled beef DUTCH

Hutzelbrot   bread made of prunes and other dried fruits GERMAN

huzarensla   salad of potatoes, hard-boiled eggs, cold meat, gherkins, beetroot and mayonnaise DUTCH

hvalbiff   whale steak NORWEGIAN

hvetebolle   sweet roll; bun NORWEGIAN

hvidkål   white cabbage DANISH

hvidløg   garlic DANISH

hvit sagosuppe   pudding NORWEGIAN

hvitkål   white cabbage NORWEGIAN

hvitløk   garlic NORWEGIAN

hvitting   whiting NORWEGIAN

hyben   rose hip DANISH

Hyderabadi   northern Indian/Pakistani culinary style with a mild yoghurty sauce with almonds INDIAN, PAKISTANI

hydrochloric acid   strong mineral acid, used diluted to turn cane sugar into glucose and fructose

hydrolysed protein   proteins are broken down by adding hydrogen and oxygen atoms, producing a different-flavoured substance

hydromel   ancient drink of honey and water, flavoured with herbs and spices; fermented it becomes mead

hydrometer   instrument used to measure density of liquids

hygiene   processes carried out to prevent the development and spread of disease

hyldebær   elderberry DANISH

hyssop   plant of the mint family with dark green, pungent, aromatic leaves and blue flowers, which may be

	used in salads and soups; an oil distilled from the leaves is used in liqueurs
hytteost	cottage cheese DANISH
hyvin paistettu	well-done FINNISH
hyytelö	jelly FINNISH
hyytelöity	jellied FINNISH

I

iahnie	ragoût; stew ROMANIAN
ibex	type of wild goat from mountain districts of Europe, *Capra caucasia*, *C. ibex*, or *C. pyrenaica*
ice	water reduced to freezing point or below, used for chilling purposes
ice cream	popular frozen confection made from a mixture based on milk or cream with a variety of flavourings
iced coffee	strong black coffee, sweetened, chilled and served in a tall glass with milk or cream
iced tea	tea, chilled and served cold
Iceland moss	lichen which grows on barren mountains, used in cooking in the same way as carrageen ICELANDIC
icing	sweet coating or covering for cakes, biscuits and pastries
icing sugar	finely powdered granulated sugar
idli	southern Indian rice and lentil flour cake
iepure	wild rabbit or hare ROMANIAN
igname	yam FRENCH
ijs	ice; ice-cream DUTCH
ikrá	caviar RUSSIAN
Ilchester cheese	Double Gloucester flavoured with mustard pickle ENGLISH
ilha, queijo da	cow's milk cheese PORTUGUESE
illallinen	supper FINNISH
imam bayildi	'fainting imam' (priest): aubergines stuffed with onions, garlic, tomatoes, garlic, parsley, bay leaves and seasonings sautéed in olive oil and cooled, casseroled in olive oil and lemon juice and served cold GREEK, TURKISH
imbir	ginger POLISH
Imbiß	snack GERMAN
impératrice, à l'	sweet dishes and cakes with a rice base FRENCH
Imperial Frischkäse	skimmed milk, soft cream cheese AUSTRIAN
impériale, à la	dish with a garnish of foie gras, truffles, cocks' combs or kidneys FRENCH
incasciata	layers of dough, meat sauce, hard-boiled eggs and grated cheese ITALIAN

indeyka	turkey RUSSIAN
Indian corn	another name for sweet corn
Indian lettuce	two plants eaten as a winter vegetable in the US AMERICAN
Indian mustard (greens)	see Chinese celery cabbage, Chinese mustard (greens), Chinese mustard cabbage, Chinese white cabbage, chingensai, gai choy, green in snow, kai tsoi, leaf mustard, mustard cabbage, taisin
Indian pudding	sweet pudding of cornmeal boiled in milk
Indian rice	rice grown in India
indianky	popular, rich little cakes CZECH
Indian spinach	see basella, Malabar spinach, Ceylon spinach
indienne, à l'	dishes influenced by Indian styles of cooking FRENCH
indienne, sauce	classical curry sauce FRENCH
indivia	chicory ITALIAN
indvolde	tripe DANISH
indyk	turkey POLISH
in-far cake	old cake, like a rich oatcake but containing flour and butter SCOTTISH
infusing	method of imparting flavour to liquid
ingberlach	small honey cake eaten at Passover JEWISH
ingefær	ginger DANISH
ingefærbrød	ginger bread DANISH
ingefära	ginger SWEDISH
ingladsild	pickled herring NORWEGIAN
inglesa	underdone; boiled; served with boiled vegetables SPANISH
Ingwer	ginger GERMAN
inhame	yam; variety of sweet potato PORTUGUESE
injera	yeast bread made from millet flour shaped like a large pancake EAST AFRICAN
inkivääri	ginger FINNISH
inkokt	boiled and served cold SWEDISH
inky caps	genus of fungus
inky pinky	hash made from slices of cold roast beef SCOTTISH
inlagd	marinated in vinegar, sugar and spices SWEDISH
insalata	salad ITALIAN
insects	source of protein in some parts of the world such as Africa, Japan and South East Asia
inspissing	thickening by evaporation

interlarding	lardoons are sewn through the outer surface only of meats to flavour and decorate
invert sugar	mixture of simple sugars, glucose and fructose, occurring naturally in many fruits
involtino	stuffed meat or ham roll ITALIAN
iodine	naturally occurring trace element essential to human diet
iridée	edible seaweed FRENCH
Irish coffee	freshly brewed coffee with Irish whiskey IRISH
Irish mist	liqueur made from Irish whiskey and heather honey IRISH
Irish pease pudding	classical accompaniment to hot pickled pork IRISH
Irish stew	traditional dish IRISH
iron	mineral vital to health to make haemoglobin in red blood cells; shortage leads to the condition known as anaemia
irradiation	method of preserving food by exposing it to gamma rays, thus destroying micro-organisms
is	ice-cream; ice DANISH, NORWEGIAN, SWEDISH
isabelita	angel fish SPANISH
iscas	thinly sliced liver PORTUGUESE
ischl	biscuit containing hazelnuts, sandwiched together with jam and covered with chocolate glaze HUNGARIAN
ishsalata	salad TURKISH
isinglass	substance produced from fish, formerly used as a setting agent but now virtually replaced by gelatine
islandssill	Iceland herring SWEDISH
Islay cheese	miniature Dunlop cheese excellent for melting
issues	the pluck (of an animal, rather than of a bird) FRENCH
isterband	coarse, very tasty pork sausage SWEDISH
istiridyè	oysters TURKISH
Italiaanse salade	mixed salad, with tomatoes, olives and tuna DUTCH
italiansalaatti	boiled vegetables in mayonnaise FINNISH
Italienischer Salat	finely sliced veal, salami, tomatoes, anchovies, cucumber and celery in mayonnaise GERMAN
italienne, à l'	dishes made partly or wholly from pasta, often flavoured with cheese or tomato; applies to other dishes of Italian origin FRENCH
italiensk salat	mayonnaise mixed with peas, chopped carrots and asparagus, served with ham on smørrebrød DANISH

italiensk salat	salad of diced cold meat or ham, apples, potatoes, gherkins and other vegetables in mayonnaise
	NORWEGIAN
ivoire, sauce	white wine sauce FRENCH
ivrogne de mer	'drunkard of the sea'; small, tough fish usually used in soups and stews FRENCH
izard	goat-like antelope, also known as the chamois
Izarra	various green and yellow herbal liqueurs based on armagnac, scented with mimosa honey
izmir köftesi	a chopped mutton and bread and egg mixture, fried as sausage-shaped rolls and served with a tomato sauce TURKISH

J

jaadyke	water ice (US: sherbet) FINNISH
jäätelö	ice-cream FINNISH
jabłka	apple POLISH
jabalí	wild boar SPANISH
jablečny štrůdl	apple tart, pie CZECH
jabuticaba	bing cherry PORTUGUESE
jachtschotel	dish made from left over game or meat DUTCH
jack bean	native of tropical America, which can be eaten as a green bean
jack cheese	alternative name for Monterey jack cheese AMERICAN
jacket potato	restaurant term for baked potato
jackfruit	tropical fruit with a rough, spiky green skin and yellow fibrous flesh, which can weigh up to 70lb
jack snipe	smaller bird than the common snipe
jägarschnitzel	veal cutlet with mushrooms SWEDISH
Jägerart, nach	sautéed with mushrooms and sometimes onions GERMAN
Jägersuppe	stew of partridge, ham, carrots, celery, stock, and red wine GERMAN
Jägerwurst	minced pork and paprika sausage GERMAN
jaggery	crude brown sugar, made from palm juice or brown cane sugar INDIAN
jagody	bilberries; blueberries POLISH
jag-ong	corn BM
jahody	strawberries CZECH
jaiphal	equivalent of nutmeg INDIAN
jaja	eggs POLISH
jajecznica	scrambled eggs POLISH
Jakobsmuschel	scallop GERMAN
jalapeño chilli	small tapered, fiery-tasting chilli, 3,000 Scoville
jalea	jelly SPANISH
jalebi	sweet, deep-fried doughnuts in syrup INDIAN
jal farezi/jalfresi	marinated and charcoal grilled with tomatoes and capsicum, or green chillies – very hot INDIAN
jälkiruoka	dessert FINNISH
jälkiuunileipä	rye bread baked in a slow oven FINNISH

jalousie   a sweet filling spread on to a strip of puff pastry and covered by another strip of pastry, which is slashed diagonally, and baked FRENCH

jam   fresh fruit preserved by cooking it with sugar

jambalaya   dish based on rice, which may include chicken, ham, sausage, prawns, crayfish and tomatoes   Creole

jambe   leg of meat FRENCH

jambon   ham FRENCH

jambon blanc   cooking ham, available unsmoked or lightly smoked FRENCH

jambon d'ardennes   cured ham BELGIUM

jambon de bayonne   dry-cured and lightly smoked ham FRENCH

jambon de poulet   chicken leg FRENCH

jambon de toulouse   unsmoked, salted and dried ham FRENCH

jambonneau   foreleg of pork FRENCH

jambonneau de volaille large chicken leg FRENCH

jambonnettes   dish consisting of ham and pork FRENCH

jambons de campagne   hams prepared according to local recipes, usually sweet-cured and smoked, intended for cooking FRENCH

jambu   variety of cress PORTUGUESE

jamdani   a mild dry dish containing yoghurt and tomatoes BANGLADESHI

jamón   ham SPANISH

jamón serrano   high quality, salted and air dried ham, eaten raw SPANISH

jänis   hare FINNISH

jänispaisti   casserole of hare FINNISH

Jansson's frestelse   'Jansson's temptation'; layers of sliced potatoes, onions and marinated sprats, baked with cream SWEDISH

Janssonin kiusaus   'Jansson's temptation' (*see* above) FINNISH

jantar   dinner PORTUGUESE

jānu siers   'St John's cheese'; a cheese eaten on the Latvian holiday, St John's Day, with bacon and beer LATVIAN

Japanese artichoke   *Stachys sieboldi*, also known as Chinese artichoke, knotroot, crosnes, and in Oriental markets as choroqi, its tubers taste similar to Jerusalem artichoke

Japanese greens   *see* chrysanthemum greens, chop suey greens, and shunguki

Japanese bunching onion   similar to the Welsh onion

Japanese quince   ornamental shrub JAPAN

japonaise, à la   dish containing or garnished with Chinese artichokes
FRENCH

japonica   the fruit of the japonica tree is an ornamental quince with a distinctive flavour, often mixed with apples in a pie or stew, but it cannot been eaten raw

japata   sea bream SPANISH

jardineira   mixed vegetables PORTUGUESE

jardinière   dishes garnished with mixed spring vegetables or green peas and sprigs of cauliflower FRENCH

jarlsberg   wheel-shaped semi-hard, pasteurised cow's milk cheese with a sweet, nutty flavour

jarmuż   stewed cabbage POLISH

jarosse, jarousse   everlasting pea, known in the Auvergne as the Auvergne lentil FRENCH

järpe   hazelhen SWEDISH

jarret   shin or knuckle FRENCH

jarrett steak   popular dish from Cornwall, made with shin of beef

jarzyny   vegetables POLISH

jaseur   waxwing FRENCH

játra   liver CZECH

játra dušená   braised liver CZECH

játra na roštu   grilled liver CZECH

játra telecí   calf liver CZECH

játrová paštika   liver pâté CZECH

jauheliha   minced meat FINNISH

jauhettu   minced FINNISH

jauphull   cinnamon INDIAN

javali   wild boar PORTUGUESE

javithri   equivalent of mace INDIAN

jawatrie   mace INDIAN

jay   common European bird, normally eaten when young

jazyk   tongue CZECH

jazyks omáčkou   tongue in gravy CZECH

ječmen   barley CZECH

jeera   cumin seed INDIAN

jehnečí   lamb CZECH

jehnečí hrudí   breast of lamb CZECH

jehnečí kotleta   lamb chop CZECH

jehněči pečene   roast lamb CZECH

jeleń	venison POLISH
jelito	blood sausage CZECH
jelly	(US: jello); flavoured liquid combined with a setting agent in a mould; a preserve made as jam, but strained to produce a clear jelly; a savoury food preparation set with gelatin or a strong gelatinous stock eg calf's foot jelly
jelly (sweet)	various sweets, including fruit jellies, Turkish delight and jujubes, set with geLatin
jem	jam BM
jemný drobenkový koláč	cheese crumble pie CZECH
jengibre	ginger SPANISH
Jenny Lind	a game consommé FRENCH
jérce koktél	chicken cocktail HUNGARIAN
jerez, al	braised in sherry SPANISH
jerky	meat preserved by cutting into thin slices and drying in the sun (from Spanish: 'from Quechuan', via charquin)
jeroboam	bottle of wine equivalent to four normal-sized bottles
Jersey wonder	small doughnut-like cake JERSEY
Jerusalem artichoke	form of artichoke, similar to the globe artichoke
jeseter	sturgeon CZECH
jesiotr	sturgeon POLISH
jesse	carp like fish, found in European rivers
jésuite	small French pastry, popular name for a turkey FRENCH
jésus	pig's liver sausage SWISS
Jew's ears	fungus resembling a human ear
jewfish	any of the large groupers found off the west coast of Mexico MEXICAN
jezyny	blackberries POLISH
jhalfry	see jal farezi INDIAN
jhinga, jinga	prawns INDIAN
jibiones	local name in Santander for calamary SPANISH
jicama	root vegetable with thin, brown skin and crisp, juicy white flesh, used in Oriental cooking
jídelní lístek	menu CZECH
jídlo	food CZECH
jinga praj pati	prawn butterfly; marinated and fried in butter INDIAN
jitrnice	white sausage CZECH

Job's tears	a course grass, with hard seeds used to made coarse bread SPANISH, PORTUGUESE
joghurt	yoghurt HUNGARIAN
jogurt	yoghurt CZECH
Johannisbeere	redcurrant GERMAN
John Dory	ugly, flat, large jawed sea fish (*Zeus faber*) with firm, white flesh and a delicate flavour
Johnny cake	speciality of Rhode Island, a cornmeal griddle-fried cake AMERICAN
joint	carcasses of animals intended for human consumption are cut into sections known as joints or cuts
joinville, sauce	classical sauce made from sauce normande and coulis of crayfish and shrimps FRENCH
Jókai bableves	bean soup HUNGARIAN
jól ásütve	well-done HUNGARIAN
jomfruhummer	Norway lobster DANISH
jonatán alma	Jonathan apple HUNGARIAN
jonge kaas	fresh cheese DUTCH
Jorbkäse	sour milk cheese GERMAN
jordärtskocka	Jerusalem artichoke SWEDISH
jordärtskockspuré	purée of Jerusalem artichoke SWEDISH
jordbaer	strawberry DANISH, NORWEGIAN
jordgubbe	strawberry SWEDISH
jordgubbstårta	sponge cake with whipped cream and strawberries SWEDISH
jordnöt	peanut SWEDISH
joue de porc fumée	smoked pig's cheek FRENCH
joule	SI unit of energy equivalent to 1 watt-second, or 4.187 calories, named for the English physicist James Prescott Joule (1818–89) FRENCH
joulukinkku	ham baked with mustard and breadcrumbs FINNISH
joulutortut	small pastry cases stuffed with pulped prunes FINNISH
jowl	alternative name for the butt cut of pork
judas tree	flower buds of this tree can be pickled in vinegar, like capers
judía	bean SPANISH
judic, à la	garnish for entrées containing braised lettuce, cocks' combs, truffles and pommes château; consommé garnished with truffles, quenelles of chicken and braised lettuces FRENCH

judru	cured pork sausage, a speciality of Chagny FRENCH
jugged	traditional method of cooking hare in a tall covered pot
juggery	dessert of tapioca, treacle, sugar, cream and coconut INDIAN
jugo	gravy, meat juice SPANISH
jugurtti	yoghurt FINNISH
Juhla	kind of cheddar cheese FINNISH
juice	liquid extracted from fruits and vegetables
jujube	a shrub, the fruit of which is eaten candied or made into jelly; sweet made of gelatine, water, sugar and flavouring, sometimes medicated or scented
julbord	buffet of Christmas specialities SWEDISH
julekake	rich fruit cake NORWEGIAN
julep	drink based on whiskey or fruit brandy, often flavoured with mint and served with ice and a slice of lemon
Jules Verne, à la	garnish for meat of stuffed potatoes and turnips FRENCH
julesalat	chicory (US: endive) DANISH
julgröt	Christmas dish of rice pudding cooked in milk, containing a single almond – the person who gets the almond will marry during the coming year SWEDISH
juliana	with shredded vegetables SPANISH
julienne	rind from vegetables or fruit cut into fine equal length strips FRENCH
julskinka	Christmas ham SWEDISH
jultallrik	plate of specialities from the julbord SWEDISH
jumble	small biscuit flavoured with lemon or almond, usually baked in an 'S' shape or tiny rock-like heaps
juneberry	shrub with sweet and juicy fruit AMERICAN
jung	young; spring GERMAN
Jungfernbraten	fillet of pork braised on sautéed onions and carrots, stock and sour cream AUSTRIAN
Jungschweinskaree	loin of pork, scored, rubbed with salt and caraway seeds and roasted AUSTRIAN
juniper	tree with aromatic purple-black berries used to flavour gin, in cooking, and marinades; Limerick ham is smoked over juniper branches and berries
junket	old fashioned milk pudding made by adding rennet to pasteurised milk causing it to set; it may be flavoured and the surface sprinkled with grated nutmeg

juomaraha	tip FINNISH
juottoporsas	suck(l)ing pig FINNISH
Jura	a soft cheese from the mountainous Jura region FRENCH
jurel	old English milk pudding ENGLISH
jurel	horse mackerel SPANISH
jus	liquid exuded from meat during cooking; fruit or vegetable juice; the juices extracted from compressed meat, poultry or game FRENCH
jus lié	fatless veal gravy thickened with arrowroot. FRENCH
jus, au	meat served with its juices or gravy FRENCH
juurekset	root vegetables FINNISH
juusto	cheese FINNISH
jydske terninger	sandwich made from shortcrust pastry DANISH

K

kaai laan tsoi	*see*, Chinese broccoli, Chinese kale, gai lan, kailan
kaai tsoi	*see* Chinese mustard cabbage, Chinese mustard (greens), gai choy, green in snow, Indian mustard (greens), leaf mustard, mustard cabbage, pak choi
kaali	cabbage FINNISH
kääresyltty	salted brawn FINNISH
kääryle	thin slice of meat, stuffed and rolled FINNISH
kaas	cheese DUTCH
kaas balleetje	baked cheese ball DUTCH
kabab	charcoal-grilled sausage of minced meat INDIAN
kabaczki	vegetable marrow POLISH
kabak	courgettes TURKISH
kabanosy	very thin dried pork sausage POLISH
Kabeljau	young cod or codling GERMAN
kabeljauw	young cod DUTCH
kabeljo	dried or cured cod SWEDISH
kabli chenna	Bengal beans; blackeyed peas INDIAN
kabocha	round, medium sized squash, with dark green ridged skin
kabul sauce	very strong commercially-produced sauce RUSSIAN
kabuní	traditional dish made with rice ALBANIAN
kaccavia, kakavia	fish or soup; bouillabaisse GREEK
ka-chang	bean BM
kachiri	powdered green papaya used to tenderise lamb INDIAN
kachna	duck CZECH
kachori	bread, stuffed, (usually with dal) and deep fried INDIAN
kačkavalj	ewe's milk cheese YUGOSLAVIAN
kacsa	duck HUNGARIAN
kaczka	duck POLISH
kadayif	traditional sweetmeat made from noodles, butter, almonds, honey and salt TURKISH, MIDDLE EASTERN
kaddu	equivalent of pumpkin INDIAN
kadeřavá kapusta	cabbage CZECH
kadin budu	traditional beef and rice patties TURKISH

kaerlinghedskranser	biscuit rings DANISH
kaernemaelk	buttermilk DANISH
kærnemælkskoldskal	chilled buttermilk soup, served with rusks (US: zwieback) DANISH
kage	cake DANISH
kager	pastry DANISH
kagyló	shellfish HUNGARIAN
kahlua	coffee liqueur based on rum MEXICAN
kahvi aamiaine-n	continental breakfast FINNISH
kailan	*see* white flowering broccoli, Chinese broccoli, Chinese kale, gai lan, kaai laan tsoi
kai tsoi	*see* Chinese celery cabbage, Chinese mustard (greens), Chinese mustard cabbage, Chinese white cabbage, chingensai, gai choy, green in snow, Indian mustard (greens), leaf mustard, mustard cabbage, taisin
kail	alternative spelling for kale
kaēmaki	cream, thick enough to be cut into slices GREEK
Kaiserfleisch	boiled rack of smoked pickled pork AUSTRIAN
Kaiserschmarren	fluffy pancakes with raisins, served with a compôte or chocolate sauce GERMAN
kajgana	omelette-like dish YUGOSLAVIAN
kajmak	thick ewe's milk cream YUGOSLAVIAN
kajzerka	bread roll POLISH
kaka	cake; biscuit SWEDISH
kake	cake; tart NORWEGIAN
kakku	cake FINNISH
kakri	cucumber INDIAN
kakukkfü	thyme HUNGARIAN
kål	cabbage DANISH, NORWEGIAN, SWEDISH
kala	fish FINNISH, ESTONIAN
kalács	fluffy white milk bread, or made into rolls called 'puffancs' HUNGARIAN
kalafjory	cauliflower POLISH
kalamaria	squid GREEK
kalamary	squid POLISH
kala mirchi	black pepper, *Piper nigrum* INDIAN
kalarepka	kohlrabi POLISH
Kalb	veal GERMAN
Kalbsbries	veal sweetbread GERMAN
Kalbskopf	calf's head GERMAN

Kalbsmilch	veal sweetbread GERMAN
Kalbsnierenbraten	roast veal stuffed with kidneys GERMAN
Kaldaunen	tripe GERMAN
kale	leafy winter vegetable, which may have flat or curly leaves, a tough texture and stronger flavour than cabbage
kalfslapje	veal cuts DUTCH
kalfsrollade	roast veal DUTCH
kalfsvlees	veal DUTCH
kalia	hot chilli sauce INDIAN
kalia	traditional soup made from chicken broth, flavoured with the juice of pickled cucumbers, garnished with diced chicken, celery root, parsley root, and carrots POLISH
kalkkuna	turkey FINNISH
kalkoen	turkey DUTCH
kalkon	turkey SWEDISH
kalkun	turkey DANISH, NORWEGIAN
kall	cold SWEDISH
kallskuret	cold meat SWEDISH
kallun	tripe DANISH
kalmar	squid CZECH
kalocsai halászlé	fish soup in red wine HUNGARIAN
kalops	beef stew flavoured with bay leaves SWEDISH
kalorifattig	low calorie SWEDISH
kalt	cold GERMAN
kalteszal	beer soup POLISH
Kaltschale	'cold bowl'; chilled fruit soup GERMAN
kalv	veal; calf SWEDISH
kalvebrisler	sweetbreads DANISH
kalvekjøtt	veal NORWEGIAN
kalvekød	veal DANISH
kalvekotelett	veal chop NORWEGIAN
kalvemedaljong	small round fillet of veal NORWEGIAN
kalvetunge	calf's tongue NORWEGIAN
kam-bing	goat BM
Kammuschel	scallop GERMAN
kampela	flounder FINNISH
kamper steur	hard boiled eggs covered with mustard sauce DUTCH
kana	hen FINNISH
kanan koipi	chicken thigh FINNISH

kanan maksa	chicken liver FINNISH
kanan muna	chicken egg FINNISH
kanan poika	spring chicken FINNISH
kanan rinta	chicken breast FINNISH
kanapka	sandwich POLISH
kandierte Frucht	crystallised fruit GERMAN
kandované ovoce	candied fruit CZECH
kanel	cinnamon NORWEGIAN
kanel	cinnamon SWEDISH
kaneli	cinnamon FINNISH
kangaroo	lean, dark, meat; high in protein; kangaroo tail soup is very fatty
kanin	rabbit NORWEGIAN, SWEDISH
Kaninchen	wild rabbit GERMAN
kantarel	chanterelle mushroom DANISH
kantarell	chanterelle mushroom SWEDISH
kantarelli	chanterelle mushroom FINNISH
kanter	a cheese resembling friesian, but unspiced DUTCH
kantola	small, bitter gourd, with thick, green knobbly skin and seeds that are edible when young
kapłon	capon POLISH
kapakoti	'with the cover on'; pot roasting GREEK
kapamà	large slices of lamb, lettuce and spring onions BALKAN
kaparki	capers POLISH
kapary	capers CZECH
Kapaun	capon GERMAN
kapers	capers DANISH
kapie	pickled sweet peppers CZECH
kapor	dill HUNGARIAN
kapostu	cabbage LATVIAN
káposzta	cabbage HUNGARIAN
káposztás rétes	cabbage strudel HUNGARIAN
káposztás ürü	mutton with cabbage HUNGARIAN
kappan	capon HUNGARIAN
kapr	carp CZECH
kapr na černo	carp in a black sauce of peppercorns, prunes and dark beer CZECH
kapr na kmíně	carp baked with caraway seeds CZECH
kapr na modro	carp cooked in stock with wine and spices, and served in vinegar CZECH

kapribogyó	caper HUNGARIAN
kapris	caper FINNISH
kapris	caper SWEDISH
kapros túrógombóc	dill-flavoured cottage cheese dumplings HUNGARIAN
kapros túrós rétes	curd strudel with dill HUNGARIAN
kapros zöldborsófőzelék	green peas with dill HUNGARIAN
kapucijners met spek	peas served with fried bacon, boiled potatoes, onion and green salad DUTCH
kapucineres felfújt	mocha soufflé HUNGARIAN
kapuśniak	sauerkraut and cabbage soup POLISH
kapusta	cabbage RUSSIAN, POLISH
kapusta	Brussels sprouts CZECH
kapusta czerwona	red cabbage POLISH
kapusta kiszona	sauerkraut POLISH
kapustová polévka	cabbage soup CZECH
kapuziner	nasturtium leaves GERMAN
karabanátek	hamburger CZECH
karaś	crucian, a freshwater fish POLISH
karai/karahi	two-handled cooking pan INDIAN
karaj	chop or cutlet HUNGARIAN
karakot	sweetmeat made from stewed fruit, sugar, ground almonds, vanilla and water, egg yolks, and stiffly-whipped egg whites, dried in a cool oven, sliced and eaten cold with lemon tea UZBEKISTANI
karalábé	green-leafed vegetable HUNGARIAN
karamel	caramel CZECH
Karamelkrem	caramel cream GERMAN
karamellpudding	caramel blancmange NORWEGIAN
karamelrand	caramel custard DANISH
karaoloi	snails GREEK
karbonade	breaded minced steak of pork or veal DANISH
karbonade	chop; cutlet DUTCH
karbonadekake	hamburger steak NORWEGIAN
karczochy	globe artichokes POLISH
kardemomme	cardamom NORWEGIAN
karela	courgettes; squashes INDIAN
karella	long pod-like vegetable, similar to okra, with knobbly skin and edible red seeds
Karfiol	cauliflower GERMAN
karfiol	cauliflower HUNGARIAN
karfy	chard POLISH

karhun liha	bear meat FINNISH
kari	curry CZECH
karides	shrimps TURKISH
karithopita	walnut cake, a speciality of Athens GREEK
karitsanliha	lamb FINNISH
karjalan paisti	Karelian stew of beef, mutton, pork, kidneys, liver and onion FINNISH
karjalan piirakk-a	'Karelian pasties'; thin, crisp, rye pastry shells filled with rice or mashed potatoes, served with finely chopped hard boiled eggs mixed with butter FINNISH
Karl XV tårta	almond and apricot tart SWEDISH
karljohanssvamp	boletus mushroom SWEDISH
karmazyn	haddock POLISH
karmonadle	pork schnitzels POLISH
karnemelk	buttermilk DUTCH
karni yarik	vegetable dish TURKISH
kärntner Nudeln	noodle paste rolled into oval shapes, filled with a mixture of chopped dried fruit, sugar and cinnamon GERMAN
Karotte	carrot GERMAN
karp	carp POLISH
karpalo	cranberry FINNISH
karpe	carp DANISH
karper	carp DUTCH
Karpfen	carp GERMAN
karpouzi	watermelon GREEK
karri	curry NORWEGIAN
karry	curry DANISH
karse	cress DANISH
kartofel	potato RUSSIAN
Kartoffel	potato GERMAN
kartoffel	potato DANISH
kartoflanka	potato soup POLISH
kartofle	potato POLISH
karve	caraway seed NORWEGIAN
karveli	coarse brown bread GREEK
karviaismarja	gooseberry FINNISH
Käse	cheese GERMAN
Kasen	curds GERMAN
kaser	popular semi-hard pressed cheese, made from ewe's milk TURKISH

Käsestangen	cheese twists SWISS
kasha	boiled or cooked cereal RUSSIAN
kasher	*see* kosher
Kashmir chicken	stuffed with minced meat INDIAN
Kashmiri	mild and sweet fruity sauce INDIAN
Kasseler Rippenspeer	smoked spare ribs of loin of pork GERMAN
kasseri	goat's or ewe's milk cheese GREEK
kassler	lightly smoked loin of pork SWEDISH
kastana	chestnuts GREEK
Kastanie	chestnuts GERMAN
kastanj	chestnut SWEDISH
kastanja	chestnut FINNISH
kastanje	chestnuts DUTCH, NORWEGIAN
kastanjepuré	chestnut purée SWEDISH
kaštanové pyre	chestnut purée CZECH
kaštanové pyré se šlehačkou	chestnut purée with whipped cream CZECH
kaštany	chestnuts CZECH
kastike	sauce; gravy FINNISH
kasvis	vegetable FINNISH
kasza	buckwheat POLISH
kaszanka z cebulą	black pudding braised with onions POLISH
kaszinó tojás	eggs with mayonnaise HUNGARIAN
kasztany	chestnuts POLISH
kataifi	pastry made by professional pastry makers GREEK
katajanmarja	juniper berry FINNISH
katalu	vegetable dish of egg plant, green peppers, tomatoes, and green beans TURKISH
kateenkorva	sweetbread FINNISH
katemaksu	cover charge FINNISH
Katenrauchschinken	country-style smoked ham GERMAN
Katenwurst	country-style smoked sausage GERMAN
katkarapu	shrimp FINNISH
Katmandu	medium-heat sauce INDIAN
katori	small dishes for traditional thali (tray meal) INDIAN
katrinplommon	prune SWEDISH
katsikaki	kid GREEK
katsoubushi	boned and dried bonito fish
Katzenjammer	beef in mayonnaise with cucumbers or gherkins GERMAN, AUSTRIAN
kaura	rolled oats FINNISH

kauris	deer FINNISH
kavalli	whole mackerel baked between layers of potato, moistened with olive oil MALTESE
kaviaar	caviar DUTCH
kaviaari	caviar FINNISH
kaviar	caviar DANISH, SWEDISH
Kaviar	caviar GERMAN
kaviár	caviar HUNGARIAN
kawior	caviar POLISH
käx	biscuit SWEDISH
kaymak	thick cream TURKISH
kdoule	quince CZECH
kečup	ketchup CZECH
kebab	cubes of meat, fish, shellfish, fruit and vegetables cooked on skewers; doner kebab is marinated, boned leg of lamb roasted on a vertical spit, sliced thinly and served in pitta bread with salad; shish kebab comprises cubes of lamb, tomato and onion threaded on to a skewer TURKISH
kebàp	kebab BULGARIAN
kecsege	sterlet HUNGARIAN
kecske	goat HUNGARIAN
kecskeméti barackpuding	apricot pudding with vanilla cream HUNGARIAN
kedgeree/khichari	English dish of Indian origin of rice mixed with flaked, cooked or smoked fish and hard boiled eggs, traditionally served for breakfast
ked-joo	cheese BM
kedlubna	green leafed vegetable CZECH
keema	dry minced meat (as in keema curry, keema nan) INDIAN
kefalotyri	hard, very salty cheese GREEK
kéfir	sour-milk product originating in the Caucasus, made with cow's milk RUSSIAN
keftedakia	very small meat balls, served as mezes GREEK
keftedes	meat balls GREEK
keitetty	boiled; cooked FINNISH
keitetyt perunat	boiled potatoes FINNISH
keitinpiiraat	small pasties made with rye flour pastry FINNISH
keitto	soup; cream FINNISH
Keks	biscuit GERMAN
keksi	biscuit FINNISH

keksy	biscuits CZECH
keksz	biscuits HUNGARIAN
kela	equivalent of banana INDIAN
kelbimbó	Brussels sprouts HUNGARIAN
keley	banana INDIAN
kelkáposzta	Savoy cabbage HUNGARIAN
kelt tészta	puff pastry HUNGARIAN
keltasieni	chanterelle mushroom FINNISH
kenyér	bread HUNGARIAN
kephalos	grey mullet GREEK
képviselöfánk	cream puff HUNGARIAN
Kerbel	chervil GERMAN
kerma	cream FINNISH
kermajuusto	a strongly flavoured cream cheese FINNISH
kermakakku	sponge layer cake with cream and jam filling FINNISH
kermakastike	cream sauce FINNISH
kermaleivos	cream pastry FINNISH
kermavaahto	whipped cream FINNISH
kermaviili	kind of sour cream FINNISH
kermes	ancient red dye, made from dried bodies of a female scale insect
kernhem	cream cheese DUTCH
kerrie	curry DUTCH
kers	cherry DUTCH
kervel	chervil DUTCH
kesäkeitto	'summer soup'; a mixed vegetable soup FINNISH
kesar	equivalent of saffron INDIAN
kesar chaval	saffron rice fried in ghee INDIAN
keserü	bitter HUNGARIAN
keso	type of cottage cheese SWEDISH
Kesselfleisch	boiled pork served with vegetables GERMAN
Kesti	hard cheese flavoured with caraway seeds FINNISH
keszeg	bream HUNGARIAN
készétel	ready-made meal HUNGARIAN
ketchup	spicy sauce or condiment, made from the juice of cooked fruits or vegetables (US: catsup)
ketsuppi	ketchup, catsup FINNISH
kettle	vessel with handle and spout for boiling water; specially shaped vessel for a particular purpose eg fish kettle

Keule leg of meat GERMAN

kevyt kerma coffee cream FINNISH

kewra tree with rose scented flowers, that grows in swampy, humid areas; the flowers are used for flavouring sweet and savoury dishes

khamira roti nan bread INDIAN

kharcho Caucasean soup made from cooked boiled brisket of beef RUSSIAN

khas-khas aromatic grass; used as a flavouring INDIAN

khatta acid INDIAN

kheema beef INDIAN

kheer milk pudding INDIAN

khichari *see* kedgeree

khlodnik any cold soup RUSSIAN

khoresh similar to soup or stew of meat cooked with fruit and nuts, served with rice IRANIAN

khren horseradish RUSSIAN

khubani apricot INDIAN

khurzi whole lamb or chicken stuffed with spicy filling INDIAN

khus khus, khush-khush equivalent of poppy seed INDIAN

khvorost 'twigs'; sweet biscuits cut into strips and twisted together RUSSIAN

kibbi lean lamb, cracked wheat and onion MIDDLE EASTERN

kibbling grinding or chopping coarsely

kichlach traditional pastry cooked like drop scones JEWISH

kid young goat, popular meat in the Mediterranean

kiddley broth a traditional Cornish soup containing bread and marigold heads

kidney classified as offal, it is nutritious and economical, popularly served with steak

kidney bean type of dried red bean with white flesh and a full, strong flavour

kiełbasa sausage POLISH

Kieler Sprotte smoked sprat GERMAN

kieli tongue FINNISH

kievitsei plover's egg DUTCH

kiisseli berry and fruit juice thickened with potato flour FINNISH

kiks biscuit DANISH

kiliç şiş fish cooked on a spit TURKISH

kilki	a Norwegian variety of anchovy RUSSIAN
kima	minced meat used for making a sauce RUSSIAN
kimichi	relish of finely chopped vegetables, such as cabbage, onions, garlic and chillies, pickled in brine, traditionally buried in a jar for several weeks to ferment KOREAN
king, à la	rich cream sauce, containing mushrooms and green peppers
kingdom of Fife pie	traditional pie containing rabbit and pickled pork SCOTTISH
kingfish	large sea fish
kinkku	ham FINNISH
kip	fowl or hen DUTCH
kipfler	a Dutch potato, particularly good for making chips DUTCH
kippeborst	breast of chicken DUTCH
kippebout	leg of chicken DUTCH
kipper	split, mildly salted, smoked herring
kirjolohi	salmon trout FINNISH
kirsch	an eau-de-vie rather than a liqueur, a cherry brandy in which the crushed kernels are included with the fruit juice
Kirsche	cherry GERMAN
kirsebær	cherry DANISH, NORWEGIAN
kirsikka	cherry FINNISH
kirxa bil-haxix	hot-pot of tripe and vegetables MALTESE
kisel	a dessert containing fruit juice and sugar RUSSIAN, BALTIC
kish mish	equivalent of raisin INDIAN
kishk	bulgar wheat, milk and yoghurt, fermented, dried, and turned into fine powder to make a type of porridge
kishmish	dried fruits ARMENIAN
kisiel	jam; dessert of puréed fruit, thickened and sometimes flavoured with white wine POLISH
kisielius	porridge-like gruel of fermented oatmeal Lithuanian
kissel, kisel	dessert made from sweetened fruit juice thickened with corn flour or arrowroot (the name comes from the Slavonic word kisly, which means 'sharp, sour') RUSSIAN, BALTIC
kiszka krwawa	black pudding POLISH
Kitz	kid GERMAN

kiwano	small fruit with tough reddish-orange spined skin, with green, watery flesh
kiwi fruit	egg-shaped fruit with brown skin and sweet green flesh full of black edible seeds
kiymali börek	pancake filled with chopped meat or mushrooms TURKISH
kizartma	meat stew TURKISH
kizil	cornelian cherry RUSSIAN
kjeks	biscuit NORWEGIAN
kjot	meat ICELANDIC
kjøtt	meat NORWEGIAN
klap-a; nee-or	coconut BM
klar suppe	consommé; clear soup DANISH
klar suppe med boller og grønsager	consommé with meat balls and vegetables DANISH
kléber	a beef consommé FRENCH
kleik	gruel of barley and bouillon POLISH
klejner	pastry crullers DANISH
klephtes	a traditional method of cooking, where the food is rubbed with herbs and oil and wrapped in parchment GREEK
kletski	general term for dumplings or quenelles RUSSIAN
klevera	sweet sauce made from minced plums CZECH
Kliesche	dab GERMAN
klikva	cranberries CZECH
klimp	dumplings SWEDISH
klip	cod which has undergone a special salting and smoking process peculiar to Norway NORWEGIAN
klipfisk	salted, smoked cod DANISH
klippfisk	salted, dried cod NORWEGIAN
klobase	sausage SLOVENE
klobásy	sausage CZECH
klobásy bílé	white pork sausages CZECH
klobásy domácí	home made sausages CZECH
klobásy opečené	fried sausages CZECH
klops czyli zając falszywy	'false hare'; meat loaf POLISH
klops z cielęciny	veal meatballs POLISH
Kloß	dumpling GERMAN
Kloßchen	small dumpling GERMAN
Kluftsteak	rump steak GERMAN
kluseczki z wątróbki	minced calf's liver POLISH

kluski	light dumplings POLISH
klyukva v sakhare	cranberries coated with beaten egg whites and icing sugar RUSSIAN
kmín	caraway CZECH
kminek	cumin POLISH
kminová polévka	caraway seed soup CZECH
knäckerbröd	crispbread SWEDISH
knackworst	small frankfurter sausage DUTCH
Knackwürst	pork and beef sausage GERMAN
knaidlach	traditional small dumpling JEWISH
knaidle	large dumpling JEWISH
knead	to mix flour with a liquid to form dough
kneading	method of combining ingredients of a dough too thick to stir
knedle	dumplings POLISH
knedlíky	dumplings CZECH
knekkebrød	crispbread NORWEGIAN
knelki	quenelles POLISH
knickerbocker glory	ice cream sundae of jelly, fruit, ice cream and whipped cream served in a tall glass
knishes	traditional dish, similar to Irish potato cake JEWISH
Knoblauch	garlic GERMAN
knobs	small marine molluscs, similar to whelks
knock back	to knead a yeast dough for a second time after rising
Knödel	very light dumplings GERMAN
Knöderl	a smaller version of knödel, used mainly in soups GERMAN
knoflook	garlic DUTCH
Knöpfli	thick noodle GERMAN
knot, knott	a European sandpiper
knuckle	joint of pork or veal, the lower part of the leg; knuckle of lamb (ie the lower part of the shoulder)
knundzar	a dish eaten by the Ten'a Indians ALASKAN
knysz	kasha cake; strudel POLISH, RUSSIAN
knyte	filled puff pastry SWEDISH
kobliha	doughnut CZECH
Köche	light steamed or baked puddings GERMAN
kocsonyázott halászlé	jellied fisherman's soup HUNGARIAN
kød	meat DANISH
kości	bones POLISH
koek	cake; gingerbread DUTCH

koekjes	sweet cakes or biscuits served with mid-morning coffee DUTCH
koffietafel	light lunch of bread and butter with a variety of garnishes, served with coffee DUTCH
kofta	meat balls INDIAN
köfte	meat balls TURKISH
kogel-mogel	beaten egg yolk with sugar POLISH
kogt	boiled DANISH
Kohl	cabbage GERMAN
kohlrabi	unusual vegetable of the cabbage family; rather like a turnip, with a swollen stalk rather than a root; it may be white or purple skinned
kohokas	soufflé FINNISH
kokad	boiled, cooked SWEDISH
kokilki z ryb	dish made from left over cooked fish POLISH
kokkelipiimä	clotted, thicker variety of viilipiimä, served with porridge, or as a drink FINNISH
kokkina avga	Easter eggs, coloured scarlet with vegetable dyes GREEK
kokojyväleipä	wholemeal bread FINNISH
kokorétsi	spiced sausage GREEK
kokos	coconut CZECH
kokos	grated coconut SWEDISH
kokòshka	chicken BULGARIAN
kokosky	coconut meringues CZECH
kokosmakron	coconut macaroon NORWEGIAN
kokosnoot	coconut DUTCH
kokosnøtt	coconut NORWEGIAN
kokospudding	a coconut pudding SWEDISH
kokt	cooked, boiled NORWEGIAN, SWEDISH
kokum	tree fruit of the same family as the mangosteen; the seeds make kokum butter and the flesh is dried for use in cooking SOUTHERN INDIAN
kókusz	coconut HUNGARIAN
koláč	cake CZECH
koláč ky	sweet buns CZECH
kolacja	supper POLISH
kolasås	caramel sauce SWEDISH
kolbasa	sausage RUSSIAN
kolbász	sausage HUNGARIAN
kold	cold DANISH

koldūnai	meat-filled dumplings LITHUANIAN
kołduny litewskie	dumpling of meat, suet, marjoram and onions POLISH
koldtbord	buffet of cold dishes such as fish, meat, salad, cheese and dessert NORWEGIAN
koleno	knuckle CZECH
koleno ovarové	boiled pig's knuckle CZECH
koleno uzené	smoked pig's knuckle CZECH
kolja	haddock SWEDISH
kolje	haddock NORWEGIAN
kolokassi	sweet potatoes GREEK
kolokithakia	vegetable marrow GREEK
kolozsvári káposzta	pork and sauerkraut HUNGARIAN
kolyva	traditional dish made from wheat and dried fruit, garnished with pomegranate seeds, eaten by families belonging to the Eastern Orthodox Church 40 days after a death and on the first and fourth anniversaries of a death; the wheat represents everlasting life, the fruit – joy and sweetness, and the pomegranate seeds – plenty GREEK
komijnekaas	cheese flavoured with cumin seeds DUTCH
komkommer	cucumber DUTCH
komló	hops HUNGARIAN
kompot	stewed fruit CZECH, POLISH
kompót	stewed fruit; compôte HUNGARIAN
kompot broskvový	stewed peaches CZECH
kompot hruškový	stewed pears CZECH
kompot jablkový	stewed apples CZECH
kompot mandarinkový	stewed tangerines CZECH
kompot míchaný	stewed mixed fruit CZECH
kompot švestkový	stewed plums CZECH
Kompott	stewed fruit; compôte GERMAN
kompott	stewed fruit SWEDISH
koncentrat pomidorowy	tomato paste POLISH
konfektbröd	macaroons SWEDISH
konfitura	jam POLISH
konfitüre	jam GERMAN
kongesuppe	'royal soup'; traditional soup of stock, peas, carrots, parsley, butter flavoured with sherry, served with meat balls NORWEGIAN
Königinpastetchen	vol-au-vent; puff-pastry shell filled with chicken and mushrooms GERMAN

Königinsuppe creamy chicken soup with pieces of chicken breast GERMAN

Königsberger Klopse meat dumplings GERMAN

Königswurst large 'royal' sausage GERMAN

konijn rabbit DUTCH

konina horse meat POLISH

koninginnesoep cream of chicken DUTCH

könnyü light HUNGARIAN

könnyü ételek snacks HUNGARIAN

konserwa tin POLISH

konzerva tin (US: can) CZECH

koo-biss cabbage BM

kool cabbage DUTCH

kool schotel met gehakt casserole of meatballs and cabbage DUTCH

koo-lit bark BM

kopanisti cheese GREEK

ko-pee coffee BM

koper dill POLISH

Kopfsalat green salad; lettuce GERMAN

koppen sour milk cheese from the Sudetic mountains CZECH

kopr dill CZECH

kopūstai su grybais traditional dish of mushrooms, bacon, onion, apple and sauerkraut LITHUANIAN

kopytka potato dumplings served with bacon bits POLISH

korai see karai INDIAN

koření seasoning CZECH

köret garnish HUNGARIAN

korint dried currant NORWEGIAN, SWEDISH

Korinthe currant GERMAN

korki ze śledzia small rolled herring POLISH

korma/koorma similar to braising; the meat is often marinated in yoghurt and spices and cooked very slowly in the marinade INDIAN

korniszony gherkins POLISH

koroptev partridge CZECH

koroptev pečená v červeném zeli roast partridge with red cabbage CZECH

körözött juhtúró ewe's cheese spread HUNGARIAN

korppu rusk FINNISH

körsbär cherry SWEDISH

körte pear HUNGARIAN

korv sausage SWEDISH

korva puusti	cinnamon roll FINNISH
korvasienet	morel mushroom FINNISH
körvel	chervil SWEDISH
kørvelsuppe	chervil soup DANISH
koryushki	smelts RUSSIAN
korzhiki	biscuits RUSSIAN
kos	sour milk ALBANIAN
košeliena	pig's trotters and goose giblets LITHUANIAN
kosher	food prepared according to orthodox Jewish dietary laws JEWISH
kost	bone CZECH
kotelet	cutlet; chop DANISH, DUTCH
Kotelett	chop; cutlet GERMAN
kotelett	NORWEGIAN
kotiruoka	home cooking; plain food FINNISH
kotitekoinen	home made FINNISH
kotlet	cutlet POLISH
kotlety	patties; rissoles of minced foods RUSSIAN
kotopoulo	chicken GREEK
kött	meat SWEDISH
köttfärs	minced meat SWEDISH
koud	cold DUTCH
koukia	dried broad beans GREEK
koulourakia	small Easter cakes GREEK
koulouria	sweet bread shaped like a large ring GREEK
koumiss	sour-tasting weak alcoholic beverage, made from mares' milk to which a culture and yeast are added
kouneli	rabbit GREEK
kounoupidi	cauliflower GREEK
koupepia	vegetable marrow stuffed with minced ground meat and baked GREEK
kourabiédes	a form of shortbread made for Christmas and New Year GREEK
kovaksi keitetty muna	hard-boiled egg FINNISH
kovászos uborka	dill gherkins HUNGARIAN
köyhät ritarit	'poor knights'; rye or wheat bread dipped in a mixture of egg and milk, fried in butter and served with cream and jam FINNISH
kozaitai (purple flowered)	see brocoletto, choy sum, flowering pak choi, flowering white cabbage, hong tsoi sum, hon tsai tai, pak tsoi sum, purple flowered choy sum, rape

közepesen átsütve	medium HUNGARIAN
kozunàk	traditional Easter cake BULGARIAN
krab	crab DUTCH
krabba	crab SWEDISH
Krabbe	crab GERMAN
krabbe	crab DANISH, NORWEGIAN
krabbetje	spare rib DUTCH
krabi	crab CZECH
krabi říční	fresh water crayfish CZECH
krabi mořští	saltwater crawfish CZECH
kræmmerhus med flødeskum	pastry cone filled with whipped cream and topped with jam DANISH
Kraftbrühe	soup of beef, carrot, onion, parsley, and leek GERMAN, AUSTRIAN
kräftor	freshwater crayfish boiled with salt and dill, and served cold SWEDISH
Krainer	spiced pork sausage GERMAN
králík	rabbit CZECH
kräm	cream custard; stewed fruit or syrup thickened with potato flour SWEDISH
kransekage	pyramid of almond macaroons DANISH, NORWEGIAN
Kranzkuchen	ring-shaped cake GERMAN
Krapfen	small pastry GERMAN, AUSTRIAN
krapiva	traditional nettle soup RUSSIAN
kråse	giblets DUTCH
krashenyie jajtza	decorated eggs served at Easter RUSSIAN
krasnice	yeast CZECH
krasse	cress SWEDISH
Krauskohl	kale GERMAN
Kraut	cabbage GERMAN
Kräuter	herbs GERMAN
Kräutersoße	herb dressing GERMAN
Krautsalat	coleslaw GERMAN
Krautsteil	white beet; Swiss chard GERMAN
Krautwickel	stuffed cabbage GERMAN
kreas	meat GREEK
Krebs	crayfish GERMAN
krebs	crayfish DANISH
Kreivi	semi-hard mildly pungent cheese FINNISH

krem	whipped cream; dessert of whipped cream with raisins or other fruits NORWEGIAN, POLISH
kremidia	onions GREEK
Kren	horseradish GERMAN
křen	horseradish CZECH
křepelka	quail CZECH
krendel	a birthday cake, made with yeast and shaped as a letter B RUSSIAN
krent	currant DUTCH
kreplach	traditional dish; similar to ravioli JEWISH
kreps	crayfish NORWEGIAN
Kresse	cress GERMAN
krev	blood CZECH
krevetky	scampi; prawns; shrimps CZECH
krevhusí	goose blood CZECH
krewetki	shrimp POLISH
kringle	variety of Danish pastry DANISH
kringle	ring-twisted bread with raisins NORWEGIAN
kritharaki	fine barley kernel, used in casseroles and soups GREEK
krocan	turkey CZECH
krocan s kaštanovou nádivkou	roast turkey stuffed with chestnuts CZECH
kroepoek	large, deep fried shrimp wafer DUTCH
krofne	small fried yeast cakes YUGOSLAVIAN
krogvärdens sås	cold sauce for boiled or steamed fish SWEDISH
kroket	croquette DUTCH
krokety	croquette CZECH
krolik	rabbit RUSSIAN
królik	rabbit POLISH
kromesky	minced poultry, game or meat, bound to a stiff paste and wrapped with bacon, coated in batter and fried RUSSIAN, POLISH
kronans kaka	crown cake SWEDISH
kronärtskocka	globe artichoke SWEDISH
kronärtskocksbotten	artichoke bottom SWEDISH
Kronfleisch	a cheap beef cut such as brisket or flank GERMAN
kroppkakor	potato dumplings stuffed with minced bacon and onions, served with melted butter SWEDISH
kruid	herb DUTCH
kruiderijen	spices DUTCH
kruidnagel	clove DUTCH

kruisbes	gooseberry DUTCH
krupek	crisp pancake made from dried prawns INDONESIAN
krupnik	barley soup POLISH
krupovka	country dish made from puréed barley served withsausage or smoked meat CZECH
krusbär	gooseberry SWEDISH
krusbärspaj	gooseberry tart or pie SWEDISH
Krustentier	shellfish GERMAN
krůta	turkey CZECH
krydda	spice SWEDISH
krydder	toasted bun DANISH
krydderfedt	spiced lard, very popular with cooks DANISH
krydderi	spice DANISH
kryddersild	pickled herring DANISH, NORWEGIAN
kryddersmør	herb butter DANISH
kryddnejlika	clove SWEDISH
kryddost	hard semi-fat cheese with cumin seeds SWEDISH
kryddpeppar	allspice SWEDISH
kryddsmör	herb butter SWEDISH
kubani	equivalent of apricot INDIAN
Kuchen	cake GERMAN
kugel	a holiday pudding JEWISH
kugelhupf	an Alsatian speciality yeast cake FRENCH
kuha	pike-perch FINNISH
kuiken	chicken DUTCH
kuivattu luumu	prune FINNISH
kukkakaali	cauliflower FINNISH
kukkoa viinnissä	chicken stewed in red wine FINNISH
kukorica	sweet corn HUNGARIAN
kukoricapehely	corn flake HUNGARIAN
kukuřice	corn CZECH
kukuiné vloky	corn flakes CZECH
Kukuruz	maize (US: corn) GERMAN
kukurydza	maize POLISH
kulajda	soup containing mushrooms and caraway seeds CZECH
kulcha	leavened bread, sometimes stuffed with onions potatoes, egg and coriander INDIAN
kulebiak	pasty; pie POLISH
kulebiak z kapustą i grzybami	rice short crust pastry POLISH
kulebyaka	traditional fishpie RUSSIAN
kulfi	ice cream INDIAN
kulibjaka	pie containing salmon, rice, hard-boiled eggs and dill; served in slices with melted butter FINNISH

kulich	cylindrical yeast dough cake, traditionally eaten at Easter RUSSIAN
kulkuts	small coconut cakes INDIAN
kulmie darchini	cinnamon INDIAN
különlegesség	speciality dish HUNGARIAN
kumina	caraway FINNISH
kumle	potato dumpling NORWEGIAN
Kümmel	caraway; a Dutch caraway-flavoured, colourless liqueur GERMAN, DUTCH
Kümmelkase	cheese flavoured with caraway GERMAN
kummin	cumin SWEDISH
kumquat	a close relative of the citrus family, a tiny fruit with a smooth orange edible skin and an unusual sweet sour flavour
kungull me kos	vegetable marrow fritters ALBANIAN
kunsági pandúrleves	chicken or pigeon soup HUNGARIAN
kun-tu	fermented salmon roe eaten by the Ten'a Indians instead of Russian caviar ALASKAN
kuoriperunat	potatoes in their jackets FINNISH
kuorrutettu	oven-browned FINNISH
kuorukka	croquette FINNISH
kura w potrawce	chicken fricassé POLISH
Kürbis	pumpkin; squash GERMAN
kurczę	chicken POLISH
kuře	chicken CZECH
kuře na paprice	stewed chicken with red peppers CZECH
kuře peciné s nádivkou	roast chicken with chicken liver stuffing CZECH
kúritsa	chicken RUSSIAN
kurka wodna	coot POLISH
kurki	chanterelle mushrooms POLISH
kurkku	cucumber FINNISH
kurleachi	crab INDIAN
kur-ma	date BM
kurnik	an elaborate chicken pie POLISH
kuropatwa	partridge POLISH
kurpitsa	gourd; pumpkin; squash FINNISH
kush kush	mild dish from the far north with dried fruit and nuts INDIAN
kutja	sweet wheat pudding BYELORUSSIAN
Kuttelfleck, Kutteln	tripe GERMAN
kutunjuusto	brown goat's cheese FINNISH

kuvertbröd	French roll SWEDISH
kuvertbrød	French roll DANISH
kuzu	thickening agent from the edible roots of a type of vine CHINESE, JAPANESE
kuzu	lamb TURKISH
kvæde	quince DANISH
kvargli	a soft cheese, usually highly spiced, made by peasants and small farmers for their own use HUNGARIAN
kvass	non-alcoholic beer made from rye, malt and yeast, often flavoured with mint or jumper RUSSIAN
květák	cauliflower CZECH
kwaśne	sour POLISH
kwark	freshwhite cheese DUTCH
kwartel	quail DUTCH
kway	cake BM
kweepeer	quince DUTCH
kyckling	chicken SWEDISH
kydonia	quinces GREEK
kyjevský kotlet	boned breast of chicken stuffed with butter, breaded, and deep fried, kiev-style CZECH
kyljys	chop FINNISH
kylkipaisti	spare-rib FINNISH
kylling	chicken DANISH, NORWEGIAN
kylmä	cold FINNISH
ky-oo ma-nis	cinnamon BM
kypsä	well-done FINNISH
kyrynga	sour cow's milk product CENTRAL ASIAN
kysané zelí	sauerkraut CZECH
kyselý	sour CZECH
kyselá	pickled CZECH
kyselé okurky	gherkins CZECH
kýta	leg; haunch CZECH
kyufté	a version of the ubiquitous Balkan meat ball or rissole BULGARIAN
kyyhkynen	pigeon FINNISH

L

laatikko	casserole; gratin FINNISH
laberdan	salted cod, packed in barrels
labiates	generic term for a group of plants with a corolla or calyx divided into two parts, suggesting lips; they often have aromatic leaves and include many common herb
lablab bean	small bean which can be used dried or green
labro	wrasse; type of fish SPANISH
labrus	brilliantly coloured sea fish; wrasse EUROPEAN
Labskaus	fisherman's dish from Oldenburg on the north coast, a type of fish cake (*cf* lobscouse) GERMAN
labskovs	(*cf* lobscouse) a casserole of potatoes, meat and vegetables DANISH
lábszár	shank HUNGARIAN
lache	small sea fish, cooked like smelt FRENCH
Lachs	salmon GERMAN
Lachsforelle	salmon trout GERMAN
Lachsschinken	smoked foreloin of pork wrapped in white pork fat GERMAN
lacón	shoulder of pork SPANISH
lacón con grelos	boiled shoulder of salt pork and white cabbage SPANISH
lacqua	thick prune butter JEWISH
lactic acid	naturally-occurring acid produced by bacteria in fermenting food; it is produced in milk as it goes over and acts as a preservative preventing the growth of other micro-organisms
lactose	natural sugar of milk
la-da	chillies, pepper BM
låda	casserole SWEDISH
laderes	foods braised in olive oil GREEK
ladies' delight	home made pickle ENGLISH
ladoxido	salad dressing; viniagrette GREEK
lady's bedstraw	wild plant, the flowers once much used as a vegetable
lady's smock	a crucifer with a cress-like flavour, it can be used in a salad

ladies' fingers   okra

ladies on horseback   chicken liver wrapped in streaky bacon and grilled

laffitte   chicken consommé FRENCH

la frita   general term for fried food SPANISH

lager   a carbonated hop-based beer that can be pale or dark, and is best served chilled

lagerblad   bay leaf SWEDISH

lagkage   layer cake, usually filled with whipped cream, jam, fruit purée or custard DANISH

lagopède   Pyrenean partridge FRENCH

lagosta   lobster PORTUGUESE

lagostim   crawfish; Norwegian lobster PORTUGUESE

lagostinhas   Dublin Bay prawns PORTUGUESE

laguiole   cow's milk cheese FRENCH

laguipière   consommé of game, garnished with poached pigeons' eggs and game royale FRENCH

laguipiére, sauce   classical sauce made from fish fumet, butter and glaze, seasoned with lemon juice FRENCH

lahana   cabbage GREEK

lahanika   vegetables GREEK

lahna   bream FINNISH

lait   milk FRENCH

laitance   fish roe FRENCH

laitue   cabbage (head); lettuce FRENCH

lake   burbot SWEDISH

lake trout   large trout found mainly in Swiss lakes

lakerda   a speciality dish of pickled fish GREEK

lakka   Arctic cloudberry FINNISH

lakror   black bird of the thrush family, eaten in pies ALBANIAN

laks   salmon DANISH, NORWEGIAN

laksørred   salmon trout DANISH

lal mirchi   chillies INDIAN

lamb   meat of young lambs slaughtered before they are a year old

lamb's fry   the collective name for lamb's liver, sweetbread, heart and some of the inside fat

lamb's lettuce   small leafed, green, winter plant, the leaves a sweet addition to salads; corn salad

lamb's wool   a drink of hot ale poured over pulped, roasted apples, with sugar and spices added to taste

lamballe   name for several dishes, particularly soup FRENCH

lambasteik	a lamb dish ICELANDIC
lambropsomo	Easter bread GREEK
lamington	small cube of sponge or butter cake, dipped in thin chocolate icing and desiccated coconut; named for Baron Lamington, Governor of Queensland (1896–1901) AUSTRALIAN
lamm	lamb SWEDISH
Lamm(fleisch)	lamb GERMAN
lammas	mutton FINNISH
lammebog	shoulder of lamb NORWEGIAN
lammebov	shoulder of lamb DANISH
lammebryst	breast of lamb DANISH, NORWEGIAN
lammekjøtt	lamb NORWEGIAN
lammekød	lamb DANISH
lammekolle	leg of lamb DANISH
lammekotelett	lamb chop NORWEGIAN
lämmin	warm FINNISH
lampaan kyljys	lamb chop FINNISH
lampone	raspberry ITALIAN
lamprea	lamprey SPANISH
lampreda	lamprey ITALIAN
lampreia	lamprey PORTUGUESE
lamprey	eel-like sea fish, prepared like an eel, but needing longer to cook
lamproie	lamprey FRENCH
lamsbout	leg of lamb DUTCH
lamsvlees	lamb DUTCH
Lancashire cheese	hard, crumbly cheese, with a mild tangy flavour that develops as the cheese matures ENGLISH
Lancashire foot	foot-shaped turnover from northern England ENGLISH
Lancashire hot-pot	warming stew of lamb, onions, and potatoes ENGLISH
lances	another name for sand eels – a traditional Cornish delicacy ENGLISH
lanche	snack PORTUGUESE
land cress	originating as a weed, it tastes a bit like watercress, but does not need the damp conditions required by watercress to grow
landgång	long, open sandwich with different garnishes SWEDISH
landrail	another name for the corncrake, a small bird protected in England

lane ciasto	soup garnish of batter noodles made from flour and eggs POLISH
langoše	fried pastry coated in garlic CZECH
langosta	spiny lobster SPANISH
langostina	large deep-sea prawns SPANISH
langostino	Norway lobster; Dublin Bay prawn SPANISH
langouste	spiny lobster FRENCH
langoustine	small lobster FRENCH
langrès	a soft cow's milk cheese from the Haute-Marne FRENCH
langue	tongue FRENCH
langue de boeuf	ox tongue FRENCH
languedocienne, à la	garnish for meat from the Languedoc region, of stuffed aubergines, minced cèpes, tomatoes, parsley, and pommes de terre château FRENCH
langues de chats	(cat's tongues) small, flat biscuits, a popular accompaniment to creamy desserts FRENCH
languste	spiny lobster; crawfish GERMAN
lankkupihvi	steak served on a board (US: plank steak) FINNISH
lansirannikon salaati	seafood salad FINNISH
lantern flounder	flat fish of the flounder family
lanttu	swede; Swedish turnip FINNISH
lanyĬ	truffles CZECH
lapa	shoulder FINNISH
lapereau	young rabbit FRENCH
lapin	fully grown, adult rabbit FRENCH
lapskaus	boiled, salt meat, potatoes, onions and other vegetables (cf lobscouse) NORWEGIAN
lapskojs	casserole of potatoes, meat and vegetables (cf lobscouse) SWEDISH
lăptucă	lettuce ROMANIAN
lapwing	see plover
laranja	orange PORTUGUESE
lard	the inside fat of a pig melted down, freed of any fibrous material, and stored
lard	bacon FRENCH
larding	inserting small strips of bacon fat (lardoons) into the flesh of game birds before roasting to prevent drying out
lardo	bacon ITALIAN
lardons	lardoons FRENCH

lardoons	strips of fat cut into varying shapes and thicknesses
lardy cake	cake of bread dough, lard, sugar and dried fruit
lark	small, wild bird, seldom eaten today; but once served in pies, roasted, grilled or set in aspic
larron, le	cow's milk cheese made from skimmed milk FRENCH
lasagne	thin layers of noodle dough with tomato, sausage meat, ham, white sauce and grated cheese ITALIAN
lasimestarinsilli	pieces of herring fillets marinated in sweetened vinegar with onion, carrot, black and white peppercorns and bay leaves FINNISH
lasinieitis	white yeast bread containing peppercorns and crisp bacon rinds LITHUANIAN
laskiaispulla	bun filled with almond paste and whipped cream FINNISH
lasku	bill; check FINNISH
lassi	nutritious, refreshing and cooling sweet or savoury yoghurt drink INDIAN
lassi meethi	sweet curd drink INDIAN
lassi namkeen	savoury curd drink INDIAN
lassoon	garlic INDIAN
lasten ruokalista	children's menu FINNISH
lath	legume grown for fodder and as a pulse
latholémono	sauce of olive oil and lemon juice GREEK
latkes	traditional dish eaten at the feast of Channukah, made from grated potato mixed with eggs, flour and seasoning JEWISH
latte	milk ITALIAN
Lattich	lettuce GERMAN
lättstekt	underdone SWEDISH
lattuga	lettuce ITALIAN
łatwy i tani piernik	honey cake POLISH
Laubfrösche	'tree frogs'; method of serving large spinach leaves, blanched, stuffed, and served with sauce crème SWISS
Lauch	leek GERMAN
Launceston pie	traditional Cornish pie containing sliced meat and sliced potatoes ENGLISH
launce	*see* sand eel
laurel	bay leaf SPANISH
laurier	bay leaf FRENCH
lauro	bay leaf ITALIAN

lautanen plate FINNISH

lavagante lobster PORTUGUESE

lavallière, à la garnish for fowl and sweetbreads of sautéed truffles, lamb's sweetbreads and small crayfish; garnish for tournedos and noisettes of artichoke bottoms filled with asparagus tips, pommes château and sauce bordelaise FRENCH

lavallière, sauce classical sauce; sauce madère or demi-glace flavoured with game essence, julienne of tarragon and truffle, with cream to thicken FRENCH

lavaret name for white fish found in the deep waters of the Savoy lakes FRENCH

lavender fragrant, spiky-leafed plant from Europe and the Far East

laver edible seaweed found on many of Britain's shores

laver bread laver which is fried and served as a breakfast food; it is popular in Wales WELSH

lavraki method of baking fish with butter GREEK

lax salmon; generally applied to smoked salmon packed in oil SWEDISH, ICELANDIC, NORWEGIAN

laxöring salmon trout SWEDISH

layer cake sponge cake baked in two or three tins, sandwiched together with cream, jam or other filling

layos hare GREEK

lazanki lasagne; thin noodles POLISH

laziale, alla with onions ITALIAN

laziz medium-hot sauce BANGLADESHI

leaf mustard see Chinese celery cabbage, Chinese mustard (greens), Chinese mustard cabbage, Chinese white cabbage, chingensai, gai choy, green in snow, Indian mustard (greens), kai tsoi, mustard cabbage, taisin

leaven originally a piece of dough saved from one batch, refreshed and used to ferment and give rise to the next; today it is any raising agent used in a dough

lebbencs broken pasta HUNGARIAN

Leber liver GERMAN

Leberwurst liver sausage made from pigs' liver, onions and seasonings GERMAN

Lebkuchen small cakes made from honey, treacle, spices, sugar and peel GERMAN

lebre hare PORTUGUESE

leche milk SPANISH

lechefrite	tin placed under spit-roasted food to catch the fat and juices FRENCH
lechón	suckling pig SPANISH
lechuga	lettuce SPANISH
Leckerli	rectangular honey and almond biscuit, sometimes flavoured with Kirsch SWISS
Lecrelet	light pastry from Basel, flavoured with orange or lemon and sweetened with honey SWISS
lecsó	puréed pepper slices, onions and tomatoes, to which eggs are added and scrambled, served with potatoes or rice HUNGARIAN
lecsós borjúmáj rántva	breaded veal liver, garnished with pepper, tomatoes and rice HUNGARIAN
lecsós rostélyos	sirloin steak in lecsó HUNGARIAN
led	ice CZECH
ledvinky	kidneys CZECH
ledvinky veprové	tenderloin CZECH
lee-dah	tongue BM
leek	vegetable from the onion and garlic family, with a mild, distinctive flavour
leem-ow	lime BM
leem-ow ma-nis	orange BM
leem-ow nip-pis	lemon BM
lees	sediment in wine bottle
lefse	thin, eggless pancake NORWEGIAN
lefser	'soft cake'; flat potato and rye bread NORWEGIAN
legeret suppe	cream soup DANISH
legiert	thickened, usually with egg-yolk (sauces or soups) GERMAN
legumbres	vegetables SPANISH
legume	generic name for a group of bi-valved pods enclosing seeds attached along one join (peas, beans, *etc*)
legumes	vegetable ITALIAN, PORTUGUESE
legumina	sweet pudding POLISH
legymsallad	blanched vegetables, served in mayonnaise sauce swedish
lehti pihvi	very thin slice of beef FINNISH
Leicester cheese	also known as Red Leicester, it is a hard, mild, slightly sweet cheese, with an orange-red colour ENGLISH
Leidse kaas	cheese flavoured with cumin seeds DUTCH

leike	cutlet FINNISH
leikkeleet	cold meat FINNISH
leikkelelautane-n	plate of cold meat FINNISH
leipä	bread; loaf FINNISH
Leipziger Allerlei	speciality dish from Leipzig, of diced cooked root vegetables, peas, green beans, asparagus and morels GERMAN
leitão	suckling pig PORTUGUESE
leitão assado	traditional Barradan dish of roast suckling-pig cooked with herbs and spices PORTUGUESE
leite-creme	blancmange PORTUGUESE
leivitetty	breaded FINNISH
leivos	cake; pastry FINNISH
lekach	traditional honey cake eaten at the Jewish New Year JEWISH
lekkerbekje	fried, filleted haddock or plaice DUTCH
lekvár	jam HUNGARIAN
lem-mah	cooking fat BM
lemon	member of the citrus family; too sour to eat raw, it is used in many savoury and sweet dishes
lemon balm	member of the mint family, with green, heart-shaped lemon-scented leaves
lemon butter	sweet spread made with lemon juice
lemon grass	tropical and sub-tropical plant with thick, grass-like leaves which taste and smell strongly of lemons
lemon sole	saltwater flat fish EUROPEAN
lemon verbena	lemon flavoured herb from a woody shrub
lemonade	originally a refreshing drink made from lemons, sugar and water (as home-made lemonade still is), today it more usually refers to a sweet, fizzy, often synthetic-tasting drink in a can or plastic bottle
lemoni	lemon GREEK
lencse	lentils HUNGARIAN
Lende	loin GERMAN
Lendenbraten	roast fillet of pork or beef GERMAN
Lendenstück	fillet of beef (US: tenderloin) GERMAN
lendestuk	sirloin DUTCH
lengua	tongue SPANISH
lenguado	sole, flounder SPANISH
leniwe pierogi	white-cheese dumplings POLISH
lenteja	lentil SPANISH

lenticchia	lentil ITALIAN
lentil	pulse; the small, dried, red, brown or green seed from a variety of leguminous plants
lentilha	lentil PORTUGUESE
lentille	lentil FRENCH
léopold	a meat consommé, thickened with semolina, with added sautéed sorrel and chopped chervil FRENCH
lepiote	parasol mushroom FRENCH
lepre	hare ITALIAN
leprotto	leveret ITALIAN
les choesels	stew containing oxtail, mutton, veal, sheep's trotters, ox kidney, and sweetbreads BELGIAN
leshch	bream RUSSIAN
leshta yahnìya	dish made with lentils BULGARIAN
lesní jahody	wild strawberries CZECH
lesso	boiled; meat or fish stew ITALIAN
lesso rifato	reheated meat ITALIAN
leszcz	bream POLISH
lettstekt	sautéed NORWEGIAN
lettuce	leaf vegetable used raw in salads, stir-fried or braised; many new leaves of different colours and curly habits have lately appeared on the market; the lettuce is supposed to be soporific
lever	liver DANISH, NORWEGIAN, SWEDISH
leveret	young hare
leves	soup HUNGARIAN
levraut	leveret FRENCH
levroux	goat's milk cheese FRENCH
Leyden cheese	semi-hard, pasteurised cow's milk cheese, usually containing cumin and caraway seeds DUTCH
liaison	combination of ingredients which thicken or bind sauces, soups or stews
lički kupus ribanac	alternate layers of sauerkraut and pork chops, cooked in a casserole YUGOSLAVIAN
liarder	to cut foods into thin round slices FRENCH
liba	goose HUNGARIAN
libamáj	goose liver HUNGARIAN
libovy	lean CZECH
liche	tuna-like fish from the deep Mediterranean
licorice	herb used for its roots as a flavouring
lié	thickened FRENCH

liebre	hare SPANISH
Liederkranz cheese	soft whole cow's milk cheese made in Ohio AMERICAN
liégeoise, à la	classical method of cooking with juniper berries FRENCH, BELGIAN
liekitetty	flamed FINNISH
liemi	broth FINNISH
lieu	pollack FRENCH
lièvre	hare FRENCH
lights	lungs of sheep, bullock, calves or pigs, rarely used for human consumption (so called from their low density)
ligueuil	cow's milk cheese from Touraine FRENCH
liha	meat FINNISH
likky pie	traditional Cornish pie containing leeks, green bacon, cream, eggs and milk ENGLISH
lilek	aubergine CZECH
lilleoise, à la	consommé of beef with chopped tarragon and chervil, garnished with chopped roasted almonds and julienne of truffles and mushrooms FRENCH
lima	lime; sweet lime SPANISH
lima bean	fast climbing, short kidney-shaped bean from South America
limande	dab FRENCH
limandelle	saltwater flat fish FRENCH
limão	lemon PORTUGUESE
limãoverde	lime PORTUGUESE
limassade	Provençal name for sauce vinaigrette to accompany snails FRENCH
Limburger cheese	soft, whole cow's milk cheese, full and strong flavoured AUSTRIAN
lime	small, green citrus fruit; with a stronger, sharper flavour than lemon
lime blossom	dried flowers of the lime tree can be infused to make a delicately-flavoured tea
lime water	liquid made of lime and water; often used to soak dried fish BELGIAN, DUTCH, GERMAN
lime, dried	often used in cooking especially in the Middle and Far East
limequat	hybrid citrus fruit with a very sour flavour produced by crossing a lime and kumquat
limón	lemon SPANISH
limone	lemon ITALIAN

limousine, à la	red cabbage in bouillon with bacon fat, garnished with braised chestnuts FRENCH
limpa	a rye bread containing molasses, fennel, candied peel and warm ale SWEDISH
limpet	two types of univalve sea creatures, one common on the Atlantic coast, the other in the Mediterranean
limppu	sweetened rye bread FINNISH
lin	tench POLISH
Lincoln cheese	soft cream cheese from Lincolnshire
Lincolnshire poacher	cheese made from unpasteurised cow's milk in Louth (Lincolnshire); ripe, tangy and packed with savoury flavours
linden	tree with scented flowers which can be infused to make a tea, or flavour honey AMERICAN, EUROPEAN
Lindströmin pihvi	amburger steak, flavoured with pickled beetroot and capers FINNISH
line	protective or decorative covering to the base and sides of a cooking container when baking
ling	sea fish resembling cod
lingon	lingonberry; small cranberry SWEDISH
lingonberry	small, wild cranberry used in purées, compotes and fruit soups
lingua	tongue ITALIAN
língua	tongue PORTUGUESE
língua de vaca	calf's tongue PORTUGUESE
lingua di bue	ox tongue ITALIAN
lingua di castagno	an edible fungus (*literally* the tongue of the chestnut tree) ITALIAN
linguado	sole PORTUGUESE
lingue	ling, an eel-like sea fish FRENCH
linguíça	thin pork sausage flavoured with paprika PORTUGUESE
linguine	flat noodles ITALIAN
link (verb)	to twist the continuous sausage *ex maduna* into individual sausages, often linked in fours
link (noun)	a sausage
linnapaisti	pot roast flavoured with brandy, molasses and marinated sprats FINNISH
linse	lentils; custard pastry DANISH
Linse	lentil GERMAN
linser	small custard tarts SWEDISH
linturuoka	fowl course FINNISH

linze

lentil DUTCH

Linzer Torte

flan with an almond flavoured pastry base filled with strawberry jam, decorated with a pastry lattice

AUSTRIAN

lipeäkala

traditional fish dish known as lye fish, consisting of dried cod or pike FINNISH

lipski sir

a soft cheese YUGOSLAVIAN

Liptauer

cheese spread, traditionally made from fresh ewe's milk cheese mixed with cream, paprika, capers, anchovies, onions or other flavourings, according to taste GERMAN

liptói túrú

a soft, ewe's milk cheese HUNGARIAN

liqueur

alcoholic drink served at the end of the meal; also used in cooking

liquorice

leguminous plant that grows wild in Europe; black liquorice juice is prepared from the roots, and is used to make sweets

lisa

grey mullet SPANISH

lískové ořišky

hazelnuts CZECH

lista dei vini

wine list ITALIAN

listek laurowy

laurel POLISH

liszt

flour HUNGARIAN

lithrini

sea bass GREEK

litorne

fieldfare FRENCH

litovski sup

potato soup LITHUANIAN

lívance

cakes or pancakes made from wheat flour dough

CZECH

livarot

traditional soft cow's milk cheese from Normandy

FRENCH

liver

most popular offal meat, a good source of iron; commonly cooked with bacon and onions

liver fungus

large, rather tasteless edible fungus – the beefsteak fungus AMERICAN

liver sausage

usually made from finely minced pig's liver, pork and flavourings, with a soft spreadable texture

liverwurst

soft sausage, of liver, ground pork, onion and seasoning GERMAN

loach

freshwater fish of the carp family

loaf

bread baked in a particular form, usually of standard weight; also describes other dishes cooked in a loaf tin

loaf cheese

cheeses resembling a cottage loaf

loaf sugar

sugar crystallised en masse in a mould; it retains its shape when turned out

lo-bah	radish BM
lobarro	variety of bass SPANISH
lobio	puréed bean salad from Georgia RUSSIAN
lobscouse	18th-century sailors' stew of meat and vegetables, now considered a Liverpudlian speciality (but *see* Labskaus, labskous, lapskaus, lapskojs) ENGLISH
lobster	several types of sea crustacean – best bought alive and killed at home
lodigiano	type of Parmesan cheese ITALIAN
lody	ice-cream POLISH
loempias	a Dutch-Indonesian dish, now a speciality of Holland, consisting of pancakes containing fried chicken, bean sprouts, chopped celery, chives and roasted pork, moistened with soya sauce and oil, and deep fried DUTCH
loff	white bread NORWEGIAN
løg	onion DANISH
logan	small, round tropical fruit, a member of the lychee family with brittle brown skin and sweet, aromatic, white flesh
loganberry	hybrid fruit produced by crossing a blackberry with a raspberry
lohi	salmon, *see* graavi FINNISH
lohi piirakka	pie stuffed with salmon, rice, hard boiled eggs and dill, served in slices with melted butter FINNISH
loimu lohi	salmon grilled on an open fire FINNISH
loin	joint of lamb, pork or veal – part of the backbone and some of the lower ribs from one side of the animal
löjrom	vendace roe, which may be served on toast with onions and sour cream SWEDISH
lök	onion SWEDISH
løk	onion NORWEGIAN
loksinu su aguonais	national dish of egg noodles with poppy seeds LITHUANIAN
l'ollada	national soup named after the dish in which it is made CATALAN
lollipop	a boiled sweet or toffee on a stick
lombarda	red cabbage SPANISH
lombata	loin ITALIAN
lombo	loin PORTUGUESE
lomo	loin SPANISH

lompe	type of potato pancake NORWEGIAN
lonac	traditional dish of meat, whole spices, dried peppers, and whole vegetables YUGOSLAVIAN
London broil	term for beefsteak AMERICAN
Long Island buck	savoury made with cheddar cheese, beer, egg yolks, paprika and Worcestershire sauce AMERICAN
Long Island duck	the first American domestic duck AMERICAN
longan	an oval-shaped fruit of Asian origin ASIAN
longaniza	lean pork sausage with garlic, wild marjoram and seasoning SPANISH
longchamp	Parisian soup of sorrel and vermicelli cooked in consommé, adding puréed green peas before serving FRENCH
longe	top end of a loin of veal FRENCH
longe de veau	loin of veal, usually braised in red wine with red cabbage FRENCH
lonja	a slice of meat SPANISH
lonza	speciality dish of spiced fillet of pork, cured like ham ITALIAN
lonzo	speciality dish of boned fillet of pork steeped in brine, air dried and eaten raw, cut very thin CORSICAN
lopatka	shoulder POLISH
loquat	like a small, yellow plum, it has sweet, scented, slightly tart orange flesh
lord of the hundreds	sweet, nutty-flavoured cheese made from unpasteurised ewe's milk
lorette	garnish for entrées of chicken croquettes, asparagus tips, and truffle; chicken consommé containing paprika and asparagus tips; corn salad with cooked red beetroot and raw celery; method of serving potatoes of braised red cabbage and pommes fondantes FRENCH
Lorraine	cheese made in the Lorraine region; garnish for meat FRENCH
Lorraine soup	soup made with chicken, veal, almonds and egg yolks SCOTTISH
losos	salmon RUSSIAN
łosós	salmon POLISH
lote	another name for freshwater burbot
lotier	bird's-foot trefoil FRENCH
lotte	lote FRENCH
lotte de mer	anglerfish FRENCH

lotus	member of the waterlily family cultivated for its roots, seeds, leaves and flowers; the roots are used as a vegetable, the seeds have a slightly almond flavour and are often used in Thai cooking THAI
lou trebuc	preserved goose or pork, from the Béarn district FRENCH
Louisberg chicken pie	a regional chicken pie, containing mushrooms, sausage meat balls, and potato balls, covered with stock and puff pastry AMERICAN
louise-bonne	variety of pear FRENCH
Louisiana hot sauce	commercially-made chilli sauce, similar to Tabasco, but thicker AMERICAN
Louisiana rice pudding	rice pudding with meringue topping, from the southern States AMERICAN
Louisiana soup	regional soup made with clear chicken broth, to which chopped okra, crab meat, rice, shrimps or lobster and sweet peppers are added AMERICAN
Louisiana yam nuggets	cooked, mashed, yams balls AMERICAN
louisiane, à la	garnish for fowl or meat, of sweet corn fritters and rice darioles on sautéed sweet potatoes and rounds of fried banana FRENCH
loukanika	Greek sausages GREEK
lou-kenkas	small spicy sausages from the Basque and Bordelais coasts SPANISH
loukoumades	yeasted honey fritters GREEK
loukoumi	version of turkish delight GREEK
lounas	lunch FINNISH
loup de mer	Provençal name for sea bass FRENCH
loup marin	wolf fish FRENCH
louro	bay leaf PORTUGUESE
lovage	sharp, peppery flavoured herb, which tastes a little like celery
lövbiff	thinly sliced beef SWEDISH
love-in-a-mist	*see* nigella
Löwenzahn	young dandelion greens GERMAN
lubina	bass SPANISH
luccio marino	hake ITALIAN
luchon	cow's milk cheese from the Pyrenees FRENCH
lucullus, à la	garnish for fowl and sweetbreads; velouté soup of chicken with puréed calf's brains; consommé of beef FRENCH
luganeghe	pure pork sausages from Romagna NORTHERN ITALIAN

lukànka   pork sausages BULGARIAN

lukewarm   moderately warm, or tepid, liquid

lula   small squid PORTUGUESE

lumaca   snail ITALIAN

lumpfish   large sea fish with a lump-like dorsal fin; source of
                       lumpfish roe (poor man's caviar)

lumpia   egg rolls INDONESIAN

luncheon cheese   variety of brick shaped Gouda cheese

Lunge   lights (lungs of an animal) GERMAN

lungemos   hash of pork lungs and onions NORWEGIAN

lupo di mare   sea perch ITALIAN

lurifakser   pastry-layer slices made of sugar, butter, flour and
                       egg NORWEGIAN

lute   flour and water paste used to seal the lid of a
                       casserole or terrine before cooking; strip of pastry
                       placed around the rim of a pie dish to seal on a
                       pastry lid

lutefisk   dried cod, preserved in a lye of potash - an acquired
                       taste NORWEGIAN

lutfisk   a traditional Christmas dish of fish soaked in wood
                       ash, lime, soda and water until four times its original
                       size, then dried – an acquired taste SWEDISH

luting paste   paste used to seal the lid of a terrine to keep the
                       steam in

luumu   plum FINNISH

luuydin   bone marrow FINNISH

lychee   stone fruit, about the size of a plum, which grows in
                       bunches, has a hard, bumpy skin and sweet, aromatic,
                       juicy white flesh

lye   solution of water alkalised by lixivation (leaching) of
                       vegetable or wood ashes; used for the preservation of
                       fish SCANDINAVIAN, FINNISH

Lymeswold   the first soft blue British cheese, made in Somerset,
                       but now deceased ENGLISH

lyonnaise, à la   garnish from the Lyonnais region of onions fried in
                       butter, white wine and wine vinegar and demi-glace
                       and sliced potatoes tossed in butter are mixed with
                       fried onions FRENCH

lyonnaise, sauce   classical sauce of chopped onions fried in butter,
                       white wine and wine vinegar, and demi-glace FRENCH

lyutenìtsa   salad of green vegetables, garlic and hot peppers,
                       which are boiled, drained, chopped and seasoned
                       with vinegar BULGARIAN

M

maa-artisokka	Jerusalem artichoke FINNISH
maapähkinä	peanut FINNISH
maas, mahns	lamb INDIAN
maatjes	cured herring DUTCH
maçã	apple PORTUGUESE
macadamia nut	large nut native to Australia, similar to hazel AUSTRALIAN
maçapão	marzipan; almond macaroon PORTUGUESE
macaroni	English name for maccheroni, a tube-shaped pasta
macaronischoteltje	macaroni with ham and cheese DUTCH
macaróny	macaroni CZECH
macaróny s masem	macaroni with meat CZECH
macaroon	small cake made from ground almonds, sugar and egg whites, baked on rice paper
macarrão	macaroni PORTUGUESE
macarrones	macaroni SPANISH
macaxeira	cassava root PORTUGUESE
maccheroni	macaroni ITALIAN
macdonald	meat consommé garnished with lamb's brains, chopped cucumber and small ravioli FRENCH
mace	outer covering of nutmeg with a stronger flavour
macédoine	mixture of raw or cooked fruit or vegetables FRENCH
macedonia di frutta	fruit salad ITALIAN
macerating	softening and flavouring raw or dried foods by soaking in a liquid
macérer	to soften by soaking FRENCH
maceron	the herb alexander FRENCH
mâche	corn salad FRENCH
machengo	ewe's milk cheese with a strong flavour and a firm texture SPANISH
machi, macchli	fish INDIAN
mackerel	fairly small, round, oily sea fish with a distinctive flavour
mâconnaise, à la	meat dish flavoured with red wine FRENCH
macreuse	widgeon; cut of beef, part of the neck and shoulder FRENCH

macrobiotic	style of eating adopted by followers of the Zen sect of Japanese Buddhism taking into account spiritual and physical needs; the major foods are whole grain cereals and vegetables – fruit and meat are excluded
made	burbot FINNISH
madeira	wine fortified with cane spirit, produced on the island of Madeira MADEIRAN
madeira cake	rich lemon-flavoured sponge cake, served in Victorian times with a glass of madeira
madeleine	small fancy cake baked in a dariole mould, coated with jam and coconut and often decorated with glacé cherries and angelica FRENCH
madeleine, à la	garnish for meat of artichoke bottoms of sauce soubise and puréed haricot beans in tartlets; a crayfish sauce garnish for fish; a cake invented by the pastrycook Avice; a small English sponge cake FRENCH
madère, au	mixture of demi-glace and madeira wine; fruit pie FRENCH
madère, sauce	classical sauce, made with madeira wine FRENCH
ma-doo	honey BM
Madras	hot curry, south Indian style INDIAN
madrileña	chorizo sausage, tomatoes and paprika SPANISH
madrilena, salsa a la	sauce for roast chicken, from Madrid SPANISH
madrilène, à la	flavoured with tomato, particularly a tomato-flavoured chicken consommé, usually served chilled FRENCH
madrileno	a dish traditional to Madrid SPANISH
madrzydi	fried cheese pastry POLISH
maślaki	boletus mushrooms POLISH
Maggi	proprietary name of a hydrolysed vegetable protein preparation
maggiorana	sweet marjoram ITALIAN
magistères	nourishing soup containing root vegetables, fowl and beef, reduced so that the essence remains, strained and served, often to invalids FRENCH
máglyarakás	apple and jam pudding HUNGARIAN
magnesium	naturally occurring mineral found in whole grain cereals, nuts and soya beans
magnum	wine bottle equivalent to two normal-sized wine bottles (1.5l)
magok	nuts HUNGARIAN

magro	lean; dish without meat ITALIAN
magyar gulyásleves	traditional gulyás soup HUNGARIAN
magyar halleves	traditional fish soup HUNGARIAN
magyaros csirkeaprólék leves	chicken giblets soup with mushrooms, diced potatoes pepper rings and tomatoes HUNGARIAN
magyaros ízelítö	a choice of salami, sausages, goose liver, eggs and green pepper HUNGARIAN
mahallebi	rose cream, a moulded, chilled, ground rice pudding flavoured with rose water and served with cinnamon or chopped nuts TURKISH
mahleb	spice made from ground cherry kernels, used in baking GREEK
Mahlzeit	meal GERMAN
maia	soured milk BALKAN
maiale	pork ITALIAN
maida	equivalent of flour INDIAN
maidenhair fern	houseplant, sometimes used to make a flavoured syrup called capillaire
maid of honour	small tartlet with a filling made from flavoured milk curds ENGLISH
maigre	without meat; large sea fish found in European waters FRENCH
maillot, à la	garnish for meat containing carrot and turnip cooked in broth, mixed with French beans tossed in butter FRENCH
Mainauer Käse	cow's milk cream cheese GERMAN
maintenon, à la	veal cutlets stuffed with sliced mushrooms, puréed onions and cream, sautéed and served with truffle sauce; rich sauce containing mushrooms, served with veal or lamb FRENCH
Mainzer Handkäse	soft, sour-milk cheese AUSTRIAN
Mainzer Käse	soft, sour-milk cheese from the Western Province
maionese	mayonnaise ITALIAN, PORTUGUESE
maioneza	mayonnaise GREEK
Mais	maize GERMAN
maēs	sweet corn; maize FRENCH
maiskolbe	corn on the cob NORWEGIAN
maiskolf	corn on the cob DUTCH
maison	'house'; dishes on a menu cooked in the style of a particular restaurant FRENCH
maissi	maize FINNISH

maissintähkä	corn on the cob FINNISH
maito	milk FINNISH
maître d'hôtel, maître d'	person in charge of the dining room or restaurant ; simply prepared dishes garnished with maître d'hôtel butter – sauce made with butter, parsley, lemon juice and cayenne pepper FRENCH
maíz	maize SPANISH
maize	corn kernels INDIAN
máj	liver HUNGARIAN
majeranek	mayonnaise POLISH
majoneesi	mayonnaise FINNISH
majonez zwykły	mayonnaise POLISH
majonéza	mayonnaise CZECH
majonézes kukorica	sweet corn with mayonnaise HUNGARIAN
majonnäs	mayonnaise SWEDISH
Majoran	marjoram GERMAN
majoránna	marjoram HUNGARIAN
majs	maize (US: corn) DANISH, SWEDISH
majs kolbe	corn on the cob DANISH
mak	poppy seed POLISH
mák	poppy seed HUNGARIAN
mąka	flour POLISH
makagigi	almond and honey biscuits POLISH
makai	sweetcorn INDIAN
ma-kan	dinner; to eat BM
ma-kan pag-ee	breakfast BM
makaron	macaroni; noodles POLISH
makaronada	macaroni and meat sauce GREEK
makaroner	macaroni SWEDISH
makaroni	macaroni FINNISH
makaróny se sýrem	macaroni with cheese CZECH
makea	sweet FINNISH
makhani	tandoori chicken cooked in ghee with tomatoes INDIAN
makhanwalla	butter-rich curry INDIAN
makkara	sausage FINNISH
mákos	poppy seeds HUNGARIAN
makový koláć	poppy seed cake CZECH
makowiec	a traditional Christmas roll, sprinkled with poppy seeds before baking POLISH

makreel	mackerel DUTCH
makrel	mackerel DANISH
makrela	mackerel CZECH, POLISH
makrele	mackerel GERMAN
makrell	mackerel NORWEGIAN
makrill	mackerel SWEDISH
makrilli	mackerel FINNISH
makron	macaroon DANISH
Makrone	macaroon GERMAN
maksa	liver FINNISH
Malabar spinach	see basella, Ceylon spinach, Indian spinach
malác	pork; suckling pig HUNGARIAN
malackocsonya	jellied pork HUNGARIAN
malacpecsenye	roast pig HUNGARIAN
malaga	sweet, fortified wine SPANISH
Málaga raisins	large raisins from the muscat grape
malagueta	hot pepper PORTUGUESE
malai	cream INDIAN
mălai	cornmeal bread containing eggs and buttermilk, popular with Romanian Jews ROMANIAN
malaxer	culinary term meaning to knead a substance to soften it FRENCH
Malaya curry	cooked with coconut, ginger and chilli INDIAN
maldive fish	frequently-used dried fish SRI LANKAN
Malibu	alcoholic drink made from a mixture of coconut and rum
malic acid	sharply sour organic acid
maliny	raspberries CZECH, POLISH
malisniki	pancakes filled with a mixture of tvorog and butter RUSSIAN
mallard	the most common species of wild duck, it makes good eating
mallorquina	traditional fish or vegetable soup from Mallorca SPANISH
mallow	flowering plant which grows wild in Europe; the flowers may be dried to make tea, and the leaves can be cooked like spinach
málna	raspberries HUNGARIAN
malt	barley grains are soaked and allowed to germinate, slowly dried and they become malt

maltaise, à la	various garnishes containing the juice of blood oranges FRENCH
maltaise, sauce	classical sauce made from hollandaise or mayonnaise sauce, the juice and some shredded peel of blood oranges FRENCH
måltid	meal DANISH
maltose	crystalline sugar, the main sugar in malt
Malvern pudding	hasty pudding mixture layered with apple purée, lemon peel and sugar ENGLISH
mămăligă	very thick type of porridge ROMANIAN
mamão	papaya PORTUGUESE
mammella	udder ITALIAN
mämmiä	traditional Easter Sunday dessert containing dried orange peel, malt, rye flour and treacle FINNISH
manatee	herb-eating mammal living in tropical coastal water and estuaries; the sea cow
mancelle	game consommé, garnished with cubes of game royale and poached chestnuts FRENCH
manche	cutlet bone FRENCH
manchego	hard sheep's milk cheese from La Mancha SPANISH
Manchester pudding	regional dish made from breadcrumbs, milk, lemon and sugar
manchet bread	14th-century name for a hand-made loaf using the finest wheat flour
manchette	small paper frill which decorates exposed bones on a crown of lamb or pork or on lamb cutlets FRENCH
manchon	petit four shaped like a muff, filled with praline cream and dipped in chopped green almonds; small muff-shaped cake using flaky pastry FRENCH
mandariini	mandarin FINNISH
mandarijntje	mandarin DUTCH
mandarin	small loose-skinned citrus fruit
mandarin	tangerine; an easy-peel or Christmas orange HUNGARIAN
Mandarin Napoleon	liqueur made from tangerines macerated in aged Cognac BELGIUM
Mandarine	mandarin GERMAN
mandarino	mandarin ITALIAN
mandarynki	tangerines POLISH
mandel	almond DANISH, NORWEGIAN, SWEDISH
Mandel	almond GERMAN

mandioca	cassava root PORTUGUESE
mandle	almonds CZECH
mandolin	vegetable slicer with one or more metal blades fixed in a frame FRENCH
mandorla	almond ITALIAN
mandula	almond HUNGARIAN
mandulá felfujt	almond soufflé HUNGARIAN
mandulás rétes	almond strudel HUNGARIAN
manestra	pasta, similar to barley GREEK
mangel, mangel wurzel	coarse type of beet grown for winter cattle feed and for human consumption
mange-tout	stringless haricot verts FRENCH
mang-ga	mango BM
mang-gis	refreshing fruit which is white inside, and has a reddish coloured skin BM
mango	large tropical and sub-tropical stone fruit, with a juicy, fibrous, orange flesh and distinctive, delicate flavour
mango powder	dried, raw, green mangoes, with a piquant flavour INDIAN
mango, dried	available in slices, it is used as flavouring in curries, fruit salads, cakes or as a snack
Mangold	white beet; Swiss chard GERMAN
mangosteen	tropical fruit with a deep purple, fibrous outer shell enclosing juicy segments of creamy-white flesh
Manhattan clam chowder	traditional clam soup with tomatoes AMERICAN
maní	peanut SPANISH
manicamp	cow's milk cheese from Picardy FRENCH
manicotti	home-made cappelletti ITALIAN
manier	to work a mixture by hand FRENCH
manioc	tropical euphorgeaceous plan of the *Manikot* genus, especially the cultivated American *M. esculenta* (bitter cassava) and *M. dulcis* (sweet cassava) from whose roots is made a starchy food eaten in the tropics; also the source of tapioca; cassava
manitas de cerdo rehogadas	pig's trotters which are boiled, boned, dipped in egg and breadcrumbs and fried SPANISH
manjar de coco	coconut blancmange topped with plum syrup PORTUGUESE
manjericão	basil PORTUGUESE
manna kasza	cream of wheat POLISH
mannavelli	semolina gruel FINNISH

manos de ternera	calves' feet SPANISH
manouri	sweet soft cheese which hardens as it matures; when fresh, it is eaten with honey GREEK
manqué	'failed'; a type of sponge cake so named because the pastry-cook intended to make a savoy cake but it went wrong FRENCH
mansikka	strawberries FINNISH
man-tay-ga	butter BM
mantecado	small butter cake; custard ice-cream SPANISH
manteche	flask-shaped cheese with a small amount of butter sealed inside ITALIAN
manteiga	butter PORTUGUESE
manteli	almond FINNISH
mantequilla	butter SPANISH
manti	minced meat and onion pasty; when cooked, chicken broth is poured over and is absorbed GREEK
mantis shrimp	crustacean similar in appearance to the praying mantis, sharing the habitat of the shrimp; it is prepared in the same way as shrimp and prawn
Manx broth	traditional soup made with shin of beef, ham, cabbage, turnip, carrot and leeks MANX
manzana	apple SPANISH
manzo	beef ITALIAN
maple	large tree which produces natural syrup CANADIAN
maple sugar	sap of various species of maple tree with a characteristic flavour
maple syrup	very sweet syrup made from maple sugar, with a distinctive but delicate flavour
maquée	soft cow's milk cheese BELGIAN
maquereau	mackerel FRENCH
maracujá	passion fruit PORTUGUESE
maraîchère, à la	garnish for roast or braised meats of braised onions, stuffed cucumber, salsify and artichokes, with pommes château; sautéed veal cutlets served with salsify and Brussels sprouts FRENCH
maräng	meringue SWEDISH
marängsviss	meringue with whipped cream and chocolate sauce SWEDISH
marasca	morello cherry ITALIAN
Maraschino	bitter-sweet, water-white liqueur made from maraschino cherries and their crushed kernels
marble cake	cake with marble-like appearance when cut

marc course spirit, produced from the remains of the grapes after they are pressed to make wine FRENCH

marc de raisin semi-hard cheese with a crust of grape skins and pips FRENCH

marcassin young wild boar FRENCH

marchand de vin, sauce popular sauce for beef, similar to bordelaise AMERICAN

marchew carrots POLISH

marchpane an archaic word for marzipan

marcipán marzipan CZECH

maréchale, à la garnish for entrées of truffles and asparagus tips; garnish for meats of chicken quenelles with chopped truffles in sauce Italienne, cocks' combs and demi-glace with Madeira; escalopes cooked in egg and breadcrumbs and garnished as above FRENCH

marée all sea food sold at a fish market FRENCH

marena freshwater fish of the salmon family

marengo dish named after the Battle of Marengo, comprising chicken sautéed in oil, flavoured with tomato, garlic and brandy, garnished with crayfish and fried eggs ITALIAN

marengs meringue NORWEGIAN

marenki meringue FINNISH

marennes oysters from Marennes FRENCH

marette special bread made in Marseilles for use in bouillabaisse FRENCH

märg marrow SWEDISH

margarine yellow fat substitute for butter, containing polyunsaturated fat

marguéry, à la garnish for tournedos of artichoke hearts filled with truffles à la crème, morels, cocks' combs, and cocks' kidneys FRENCH

marguéry, sauce classical sauce, made from sauce hollandaise flavoured with fish essence and oyster purée FRENCH

maribo large round cheese DANISH

marides whitebait; small smelts GREEK

Marie Stuart garnish for entrées of tartlets containing purée of turnips or onions covered in marrow bone fat and demi-glace FRENCH

Marie-Jeanne, à la garnish for noisettes and tournedos of tartlets containing mushroom purée and a slice of truffle FRENCH

Marie-Louise, à la   garnish for entrées of artichoke bottoms filled with mushroom purée covered with grated cheese and gratinéed; consommé of chicken with royale and peas FRENCH

marignan   Parisian cake, a baked savarin soaked in liqueur-flavoured syrup covered in meringue FRENCH

marigny, à la   garnish for entrées of tartlets filled with green peas and French beans, and pommes fondantes; a sauce of demi-glace with tomato purée, mushroom stock and white wine, mushrooms and stoned olives; chicken consommé with chicken quenelles, chopped cucumber and chervil FRENCH

marigold   cultivated in mediaeval monastery gardens, the bright orange flowers were used in possets, broths and drinks, and may be used in salads or as an alternative to saffron in rice dishes

Marille   apricot GERMAN

marinade (n)   the liquid in which food is marinaded

marinade, marinate (v)   to steep raw meat, game, poultry or fish in oil, wine or vinegar and seasoning to tenderise and give flavour

marinado   marinated PORTUGUESE

marinara, alla   sauce of tomatoes, olives, garlic, clams and mussels ITALIAN

marinato   marinate ITALIAN

mariné   marinated; pickled FRENCH

Marinebraten   fillet steak on onions, carrot and celeriac AUSTRIAN

marinera, a la   served with mussels, onions, tomatoes, herbs and wine SPANISH

marinerad   marinated SWEDISH

marineret   marinated DANISH

marineretsild   marinated herring DANISH

marinert   marinated NORWEGIAN

marinheira, à   with white wine, onions, parsley and sometimes tomatoes PORTUGUESE

marinière, à la   fish or shell fish in white wine; garnish for fish; sauce made from sauce bercy and mussel stock FRENCH

mariniert   marinated; pickled GERMAN

marinoitu   marinated FINNISH

marinovaný   marinated CZECH

marinovannye   marinated or pickled RUSSIAN

marisco	seafood PORTUGUESE, SPANISH
mariscos	mussels SPANISH
maritozzo	soft roll ITALIAN
marja	berry FINNISH
marjolaine	marjoram FRENCH
marjoram	small-leaved herb, with a spicy, slightly bitter, nutmeg-like flavour
Mark	bone marrow GERMAN
marketspeak	adjectives chosen to woo a prospective buyer into purchasing a foodstuff, including: Auntie's, baby, bitesize, chef's choice, chef's kitchen, creamy, crispy, crunchy, crusty, dark, encrusted, enrobed, farmhouse, Farmer's wife, free range, fun size, golden, golden brown, Granny's, healthy, Home Farm, homemade, honeydew, luscious, Milkmaid, Mother's, mouthwatering, nourishing, nugget, nutty, platter, rich, smooth, traditional, velvet – often demonstrating a triumph of hope over experience
Marlborough pie	Massachusetts speciality containing apple, lemon juice, sugar and eggs AMERICAN
marling	old English name for whiting ENGLISH
marly	chicken consommé with julienne of leek, celery, chicken, shredded lettuce, chopped chervil and croûtons, sprinkled with Parmesan FRENCH
marmalade	traditional breakfast preserve made from Seville oranges, though it may be made from other citrus fruits
marmelaati, marmeladi	marmalade FINNISH
marmelad	marmalade SWEDISH
marmelada	quince paste PORTUGUESE
marmeláda	jam CZECH
marmelade	name in most European countries for thick jam made from various types of fruit; French name for thick fruit purée FRENCH
marmellata	jam ITALIAN
marmite	metal or earthenware pot used for long slow cooking of casseroles; clear, strong, savoury broth; yeast and vegetable extract used as a drink, on bread and for flavouring soups and stews FRENCH
Marmite™	British trademark for a yeast and vegetable extract spread; the name is derived from the French cooking pot as illustrated on the label

marmolada — jam POLISH

marmot — cat-sized edible rodent of the Alps and Pyrenees, meatiest before hibernation, marinated to reduce its musky flavour

marmotte — marmot FRENCH

maroilles — semi-hard cheese made from unskimmed cow's milk, slightly salted and fermented FRENCH

maroilles gris, le — rindless cow's milk cheese; of the maroilles type FRENCH

marokánky — macaroons CZECH

Marone — chestnut GERMAN

marquer — to prepare foods before cooking FRENCH

marquise, à la — garnish for noisettes and tournedos containing calf's marrow, asparagus tips, julienne of truffles and sauce suprême; sauce hollandaise with caviar; variety of pear; consommé of beef with celery and chicken quenelles, beef marrow, and chopped hazelnuts FRENCH

marron — chestnut FRENCH

marrone — chestnut ITALIAN

marrons glacés — chestnuts in syrup, served as a dessert or as decoration, beaten into a meringue mixture or blended with cream as a dessert FRENCH

marrow, vegetable marrow — popular summer squash; allowed to grow quite large, it may be braised, cooked with other vegetables or stuffed with mince

marrow bone — a bone containing edible marrow (the fatty network of connective tissue found in bones)

marrow fat, marrow pea — large variety of pale green pea, the principle of mushy peas

marrow (squash) — any of several oblong squashes with a hard, smooth rind, especially the vegetable marrow AMERICAN

marsala — fortified wine, a blend of local wines, brandy and unfermented grape juice SICILIAN

marseillaise — garnish for noisettes and tournedos of stuffed olives with anchovy fillets in hollowed tomatoes, potato chips, and sauce provençale; mayonnaise mixed with puréed sea-urchins FRENCH

marsepein — marzipan DUTCH

marshmallow — sweetmeat with a spongy elastic texture, which may be tinted pale colours, usually cut into cubes and rolled in icing sugar

marsipan	marzipan SWEDISH
marsouin	porpoise FRENCH
mártások	sauces HUNGARIAN
maruzze	shell-shaped pasta ITALIAN
Maryland	served with a butter and cream sauce often containing wine
marynowane	marinated POLISH
marzipan	firm paste of ground almonds, sugar and egg whites
masło	butter POLISH
masa	dough SPANISH
masala	cooked in a spice mixture INDIAN
mascarpone	rich unsalted cow's milk cream cheese; eaten fresh, often used to make cakes and desserts ITALIAN
mascotte	garnish for fowl or meat of artichoke bottoms, pommes cocotte and truffles; sauce of meat juice and white wine; cake using mocha butter cream and roast hazelnuts FRENCH
mash	mixture of mashed malt, grains and hot water from which malt is extracted in brewing; mashed potatoes, as in sausage and mash
mashing	crushing or pounding; Northern England – brewing tea
mashlum bannock	bannock made from mixed flours SCOTTISH
masking	covering cooked meat or a similar dish with savoury jelly, glaze or sauce; coating the inside of a mould with jelly
maso nu grilu	grilled meat CZECH
masoor	type of lentil, available whole or split INDIAN
masoor dal	split red lentils INDIAN
massala	a mixture of spices cooked with a dish INDIAN
massa	dough; pastry; pasta; all types of noodles PORTUGUESE
massa	cornmeal MEXICAN
mass-ah	to cook BM
massena quail	a partridge AMERICAN
masséna, à la	garnish for tournedos and noisettes of artichoke bottoms with sauce périgueux and slices of poached marrow bone fat or truffle FRENCH
massepain	marzipan FRENCH
massillons	tartlet-shaped petit four made from marzipan FRENCH
mas-tad; sa-sa-wee	mustard BM
Mastente	fattened duckling GERMAN

Masthühn	pullet GERMAN
Masthühnchen	broiler; spring chicken GERMAN
mastic	sticky resinous substance obtained from a Mediterranean plant used as a flavouring in some Greek dishes and as an ingredient in Turkish delight
mastiha	mastic GREEK
matambre	rolled beef stuffed with vegetables SPANISH
matar, matter	green peas INDIAN
maté	*see* yerba maté SOUTH AMERICAN
mateenmäti	skinned, mashed burbot roe FINNISH
matefaim	coarse pancake FRENCH
matelote	rich, well seasoned fish stew containing red or white wine FRENCH
matelote, sauce	classical sauce of reduced fish stock, demi-glace, butter and a dusting of cayenne FRENCH
mäti	fresh roe FINNISH
matignon	garnish of fondue of root vegetables and celery FRENCH
Matjesheringe	young salted herrings GERMAN
matjessill	marinated herring fillets SWEDISH
Matrosenbrot	sandwich containing chopped boiled eggs, anchovies and seasoning GERMAN
mattar dal	split peas INDIAN
mattar paneer	peas and cheese INDIAN
matzo	unleavened bread, a large, brittle, very thin biscuit which can be crushed to make matzo meal JEWISH
maubeche	sandpiper FRENCH
Maulbeere	mulberry GERMAN
Maultaschen	ravioli dish, traditionally eaten in Wurtemburg on Good Friday GERMAN
mauste	spice; condiment FINNISH
mauviette	lark FRENCH
may bowl	wine cup of German origin
mayieritsa	traditional Easter soup made from odd bits and pieces left from the lamb to be roasted later in the day GREEK
mayonesa	mayonnaise SPANISH
mayonnaise	rich thick sauce, an emulsion of oil and vinegar, combined with egg yolks and flavourings, which forms the basis of many other sauces FRENCH

mazagran	tartlet made from pommes duchesse filled with salpicon; cold coffee served in a glass FRENCH
mazanotz	traditional Easter cake made from yeast, flour, sugar, butter, egg yolks, sultanas, almonds and lemon CZECH
mazapán	marzipan; almond paste SPANISH
mazarin	elaborate round cake, hollowed and filled with crystallised fruit, syrup and kirsch-flavoured apricot jam FRENCH
mazarine, à la	garnish for entrées of vegetable-stuffed artichoke bottoms; garnish for fish of tartlets filled with diced truffles, and shrimps in shrimp sauce FRENCH
mazurek	square almond-flavoured cake POLISH
mazurek pomaranczowy	mazurek with oranges POLISH
mazurki	sweetmeat of raisins, almonds, walnuts, figs, prunes, candied fruit and flour RUSSIAN
mazzancolle	variety of very large prawn ITALIAN
mead	old-fashioned drink of honey fermented with hops or yeast; spices or wild flowers were added for flavouring
meadow cress	free growing European plant with peppery leaves
meadow-sweet	wild plant; the leaves can be chopped and used in soups
meal	edible parts of any grain that has been milled or ground to a powder; generally coarser than flour
mealie	maize or corn SOUTH AFRICAN
mealy pudding	suet and oatmeal, onion-flavoured pudding, possibly stuffed into skins, served with grilled sausages, bacon or herring
mearns quail	lighter relative of the massena quail AMERICAN
meat	in particular the flesh of the ox (beef), pig (pork), and sheep (lamb or mutton); part of the human diet since ancient times
meat balls	small round balls of minced meat
meat extract	produced by skimming minced, boiled meat, filtering it and reducing it to a concentrated liquid
meat loaf	minced meat mixture baked in a loaf tin
meaty fuggan	Cornish dish of dough made with water, flour, salt and lard or suet, made into a pastry case
Mecklenburger Bratwürst	sausage from Mecklenburg GERMAN
med	honey CZECH
medaglione	round fillet of beef or veal ITALIAN

médaillon	small round or oval pieces of meat FRENCH
medalhão	medallion PORTUGUESE
medalion	small, round or oval cut of veal POLISH
medaljonger	fritters or médaillons SWEDISH
medg	whey IRISH
médicis, à la	garnish for tournedos and noisettes of artichoke bottoms filled with vegetables, pommes noisette and sauce choron; sauce béarnaise flavoured with tomato purée and red wine; consommé of beef thickened with tapioca, garnished with puréed carrots, sorrel and peas FRENCH
medisterkake	hamburger steak made of pork NORWEGIAN
medisterkaker	fried meat cakes NORWEGIAN
medisterpølse	sausages DANISH
medlar	sharp-flavoured brown fruit resembling an apple
Médoc	region of France famous for its red Bordeaux wines FRENCH
medronho	arbutus berry PORTUGUESE
medved	bear RUSSIAN
mee kook	honey cake ESTONIAN
mee-num	drink BM
Meerrettich	horseradish GERMAN
meetvursti	kind of salami FINNISH
meggy	morello HUNGARIAN
megrim	flat fish of the flounder family
Mehl	flour GERMAN
Mehlnockerl	small dumpling GERMAN
Mehlsuppe	brown flour soup GERMAN
mehu	juice FINNISH
mehukeitto	dessert of berry or fruit juice, thickened with potato flour FINNISH
meia desfeita	poached dried cod fried with chickpeas, onions and vinegar, topped with hard-boiled eggs and chopped garlic PORTUGUESE
meikaas	creamy cheese with a high fat content DUTCH
mejillón	mussel SPANISH
mejorana	sweet marjoram SPANISH
mejram	marjoram SWEDISH
mel	flour NORWEGIAN
mel	honey PORTUGUESE
mela	apple ITALIAN

melachrino	traditional spiced cake eaten at Easter and other festivals GREEK
melacotogna	quince ITALIAN
melancia	watermelon PORTUGUESE
melanzana	aubergine ITALIAN
melão	melon, usually honeydew PORTUGUESE
melaza	treacle; molasses SPANISH
melba	ice-cream with fruit POLISH
melba sauce	sweet, fresh raspberries sauce, served with fruit sundaes and similar desserts; garnish for small cuts of meat FRENCH
Melba toast	light, crisp toast; bread is cut into thin slices and toasted very slowly (named after the Australian operatic soprano Dame Nellie Melba 1861–1931)
melboller	choux pastry balls used to garnish soup DANISH
Melbury cheese	mild, white mould-ripened, loaf-shaped cheese ENGLISH
meli	honey GREEK
melilot	rare herb, a member of the clove family, used in stuffing and to flavour home-made wines
melisa	aubergine (US:eggplant) TURKISH
melitzanes	aubergine (US:eggplant) GREEK
mellemsteg	medium (done) DANISH
melocotón	peach SPANISH
meloen	melon DUTCH
melomakarona	see finikia
melon	fruits with perfumed, sweet, juicy flesh
melon de malabar	Siamese pumpkin FRENCH
melone	melon ITALIAN
Melone	GERMAN
meloni	melon FINNISH
meloun	melon; watermelon CZECH
melt	spleen of certain animals, classified as offal
melting	converting a solid into a liquid by applying heat
melwel	old name for hake ENGLISH
membrillo	quince SPANISH
men-dik-eye	melon BM
menestra	boiled green vegetable soup SPANISH
menestra de legumbres frescas	a vegetable and egg dish SPANISH
menta	mint HUNGARIAN, ITALIAN, SPANISH
menthe	mint FRENCH

mentonnaise, à la method of cooking foods using garlic, tomatoes and black olives; garnish of chard stuffed with duxelles, artichoke bottoms filled with potato balls and meat gravy; garnish of sliced courgettes stuffed with rice and tomato purée FRENCH

Menü meal at a set price GERMAN

menu van de dag set menu DUTCH

menudillos giblets SPANISH

menudos gitanos 'gypsy tripe', a tripe dish from Andaluz SPANISH

mérce sauce LATVIAN

mercedes, à la garnish for meat of grilled tomatoes and mushrooms, braised lettuce, potato croquettes and sauce madère; chicken or beef consommé with sherry, garnished with cocks' combs and cocks' kidneys FRENCH

merengue meringue PORTUGUESE, SPANISH

merguez spicy goat or mutton sausage

meriantura sole FINNISH

merienda snack SPANISH

merimiespihvi sliced beef, onions and potatoes, braised in beer
                                                              FINNISH

meringa meringue ITALIAN

Meringe(l) meringue GERMAN

meringue egg whites are whisked and sugar is folded in to make a sweet, light mixture which is dried in a very low oven so it becomes crisp and firm FRENCH

merlan Provençal name for hake; whiting FRENCH

merlango whiting SPANISH

merlano whiting ITALIAN

merlin local name for Washington navel orange, introduced to the island by a British Consul called Merlin

merluche dried hake FRENCH

merluza hake SPANISH

merluzzo cod; haddock; whiting ITALIAN

mermelada jam SPANISH

mero red grouper PORTUGUESE

mérou sea fish with firm white flesh FRENCH

merrythought forked bone between the neck and breast of chicken and turkey, usually known as a wishbone or furcula

meruňkové knedlíky apricot dumplings made from sweet dough filled with fruit, boiled and served with sugar and sour cream CZECH

meruňky	apricots CZECH
merveille	a pastry FRENCH
mescal	alcoholic drink similar to tequila, made from the Maguey or American sloe MEXICAN, SOUTH AMERICAN
mesentery	a fold of the peritoneum attached to part of the intestine in mammals
mesimarja	Arctic raspberry FINNISH
mesost	cow's milk whey cheese SWEDISH
mesquite	leguminous tree grown for its pods, added to barbecue fuel when cooking fish to impart a potent flavour NORTH AMERICAN
messicani	veal scallops rolled around a meat, cheese or herb stuffing ITALIAN
messine	petite marmite consommé garnished with small poached sausages and cabbage rolls FRENCH
messmör	soft whey cheese SWEDISH
metabolism	the process by which the body converts the nutritive value of food to supply its needs
methi	intoxication GREEK
methi	fenugreek seed INDIAN
méthode	Bayonne name for confit de porc FRENCH
mets	any food prepared for eating FRENCH
metsästäjänleike	veal scallop with mushroom sauce FINNISH
metso	capercaillie; wood-grouse FINNISH
metternich	pheasant consommé garnished with artichoke royale and julienne of pheasant FRENCH
metton	cow's milk cheese from the Franche-Comté FRENCH
Mettwürst	'spreading sausage'; smoked sausage made from pork and spices GERMAN
meunière, à la	food cooked in butter, seasoned with salt, pepper and lemon juice and garnished with parsley FRENCH
mexerica	tangerine PORTUGUESE
mexicaine, à la	garnish for meat of grilled mushrooms, sweet peppers, tomatoes and aubergines served with tomato-flavoured meat gravy; mayonnaise flavoured with anchovy essences and garnished with red and green peppers FRENCH
Mexican saffron	plant with large orange flowers; the stigmas make an inferior substitute for saffron
mexilhão	mussel PORTUGUESE
méz	honey HUNGARIAN
mezclado	mixed SPANISH

mezes	hors d'oeuvres GREEK
mézes csók	'honey kisses'; a type of honey biscuit HUNGARIAN
mezzaluna	a two-handled crescent-shaped chopping blade ITALIAN
mięso	meat POLISH
mięta	peppermint POLISH
miala	brains GREEK
míchaný	mixed; assorted CZECH
míchaná vejce	scrambled eggs CZECH
míchaná zmrzlina	mixed ice cream CZECH
michihili	*see* bok choy, Chinese leaves, headless Chinese cabbage, pe-tsai, wong bok
micishja, la	method of preparing young goat; strips of meat are slightly salted and dried CORSICAN
microwave cooking	convenient and economical way to heat, thaw and cook food; some foods are not suitable for microwave cooking
microwave thermometer	useful when cooking meat in the microwave; it is not equipped with a temperature probe
microwaves	electrical energy used to cook food which makes the molecules vibrate so rapidly they produce intense heat which cooks the food
middag	dinner NORWEGIAN, SWEDISH
midia	mussels GREEK
midollo	marrow ITALIAN
midye	mussels TURKISH
mie-de-pain	fresh breadcrumbs rubbed through a coarse sieve, used with eggs for coating fish or meat FRENCH
miel	honey FRENCH, SPANISH
miele	honey ITALIAN
Miesmuschel	mussel GERMAN
mieszane	mixed POLISH
miga	'crumb'; large Andalusian pancake often eaten for Sunday lunch with white grapes SPANISH
migas	mediaeval dish of bread soaked in milk and fried; an Andalusian garlic soup SPANISH
migas	meat or fish fried in olive oil with onions and garlic and thickened with bread PORTUGUESE
migdały	almonds POLISH
migliaccini	small versions of migliaccio ITALIAN
migliaccio	bread-like cake made from chestnut flour sprinkled with pignoli ITALIAN

migliassis	chestnut flour cake baked on chestnut leaves CORSICAN
mignardise	various small, dainty made-up dishes FRENCH
mignon	small and dainty; often describes small, tender portions of meat FRENCH
mignonette	coarsely ground white pepper FRENCH
mignot	soft cow's milk cheese from Calvados; dry biscuit from Paris FRENCH
mihaliç	soft cheese TURKISH
mijo	millet SPANISH
mijoter	to cook gently over low heat; to simmer FRENCH
mikado, á la	garnish for tournedos and noisettes of fried tomatoes, Chinese artichokes and sauce provençale; garnish for escalopes or chicken of small mounds of curried rice or tartlets filled with bean shoots and cream FRENCH
milanais	cake made like a génoise, flavoured with anisette liquor FRENCH
milanais, à la	garnish for escalopes of julienne of tongue, mushrooms, truffles and ham in spaghetti or macaroni with a little tomato sauce, grated cheese and butter; sauce allemande mixed with tomato purée, tomatoes and pignoli; demi-glace mixed with tomato purée and meat glaze, flavoured with garlic; method of preparing risotto; dishes cooked à la milanaise are usually dipped in egg, breadcrumbs and Parmesan and fried FRENCH
milanesa	with cheese, generally baked SPANISH
milanese	Milanese-style cooking; breaded ITALIAN
Milch	milk GERMAN
milchig	dish containing a dairy product JEWISH
mil-folhas	flaky pastry with cream filling PORTUGUESE
milho doce	sweet-corn PORTUGUESE
milho frito	a Madeiran dish of fried maize PORTUGUESE
milieu de tendron	cut of beef, comprising part of the brisket FRENCH
milk	usually applies to cow's milk, it can be used fresh and to make dairy products; in some countries goats and ewes provide an important source of milk and it can also be obtained from mares, buffaloes and camels; soya milk is becoming increasingly popular as a substitute

milk pudding	grains such as rice, tapioca or sago cooked in milk and served hot or cold, enriched with cream or eggs, flavoured with dried fruit or spices or given a caramel topping
milk shake	refreshing drink of milk whisked with a flavouring, served chilled, possibly with a scoop of ice cream
milk substitutes	various powdered substitutes are available
Milke	sweetbread GERMAN
milkweed	group of plants whose stems contain a milky juice
mill	to reduce foods to a powder or a paste
millas	corn meal polenta or porridge from the Languedoc region FRENCH
millefanti	traditional bread soup ITALIAN
millefeuille	'a thousand leaves'; sweet pastry made from thin layers of puff pastry sandwiched together with jam and whipped cream FRENCH
millefoglie	custard slice ITALIAN
miller's thumb	local name for a bullhead, a freshwater fish ENGLISH
millet	variety of grasses with edible grain, which can be cultivated in arid environments, important in African and Asian diets
millionbøf	minced meat in cream sauce DANISH
millsén	sweet curd cheese IRISH
milosti	thin, lightly-fried pastry sprinkled with sugar BOHEMIAN
milt	fish roe, another name for the spleen
mimosa salad	salad of almost any variety of raw or cooked vegetables
mince	finely ground or chopped meat
mince pie	pastry filled with mincemeat, traditionally served at Christmas, often with cream
mincemeat	dried fruit preserve used to fill mince pies, made from a mixture of currants, sultanas, raisins, mixed peel, almonds, apple, nutmeg and cinnamon, possibly fortified with brandy
mincing	chopping or cutting food into very small pieces
mineola	hybrid citrus fruit, a cross between grapefruit and tangerine
mineral water	water bottled from a natural spring which contains minerals
minerals	chemical substances naturally occurring in food essential to a healthy diet

minestra	thick soup usually made from root vegetables, mushrooms or lentils MALTESE
minestrone	soup of vegetables and pasta, served with Parmesan cheese ITALIAN
minnow	small freshwater fish found in most streams
mint	a common herb; there are a number of varieties, each with there own individual flavour and scent; traditionally served as a sauce with lamb
minute, à la	quickly cooked food FRENCH
min-ya	oil BM
miód pszczeli	honey POLISH
mioleira	brains PORTUGUESE
miolos	brains PORTUGUESE
miques de mais	stiff corn meal and wheat flour dough made into dumplings and eaten in place of bread in the Périgord region FRENCH
mirabeau, à la	garnish for grilled meat made of anchovy fillet, stoned olives, and chopped tarragon with beurre d'anchois; sauce allemande flavoured with garlic FRENCH
mirabelki	yellow plums POLISH
mirabelle	small yellow plum FRENCH
Mirabelle	small yellow plum GERMAN
mirchi, mircha	green or red chilli peppers INDIAN
mirepoix	chopped vegetables with a little ham or bacon, used as a bed on which to braise meat FRENCH
mirette	beef consommé garnished with chicken quenelles and a julienne of lettuce and chervil; method of serving potatoes FRENCH
mirlitons de Rouen	small tarts, a speciality of Rouen, filled with egg custard flavoured with orange flower water FRENCH
miroir, au	eggs baked in the oven or finished under a grill FRENCH
miroton	stew of meat, usually beef, flavoured with onions FRENCH
mirtillo	bilberry ITALIAN
mirto	myrtle ITALIAN
Mischlingkäse	hard cheese from the western highlands Austrian
mish me bamje	traditional dish of stewed lamb or mutton Albanian
miso	thick, salty, nutty-flavoured red bean paste JAPANESE
místní speciality	local speciality CZECH

misto	mixed ITALIAN, PORTUGUESE
mitan	old culinary term meaning middle, now meaning the middle cut of salmon FRENCH
mitili	local Tuscan name for mussels ITALIAN
mititei	pork sausages ROMANIAN
mitonner	to simmer bread in soup or stock FRENCH
mitsuba	Japanese parsley
Mittagessen	midday meal; lunch GERMAN
miúdos de galinha	chicken giblets PORTUGUESE
miêzu putra	traditional stew LATVIAN
mixed grill	informal dish containing a number of grilled meats such as chops, sausages and bacon served with grilled tomatoes, mushrooms and chips
mixed herbs	ready-made mixture of dried herbs, usually containing parsley, sage, thyme, marjoram and tarragon
mixed spice	mixture of sweet-flavoured ground spices, usually cloves, allspice, cinnamon, nutmeg, and ginger
mixto	mixed SPANISH
mizerja	chopped cucumbers with sour cream and dill POLISH
mizithra	mild, soft, moist cheese GREEK
mizuna	salad leaf with peppery flavour
mjukost	soft white cheese made from whey drained from féta SWEDISH
mleczko	sweetbreads POLISH
mleczko waniliowe	vanilla custard pudding POLISH
mleko	milk POLISH
mléko kyselé	sour milk CZECH
mleté maso	minced meat CZECH
młode	young; spring POLISH
mlyàko	milk BULGARIAN
móżdżek	brains POLISH
móżdżek cielęcy	calf's brains POLISH
mocha	strongly-flavoured coffee; cakes flavoured with coffee; a mixture of coffee and chocolate flavourings
mock angels on horseback	tinned smoked oyster or mussel wrapped in streaky bacon and grilled
mock cream	fresh cream substitute used as a substitute for cake fillings
mock goose	country dish made from bullock or ox heart ENGLISH
mock turtle soup	an imitation turtle soup made from a calf's head

mocotós	stewed calves' trotters PORTUGUESE
mode, à la	most often applied to braised beef cooked with veal, carrots and onions FRENCH
moderne, à la	garnish of layered carrot, turnip, green beans and peas FRENCH
moelle	bone marrow FRENCH
moelle, sauce	classical sauce made from sauce bordelaise with white wine and poached beef marrow-bone fat FRENCH
Moghul, Muglai	cooked in the style of the Moghul emperors with a sauce of cream, egg, spices and almonds INDIAN
mogyoró	hazelnuts HUNGARIAN
mogyoróhagyma	shallot HUNGARIAN
Mohn	poppy GERMAN
Möhre, Mohrrübe	carrot GERMAN
moka	mocha FRENCH
molasses	thick, brown syrupy drainings obtained from raw sugar during refinement
molbo	aromatic cheese similar to samsoe DANISH
mole	traditional savoury sauce containing peppers, spices and chocolate MEXICAN
mole poblano	chicken with a sauce of chilli peppers, spices and chocolate SPANISH
mole powder	seasoning of powdered herbs and spices with chillies and dried sweet peppers MEXICAN
molecche	soft-shelled crabs ITALIAN
molee	Goan style of cooking in spices and coconut milk INDIAN
molho	sauce PORTUGUESE
moliterno	a cheese similar to contronese ITALIAN
molleja	sweetbread SPANISH
mollet	soft FRENCH
mollusca	group of hard-shelled creatures with soft bodies
molusco	mollusc SPANISH
Monastine	yellow liqueur similar in flavour to yellow Chartreuse
moncenisio	factory-made blue-mould cheese ITALIAN
Mondseer Schlosskäse	cheese made and eaten only in the Mondsee district AUSTRIAN
monégasque, à la	chicken consommé thickened with arrowroot, garnished with cheese profiteroles; garnish for

entrées of fried calf's brains, fried ham, mushrooms and demi-glace with mushrooms and truffles; eggs on a bed of fried tomatoes and tarragon with anchovy fillets and tomato sauce FRENCH

moniatos   type of sweet potato native to Malaga SPANISH

monkey nut   another name for peanut AMERICAN

monkfish   round sea fish with a large ugly head; only the tail is eaten and the firm white flesh tastes similar to lobster

Monmouth pudding   regional pudding from Monmouth WELSH

monosodium glutamate   powder with little flavour, used to enhance the flavour of meat and vegetables

monostorer   Transylvanian ewe's milk cheese ROMANIAN

monselet, à la   cooked or garnished with artichoke hearts, truffles and pommes de terre Parisienne FRENCH

monsieur blanc   white, unfermented Normandy cheese FRENCH

monstera   decorative plant with deeply incised leaves and an edible fruit with a flavour like pineapple

mont blanc   dessert made from sieved, cooked chestnuts FRENCH

mont d'or   the best known cheese from Lyon, made from stable-fed goat's milk FRENCH

montanara, alla   served with root vegetables ITALIAN

montasio   hard, whole cow's milk cheese from the Veneto region ITALIAN

mont-bry, à la   garnish for small cuts of meat made from spinach cakes containing Parmesan, and cèpes in cream FRENCH

Mont-Cenis   blue-mould, hard cheese from the district of Mont Cenis FRENCH

mont-des-cats   cow's milk cheese from Picardy FRENCH

Monterey Jack   cow's milk cheese from Monterey AMERICAN

Monterey Spanish mackerel   fish related to the Spanish mackerel

monthéry   cow's milk cheese from Seine-et-Oise FRENCH

montmorency, à la   garnish for tournedos or noisettes of artichoke bottoms filled with vegetables and Montmorency cherries; dishes containing cherries, dedicated to the family of the same name FRENCH

montone   mutton ITALIAN

montpensier, à la   garnish for tournedos, noisettes and sweetbreads of artichoke bottoms filled with asparagus tips, julienne of truffles and pommes noisette; a flan also called Monte Cristo FRENCH

mooli	equivalent of radish INDIAN
moong	green gram INDIAN
moong dal	mung beans (beansprouts) INDIAN
moonphali	peanuts (US: groundnuts) INDIAN
moorfowl	Scottish name for grouse SCOTTISH
moorhen	small water bird, common in Britain but rarely eaten
moqueca de peixe	fish cooked in an earthenware casserole with coconut milk, palm-oil, coriander leaves, ginger and ground shrimps PORTUGUESE
mor	yoghurt-based drink INDIAN
mor monsen	cake containing almonds, with almonds and raisins sprinkled on top NORWEGIAN
mora	blackberry; mulberry ITALIAN, SPANISH
morango	strawberry PORTUGUESE
moravský salám	Moravian salami CZECH
Moravské uzené	smoked ham CZECH
moray eel	very large, dangerous eel
Moray Firth	mid-19th-century method for curing fish SCOTTISH
morbier	cow's milk cheese from the Franche-Comté FRENCH
mørbrad	fillet of meat (US: tenderloin) DANISH
mørbrad	rump steak NORWEGIAN
mørbrad bøf	small round pork fillet DANISH
mørbrad steg	porterhouse steak DANISH
morcela	black pudding (US: blood sausage) PORTUGUESE Morchel
morel mushroom	GERMAN
morcilla	black pudding SPANISH
morcilla blanca	sausage made from minced chicken, egg, bacon and black pepper; white pudding made from tripe and minced pig's lungs SPANISH
morel	edible fungus
morele	apricots POLISH
morell	morello cherry NORWEGIAN
morello	almost black, sour cherry
morgado de figos	cake of chopped dried figs, marzipan, sugar, and chocolate, flavoured with cinnamon PORTUGUESE
morgencomplet	continental breakfast DANISH
Morgenessen	breakfast GERMAN
morgenmad	breakfast DANISH
Morgenrötessuppe	thick soup of meat, tapioca, tomatoes and chicken stock GERMAN

morilla	morel mushroom SPANISH
morille	morel mushroom FRENCH
morkel	morel mushroom NORWEGIAN
morkulla	woodcock SWEDISH
mornay	béchamel sauce flavoured with Gruyère, Parmesan or cheddar cheese FRENCH
moron	carrot WELSH
moros y cristianos	rice and black beans with diced ham, garlic, green peppers and herbs SPANISH
morot	carrot SWEDISH
morpølse	sauce made with beef, mutton, and reindeer meat NORWEGIAN
morros de ternera	calves' cheeks cooked with onions, red peppers, garlic, herbs and seasoning BASQUE
mořské speciality	seafood specialities CZECH
mortadela	bologna sausage POLISH, SPANISH
mortadella	Bologna sausage ITALIAN
mortar	stone bowl in which foodstuffs are pounded or mixed with a pestle
mortifier	to hang meat or game FRENCH
morue	salt cod FRENCH
moschari	veal GREEK
moscovite, à la	cold sweet dish similar to a bavarois or a jelly FRENCH
moscovite, sauce	classical sauce made with sauce poivrade, juniper berries, almonds, raisins, and Málaga or Marsala FRENCH
Moselle	wine from vineyards surrounding the River Moselle and its tributaries in France, Luxembourg or Germany
mossala	see massala INDIAN
mossel	mussel DUTCH
mostarda	mustard ITALIAN, PORTUGUESE
mostaza	mustard SPANISH
mostek	breast portion of meat with savoury stuffing POLISH
mostelle	southern name for a fish of the whiting family FRENCH
mosterd	mustard DUTCH
Mostrich	mustard GERMAN
moth bean	a bean which grows wild in India
Mothe-St Héraye, la	goat's milk cheese made in Poitou FRENCH

mouette	gull, whose eggs are a delicacy FRENCH
moufflon	various types of wild sheep
mouka	flour CZECH
mould	hollow container of a variety of shapes used to make sweet or savoury dishes which are turned out when set; woolly growth of minute fungi; certain moulds which give flavour and colour to cheeses such as Stilton
moule	mould FRENCH
moule à manqué	cake tin resembling a deep sandwich tin with slightly sloping sides FRENCH
moules	mussels FRENCH
moules marinière	mussels white wine sauce with shallots and herbs FRENCH
mouli-légume	hand-operated food mill used to reduce cooked food to a purée FRENCH
mousquetaire, sauce	classical sauce served with boiled meats made from mayonnaise with shallots and chives, seasoned with cayenne and veal jelly; sauce provençale with chopped herbs FRENCH
moussaká	savoury dish based on sliced aubergines and minced lamb GREEK, TURKISH
mousse	light, frothy sweet or savoury dish; a sweet mousse is often served cold as a dessert FRENCH
mousseau	a whole wheat flour loaf FRENCH
mousseline	savoury sauce based on hollandaise with added beaten egg white or whipped cream to make it frothy FRENCH
mousseux	sparkling FRENCH
moustartha, saltsa	lemon and mustard sauce with garlic and olive oil GREEK
moutarde, sauce	mustard sauce FRENCH
mouton	mutton FRENCH
mouvette	wooden spoon for stirring sauces FRENCH
moya	fish of the cod family SPANISH
moyeu	old word meaning the yolk of an egg FRENCH
mozart, à la	garnish for entrées made with artichoke and celery FRENCH
mozeček	brains CZECH
mozzarella	egg shaped curd cheese, traditionally made from the milk of water buffaloes ITALIAN
mražená káva	iced coffee CZECH

mrkev	carrots CZECH
MRM	machine-recovered meat; making sure that nothing is wasted
mučkalica	stew of chopped pork, onions, sweet peppers, eggplant, and chillies YUGOSLAVIAN
mudjemeri	mutton rissoles TURKISH
muesli	a cereal mixture which may contain oats, wheat, rye, millet, barley flakes, dried fruits and nuts and is served with milk, cream or yoghurt, usually as a breakfast dish SWISS
muffin	the traditional English muffin is a thick, flat, yeast cake; the American muffin is a small, sweet sponge cake AMERICAN
muggety pie	old dish made with sheep's pluck CORNISH
mugwort	European perennial plant, which adds flavour to stews, stuffings and sweets
muhennettu	stewed; mashed FINNISH
muhennos	stew; purée FINNISH
muikku	vendace; fry of whitefish FINNISH
muikunmäti	vendace roe FINNISH
muir fowl	local name for grouse or blackcock SCOTTISH
mujdei de usturoi	garlic sauce served with meats ROMANIAN
mújol	(grey) mullet SPANISH
mulberry	the soft juicy, fragile fruit of a moraceous tree, on whose leaves silkworms live; a larger version of the blackberry
mulchán	unpressed buttermilk cheese IRISH
mule	hybrid of donkey and horse, eaten when young in some parts of Europe
mulet	grey mullet FRENCH
mullbär	mulberry SWEDISH
mullet, grey	round sea fish similar to sea bass with a mild nutty flavour
mullet, red	no relation to grey mullet; it is smaller, crimson coloured, with a unique, delicate flavour
mulligatawny	'pepper-water'; originally a Tamil pepper sauce adapted for British army officers who insisted on starting the meal with soup (of thick meat stock flavoured with the sauce) ANGLO-INDIAN
mulling	warming, sweetening and spicing ale, cider or wine
multasieni	truffle FINNISH
multe	Arctic cloudberry NORWEGIAN

mum	strong sweet ale made of wheat and malt
muna	egg FINNISH
munakas	omelette FINNISH
munakoiso	aubergine (US: egg plant) FINNISH
munakokkeli	scrambled eggs FINNISH
munariisipasteija	egg and rice pasty FINNISH
munavoi	finely chopped hard-boiled eggs mixed with butter FINNISH
mung bean	small, round green dried bean used in Indian cookery and for germinating to produce bean sprouts
munk	doughnut SWEDISH
munkki	(jam) doughnut FINNISH
Münsterkäse	semi-hard cheese from the Alsace available flavoured with caraway or aniseed FRENCH, GERMAN
munuainen	kidney FINNISH
munuaishöystö	kidney stew FINNISH
Mürbeteig	sweet pastry case GERMAN
mûre	mulberry or blackberry FRENCH
mureke	fish or meat mousse; forcemeat; stuffing FINNISH
murena	moray eel, used in a Roman fish soup ITALIAN
murgh, murag	chicken INDIAN
murkelsås	morel mushroom sauce SWEDISH
murkelstuvning	creamed morel mushrooms SWEDISH
murkla	morel mushroom SWEDISH
murol	a cow's milk cheese from the Auvergne district FRENCH
murot	breakfast cereals FINNISH
mus	mousse POLISH
Mus	stewed fruit; purée; mash GERMAN
mus z jabłek	apple sauce POLISH
musaka od plavih patlidzana	form of moussaka, made with minced pork and mutton, aubergine and onion YUGOSLAVIAN
muscade	nutmeg FRENCH
muscadelle	variety of winter pear FRENCH
Muscadet	fresh, dry white wine made from Muscadet grapes in the Loire region FRENCH
muscat	very sweet white or black grapes
muscatel	large, juicy, sun-dried raisin; sweet white wines made in France, Spain and Italy SPANISH, FRENCH, ITALIAN
Muschel	mussel GERMAN

musciame	dried dolphin meat; a speciality from the Ligurian and Tuscan coasts ITALIAN
muscoli	alternative name in Tuscany for mussels ITALIAN
muscovy duck	native duck to Central America, now domesticated throughout the world, which can be cooked as wild duck
museau	muzzle or snout FRENCH
mush	maize porridge resembling polenta AMERICA
mushroom	there are many varieties of edible fungus, cultivated and wild
mushy peas	pale green marrowfat peas served as a mush, especially in fish-and-chip shops
Muskat(nuß)	nutmeg GERMAN
muskellunge	large freshwater game fish found in Central American and Canadian lakes
muskot	nutmeg SWEDISH
muskrat	aquatic rodent which makes a good stew
musling	mussel DANISH, NORWEGIAN
mussalam	*see* massala INDIAN
mussel	common bivalve mollusc with almost black shell
mussla	mussel; clam SWEDISH
musta viinimarja	blackcurrants FINNISH
mustár	mustard HUNGARIAN
mustard	classified as a spice, the seeds are ground to make a condiment, or germinated to produce a leafy garnish
mustard cabbage	*see* Chinese mustard cabbage, Chinese mustard (greens), gai choy, green in snow, Indian mustard (greens), kaai tsoi, leaf mustard, pak choi
mustard and cress	young shoots of those seeds germinated and harvested on a small scale to provide a fresh garnish for salads, sandwiches etc
mustard greens	*see* Chinese mustard cabbage, Chinese mustard (greens), gai choy, green in snow, Indian mustard (greens), kaai tsoi, leaf mustard, mustard cabbage, pak choi
mustikka	bilberry FINNISH
musztarda	mustard POLISH
muttar	equivalent of peas INDIAN
mutton	meat of sheep, slaughtered when more than a year old
muurain	Arctic cloudberry FINNISH

mycella   green-veined, semi-soft, full fat cow's milk cheese
                                                                    DANISH

myśliwska kiełbasa   dry pork sausage POLISH

myrobalan   varieties of plum indigenous to the East Indies, now
                         grown widely in Alsace

myrtille   bilberry FRENCH

myrtle   fragrant herb which marries well with lamb and may
                         be used in marinades

mysost   brown, cow's milk whey cheese NORWEGIAN

N

na másle	sautéed CZECH
na ztraceno	poached (fish) CZECH
naan	see nan INDIAN
naartje	small tangerine SOUTH AFRICAN
nabiał	dairy products POLISH
nabiça	turnip greens PORTUGUESE
nabo	turnip SPANISH, PORTUGUESE
Nachspeise, Nachtisch	dessert; sweet GERMAN
nadívaný	stuffed CZECH
nadívané hrudí	stuffed breast CZECH
nádivka	stuffing CZECH
nadzienie	stuffing POLISH
nage, à la	shellfish cooked in a court bouillon FRENCH
nageoires de tortue	turtle flippers FRENCH
nagerecht	dessert DUTCH
nahit	traditional dish made of chick-peas, eaten at Purim (the Feast of Esther) JEWISH
nahkiainen	lamprey FINNISH
nakki	frankfurter FINNISH
näkkileipä	crispbread FINNISH
nakládacka	gherkin CZECH
nakládané houby	pickled mushrooms CZECH
nakládané papriky	pickled peppers CZECH
nákyp	pudding CZECH
naleśniki	crêpes or pancakes POLISH
nam pla	salty fish sauce used in cooking and as a condiment THAI
namak pare	see nimki INDIAN
namaycush	large char, sometimes called lake trout, found in the Great Lakes of North America
nan, naan	soft, flat, pear-shaped bread baked in a tandoor INDIAN
na-nas	pineapple BM
nang-ka	jackfruit BM
nantais	small almond biscuits; tartlet containing an almond mixture; cow's milk cheese from Brittany; Nantes duckling FRENCH

nantaise, à la	garnish for meat of glazed turnips, peas, mashed potatoes and thick meat gravy; method of serving chicken FRENCH
nantua, à la	garnished with, or made with crayfish FRENCH
nantua, sauce	classical sauce of sauce béchamel, cream, fish fumet, vegetables, crayfish butter, and tomato FRENCH
napi ajánlat	speciality of the day HUNGARIAN
napoleonka	napoleon POLISH
napoleonskake	custard slice NORWEGIAN
napoletana, alla	cooked with cheese, tomatoes, herbs and sometimes anchovies ITALIAN
napolitaine, à la	macaroni or spaghetti served in tomato sauce sprinkled with grated cheese FRENCH
napolitains	large ornamental cakes FRENCH
napper	to mask (or to cover) with a sauce FRENCH
nara nut	the seed of a gourd from arid South West Africa SOUTH WEST AFRICAN
narancs	orange HUNGARIAN
naranja	orange SPANISH
narceja	snipe PORTUGUESE
nargisi kebab, kofta	version of Scotch eggs INDIAN
nariel	coconut INDIAN
naseberry	the fruit of the sapodilla tree, similar to a medlar AMERICAN
na-see	rice (cooked) BM
nasello	whiting ITALIAN
nashi	Asian pear with white apple-scented flesh, which looks like a large, round, yellow apple
nasi goreng, nassi goreng	cooked rice, pork or chicken and seafood with fried onions, garlic and chilli DUTCH-INDONESIAN
nässelkål	nettle soup SWEDISH
nastoika	galangal-flavoured liqueur RUSSIAN
nasturtium	the round, hot, young leaves are eaten in salads, the bright yellow and orange flowers are used as a garnish and the berry-like seeds make a substitute for capers
nata	fresh cream PORTUGUESE, SPANISH
natillas	custard SPANISH
natives	popular name for oysters bred in Kentish (Whitstable) or Essex (Colchester) oyster beds ENGLISH

na-tlöda   delicacy eaten by the Ten'a Indians of bear fat, moose tallow and sometimes seal oil, melted together; snow is stirred in, and the mixture is frozen before eating ALASKAN

natron   naturally occurring sodium sesquicarbonate ($Na_2CO_3 \cdot 10H_2O$)

natural, ao   plain; without dressing, sauce, stuffing etc
PORTUGUESE

naturale   plain; without sauce or filling ITALIAN

naturel, au   plain; uncooked; very simply cooked FRENCH

naturell   plain GERMAN

naudanliha   beef FINNISH

navarin   lamb or mutton stew cooked with onions and potatoes FRENCH

navet   turnip; in Britain it applies to a small, tender variety
FRENCH

navone   yellow turnip ITALIAN

navy bean   small, white dried bean from the same family as the haricot bean

neapolitan   sweets, cakes and ice creams in layers of two or more colours

neat   old name for ox ENGLISH

neck   in butchery, a term meaning the neck, shoulder and ribs of an animal

nécoras   spider crabs SPANISH

nectarine   variety of peach with a smooth skin

nedopečené maso   rare meat CZECH

neep   root vegetable, particularly a turnip SCOTTISH

nèfle   medlar FRENCH

negus   mulled wine made of port, claret or sherry, spice, lemon, sugar and hot water (named after Col Francis Negus d1732)

neige   grated ice FRENCH

neige de Florence   very fine type of white pasta FRENCH

Nelke   clove GERMAN

nelusko   petit four made with stoned cherries in brandy; soup made with chicken-based velouté FRENCH

nemes édes   'noble and sweet'; a variety of paprika HUNGARIAN

Nemours, à la   garnish for entrées of green peas, carrots and pommes duchesse; soup of puréed potatoes and mushrooms; small tartlets filled with jam and chou pastry FRENCH

nerandzi giristo preserved orange rolls GREEK

nerki kidney POLISH

nerkówka cięleca nadziewana roast veal stuffed with kidneys POLISH

neroli oil distilled from orange blossoms, used as a flavouring

néroli neroli, a small cake containing almonds and orange water FRENCH

nêspera medlar PORTUGUESE

nesselrode frozen dessert of chestnut purée, egg yolks and cream; other dishes containing chestnut purée (named after Count Nesselrode whose chef invented it)

nesselrode, à la fish with a stuffing of pike and lobster forcemeat wrapped in puff pastry, baked and served with lobster sauce with oysters; garnish for meat of glazed chest-nuts, mushrooms, and truffles in sauce madère; soup of puréed woodcock and chestnuts; game consommé garnished with chestnuts, hazel hen, and mush-rooms; iced pudding containing chest-nuts; an American chilled pudding containing milk, gelatine, dried fruits, macaroons, brandy or rum, and egg whites FRENCH, AMERICAN

nettle young stinging nettles have a pleasant slightly bitter taste and can be cooked as a vegetable or made into soup

neufchâtel soft creamy cow's milk cheese from the Pays-de-Bray region FRENCH

neva, à la cold stuffed chicken served with Russian salad and mayonnaise FRENCH

New Brunswick stew casserole of string beans, wax beans, new potatoes, onions, peas, carrots, ham, roast lamb or beef, water, salt and pepper CANADIAN

New England boiled dinner speciality dish from New England of corned beef, onions, carrots, turnips, cabbage, parsnips, potatoes and bay leaf AMERICAN

New England clam chowder soup of onions, leeks, green peppers, and pork AMERICAN

New England spinach annual herb similar to ordinary spinach AMERICAN

New England stew stew of salt pork, turnips and onions AMERICAN

New England stuffing stuffing for poultry consisting of bread soaked in water or stock and mixed with diced salt pork, chopped herbs, egg and seasoning AMERICAN

newburg sauce sauce for shellfish containing butter, dry sherry and cream AMERICAN

newburg, à la   method for serving lobster or other seafood, sautéed and served with a rich sauce of cream, sherry and egg yolk FRENCH

Newport pound cake cake popular in the US AMERICAN

ngapi   dark grey paste made from decomposed fish BURMESE

niçoise, à la   dishes made from or garnished with tomatoes and other ingredients typical of the area around Nice

FRENCH

Nidel, Nidle   cream GERMAN

Nieheimer Hopfenkäse   sour milk cheese from the city of Nieheim

GERMAN

nier   kidney DUTCH

Niere   kidney GERMAN

Nierenstück   loin GERMAN

nigella   small, hard, black seeds with a peppery taste, used as a spice – popular name: love-in-a-mist

nigger-fish   large grouper from warm waters AMERICAN

nimki   deep-fried, seasoned crispbreads INDIAN

nimrod, à la   garnish for game birds of mushrooms and chestnut purée, French beans, rissoles of marrow bone fat and pommes croquettes; light game soup flavoured with sherry or port and garnished with profiteroles stuffed with game purée FRENCH

niolo   goat's milk cheese CORSICAN

nipplewort   wild plant sometimes used in raw salads

niramish   dish of thinly-sliced potato and onion fried with spices INDIAN

níspola   medlar SPANISH

niter kebbeh   spiced ghee, produced as ghee but with added spices

ETHIOPIAN

Nivernais   French province which has given its name to a classical garnish which contains root vegetables

FRENCH

nivernaise, à la   various garnishes for entrées containing various vegetables; sauce allemande garnished with carrot and turnip balls; beef consommé; thick soup of puréed carrots and turnips FRENCH

niza, queijo de   farmhouse variety of serra cheese PORTUGUESE

nízkokalorický   low calorie CZECH

njure   kidney SWEDISH

nóżki cielęce   calf's trotters POLISH

nocciolo   dogfish ITALIAN

noce	walnut ITALIAN
noce moscato	nutmeg ITALIAN
Nockerl	small dumpling GERMAN
noggin	liquid measure, usually one gill (150 ml) often taken to mean a portion of liquid, usually liquor; the vessel in which it is served
noisette	neatly trimmed, tied, boneless piece of lamb cut from the loin or best end of neck FRENCH
noisettines	small cakes made from short crust pastry sandwiched together with hazelnut-flavoured cream FRENCH
noix	nut; walnut; pancreas FRENCH
noix (de) muscade	nutmeg FRENCH
noix de veau	one of three major muscles in the leg of veal FRENCH
noix patissière	top rump or thick end of the loin of veal FRENCH
nokedli	noodles HUNGARIAN
nøkkelost	semi-hard, rennetted, spiced cow's milk cheese NORWEGIAN
nonat	tiny Mediterranean fish
nonnette	small iced gingerbread from Dijon and Rheims FRENCH
nonpareille	variety of pear; tiny sugar balls used for cake decoration FRENCH
noodles	ribbons of pasta, or other starchy substances added to soup or served with a sauce
noot	nut DUTCH
nopalito	young cactus leaf served with salad dressing SPANISH
noques	Alsatian speciality similar to Nockerln FRENCH
Norfolk hollow	small, round crisp roll NORFOLK
Norfolk plover	bird of the plover family protected in the British Isles NORFOLK
Norfolk pudding	sliced, fried apples baked in batter NORMANDY
Norfolk pippins	whole, peeled, cored and dried apples soaked before cooking and simmered in syrup
normannaost	blue cheese NORWEGIAN
nörs	smelt SWEDISH
norvégienne	thick puréed potage of cabbage and turnips; method of presenting fish, poached, skinned and decorated with prawns, salmon-stuffed cucumber, hard-boiled eggs, tomatoes and Russian salad; garnish for meat or poultry of noodles with sauce madère; sauce of mashed, hard boiled egg yolks; baked Alaska FRENCH

Norway haddock   variety of haddock SCANDINAVIAN

nostrale   home made ITALIAN

nostrano   local; home grown ITALIAN

notch-weed   purslane, which can be cooked like spinach

nøtt   nut NORWEGIAN

Nottingham batter pudding   regional pudding of peeled, cored apples in batter

nouet   culinary word for a muslin bag contained spices, herbs or other flavourings FRENCH

nougat   hard sweet, usually pink or white, made from sugar and honey containing chopped fruits and nuts

FRENCH

nougatine   similar to praline, made from light caramel syrup, crushed almonds and hazelnuts FRENCH

nougatine cakes   Génoise cake mixture FRENCH

nouille noodle   FRENCH

nouvelle cuisine   beautifully arranged dishes purportedly designed to promote healthy eating but, because of the modest portions, leaving the eaters as hungry as their wallets are empty FRENCH

noyau   sweet liqueur flavoured with fruit kernels, particularly apricot and cherry FRENCH

noz   nut PORTUGUESE

Nudel   noodle GERMAN

Nudelteig   plain noodle dough GERMAN

nudle   noodles CZECH

nudličky   small noodles CZECH

nuez   nut SPANISH

numbles   archaic word for the heart, lungs, liver etc of a deer or other animal – *see* umble pie

nun's beads   hard cheese mixed with breadcrumbs and egg yolks formed into nut-sized pieces and fried in puff pastry

SCOTTISH

nuoc-mam   salty fish sauce used as a condiment and flavouring

VIETNAMESE

Nürnberger Eier   egg dish from Nuremberg of hard-boiled eggs fried in batter, served with wine sauce GERMAN

Nürnberger Lebkuchen   Christmas cakes from Nuremburg GERMAN

Nürnberger Würste   sausage from Nuremberg GERMAN

Nuß   nut; steak similar to rump GERMAN

nut   fruit with a hard or leathery shell enclosing an edible kernel

nutmeg	brown, nut-like seed of the nutmeg fruit, which grows inside the fruit; it is available both whole and ground and is used as a flavouring
nutrient	any substance which provides the body with energy and the raw materials for growth, repair and reproduction
nutrition	the provision of nutrients; the process by which the body takes in food and uses it to provide growth
Nutwood Cheddar	cheddar cheese flavoured with cider, nuts and raisins
nye kartofler	new potatoes DANISH
nyelv	tongue HUNGARIAN
nyelvhal	sole HUNGARIAN
nype	rose hip NORWEGIAN
nypon	rose hip SWEDISH
nyre	kidney DANISH, NORWEGIAN
nyúl	rabbit HUNGARIAN

O

oat bran	course outer layers of oat
oatmeal	ground oats, used in baking
oatcakes	unleavened oatmeal bread
oats	cereal grass which can grow in more marginal environments than other cereals. Johnson's Dictionary: 'A grain, which in England is generally given to horses, but in Scotland supports the people.' (1755)
obalovaný	breaded CZECH
občerstvení	a snack, usually served with drink CZECH
oběd	lunch CZECH
Oberskren	sauce containing horseradish AUSTRIAN
obiad	dinner POLISH
obilné kličky	groats CZECH
oblade	Mediterranean fish of the family *Sparidae*, similar to grey bream FRENCH, ENGLISH
obloha	with vegetable garnish CZECH
obložená masová mísa	assorted meat; cold cuts CZECH
obloženy chléb	sandwich CZECH
Obst	fruit GERMAN
obuolainis	yeast cake, topped with apples and plums Lithuanian
oca	tuber resembling a large walnut SOUTH AMERICAN
oca	goose ITALIAN
ocet	vinegar CZECH, POLISH
ochroszka	version of Russian rye soup, made with fermented rye POLISH
Ochsenauge	fried eggs (US: sunny side up) GERMAN
Ochsenfleisch	beef GERMAN
Ochsenmaulsalat	ox muzzle salad GERMAN
octopus	largest marine cephalopod mollusc of the genera *Octopus*, *Eledone* etc, with a soft body, hard beak and eight tentacles
ocvrti piščanèc	method of cooking chicken SLOVENIAN
oedicnème	type of stone curlew FRENCH
oester	oyster DUTCH
oestrina	sturgeon RUSSIAN
œuf	egg FRENCH
œufs en cocotte	eggs cooked in earthenware moulds called cocottes

œufs meulemeester traditional method of serving eggs from Bruges: hard-boiled eggs are shredded, mixed with prawns, covered with cream sauce containing chervil, parsley and mustard, and the whole sprinkled with grated cheese and browned BELGIAN

offal edible parts of an animal other than cuts of meat, including brains, chitterlings, feet, head, heart, liver, kidneys, lungs, spleen, sweetbread, tail, tongue and tripe

ogeechee lime fruit of a gum tree which grows in the southern States AMERICAN

ogórek cucumber POLISH

ogórki ridge cucumbers; salted cucumbers POLISH

ogurtsy cucumbers RUSSIAN

ohra barley FINNISH

ohrasämpylä barley roll FINNISH

ohukaiset small thin pancakes served with jam or sugar FINNISH

oie adult goose FRENCH

oignon onion FRENCH

oignonade stew containing a large number of onions; finely chopped onions sweated in butter or cooked in white wine FRENCH

oille old name for a potée of meats, poultry and vegetables FRENCH

oils liquid fat produced from seeds, nuts and fruits

oiseaux sans têtes 'birds without heads'; a speciality dish containing sliced beef spread with a mixture of breadcrumbs, pork and veal, onion, eggs, nutmeg, cream, butter and seasoning, rolled and braised in stock BELGIAN

oison gosling FRENCH

oka cheese made by Trappist monks at Oka in Quebec
CANADIAN

ökörfarok oxtail HUNGARIAN

okoun bass CZECH

okra small, dark green stocky pod of *Hibiscus esculentus*, an important ingredient of Creole cooking; bhindi; ladies' fingers

okrochka traditional dish made from layers of aubergines, minced beef and onions cooked in stock, covered in cream and egg yolk and browned BALKAN

okroshka traditional cold sour soup made from sour cream, sour milk, kvass, seasoning, chopped meats and ice
RUSSIAN

okse OX DANISH, NORWEGIAN

oksebryst brisket of beef DANISH

oksefilet fillet of beef (US: tenderloin) DANISH, NORWEGIAN

oksehalesuppe oxtail soup DANISH, NORWEGIAN

oksekjøtt beef NORWEGIAN

oksekød beef DANISH

oksekødsuppe beef broth; consommé DANISH

oksemørbrad fillet of beef DANISH

okserull rolled stuffed beef, served cold NORWEGIAN

oksestek roast beef DANISH, NORWEGIAN

okun perch RUSSIAN

okurka cucumber CZECH

Öl oil GERMAN

oladyi yeast cake resembling a thick pancake RUSSIAN

olaj oil HUNGARIAN

Old Heidelberg cheese cow's milk cheese from Illinois AMERICAN

oldalas rib HUNGARIAN

olej oil CZECH, POLISH

olén deer RUSSIAN

óleo oil PORTUGUESE

olie oil DANISH, DUTCH

oliebollen doughnuts containing dried fruit DUTCH

oliekoeken savoury oliebollen containing cheese, ham, or spinach DUTCH

oliheň squid CZECH

oliivi olive FINNISH

olijf olive DUTCH

olio oil ITALIAN

oliv olive SWEDISH

oliva olive ITALIAN

olive small, oval fruit of the olive tree, which can be picked green or when black and fully ripe; they are often sold stoned and stuffed ENGLISH, FRENCH

olive agrodolci olives in vinegar and sugar ITALIAN

olive oil oil extracted from olives, widely used for culinary purposes

olive ripiene stuffed olives ITALIAN

oliven olive DANISH

olivet soft cow's milk cheese inoculated with blue mould FRENCH

olivette glacate	stuffed veal roll made with a large slice of veal from the top of the leg ITALIAN
olivový olej	olive oil CZECH
olivy	olives CZECH
oliwa	olive oil POLISH
oliwki	olives POLISH
olja	oil SWEDISH
öljy	oil FINNISH
olla	stew SPANISH
olla podrida	soup or stew usually containing meat or poultry, beans, and sausages SPANISH
øllebrød	beer porridge made from dark beer, pumpernickel and wholemeal bread DANISH
øllebrød	beer cream made from egg yolks, sugar, cream, water and light beer, beaten in a double saucepan until slightly thick and frothy NORWEGIAN
oloron	ewe's milk cheese from the Béarn district FRENCH
ølsuppe	beer soup made from milk, ground rice, lemon and beer NORWEGIAN
omácka	sauce; gravy CZECH
omble chevalier	char FRENCH
ombre commun	grayling FRENCH
ombre de mer	umbra FRENCH
ombrina	umbrine ITALIAN
omelet fines herbes	herb omelette DUTCH
omelet med kyllingelever	chicken liver omelette DANISH
omelet met kippelevertjes	chicken liver omelette DUTCH
omelet nature	plain omelette DUTCH
omeleta	omelette CZECH, PORTUGUESE
omeleta přirodni	plain omelette CZECH
omeleta se šunkou	ham omelette CZECH
omeleta se sýrem	cheese omelette CZECH
omelette	beaten eggs cooked in a hot frying pan until they are set; the omelette can be filled with sweet or savoury ingredients FRENCH
omeletti	omelette FINNISH
omena	apples FINNISH
omlet	omelette POLISH
omlett	omelette HUNGARIAN
ongaar	underdone (US: rare) DUTCH
onglet	cut of beef from the top of the skirt FRENCH

onion	common bulb vegetable with juicy white flesh and a pungent vapour, used in countless savoury dishes
ontbidjt	breakfast DUTCH
oo-bee	potato BM
oo-bee ky-oo	tapioca BM
oopperavoileipä	toast topped with a hamburger steak and a fried egg FINNISH
opah	deep sea fish found in all Atlantic waters
open sandwich	sandwich without a top layer of bread
opepřený	peppery; hot CZECH
opiekanki z grochu	fritters POLISH
oplatky	waffle CZECH
opletek	semi-transparent unleavened dough wafer stamped with scenes of the Nativity, eaten on Christmas Eve POLISH
opossum	small nocturnal animal from southern and eastern States AMERICAN
opphengt melk	sour cream dessert made from curdled milk and cream, skimmed and strained and served with sugar NORWEGIAN
oquassa	small delicately flavoured char
orach(e)	herbaceous plant or shrub with grey- green lobed leaves, cultivated as a vegetable; a plant widely grown in France, cooked like spinach FRENCH
orange	sweet, juicy citrus fruit containing Vitamin C, eaten raw and in sweet and savoury dishes
orange flower water	a potent flavouring distilled from Seville orange flowers
orange peel	orange rind
orange rockfish	sea fish from the coast of California AMERICAN
orangeade	drink made from fresh oranges and sugar
orangine	cake of génoise cake flavoured with orange peel, sandwiched with crème patisserie FRENCH
orata	daurade; similar to English sea bream ITALIAN
oregano	wild marjoram
oregáno	oregano HUNGARIAN
oreiller de le belle Aurore	'pillow of the beautiful Aurora'; elaborate game pie FRENCH
oreilles de porc (veau)	pig's (calf's) ears, usually served braised with root vegetables, or boiled, coated with breadcrumbs and grilled FRENCH
organ meats	term for offal AMERICAN

orgeat	a beverage, originally made from barley, later from syrup of almonds and sugar diluted with water
óriás kifli	large, flaky crescent shaped roll HUNGARIAN
orientale, à l'	dishes that use ingredients from the Mediterranean, particularly Turkey and the Balkans; often describes vegetables and fish cooked with tomato, garlic and sometimes saffron FRENCH
orientale, sauce	sauce américaine flavoured with curry powder and mixed with fresh cream
origano	wild marjoram ITALIAN
original	moose FRENCH
Orkney cheese	white, red or blue cheese originally made on Orkney farms
Orléans	chicken consommé thickened with tapioca and garnished with chicken quenelle and chervil; beef consommé garnished with chicory royale, diced French beans, flageolets and chervil FRENCH
orloff, à la	garnish for meat of braised celery, lettuce, tomatoes and pommes château; garnish for saddle of lamb or veal, which is sliced, coated with onion purée, reshaped with a slice of truffle between each slice, and covered with sauce soubise; Russian method of preparing sterlet cooked in white wine and fish stock, garnished with stuffed cucumbers, stuffed olives, stuffed crayfish heads, mushrooms and vesiga FRENCH
orly, à la	fish, deep fried in batter, served with fresh tomato sauce FRENCH
ormer	Edible marine gastropod from the Channel Islands, *Haliotis tuberculata*; sea-ear
orosz hússaláta	Russian salad with meat HUNGARIAN
orphie	garfish FRENCH
orre	black grouse SWEDISH
ørred	trout DANISH
ørret	trout NORWEGIAN
orris	dried aromatic roots of a type of iris
orsay, d'	chicken consommé garnished with egg yolks and strips of pigeon, pigeon quenelles, and chervil FRENCH
orseille	paste made from lichen, used to colour tongue pink FRENCH
ortanique	hybrid citrus fruit, probably a cross between sweet orange and tangerine

ortolan	delicately flavoured wild bird *Emberiza hortulana* now extinct in Britain
orzechy	walnuts POLISH
orzo	pasta GREEK
os	bone FRENCH
oseille	sorrel FRENCH
oshàf	dried or fresh fruit compote BULGARIAN
ossenhaas	tenderloin or fillet of beef DUTCH
ossestaart	oxtail DUTCH
ossetong	beef or ox tongue DUTCH
ossi buchi alla milanese	famous veal dish also known as osso bucho ITALIAN
osso	bone ITALIAN, PORTUGUESE
osso buco	chopped knuckle of veal, sautéed and stewed with garlic, onion and tomato ITALIAN
ost	cheese CZECH, DANISH, NORWEGIAN, SWEDISH
osteanretning	cheese board DANISH
oštěpek	plastic-cured ewe's milk cheese CZECH
osteri	oyster FINNISH
østers	oyster NORWEGIAN
ostiepok	smoked ewe's milk cheese CZECH
ostrý	hot; spicy CZECH
ostra	oyster SPANISH, PORTUGUESE
ostreon	oysters GREEK
ostrica	oyster ITALIAN
ostrich	large edible bird, *Struthio camelus*, now bred for food; the idea that it buries its head in the sand springs from a mis-translation – for 'sand' read 'bush'
ostriche	oysters ITALIAN
ostron	oyster SWEDISH
ostropel	method of cooking duck ROMANIAN
ostružiny	blackberries CZECH
ostrygi	oysters POLISH
oszczypek	smoked ewe's milk cheese POLISH
öszibarack	peach HUNGARIAN
Othellokage	layer cake filled with custard, topped with chocolate sauce and whipped cream DANISH
ou	egg ROMANIAN
ouananiche	lake salmon from a land-locked lake FRENCH-CANADIAN

oublie	sweet wafer made in waffle irons FRENCH
oude kaas	any mature, strong cheese DUTCH
ouillat	speciality soup from Béarn containing onion and garlic strained on to slices of bread FRENCH
ouriço-do-mar	sea urchin PORTUGUESE
oursins	sea urchins FRENCH
ouzo	clear aniseed-flavoured alcoholic drink, usually drunk with water which turns it milky-white GREEK
ovaší syr	sheep's milk cheese CZECH
ovalina	small buffalo's milk mozzarella cheese ITALIAN
ovarová hlava	brawn (US: head cheese) CZECH
ovarová polévka ze zabíjačky	rich pork soup flavoured with garlic and marjoram and served with boiled barley or rice, traditionally served at carnival time CZECH
ovas	fish roe PORTUGUESE
oveja	ewe SPANISH
ovesná kaše	porridge CZECH
ovesné vločky	oats CZECH
ovnbagt	baked DANISH
òvneshli ezìk	dish of lambs' tongues covered in potatoes BULGARIAN
ovnstegt	roasted DANISH
ovoce	fruit CZECH
ovoce kandované	candied fruit CZECH
ovocný protlak	puree CZECH
ovocný salát	fruit cocktail CZECH
ovocny hruškovy	pear puree CZECH
ovocny jablkový	apple puree CZECH
ovocny meruňkový	apricot puree CZECH
ovocny protlak broskvový	peach puree CZECH
ovoli	'egg-shaped'; a very small form of mozzarella cheese ITALIAN
ovolo	egg mushroom ITALIAN
ovos	eggs PORTUGUESE
owoce	fruit POLISH
ox	domesticated bovine, much used for food
oxbringa	brisket of beef SWEDISH
oxfilé	fillet of beef SWEDISH
Oxford sauce	sauce served with cold venison ENGLISH
oxjärpe	minced beef meatball SWEDISH
oxkött	beef SWEDISH

Oxo™ century-old meat extract, formerly Liebig's Extract of Meat, sold first as a liquid, then in a compressed cube; the name now extends to chicken Oxo, curry Oxo, *etc*

oxrulad beef olives, slices of beef rolled and braised in gravy SWEDISH

oxstek roast beef SWEDISH

oxsvanssoppa oxtail soup SWEDISH

oxtail the skinned tail of an ox or cow used especially in soups and stews

ox-tongue plant of the genus *Picris* with bristly oblong leaves and dandelion-like flowers; similar plants such as alcanet

oxtunga beef tongue SWEDISH

oxymel drink made from a syrup of four parts honey and one part vinegar

oyster bivalve mollusc (said to be an aphrodisiac) which can be eaten raw with a dash of lemon, or cooked in various ways

oyster catcher black and white wading bird

oyster crabs tiny baby crabs found inside oysters, which can be stewed in cream

oyster, poultry tiny succulent portion of meat found on the back of poultry birds

oyster plant *see* salsify

öz venison HUNGARIAN

ozór tongue POLISH

P

płastuga	dab POLISH
płucka cielęce	calf's lungs POLISH
płucka cielęce z winem	veal lights in wine POLISH
pīrāgs	pastry turnovers LATVIAN
pa'an	stuffed betel vine leaves INDIAN
paški sir	soft cream cheese made from fresh curds YUGOSLAVIAN
paštika	pâté CZECH
paštika drůbeží	fowl pâté CZECH
paštika játrová	liver pâté CZECH
paahdettu	toasted; roasted FINNISH
paahto leipä	toast FINNISH
pääruoka	main course FINNISH
päärynä	pear FINNISH
pabassinos	small traditional dough cakes flavoured with aniseed SARDINIAN
pabellón criollo	beef in tomato sauce garnished with beans, rice and bananas SPANISH
paça	stewed sheep's trotters TURKISH
pacal	tripe HUNGARIAN
Pacific salmon	fish of the subgenus *Oncorhynchus*, closely related to the Altantic salmon but not as good to eat
packet	colloquial name in County Cork for drisheen IRISH
paçoca	roast carne de sol ground with cassava root and served with sliced bananas; dessert of roast peanuts crushed with sweetened cassava root meal PORTUGUESE
pácolt	marinated HUNGARIAN
paczki	doughnut POLISH
paddestoel	mushroom DUTCH
pa-dee	rice (growing) BM
padlizsán	aubergine HUNGARIAN
padr shka	Eastern European root vegetable similar to celeriac
paella	rice and a variety of other ingredients, traditionally chicken and shellfish, cooked and served in a shallow two-handled pan of the same name SPANISH
pære	pear DANISH, NORWEGIAN

paesana, alla	with bacon, potatoes, carrots, vegetable marrow and other root vegetables ITALIAN
paesana, salsa	sauce containing mushrooms and bacon, served with pasta ITALIAN
pagel	Provençal name for sea bream FRENCH
pagliarino	medium-soft cheese from Piedmont ITALIAN
pagotón	ice cream GREEK
pähkinä	nut FINNISH
pai	pie NORWEGIAN
païdakia	lamb chops GREEK
pažitka	chives CZECH
paille	straw FRENCH
paillettes	little pastry sticks; fine stick-like slices of vegetables FRENCH
pain	loaf of bread; fruit mould coated with jelly FRENCH
pain complet	loaf-shaped cake made of almond paste FRENCH
pain de gênes	almond-flavoured Genoa cake FRENCH
pain de sucre	loaf sugar FRENCH
painosyltty	brawn (US: head cheese) FINNISH
pain perdu	'lost bread'; bread soaked in a mixture of egg and milk, fried on both sides in butter, and served with sugar and cinnamon, or as the basis of savouries (US: French toast)
paio	smoked mountain ham; pork fillet PORTUGUESE
paistettu	fried; roast FINNISH
paistetut perunat	fried potatoes FINNISH
paisti	roast FINNISH
paistinliemi	gravy FINNISH
paistos	fried or baked dishes FINNISH
päivällinen	dinner FINNISH
päivän annos	speciality of the day FINNISH
paj	pie; tart SWEDISH
pak choi	*see* Chinese celery cabbage, Chinese mustard (greens), Chinese mustard cabbage, Chinese white cabbage, chingensai, gai choy, green in snow, Indian mustard (greens), kai tsoi, leaf mustard, mustard cabbage, taisin CHINESE
pakhtakhor	salad from Uzbekistan containing pickled plums, apples, peaches, cucumbers, olives and chicken paste RUSSIA
pakora	deep fried onion and potato slices INDIAN

pak tsoi sum	*see* brocoletto, choy sum, flowering pak choi, flowering white cabbage, hong tsoi sum, hon tsai tai, kozaitai, purple flowered choy sum, rape
pala	piece FINNISH
pa-la	nutmeg BM
palačinke	pancakes served with peanuts, cinnamon and sugar mixed with thick cream YUGOSLAVIAN
palačinky	pancakes CZECH
palačinky s džemem	pancakes with jam CZECH
palačinky s tvarohem	pancakes with cream cheese CZECH
palačinky s vaječným konakem	pancakes with egg brandy CZECH
palacsinta	pancakes, often spread with minced ham and mushrooms HUNGARIAN
paladru	cow's milk cheese from the Savoie FRENCH
pålæg	garnish for smorrebrød of cold meat, sausage salad, fish or cheese DANISH
palak	spinach INDIAN
palamida	palamid or bonito, a large rich fish GREEK
palamut	bonito TURKISH
palate of beef	palate of the ox
Palatschinke	pancake with a brandy-flavoured batter AUSTRIAN
Palatschinke	pancake filled with jam or cheese, or with hot chocolate and nut topping GERMAN
pale	young coalfish NORWEGIAN
paleron	cut of beef with no English equivalent but similar to chuck roast FRENCH
Palestine soup	19th-century name for a Jerusalem artichoke soup ENGLISH
palets de dames	type of petit four flavoured with vanilla, lemon or orange FRENCH
palette knife	flexible, blunt bladed knife used in pastry making
paling	eel cooked in a soup or stew DUTCH
paling	eel DUTCH
paling in't groen	eel braised in white sauce, garnished with chopped parsley and other greens DUTCH
pall	*see* phall
pallottole d'aranci	an orange sweet ITALIAN
palm	large family of trees which include date and coconut
palm hearts	firm, creamy-coloured, delicately flavoured inner parts of palm tree shoots

palm wine	wine made from the fermented sap of various palms, particularly date and coconut palms
palmier	heart-shaped cake of flaky pastry sandwiched with whipped cream or jam, resembling palm leaves FRENCH
palmito	palm heart PORTUGUESE, SPANISH
palócleves	mutton, French beans, potatoes and sour cream, seasoned with paprika, garlic and caraway seeds HUNGARIAN
paloise, sauce	sauce made like a béarnaise but flavoured with mint FRENCH
paloma	pigeon SPANISH
palomba	wood-pigeon ITALIAN
palourde	clam; name for vegetable marrow in some parts of France FRENCH
palsternacka	parsnip SWEDISH
palta	avocado SPANISH
palten	form of black pudding RUSSIAN
palvattu	cured; smoked FINNISH
palvikinkku	cured ham FINNISH
pampanito	small pompano fish SPANISH
Pampelmuse	grapefruit GERMAN
pamplemousse	grapefruit FRENCH
pan	speciality dish of betel nuts and spices folded into betel leaves to make small parcels, served as a digestif at the end of a meal INDIAN
pan	bread SPANISH
pan broiling	cooking food using dry heat in a pan on top of the stove AMERICAN
pan di Genova	almond cake ITALIAN
pan di spagna	sponge cake ITALIAN
pan dowdy	a pudding usually containing apples AMERICAN
pan dulce	'sweet bread'; an egg and flour pudding SPANISH
pan tostato	toasted Italian bread ITALIAN
pan vis	a meal made from leftovers from stock fish DUTCH
panaché	mixed; two or more of something FRENCH
panada	thick roux-based sauce or paste used to bind mixtures such as the basis of choux pastry and some soufflés
panado	breaded PORTUGUESE
panage	coating food with breadcrumbs FRENCH

panais	parsnip FRENCH
pancake	thin pouring batter cooked on both sides in a frying pan making a round thin cake which is served with lemon juice or other sweet or savoury fillings
pancetta	distinctively smoky, salted, raw belly of pork ITALIAN
panch foran	five-spice mixture which usually contains cumin seeds, nigella seeds, aniseed, fenugreek seeds and mustard seeds BENGALI
pandekage	pancake DANISH
pandolce	heavy cake containing dried fruit and pine kernels ITALIAN
pane	bread ITALIAN
panecillo	roll SPANISH
panedda	another name for casigiolu SARDINIAN
paneer, panir	fresh, soft cheese often used in Indian cooking; mixed with peas, it is called mattar panir INDIAN
paner	to coat food in breadcrumbs before frying FRENCH
panerad	breaded SWEDISH
paneret	breaded DANISH
panert	breaded NORWEGIAN
panetière	a loaf is scooped out, stuffed and finished in the oven; method of serving chicken FRENCH
panette dolce	Easter speciality sweet bread decorated with raisins CORSICAN
panettone	tall yeast cake containing candied peel, traditionally served with sparkling white wine after lunch on Christmas Day and at midnight on New Year's Eve ITALIAN
panforte	honey and fruit cake from Siena, eaten at festivals SPANISH
panforte di Siena	flat round slab cake made mostly of spiced crystallised fruit ITALIAN
pangrattato	breadcrumbs ITALIAN
panier	basket FRENCH
panierowane	breaded POLISH
paniert	breaded GERMAN
panierte Eier	eggs in breadcrumbs GERMAN
panino	roll ITALIAN
panir	type of milk curd INDIAN
pankūkas	yeast pancake LATVIAN
panna	cream ITALIAN

pannbiff   hamburger steak with fried onions SWEDISH

panne   the fat surrounding pig's kidneys and fillets FRENCH

pannekake   pancake NORWEGIAN

pannekoek   pancake DUTCH

pannekoek met stroop   pancake served with syrup DUTCH

pannequet   pancake FRENCH

Pannfisch   large fishcake GERMAN

pannkaka   pancake SWEDISH

pannonia   hard cheese made of cow's milk HUNGARIAN

pannu   sautéed dishes FINNISH

pannukakku   thick pancake FINNISH

panorato alla romana dish of bread soaked in milk, then beaten egg ITALIAN

panoufle   the under part of the top of a sirloin of beef FRENCH

pansperima   a dish signifying death, dating from pagan times, made from boiled wheat GREEK

pantin   a crescent-shaped mould used to make pâté; pork pâté FRENCH

panure   coating of egg and breadcrumbs on food before it is fried FRENCH

panzanella alla marinna   bread salad from Tuscany mixed with basil, dressed with oil and vinegar, pounded garlic, anchovies and chillies, surrounded by hard-boiled eggs or tomato ITALIAN

panzarotti   large fried or baked dough envelopes, often filled with pork, eggs, cheese, anchovies and tomatoes ITALIAN

panzarotti alla napolitana   small fried ravioli from Naples ITALIAN

pão   bread PORTUGUESE

pão-de-ló   tea bread PORTUGUESE

pãozinho   roll PORTUGUESE

pap   porridge DUTCH

papa   potato SPANISH

papanash   cheese balls made with cottage cheese, semolina, flour, butter and egg, simmered in water, and served with sugar BULGARIAN

papanaşi   cheesecakes ROMANIAN

paparot   speciality soup from Istria, containing spinach ITALIAN

papas a la huancaína with cheese and green peppers SPANISH

papaw, pawpaw   the custard apple, a tropical fruit (also called papaya, *see* below)

papaya	large pear-shaped West Indian tropical fruit with fragrant juicy, orange-pink flesh and lots of black seeds in the centre (also called pa(w)paw, *see* above)
papaz yahnisi	mutton stew TURKISH
paperissa savustettu kala	method of smoking fresh fish, wrapped in a paper parcel and placed in the embers of a fire FINNISH
papillote, en	baked and sometimes served in an envelope of greased paper FRENCH
papos de anjo	baked egg yolks topped with syrup PORTUGUESE
papoutsakia	stuffed aubergines GREEK
pappadam	*see* poppadom
pappardelle	broad crimped noodles from Tuscany ITALIAN
pappilan hatavara	trifle made with small sweet biscuits soaked in fruit juice FINNISH
paprika	mild spice made from sweet red peppers HUNGARIAN
paprika	green or red (sweet) peppers DUTCH
paprika	pepper SWEDISH
Paprika-Kalbschnitzel	dish made with sliced veal fillet, floured and fried with onions and paprika, and sour cream added before serving AUSTRIAN
paprikás	stew containing paprika and sour cream HUNGARIAN
Paprikaschote	sweet pepper GERMAN
paprikový salát	green pepper salad CZECH
papryka	pepper; sweet pepper POLISH
paprykarz	stew POLISH
papu	bean FINNISH
paradicsom	tomatoes HUNGARIAN
paradise nut	like a Brazil nut but slightly larger and with a sweeter, more delicate flavour
paragon	type of cultivated chestnut
Paraguay tea	*see* yerba (maté)
paratha	shallow-fried unleavened bread, crisp on the outside and soft on the inside; it may be flavoured with spices or filled with vegetables (stuffed paratha) INDIAN
par-boiling	boiling food for part of its cooking time and finishing it by another method
parching	browning food in dry heat in the oven or under the grill
par-cooking	half-cooking food by roasting or frying
paring	cutting peel or rind from fruit or vegetables

párek v rohlíku	hot dog CZECH
parenica	tasty hard cheese made from sheep's milk CZECH
parfait	frozen dessert like a rich mousse FRENCH
parfait amour	sweet, slightly scented and spiced citrus oil-based liqueur produced in several colours FRENCH
parfait glacé	iced sweet like a bombe but without the plain ice cream coating FRENCH
parfumé	flavoured FRENCH
pargo	large red bream PORTUGUESE, SPANISH
pariloitu	grilled; barbecued FINNISH
paring	thinly peeling skin and any irregular parts from fruit or vegetables
parisare	minced beef with capers, beetroot and onions served on toast and topped with a fried egg SWEDISH
Paris-Brest	gâteau of choux pastry ring, split and filled with praline butter cream FRENCH
pariserbøf	hamburger on toast with egg yolk and chopped capers DANISH
parisertoast	toasted ham and cheese sandwich DANISH
Paris-gênes	French layered cake, with rum-flavoured icing decorated with walnuts FRENCH
parisien	ring-shaped sponge cake, split and sandwiched with frangipane cream; the centre is filled with crystallised fruits and apricot jam and the dish is covered in meringue and set in the oven FRENCH
parisienne, à la	dishes with a garnish of potato balls fried in herb butter and vegetables, often including artichoke hearts; poached fish with mushrooms and truffles in white wine sauce, surrounded with crayfish; chicken consommé with macédoine of vegetables, rounds of royale, and chervil; sauce blonde; a method of serving potatoes FRENCH
pař* íský řízek	veal cutlet dipped in egg and flour CZECH
Parker House croûtons	croûtons made from bread toasted on one side only AMERICAN
Parker House rolls	rolls originating from the Parker House Hotel, Boston AMERICAN
parkin	moist ginger cake, usually cut into squares ENGLISH
párky	form of frankfurter, the best being those from Prague CZECH
parlies	ginger cakes thought to have been so called because they were eaten by members of the Scottish Parliament in the 19th century SCOTTISH

Parma ham	smoked ham from Parma ITALIAN
Parmentier	an 18th-century Frenchman famed for promoting the popularity of potatoes in France; his name now applies to a number of potato dishes FRENCH
Parmesan cheese	very hard unpasteurised skimmed cow's milk cheese with a strong distinctive flavour, used finely grated on soups and pasta dishes
parmesane, à la	dishes including grated Parmesan cheese FRENCH
parmezan	Parmesan cheese POLISH
parmice	red mullet CZECH
parmigiano	Parmesan cheese ITALIAN
parnossus	white ewe's milk cheese GREEK
párolt	steamed HUNGARIAN
párolt hús	pot roast HUNGARIAN
párolt húsok	stews HUNGARIAN
päron	pear SWEDISH
parówki	wiener; frankfurter POLISH
parping sugg	home made tea-time confection made from cornflakes and chocolate; chocolate crispy cake
parr	young salmon ENGLISH
parrilla, a la	grilled SPANISH
parrillada mixta	mixed grill SPANISH
parrot fish	a number of fish of the Scaridae family
parsa	asparagus FINNISH
Parsee	a race with its own style of cooking INDIAN
parsley	mild, pleasantly-flavoured herb with flat or curly leaves; the flavour is mainly in the stalks but the leaves make an attractive garnish
parsnip	common root vegetable – nutty and sweet, the flavour improves after several frosts
parson's nose	nickname for the fatty piece of meat at the tail end of chicken or turkey – that part of a duck or goose is known as the pope's nose
partan	crab SCOTTISH
partridge	greyish-brown game bird
pasa makarouna	dish of Turkish origin made from meat, pasta and cheese GREEK
pasado	done; cooked SPANISH
pasanda	mild curry with yoghurt INDIAN
pashtet	layered pie made of fish, shellfish, poultry or game RUSSIAN

paskha   sweet dish of curd cheese, cream, almonds and dried
                     fruit set in a wooden mould, traditionally served at
                     Easter RUSSIAN

passa   raisin; sultana PORTUGUESE

passa tempo man   Greek street-vendor who sells nuts and seeds from a
                     small cart GREEK

(bem) passado   well-done PORTUGUESE

(mal) passado   medium PORTUGUESE

(muito mal) passado rare PORTUGUESE

passarelle   dried muscatel grape FRENCH

passatelli   a speciality soup from Modena and Bologna; pasta
                     made from egg, parmesan cheese, breadcrumbs, and
                     often a pinch of nutmeg ITALIAN

passato   purée; creamed ITALIAN

passe-crassane   variety of sweet pear FRENCH

passe-pomme   variety of apple FRENCH

passe-purée   kitchen utensil to make purées FRENCH

passion fruit   tropical vine fruit which looks like a large wrinkled
                     plum; the yellow flesh is fragrant, sweet and juicy
                     and full of small black edible seeds; it can be eaten
                     raw or to flavour drinks and ice creams

passoire   colander or sieve FRENCH

pasta   flour-and-water dough shaped into spaghetti,
                     macaroni, lasagne and many other forms, available
                     dried or fresh and in a variety of colours ITALIAN

pasta asciutta alla marchigiana   a speciality of the Marche province it is
                     not a true pasta, but made from bread dough ITALIAN

pasta frolla   sweet short crust pastry ITALIAN

pasta ke faki   speciality dish of noodles and lentils from the island
                     of Rhodes GREEK

pastas   noodles; macaroni; spaghetti SPANISH

pastas de almendras mallorquinas   Mallorcan almond biscuits SPANISH

paste   a thick mixture of ingredients usually combining
                     ground or minced food with a little liquid

pastei   pasty; pie DUTCH

pasteija   paste; pastry; pie FINNISH

pastej   pie; patty; pâté SWEDISH

pastel   sweet or savoury dish containing pastry SPANISH

pastel   usually a type of pie PORTUGUESE

pastelaria   pastries; pâtisseries PORTUGUESE

pastelillo   small tart SPANISH

pastelinhos de anchovas   fingers of pastry spread with anchovy paste
PORTUGUESE

pastella   frying batter ITALIAN

pastelli   toffee-like, honey flavoured sweet containing sesame seeds GREEK

pastèque   watermelon FRENCH

Pastetchen   filled puff pastry case GERMAN

Pastete   pastry; pie GERMAN

pasteurising   heating a substance, usually milk, to 60°–92°C and keeping it at that temperature for 15 seconds (which destroys bacteria) and then cooling it rapidly (named for Louis Pasteur (1822–95), French chemist and bacteriologist

pastiňak   parsley CZECH

pasticciata   meat stew from Verona with herbs and vegetables
ITALIAN

pasticciata polenta   a Milanese dish made with polenta layered with sauce béchamel and mushrooms or truffles, topped with grated Parmesan and baked ITALIAN

pasticcino   tart, cake or small pastry ITALIAN

pasticcio   pie; type of pasta like lasagne ITALIAN

pastichio   popular dish with two cream sauces GREEK

pastillage   confectioners' paste of icing sugar, water and gum tragacanth, used to make cake decorations FRENCH

pastille   small gum lozenge usually flavoured with fruit juice and often coated in crystallized sugar

pastina   small pasta in various shapes, mainly used as a bouillon or soup ingredient ITALIAN

Pastinake   parsnip GERMAN

pastine   grain-like pasta shapes

pastis   liquorice or aniseed flavoured liqueur which turns milky with water

pastitsada kerireïkïa   a speciality dish made with chunks of veal, onions, tomatoes, herbs, water and seasoning; the sauce is served with macaroni and the meat on a separate place CORFIOTE

pasto   meal ITALIAN

pastokydona   quince paste GREEK

pastourmá   black-rinded smoked bacon flavoured with garlic
GREEK

pastrami   dry cured and smoked, preserved beef from the underside, a popular sandwich filling AMERICAN

pastries	fancy cakes, usually iced or decorated
pastry	mixture of flour and fat and sometimes egg bound with water; there are several types of pastry, used in sweet and savoury recipes
pastry cream	crème pâtissière ENGLISH
pastürmą	dry garlic-flavoured sausage BULGARIAN
pasty	individual pastry pie containing diced meat, potato and vegetables
paszteciki	rissole; croquette POLISH
pasztet	moulded pâté POLISH
pata	casserole FINNISH
pata	trotter SPANISH
patakukko	fish pie FINNISH
patapaisti	veal or beef pot roast FINNISH
patata	potato SPANISH
patáta	potato GREEK
patate	sweet potato FRENCH
patate	potatoes ITALIAN
patates frites	chips DUTCH
patatine	small, new potatoes ITALIAN
pâte	pastry; in English the only pastry still called by its French name is pâté sucrée FRENCH
pâté	savoury mixture of minced meat, flaked fish and/or vegetables cooked to form a solid mass FRENCH
patelle	gastropod molluscs such as limpets FRENCH
paté de foie gras	literally paste of fat liver, ie of a specially force-fed goose, supposed to be a great delicacy FRENCH
pathia/patia	seafood curry with rich dark sweet and sour sauce INDIAN
patinho	duckling PORTUGUESE
pâtisserie	highly decorated pastries FRENCH
patlagele vinete	cold cooked aubergine salad ROMANIAN
patlican	aubergine TURKISH
Patna rice	rice with a very long thin grain from the 5th-century BCE city of Patna on the River Ganges, the capital of Bihar state INDIAN
pato	duck PORTUGUESE, SPANISH
patonki	French bread FINNISH
patrani	banana leaves INDIAN
patricieni	spicy pork sausages ROMANIAN
patrijs	partridge DUTCH

patsas	soup of tripe, pig's feet, garlic and lemon GREEK
pattegris	suckling pig DANISH
pattogatott kukorica	popcorn HUNGARIAN
patty	small pie; often made of puff pastry, with a savoury mixture; a burger-like cake of minced meat
patumpeperium	19th-century English anchovy paste
pauillac	a type of unweaned lamb FRENCH
paunch	the stomach and intestines of a rabbit or hare
paupiette	thin slice of meat or fish rolled around stuffing FRENCH
pavé	cold dish; small square; sponge cake FRENCH
pavé de moyeaux	a cow's milk cheese from Normandy FRENCH
pavezky	thin slices of bread dipped in milk, beaten egg and breadcrumbs and fried CZECH
pavie	a firm fleshed peach
pavlova	dessert of meringue topped with whipped cream and fresh fruit, popular in Australia – where it is unsurprisingly shortened to Pav (named after the Russian ballerina Anna Pavlova (1885–1931)
pavo	turkey SPANISH
pavot, graines de	poppy seeds FRENCH
pawpaw	*see* papaw, papaya
pa-y-all	corruption of pain à l'ail (garlic bread); a peasant breakfast dish CATALAN
payasam	milk pudding INDIAN
paysanne, à la	prepared in simple country style; often applies to braised meat garnished with mixed chopped vegetables; a method of serving peas; a method of serving potatoes FRENCH
payusnaya	coarse, pressed form of caviar RUSSIAN
pé de moleque	peanut brittle PORTUGUESE
pé de porco	pig's trotters PORTUGUESE
pea	seeds of a climbing plant, of which there are many varieties; the pod may be eaten when young; available fresh for a short season then frozen, canned, dried and dehydrated
pea bean	variety of climbing bean FRENCH
pea flour	flour produced from ground dried peas, used for thickening sauces
peach	delicious tree fruit about the size of an apple, with yellow-red downy skin and soft, juicy, orange flesh

peacock	large bird, distantly related to the turkey, once eaten at mediaeval festivals
pečená husí játra s mandlěmi	goose liver with almonds CZECH
pečene jěhnecí	roast lamb CZECH
pečene tělecí	roast veal joint CZECH
pečene věpřová	roast pork CZECH
pečeně	roast CZECH
pečeně hovězí	roast beef CZECH
peanut	two kernels are enclosed in the dry, crinkly pod of the leguminous plant *Arachis hypogaea*, which are forced underground to ripen; they are available in their shell or shelled, and may be plain, dry roasted or roasted and salted and can be eaten as a snack or used in various dishes; they are used to make an oil; *also* goober, groundnut, monkey nut
peanut butter	brownish-yellow oily paste made from peanuts
peanut oil	oil of peanut kernels
pear	popular tree fruit eaten as a dessert fruit and in cooking; there are many varieties
pearl barley	barley with the outer husk removed
pease	archaic word for pea(s)
pease brose	porridge of pea flour SCOTTISH
pease pudding	split peas, soaked, boiled, mashed and served with ham or pork
peber	black pepper DANISH
peberbøf	beef steak with pepper corns DANISH
peberfrugt	pepper; pimiento DANISH
peberrod	pepper; horseradish DANISH
peberrod	horseradish DANISH
pebronata	speciality dish of braised beef flavoured with juniper berries CORSICAN
pec	unsmoked, applied only to herring FRENCH
pecan nut	the fruit of the South US hickory tree *Carya pecan* (or *C. illinoensis*) having an oily kernel with a walnutty flavour but sweeter and milder; also hickory nut AMERICAN
pêche	peach FRENCH
pêche Melba	peaches poached in vanilla syrup served with vanilla ice-cream (named after the Australian operatic soprano Dame Nellie Melba 1861–1931) FRENCH
pechenaia kartofel v smetane	potato and sour cream RUSSIAN
pechuga	breast SPANISH

pecorino	ewe's milk cheese ITALIAN
pecorino sardo	hard white cheese made from ewe's milk SARDINIAN
pecten	bivalve mollusc with a rounded shell, such as the scallop (*Pecten*), which swims by snapping its shell open and shut
pectin	naturally occurring substance contained in ripe fruit and vegetables; used to set jams and jellies because it solidifies to a gel when heated in a sugar solution
peel	outer skin or rind on some fruits and vegetables
peêle	mare's tail weed, which is an edible weed; the young shoots can be eaten FRENCH
peeling	removing the outer shell, rind or peel from foods
pee-nang	betel-nut BM
peer	pear DUTCH
pee-sang	banana BM
Peggy's leg	toffee containing brown sugar, molasses and syrup, butter, ginger and vinegar; a little baking soda is added to half of the mixture so the toffee has two colours; it is pulled out into sticks IRISH
pehmeäksi keitetty muna soft boiled egg FINNISH	
peinirlis	savoury pastries made from filled yeast dough boats GREEK
peito	breast PORTUGUESE
peixe	fish PORTUGUESE
pejerrey	'the king of fishes'; fish of the silverside family found off the Atlantic coast SOUTH AMERICAN
pekeltong	salt tongue DUTCH
pekelvlees	slices of salted meat DUTCH
Peking duck	roasted, marinated duck, cut into strips and served with spring onions, cucumber, pancakes and a special plum based sauce CHINESE, MANDARIN
pekoni	bacon FINNISH
pekoni pannu	fried bacon, sausages, potatoes and eggs FINNISH
péksütemény	bakery product HUNGARIAN
pélamide	bonito FRENCH
pelardou	goat's milk cheese from the Languedoc region FRENCH
pelle rouge	another name for the utensil called a salamander FRENCH
Pellkartoffeln	potatoes cooked in their skins GERMAN
pelmeni	small stuffed envelopes of thin pastry, similar to ravioli RUSSIAN

pelte	sweet dish made with corn flour, molasses, sugar and water, with added almonds and lemon juice ALBANIAN
peltopyy	partridge FINNISH
pelures	the trimming or parings of foods FRENCH
pemmican	well dried buffalo or deer meat which is ground and mixed with melted fat and berries or dried fruits to form a cake and wrapped in animal skin; once used by the Native Americans and now made chiefly for emergency rations
penetleu	cheese named after the district in which it is made ROMANIAN
pénide	a sweet similar to barley sugar FRENCH
penne	pasta tube
pennyroyal	strongly scented creeping plant related to the mint family; the traditional flavouring in black pudding
penoche, penuche	candy from the southern States, made with sugar, milk, butter and nuts AMERICAN
pentéola	scallop PORTUGUESE
peoci	Venetian name for mussels ITALIAN
pepato	a type of pecorino spiced with pepper SICILIAN
pepato	peppered ITALIAN
pepe	pepper ITALIAN
peper	pepper DUTCH
peperata, salsa	an uncooked sauce from Verona made from beef marrow, butter, breadcrumbs and Parmesan cheese, served with cold meats and poultry ITALIAN
pepernoten	ginger-nut biscuit DUTCH
peperonata	vegetable dish made from onions, red peppers and tomatoes cooked in olive oil and butter ITALIAN
peperoni	green or red sweet pepper; hot, dry coarsely chopped pork and beef sausage flavoured with hot pepper, fennel and spices ITALIAN
pepř	pepper CZECH
pepř černý	black pepper CZECH
pepinillo	gherkin SPANISH
pepino	cucumber PORTUGUESE, SPANISH
pepitoria, en	stewed with onions, green peppers and tomatoes SPANISH
peppar	pepper SWEDISH
pepparkaka	ginger snaps SWEDISH
pepparkaka	spice cake SWEDISH

pepper	a spice, the berry of a tropical vine *Piper nigrum*, which may be green (unripe), white or black; the fruit of capsicum – green, red or yellow peppers used as a vegetable
pepper dulse	red seaweed resembling dulse, dried and used as a spice SCOTTISH
pepper, sweet	fluted pear-shaped fruit, a member of the capsicum family, mainly green when first developed, turning yellow and then red when fully developed
peppercorn	fruit or berry of *Piper nigrum*
peppergrass	species of hot-tasting cress; pepperwort
pepperkake	ginger biscuit NORWEGIAN
peppermint	related to garden spearmint but with a stronger scent and flavour; oil and an essence may be extracted
pepperrot	horseradish NORWEGIAN
peppers	fruits of plants of the genus piper; fruits of any plant of the genus capsicum
pepsin	an enzyme; a creamy-white powder which can be prepared from fresh pig's stomach
pequeno almoço	breakfast PORTUGUESE
pera	pear ITALIAN, SPANISH
pêra	pear PORTUGUESE
pera di vacca	another name for a cheese called casigiolu SARDINIAN
perca	perch PORTUGUESE, SPANISH
perçebas	sessile goose-barnacle, of the genus *Lepas*, with flattened shell and feathery cirri PORTUGUESE
percebe	barnacle SPANISH
perceve	barnacle PORTUGUESE
perch	large round freshwater fish with firm, white, sweet flesh
perche	perch FRENCH
perdikes	partridge GREEK
perdiz	partridge PORTUGUESE, SPANISH
perdreau	young partridge under a year old FRENCH
perdrix	partridge over a year old FRENCH
perejil	parsley SPANISH
peren	pears DUTCH
pérgourdine, à la	garnish for fillets of beef of whole truffles cooked in Madeira, with mirepoix and sauce périgueux; poultry with truffle slices placed under the skin of the breast, poached and served with sauce suprême with truffle

	essence; all dishes with a garnish of truffles and foie gras FRENCH
perifollo	chervil SPANISH
perilla	a firm, bland cheese SPANISH
perişoare cu verdeţuri	national dish of minced meat, one part beef to three parts fat pork, mixed with fried onions, seasoning and herbs into small balls fried butter and served with demi-glace ROMANIAN
periwinkle	small, round, black or orange shell inhabited by a sea snail, *see* winkle
perkelt	chopped pork or lamb braised with onion, and with sour cream added CZECH
Perlgraupe	pearl barley GERMAN
perliczki	guinea hen POLISH
perliczki pieczone	roast guinea fowl POLISH
perlot	name in the Manche département for a small oyster FRENCH
perna	leg PORTUGUESE
pernice	partridge ITALIAN
perník	traditional honey cake CZECH
pernil	ham PORTUGUESE
Pernod	liqueur based on aniseed, usually served with water and topped with ice which turns it a milky colour
pêro	variety of eating apple PORTUGUESE
perry	alcoholic drink made from fermented juice of a hard astringent pear
persetorsk	salted, boiled and pressed cod NORWEGIAN
persicata	peach conserve ITALIAN
persika	peach SWEDISH
persikka	peach FINNISH
persil	parsley FRENCH
persilja	parsley FINNISH, SWEDISH
persiljesmör	parsley butter SWEDISH
persillade	chopped parsley and sometimes garlic sprinkled over dishes as a garnish; a dish of leftover meats fried in butter and sprinkled with parsley FRENCH
persille	parsley DANISH, NORWEGIAN
persimmon	large, sweet, tomato-like tropical fruit of a tree of the genus *Diospyros* with leathery skin that turns from yellow to red as it ripens
peru	turkey PORTUGUESE
peruna	potato FINNISH

péruvienne, à la	garnish for meat of stuffed oca and sauce allemande FRENCH
perzik	peach DUTCH
pesca	peach ITALIAN
pescada	hake PORTUGUESE
pescadilla	whiting SPANISH
pescadinhas	whiting PORTUGUESE
pescado	fish SPANISH
pescatrice	angler fish ITALIAN
pesce	fish ITALIAN
peshawari	cooked with coconut and fruits INDIAN
pêssego	peach PORTUGUESE
pestle and mortar	a bowl and a round-ended implement used to crush and grind foods
pesto	sauce of fresh basil, garlic, pine nuts, Parmesan cheese and olive oil ITALIAN
pet de nonne	soufflé fritter made from choux pastry FRENCH
peterselie	parsley DUTCH
Petersilie	parsley GERMAN
petits-fours	variety of small sweets, pastries and biscuits, often served with coffee at the end of a meal FRENCH
petit gruyère	processed Emmenthal cheese FRENCH
petit salé	salted belly or flank or pork FRENCH
petit-carré	fresh ancien impérial cheese FRENCH
petite marmite	strong savoury soup served in an earthenware dish; it is a Parisian speciality and in Paris often called petite marmite Henri IV FRENCH
petit-houx	butcher's broom (*Ruscus*); its bitter roots are used to make aperitifs FRENCH
petits pâtés	patties served hot as hors d'œuvres FRENCH
petits-pieds	term used on menus to describe small birds such as blackbirds, thrushes, larks, etc FRENCH
petit-suisse	unsalted, mild, whole milk cream cheese with added cream FRENCH
petmèz	type of treacle made from boiled grape juice and sugar, stored for the winter BALKAN
pétoncle	another name for scallop FRENCH
petrezselyem	parsley HUNGARIAN
petržel	parsley CZECH
pe-tsai	a variety of cabbage *see* bok choy, Chinese leaves, headless Chinese cabbage, michihili, wong bok CHINESE

petti di pollo chicken breasts ITALIAN

petticoat tails a cake; the name may come from the shape, like a crinoline petticoat, or from 'petites gatelles', the name of cakes introduced to Scotland by Mary Queen of Scots SCOTTISH

pettitoes old English dish made from the feet, heart, liver and lungs of a pig

petto breast ITALIAN

peu few; little FRENCH

pevide pip; salted pumpkin seed PORTUGUESE

peynir cheese TURKISH

pez espada swordfish SPANISH

pez limon Mediterranean silverfish SPANISH

Pfahlmuschel mussel GERMAN

Pfannkuchen pancake; dialect word for doughnut GERMAN

pfarvel garnish made from a stiff dough which is grated, left to dry, then added to soups JEWISH

Pfeffer pepper GERMAN

Pfefferkuchen very spicy ginger bread GERMAN

Pfeffer-Potthast 'pepperpot'; a beef stew GERMAN

Pfifferling chanterelle mushroom GERMAN

předkrm appetizer CZECH

předkrm studený cold appetizer CZECH

předkrm teplý warm appetizer CZECH

přírodní řízek breaded hamburger CZECH

Pfirsich peach GERMAN

Pflaume plum GERMAN

pflütten boulettes of semolina and potato ALSATIAN

phal(l), pall five-star hot INDIAN

pheasant game bird which should be hung for about a week before being plucked and drawn, commonly served in a brace, one male and one female

Philadelphia cinnamon buns speciality from Philadelphia AMERICAN

Philadelphia ice cream ice cream made from scalded cream, sugar, salt and flavouring AMERICAN

Philadelphia pepperpot traditional soup, said to have been created by George Washington's head cook, from what was available to him at the time – tripe, a veal bone and peppercorns AMERICAN

Philadelphia relish relish of cabbage, green peppers, celery seed and mustard AMERICAN

Philippine spinach	variety of purslane cultivated for its leaves, cooked like spinach
pholiota	genus of fungus
phoolgobi	cauliflower INDIAN
phosphoric acid	a highly corrosive acid which is found highly diluted in some synthetic drinks
phosphorus	naturally occurring mineral, essential in human diet
phyllo	paper-thin pastry, also filo GREEK
physalis	small, edible, round yellow berry of a tropical annual *Physalis peruviana* or *P. pubescens*, also known as the cape gooseberry, ground cherry, strawberry tomato or winter cherry FRENCH
pianki do zupy nic	'nothing soup', with a garnish of 'kisses'; a cold, sweet, custard-like soup with a cooked or uncooked meringue mixture dropped into it POLISH
piatto	dish ITALIAN
piaz	onion INDIAN
picadillo	minced meat; hash SPANISH
picado	minced SPANISH
picado de carne	minced meat PORTUGUESE
picalilly	pickle DUTCH
picante	sharp; spicy; highly seasoned SPANISH
picarel	small Mediterranean fish served like an anchovy FRENCH
picatoste	deep-fried slice of bread SPANISH
piccalilli	bright yellow mustard pickle made from mixed vegetables especially onions, cauliflower and cucumber
piccante	highly seasoned ITALIAN
piccante, salsa	piquant cold sauce served with cold meats ITALIAN\
piccata	thin veal scallop ITALIAN
piccione	pigeon ITALIAN
Pichelsteiner	hotpot of sliced beef, pork, veal, mutton, ox marrow, onions, carrot, celeriac, cabbage and potato GERMAN
piche-pache	stew made from turkey giblets SPANISH
picholine	large green olive FRENCH
pichoncillo	young pigeon SPANISH
pickerel	young pike; a particular variety of North American pike
pickling	preserving fresh, raw or lightly cooked meat, eggs, vegetables or fruit in brine, or spiced vinegar

pickled butter	Cornish method of pickling butter in brine
pickled eggs	method of preserving hard boiled eggs
pickled herrings	dish made with herrings, vinegar, onion and sugar SCOTTISH
pickled onions	small onions, peeled and pickled in vinegar
pickled plums	peeled plums picked in vinegar
pickled pork	pork immersed in solution of salt, sugar and water
pickled walnuts	green walnuts pickled in vinegar
pickling spice	pungent mixture of spices added to the vinegar when making pickles, which includes peppercorns, mace, red chillies, allspice, cloves, ginger, mustard seeds or coriander
picnic	meal eaten in the open air; it may be a bag of crisps and a can of lemonade taken in a haystack, or a range of foods washed down with champagne, set out on elaborate tables with tablecloths and silver candalabra
picnic shoulder	hand of pork AMERICAN
picodon	goat's milk cheese from the Dauphiné district FRENCH
piddock	edible clam-like mollusc of the family Pholadidae which bores into rock, wood and clay, unusual for its phosphorescence
pide	thin bread often served with kebab or put at the bottom of a casserole TURKISH
pie	large and small pastry cases filled with sweet or savoury mixtures
pie plant	dialect name for rhubarb AMERICAN
pièce de résistance	the main course FRENCH
pièces montées	lavish table decorations FRENCH
pieczarki	cultivated mushrooms POLISH
pieczeń	roast POLISH
pieczen barania	roast mutton POLISH
pieczone	roasted POLISH
pieczywo	bread; rolls POLISH
pied-de-cheval	large variety of oyster (*literally* horse's hoof) FRENCH
piede	trotter ITALIAN
Piedmont-style	cooked with truffles and rice
pieds de mouton	sheep's feet or trotters FRENCH
pieds de porc	pig's trotters FRENCH
pie-grièche	shrike FRENCH

piémontaise, à la	garnish for poultry, meat and entrées of risotto with shredded Italian truffles FRENCH
piemontese, alla	see Piedmont-style ITALIAN
piens	milk LATVIAN
pieprz	pepper POLISH
pierna	leg SPANISH
piernik	spiced honey cake POLISH
pieróg	pasty POLISH
pierogi	envelopes of dough stuffed with meats, cheese, cabbage or fruit; dumplings POLISH
pierozki drożdżowe	pierogi made with a yeast dough POLISH
pietruszka	parsley POLISH
pig	an animal, the source of bacon, ham and pork
piglets on horseback	half-cooked cocktail sausages wrapped in streaky bacon and grilled
pig's cheek	a part of the pig usually pickled or dried and cured
pig's ear	rarely eaten in Britain today, it can be cooked with the trotters or separately; generally used in sausages
pig's fry	dish comprising heart, liver, lungs and sweetbreads of a pig, usually fried but sometimes stewed or casseroled
pig's trotters	fresh or salted, they may be boned, stuffed and roasted or used to make brawn
pigeon	wild and tame pigeons are edible, the breasts being the easiest parts to contend with
pigeon pea	green, nutty peas with a floury texture, and coarse, curved pods; available dried and sometimes fresh
pigeonneau	young pigeon FRENCH
piggvar	turbot SWEDISH
pighvarre	turbot; a popular Danish fish DANISH
pignoli	pine kernels ITALIAN
pigwa	quince POLISH
pihlajanmarja	rowanberry FINNISH
pihti hirino	pork brawn GREEK
pihvi	beefsteak FINNISH
piimä	clotted milk FINNISH
piimäjuusto	sour milk cheese made with eggs if skimmed milk is used, or without eggs if whole milk is used FINNISH
piirakka	pie FINNISH
piiras	small pie; pasty FINNISH
pikant	spiced; highly seasoned GERMAN

pike	Large predatory fresh-water fish of the genus *Esox*, with a broad flat snout, strong teeth and a body covered with small scales; the best to eat are young pickerel
pikelet	various types of teacake BRITISH
pikkelsagurk	gherkin NORWEGIAN
pikkulämpimät	hors d'œuvres FINNISH
pikkuleipä	biscuit FINNISH
pilaf	the name in Europe for pilâv
pilafi	rice dish of Turkish origin GREEK
pilau rice	fried, spiced, yellow rice INDIAN
pilauf, pilâv	Turkish national dish of rice or bulgar wheat, oil, stock or water, meat, poultry, fish, vegetables or nuts, herbs and dried fruit, covered and cooked until all the liquid is absorbed TURKISH
pilaw	steamed rice POLISH
pilaw turecki	Polish version of pilâv POLISH
pilchard	matured sardine; a small, round, oily sea fish
pīles	duck LATVIAN
pilgrimsmussla	scallop; coquille St Jacques SWEDISH
pillede rejer	shelled shrimps DANISH
pilot fish	cross-banded amberfish found in the Atlantic; member of the horse mackerel family; Menominee whitefish AMERICAN
piltocks	dialect name for saithe or cuddy SHETLANDS
Pilze	another name for mushrooms GERMAN
piment basquais	spicy red pepper used in the Basque country SPANISH
pimenta	peppercorn PORTUGUESE
pimentão	sweet pepper PORTUGUESE
pimento	another name for allspice
pimentón	paprika; cayenne pepper; chilli pepper SPANISH
pimentos	large red and green sweet peppers
pimienta	pepper SPANISH
pimiento	sweet pepper SPANISH
pimprenelle	burnet FRENCH
piña	pineapple SPANISH
pina colada	cocktail of rum, pineapple juice and coconut cream CARIBBEAN
pinaatti	spinach FINNISH
pincho moruno	grilled meat on a skewer SPANISH
pinda	peanut DUTCH

pinda kaas	peanut butter DUTCH
pindos	cheese similar to kefalotyri GREEK
pine nuts, pine kernels	pignoli or pinoli, the small, cream-coloured seeds of the Mediterranean stone pine tree, with a resinous flavour and oily texture
pineapple	large, oval tropical fruit with hard knobbly skin surrounding sweet, juicy pale yellow flesh, the fruit of the tropical American bromeliad *Ananas comosus*
pineapple cheese	cheese shaped like a pineapple
pinée	best quality dried cod FRENCH
pinfish	fish, *Lagodon rhomboides*, found off the SE North American coast of the Atlantic; *see* sailor's choice
pingiàda	soup made with small birds, beef, tomatoes, celery, sweet basil, onions, rosemary, salt and black pepper SARDINIAN
pinhão	pine kernel PORTUGUESE
pinhoada	pine-kernel brittle PORTUGUESE
pinion	terminal segment of a bird's wing; ray-bone in the fin of a fish
Pinkelwürst	sausage from Bremen made from groats, smoked pork and spices GERMAN
pinnekjøtt	salted, fried ribs of mutton roasted on twigs NORWEGIAN
pinoccate	pine kernel and almond cake, a speciality of Perugia, traditionally eaten at Christmas and Epiphany ITALIAN
pinot blanc, pinot noir	varieties of grape FRENCH
pintada	guinea fowl SPANISH
pintade	guinea fowl FRENCH
pintadeau	young guinea fowl FRENCH
pintail	migratory wild duck *Anas acuta* with slender pointed wings and pointed tail, popular in France pinto bean variety of kidney bean, pale-coloured with bright red markings
piora cheese	cheese made only in the canton of Ticino, from whole milk from Piora Alp cows SWISS
piparjuuri	horseradish FINNISH
piparkakku	gingerbread FINNISH
piparkakut	ginger snaps FINNISH
pipérade	ragoût of eggs, peppers and tomatoes, a speciality of the Basque country SPANISH

piperies	sweet peppers GREEK
piperies yemistes	stuffed peppers GREEK
piping	forcing cream, icing and other mixtures through a nozzle fitted into the end of a bag to decorate cakes and other dishes
pipo crem'	blue veined cow's milk cheese with a flavour similar to Bleu de Bresse FRENCH
pippuri	pepper FINNISH
piquage	interlarding pieces of meat such as veal or saddle of hare with pork fat FRENCH
piquant sauce	well flavoured sharp sauce, based on sauce espagnole with added shallots, vinegar, gherkins and parsley
pir	small mackerel NORWEGIAN
piri-piri	small red chillies preserved in olive oil; dishes served with a hot pepper sauce; a mixture of hot ground spices
pirítós kenyér	toast HUNGARIAN
pirog	pasty RUSSIAN
piroshki	small savoury pastries, often served with soup RUSSIAN, POLISH
pirozhki	another name for piroshki RUSSIAN
pirozhnoye	pastry, often containing yeast or eggs RUSSIAN
pirukas	small pasty filled with minced meat, cheese or vegetables ESTONIAN
pisang goreng	baked bananas DUTCH-INDONESIAN
pisang goreng	fried banana dish which accompanies nasi goreng DUTCH
pisco	brandy made from muscat wine aged in clay jars, said to taste and smell like beeswax SOUTH AMERICAN
piselli	green peas ITALIAN
pisket krem	whipped cream NORWEGIAN
piškot	sponge finger CZECH
piškotový dort	sponge cake CZECH
piškotová roláda	Swiss roll served with redcurrant jam and whipped cream CZECH
pislicine	cake made from chestnut porridge fermented with yeast, flavoured with aniseed CORSICAN
pissaladière	traditional Provençal savoury tart filled with tomatoes, onions, black olives and anchovy fillets FRENCH

pissenlit	dandelion, *Taraxacum officinale* (a dialect name for which is pissabed) FRENCH
pistacchi	pistachio nuts ITALIAN
pistachio nut	a nut with bright green kernels, purple skins and beige-coloured shells, commonly used as flavouring in sweets
pisto	scrambled eggs mixed with diced sautéed vegetables, served with toast and grated cheese SPANISH
pistou	version of Italian pesto FRENCH
pisztácia	pistachio HUNGARIAN
pisztráng	trout HUNGARIAN
pita	paper-thin pastry similar to the Greek phyllo (or filo) YUGOSLAVIAN
Pitcaithly bannock	traditional cake similar to shortbread, containing almonds and candied peel SCOTTISH
pitchy cake	traditional Cornish currant cake
pith	white and often bitter layer under the rind of citrus fruits
pithaya	round cactus fruit, with scaly red or purple skin and red flesh speckled with little black seeds
Pithiviers	lark pâté from the town of the same name in the Orléanois; cake or tart made with puff pastry filled with an almond mixture FRENCH
Pithiviers au foin	cow's milk cheese from Orléans, ripened on hay FRENCH
piti	very spicy lamb stew, a speciality of Azerbaijan RUSSIAN
pitta bread	flat, yeast bread with a pocket designed to accept food MIDDLE EASTERN
pitte con niepita	small turnovers filled with grape jam, walnuts, grated chocolate, cinnamon and rum, a Calabrian speciality ITALIAN
pitu	baked prawns PORTUGUESE
Pitz	raw tomatoes stuffed with minced apples and celeriac, mixed with olive oil and sour cream, a speciality of the lower Valois SWISS
piviere	plover ITALIAN
pivní syr	beer cheese CZECH
piwna zupa	beer soup with cinnamon, cloves and sometimes cream POLISH

pizza	yeast dough rolled flat, covered with a variety of ingredients such as tomatoes, cheese, ham, olives and onions and baked ITALIAN
pizzaiola, salsa	Neopolitan sauce, usually served with steak ITALIAN
pizzetta	small pizza ITALIAN
placek drożdżowy z owocami	yeast cake with fresh fruit POLISH
placek serowy na kruchym spodzie	curd cake in a pastry shell POLISH, RUSSIAN
placki ziemniaczane	potato fritters POLISH
plafond	a tinned copper baking sheet FRENCH
plaice	flat sea fish *Pleuronectes platessa* with brown skin and orange or red spots on the upper side plaki fish baked with vegetables GREEK
plakia	vegetable dish containing onions, tomatoes and beans, eaten hot or cold, particularly as a Lenten dish BALKAN
plancha, a la	grilled on a griddle SPANISH
planche à découper	wooden carving board with grooves to catch juices FRENCH
planche à hacher	chopping board FRENCH
planche à pâtisserie	board for making, rolling and cutting pastry FRENCH
plank	oak board used for cooking
planking	method of cooking which usually describes serving meat or fish on a special board
plankstek	thin steak served on a wooden platter SWEDISH
plantain	large green bananas with a high starch and low sugar content, which must always be cooked
plastron	ventral part of the turtle shell
plat	plate or dish FRENCH
plat de côtes	cut of beef; cut of pork FRENCH
plat du jour	dish of the day served in a restaurant FRENCH
platýz	plaice; halibut CZECH
plátano	banana SPANISH
plate	cut of beef comprising the rear quarter flank AMERICAN
plateau	large dish FRENCH
plateau de fromages	cheese board FRENCH
platija	plaice SPANISH
platine	shallow baking tin FRENCH
platki owsiane z mlekiem	porridge POLISH
plato	plate; dish or portion SPANISH

plättar	small, thin pancakes SWEDISH
Platte	platter GERMAN
platter	large plate, often elliptical, on which food is served; restaurant marketing speak implying olde worldiness, value for money, etc
Plätzchen	biscuit (US: cookie) GERMAN
Plätzli	scallop; cutlet GERMAN
plecko	pork shoulder CZECH
plie	plaice FRENCH
pligouri	bulgar GREEK
plísňový sýr	blue cheese CZECH
pljeskavica	sausage of minced mutton, pork and veal YUGOSLAVIAN
plnené papriky	stuffed pepper CZECH
plněné papriky v rajcatové omáčce	stuffed peppers in tomato sauce CZECH
plombières	ice cream containing sieved almonds FRENCH
plomme	plum NORWEGIAN
plommon	plum SWEDISH
plommonspäckad fläskkarré	pork stuffed with prunes SWEDISH
plov	a version of pilâv RUSSIAN
plover	small, wild wading bird; varieties and their eggs have been eaten since the Middle Ages; the finest in flavour is the golden plover, then the grey plover and lastly the green plover, better known as lapwing
pluches	the leaves of herbs such as chervil or parsley FRENCH
pluck (noun)	liver, heart and lungs of a sheep or other animal or bird, especially one used for food
plucking	removing feathers from poultry and game birds
plukkfisk	poached fish in white sauce NORWEGIAN
plum	variety of hybrid fruits created from the cherry plum and the sloe; they vary in size and colour plum
pudding	rich steamed or boiled pudding containing dried fruits
pluvier	plover FRENCH
poaching	cooking food gently in liquid at simmering point
pochard	diving duck which breeds in Northern and Central Europe
poche	forcing bag FRENCH
poché	poached FRENCH
pocheret	poached DANISH

pochiert	poached GERMAN
pochki	kidneys RUSSIAN
pod	the fruit of a leguminous plant, sometimes edible, with seeds such as peas of beans attached along one of its long joins
podkvàsa	culture used to turn fresh milk into yoghurt BULGARIAN
podle jídelního lístku	a la carte CZECH
podmáslí	sour milk CZECH
podroby	giblets POLISH
podvarak	traditional way of cooking duck in a casserole of onions and sauerkraut YUGOSLAVIAN
poêlage	cooking in a pan with no liquid other than fat (usually butter) FRENCH
poêle, à la	fried FRENCH
Pofesen	version of pain perdu, bread sandwiched with jam, dipped in wine and egg, fried and served with sugar and fruit syrup AUSTRIAN
poffertje	fritter served with sugar and butter DUTCH
pogácsa	biscuit HUNGARIAN
pogne	traditional cake or tart from the Dauphiné region, usually a pastry flan containing fruit, or pumpkin FRENCH
pogne de romans	sweet rolls served with redcurrant jelly FRENCH
pohjalainen leipäjuusto	round cheese-curd loaf from Ostrobothnia FINNISH
point steak	top end of rump steak
point, à	medium cooked steak FRENCH
pointe	tip FRENCH
pointe d'asperge	asparagus tip FRENCH
pointe de culotte	rump steak or roast FRENCH
pointe de filet	cut of pork equivalent to chump end of pork loin chops FRENCH
poire	pear FRENCH
poireau	leek FRENCH
poirée	spinach; beet; chard FRENCH
pois	peas FRENCH
pois chiche	chick-pea FRENCH
poisson	fish FRENCH
poisson d'eau douce	freshwater fish FRENCH
poisson de mer	saltwater fish FRENCH

poissonnier	French chef who cooks fish dishes in a large restaurant, except those which are grilled or fried; fishmonger; fish kettle FRENCH
poitrine	breast; brisket FRENCH
poitrine fumée	generally bacon, more specifically smoked breast FRENCH
poivrade	sautéd roebuck cutlets layered in a dish with croutons and served with sauce poivrade; cold venison, beef or lamb served in sauce poivrade, with chestnut puré and gooseberry jelly; very young cooked artichokes, served with salt FRENCH
poivrade, sauce	popular sauce containing sautéed carrots, onions, shallots, bay leaf, clove, thyme, red wine and wine vinegar cooked together, freshly ground pepper is added and the sauce is strained before serving FRENCH
poivre	pepper FRENCH
poivre d'âne	Provençal name for a variety of wild savoury herb FRENCH
poivre de guinée	Guinea pepper or chilli FRENCH
poivre de la Jamaïque	allspice FRENCH
poivre mignonette	fresh, coarsely ground white peppercorns FRENCH
poivron	sweet pepper FRENCH
Pökelfleisch	pickled pork; brawn GERMAN
pokerounce	mediaeval dish of hot spiced toast spread with honey and pine nuts ENGLISH
pokeweed	native shrub of North America, the leaves of which can be cooked and eaten as asparagus NORTH AMERICAN
pokhlyobka	traditional country soup RUSSIAN
polędwica	fillet or tenderloin steak POLISH
polenta	fine golden cornmeal used to make a thick savoury porridge served with meat or vegetable dishes ITALIAN
polévka	soup CZECH
polewka	traditional rye soup POLISH
polewka z wina	sweet soup made with white wine POLISH
polipetto	Genoese name for a small tender octopus cooked gently in olive oil and white wine ITALIAN
poliporo	edible fungus ITALIAN
polita	food cooked Constantinople-style GREEK

pollack, pollock   *Pollachius pollachius*, a sea fish from the same family as the cod although lacking a little of its flavour

pollame   fowl ITALIAN

pollan   varieties of whitefish *Coregonus pollan* found in the lakes of Scotland and Northern Ireland

pollito   spring chicken SPANISH

pollo   chicken ITALIAN, SPANISH

polo   rice dish which may include lentils, beans vermicelli or cherries IRANIAN

polonaise, à la   garnish of fried white breadcrumbs sprinkled over a dish of vegetables, in particular asparagus and cauliflower, garnished with chopped hard boiled egg and parsley; method of serving chicken

FRENCH, POLISH

polony   large smoked sausage of seasoned mixed meats (US: Bologna sausage)

polpetta di carne   meatball ITALIAN

polpette   small flat meat cakes ITALIAN

polpetti   traditional cheese soup made from Parmesan cheese mixed into beef broth and served with pasta ITALIAN

polpettine   smaller versions of polpette

polpettone   meat loaf of seasoned beef or veal ITALIAN

polpo   octopus ITALIAN

pölsa   hash of boiled pork and barley SWEDISH

pølse   sausage DANISH, NORWEGIAN

polvo   octopus PORTUGUESE

polvorón   hazelnut biscuit SPANISH

polynéer   small pastry tarts filled with ground almonds, icing sugar and egg white SWEDISH

polypodium   species of edible fern

pomarańcze   oranges POLISH

pombo   pigeon PORTUGUESE

pomegranate   fruit the size of an apple with a thin, tough, shiny rind and a mass of edible seeds surrounded by red translucent flesh

pomelo   citrus fruit with firm sharp-flavoured flesh, like a large green grapefruit SPANISH

pomerană   orange CZECH

Pomeranzensoße   sauce of bitter oranges, wine and brandy, usually served with duck GERMAN

pomfret	sea fish also known as Ray's bream or sea bream CHINESE, INDIAN, SOUTH EAST ASIAN
pomfret (cake)	a corruption of Pontefract cake, which *see*
pomidoro	tomatoes ITALIAN
pomidory	tomatoes POLISH
pommarola, salsa di	tomato sauce for pasta ITALIAN
pomme	apple FRENCH
pomme de terre	potato FRENCH
Pomme frites	chips (US: French fries) GERMAN
pommel	unsalted double cream cheese FRENCH
Pommersche suppe	soup from Pomerania made from puréed haricot beans, celery, onions and stock GERMAN
pommes Anna	a cake of sliced potatoes which is dotted with butter and baked in the oven until golden FRENCH
pommes au beurre	*see* pommes château FRENCH
pommes au four	potatoes baked in their jackets FRENCH
pommes château	potatoes cut into large olive shapes, parboiled and cooked in butter - the traditional accompaniment for châteaubriand steak; also known as pommes au beurre FRENCH
pommes cocotte	as pommes château but the potatoes are cut into much smaller shapes FRENCH
pommes rôties	roast potatoes FRENCH
pommes frites	potato chips DANISH, FRENCH, NORWEGIAN, SWEDISH
pomodoro	tomato ITALIAN
pompano	small, round oily sea fish of the genera *Trachinotus* or *Palometa* found in the Mediterranean, the Caribbean and around the coasts of Louisiana and Florida
pompe	traditional cake eaten in Provence on Christmas Eve FRENCH
pompelmo	grapefruit ITALIAN
pompelmoes	grapefruit DUTCH
pomponnettes	small hors d'œuvres made from short-crust pastry pouches filled with meat, fish or vegetables and deep fried FRENCH
ponchiki	fried cakes like non-yeasted doughnuts RUSSIAN
ponczowe ciastko	sponge cake steeped in rum POLISH
ponebread	corn pone; name in the southern States for corn bread AMERICAN
pönnukökur	traditional pancakes served with jelly and whipped cream ICELANDIC

Pontefract cake	small, round liquorice confection, originally made from the roots of liquorice grown at Pontefract, Yorkshire but, sadly, no more; also pomfret
pontgibaud	cow's milk cheese from the Auvergne FRENCH
pont-l'evêque	cow's milk, rennetted cheese from Normandy FRENCH
pont-neuf	method of preparing potatoes; a pastry filled with frangipane cream and macaroons FRENCH
pontoise veal	tender veal sold in Paris, also known as river veal FRENCH
ponty	carp HUNGARIAN
poona cheese	whole cow's milk soft cheese from New York AMERICAN
poor knights of Windsor	pain perdu, with the bread sometimes sprinkled with sherry before being dipped in egg and milk and fried, and served with butter and sugar, with sherry, boiled to make a syrup, to taste
poor man of mutton	bladebone of mutton, grilled or spit-roast SCOTTISH
popcorn	type of Indian corn; when exposed to a dry heat it pops, to create a white starch mass
pope	freshwater fish like perch
pope's eye	small circle of fat in the centre of a leg of lamb or pork; in Scotland it describes a piece of prime rump steak
pope's nose	fatty tail of duck or goose – *see* parson's nose
popone	melon ITALIAN
popover	individual Yorkshire pudding served instead of bread or rolls AMERICAN
poppadom, poppadum, etc	thin, round, very light and crisp savoury biscuit or bread, served with savoury dishes, especially curries INDIAN
poppy seeds	small blue-black seeds of the opium poppy, classified as a spice
porc	pork FRENCH
porce	portion CZECH
porceddu	suckling pig split lengthways and spit-roasted over wood, then placed on a covered dish with myrtle leaves SARDINIAN
porcelet	suckling pig FRENCH
porchetta	roast suckling pig cooked with rosemary and basted with white wine ITALIAN
porcini	boletus mushrooms ITALIAN

porción	portion SPANISH
porco	pork PORTUGUESE
póréhagyma	leeks HUNGARIAN
pórek	leek CZECH
porgand	carrot ESTONIAN
porgy	Atlantic fish similar to John Dory
pork	the meat of the pig eaten fresh
porker	young pig between six months and one year old
porkkana	carrot FINNISH
pörkölt	variety of stews HUNGARIAN
pörkölt	'browned' or 'scorched'; stew containing onions and meat HUNGARIAN
pórková polévka	leek soup CZECH
poron	reindeer FINNISH
porossenok a khrenom i smetanoi	a famous dish of suckling pig simmered in water with root vegetables, served cold with a horseradish and sour cream sauce; the stock is jellied, so the dish is something like a good brawn RUSSIAN
porotos granados	shelled beans served with pumpkin and maize SPANISH
porpoise	the smaller members of the order *Cetacea*, which used to be eaten in France and England at banquets and festivals
porre	leek DANISH
Porree	leek GERMAN
porridge	a dish of oatmeal or other cereal cooked in water or milk to a thick consistency, often seasoned with salt in Scotland and with jam, syrup etc in England; in Malaysia, a broth of rice
porringer	round bowl in which to serve porridge or other similar foods
porro	leek ITALIAN
porsaansorkat	pig's trotters FINNISH
port	fortified wine made from grapes from the upper Douro valley, exported from Oporto PORTUGUESE
port wine sauce	sauce of gravy, redcurrant jelly, port wine and lemon juice, boiled, strained and served with mutton or venison ENGLISH
Port-du-Salut	semi-hard cow's milk cheese, originally made by Trappist monks in western France FRENCH

porter	dark brown beer, coloured and flavoured with roasted malt; stout can be made by adding molasses to porter
porter cake	traditional Cornish and Irish cake made with porter
porterhouse steak	another name for T-bone steak, cut from wing-rib of beef
portie	portion DUTCH
porto	port FRENCH
portugaise, sauce	classical sauce containing tomatoes, garlic, salt, pepper and olive oil, sauce espagnole and tomato sauce FRENCH
portuguaise, à la	small stuffed tomatoes and pommes château; a method of serving chicken FRENCH
pory	leeks POLISH
poshin tang	dog-meat soup, believed to have energy-enhancing qualities KOREAN
porzeczki	currants POLISH
posset	drink of sweetened milk curdled with treacle, ale or wine
posta	slice of fish or meat PORTUGUESE
postei	vol-au-vent; meat or fish pie NORWEGIAN
postelein	purslane DUTCH
postre	dessert; sweet SPANISH
pot barley	barley with the hull or outer husk removed
pot cheese	type of cottage cheese made from sour milk and buttermilk
pot herbs	herbs used in cooking
pot roasting	cooking meat slowly in a covered pan with fat and very little liquid, often with vegetables
potage	a thick meat or vegetable soup; old French word meaning the contents of a pot; also known as pottage FRENCH
potaje	vegetable soup SPANISH
potassium	mineral which helps the cells of the body to maintain a correct fluid balance; bananas are a good source
potatis	potato SWEDISH
potato	originally from South America, there are many varieties of this staple food, grown for its starchy underground tubers
potato flakes	commercial product made from potatoes, which can be used as a substitute for fresh potato
potato flour	flour extracted from potatoes by pulverizing and washing

pot-au-feu	meat or poultry and vegetables, often separated into two dishes, the broth being served as a soup and the meat and vegetables as the main course FRENCH
pote	stew made with white haricot beans, named after the pot in which it is cooked SPANISH
potée	food cooked in an earthenware pot FRENCH
potet	potato NORWEGIAN
potetmel	potato flour NORWEGIAN
potiron	pumpkin FRENCH
potka	leg; shank FINNISH
potrawka	dish cooked in a casserole in the oven POLISH
potrokha	giblets RUSSIAN
pottage	*see* potage
potting	cooking or preserving food in a pot eg potted shrimps
poteen	whiskey illicitly distilled from potatoes or barley – it can be bad for the health! IRISH
pouding	pudding FRENCH
pouillard	another name for partridge FRENCH
poularde	neutered, fattened hen chicken FRENCH
poule	boiling fowl FRENCH
poulet	spring chicken FRENCH
poulet à la Wallone	method of cooking a jointed chicken with a knuckle of veal, chopped root vegetables, stock, and calf's sweetbreads served with a sauce of cream, egg yolks and sweet white wine WALLOON
poulette, à la	method of serving many foods with sauce poulette FRENCH
poulette, sauce	classical sauce which is a variant of sauce allemande, made from egg yolks, white stock, lemon juice, butter and chopped parsley FRENCH
Pouligny-Saint-Pierre	goat's milk cheese from Pouligny FRENCH
poulpe	octopus FRENCH
poultry	domestic birds bred for their eggs or for the table
pound cake	old English fruit cake, also popular in the States, which gets its name because all the ingredients are traditionally added in 1lb quantities
poupart	giant crab FRENCH
poupelin	chouxx pastry cake in a round mould filled with crème chantilly, ice cream or fruit mousse FRENCH
poupeton	several meats, layered and rolled up, braised, and served cold FRENCH

pourgouri	coarse porridge made from ground wheat, used instead of rice CYPRIOT
pourpier	purslane FRENCH
poussin	young chicken 4 to 6 weeks old FRENCH
poutine	small, undeveloped fish FRENCH
pouting	species of copper-coloured cod found in the North Atlantic
powan	a whitefish found only in Loch Lomand and Loch Eck SCOTTISH
powidła	damson jam POLISH
powsowdie	stew made of sheep's head and feet, neck of mutton, pearl barley, dried fresh peas, carrot, turnip, onions, chopped parsley, salt and pepper SCOTTISH
poziomki	wild strawberries POLISH
pršut	smoked air-dried ham YUGOSLAVIAN
prażone	traditional picnic stew POLISH
praetud vasikaliha hapukoore soustiga	traditional stew of veal, butter, onions, and water, adding sour cream when almost cooked ESTONIAN
Pragerschinken	delicately-smoked ham salted in a mild brine for several months before being smoked; the recipe actually comes from the former Czechoslovakia GERMAN
pragon	butcher's broom (*Ruscus*), the young shoots of which are eaten in France FRENCH
pražená kukuřice	popcorn CZECH
praire	clam FRENCH
prairie chicken	game bird, similar to grouse AMERICAN
prairie oyster	drink of shelled, unbroken egg, flavoured with Worcestershire sauce, lemon juice and salt, said to be a cure for a hangover
praties	potatoes IRISH
pražská šunka	Prague Ham; smoked ham used in various dishes POLISH
pražská pečene na smetaně	tasty cut of beef cooked in sour cream and spice sauce CZECH
pražské telecí hrudí	Prague-style breast of veal, stuffed with eggs, ham, peas and whipped cream, and roasted with butter CZECH
pralin	nut-sugar mixture, added to creams, ices, cakes and soufflés FRENCH
pralinate	pralin ITALIAN
praline	almonds caramelised in sugar, left to harden,

	crushed, and used to flavour or decorate sweet dishes
pranzo	lunch or dinner ITALIAN
prasa	leeks TURKISH, GREEK
prasèntse pūlneno	roast stuffed suckling pig BULGARIAN
pratelle	horse mushroom FRENCH
prato	plate; dish PORTUGUESE
prawn	small, delicately flavoured crustaceans, available in a variety of sizes
prawn puree, puri	prawns served in a hot sauce on a puri INDIAN
praz	leek ROMANIAN
Prebkohlsuppe	traditional beef broth with stuffed cabbage AUSTRIAN
pregado	turbot PORTUGUESE
prego	small steak, often served in a roll PORTUGUESE
prei	leek DUTCH
Preiselbeere	cranberry GERMAN
prejt	black pudding CZECH
pré-salé	mutton and lamb from salt marshes considered to be particularly well-flavoured FRENCH
present	Edam cheese FRENCH
presentoir	dish on which a tureen stands FRENCH
preservation	storing fresh food in such a way that it will remain in good condition for long periods
preservatives	any substances added to food to help to prevent or slow fermentation, acidification or other decomposition
preserve	another name for jam
presnitz	Easter cake, originally from Castagnevizza ITALIAN
pressing	shaping meat by pressing under a weight
pressato	sweetish asiago-type cheese ITALIAN
pressed beef	beef cooked with herbs, calf's foot, onion and seasoning
pressgurka	marinated, sliced, fresh cucumber SWEDISH
Preßkopf	brawn (US: head cheese) GERMAN
pressure cooking	to cook food quickly in steam under pressure, which raises the boiling point of the water; lower pressures reduce the boiling point of water, which makes it difficult to cook eggs for mountaineers
pressylta	brawn SWEDISH
prestost	cow's milk cheese, cured with aquavit SWEDISH
presunto	cured, smoked ham PORTUGUESE

pretzel	savoury biscuit shaped in a loose knot, sometimes sprinkled with salt or cumin seeds GERMAN
prezpiórka	quail POLISH
prezzemolo	parsley ITALIAN
prezzo	price ITALIAN
prickly pear	small pear-shaped fruit of cacti of the genus *Opuntia*, with greenish-orange skin, covered with sharp prickles, and pink and juicy flesh
prima colazione	breakfast ITALIAN
primeur	early forced fruit and vegetables FRENCH
primizie	forced fruit or vegetables ITALIAN
primrose	the flower petals can be candied and the young leaves can be boiled like sorrel
primula cheese	processed cheese made from caramelised whey NORWEGIAN
princesse, à la	garnished with asparagus tips and truffles or noisette potatoes FRENCH
prinsefisk	cod with egg sauce NORWEGIAN prinsessenboon FRENCH bean (US: green bean) DUTCH
prinsesstårta	sponge cake with vanilla custard and whipped cream, covered with green almond paste SWEDISH
prinskorv	cocktail sausage; small frankfurter SWEDISH
printanière, à la	garnish of vegetables arranged in their separate kinds round a dish; ragoût of root vegetables; consommé with root vegetables and pearl sago cooked in stock FRENCH
Printe	honey-flavoured biscuit (US: cookie) GERMAN
printemps	spring FRENCH
prošpikovaný	larded CZECH
processed cheese	preserved cheese made by blending cheeses by heating and emulsifying them
profiterole	small choux pastry bun filled with cream or custard, sometimes topped with rich chocolate sauce FRENCH
pronghorn	horned ruminant from western States and Mexico, prepared and cooked as venison AMERICAN, MEXICAN
proof spirit	measure of alcohol strength in spirit
prorostlá slanina	bacon with strips of meat CZECH
prosciutto	fresh ham, and in particular various types of raw smoked ham ITALIAN
prosi´	suckling pig POLISH
prostokvasha	thick sour milk used for cooking RUSSIAN

protein	body-building nutrient
provatura	soft, mild cheese made from buffalo's milk ITALIAN
provençale, à la	dishes typical of the Provence region, usually containing olive oil, garlic and tomatoes FRENCH
providence	cow's milk cheese made in the monastery of Bricquebec in the Manche department FRENCH
proving	leavening bread to ensure an even-textured loaf
provola	originally buffalo's milk cheese, it is now made from cow's milk because you don't see many buffalo around these days ITALIAN
provolone	white medium-hard cheese ITALIAN
prsíčka	breast CZECH
prugna	plum ITALIAN
prugna secca	prune ITALIAN
pruim	plum DUTCH
prune	dried plum
prune	plum FRENCH
prune jam knaidlach	traditional Jewish Passover dish HUNGARIAN
pruneau	prune FRENCH
pryaniki	traditional biscuit RUSSIAN
przepiórka	quail POLISH
przystawki	appetisers POLISH
psari	fish GREEK
psomi	bread GREEK
pstràg	trout POLISH
ptarmigan	small game bird of the Grouse family from Northern Europe and Scotland
puant macéré	puant means 'stinking'; a strongly-flavoured cow's milk cheese made in Flanders FRENCH
puchero	a national soup made from beef and ham or chicken cooked with chick-peas and seasoning; chorizo is added and the soup is served with small dumplings made of chopped ham, eggs, breadcrumbs and garlic, fried in oil SPANISH
pudding	wide range of sweet and savoury dishes, usually served hot and made in a pudding basin or other mould; any sweet dish served at the end of the meal
Pudding	custard; pudding GERMAN
pudding	mould; baked casserole SWEDISH
puddinghos a pienu	roast chicken stuffed with the chopped giblets and herbs SARDINIAN

pudena	equivalent of mint INDIAN
pudim	pudding PORTUGUESE
pudín	pudding SPANISH
pudink	custard cream CZECH
puerro	leek SPANISH
puff pastry	rich, crisp, flaky pastry used for both sweet and savoury dishes
puffball	largest of a family of fungi, rounded in shape with white cheesy flesh
puftaloon	small cakes of deep-fried rounds of a type of scone dough
pui	chicken ROMANIAN
puits d'amour	small cakes of pâte feuilletée filled with gooseberry jelly or crème pâtissière FRENCH
pularda	fattened neutered hen POLISH
pulardy	fattened pullet POLISH
pulasan	tropical fruit of the lychee family with skin is covered with short red or yellow projections and strongly-scented, sweet, juicy flesh
pulë	chicken ALBANIAN
pulla	bun FINNISH
pullataikina	yeasted dough FINNISH
pulled bread	bread cut very thinly and dried in a low oven until golden brown
pullet	young hen or female fowl
pulpety	croquette of meat, fish, vegetables or dough coated with breadcrumbs or batter and deep-fried POLISH
pulpo	octopus SPANISH
pulque	light alcoholic drink made from agave juice Mexican
pulses	generic name for all dried peas, beans and lentils
pultost	soft, sometimes fermented cheese, usually flavoured with caraway seeds NORWEGIAN
pulyka	turkey HUNGARIAN
Pumpernickel	black bread made from coarse rye flour GERMAN
pumpernikiel	black bread POLISH
pumpkin	one of the largest of the winter squashes, green or orange in colour, round in shape with flattish tops and bottoms
pumpkin seeds	large, flat green seeds which can be eaten raw or cooked in sweet or savoury dishes

puna, juuri	beetroot FINNISH
punainen viinimarja	redcurrant FINNISH
punčový dort	frosted sponge cake sprinkled with rum CZECH
punch	drink made from a mixture of ingredients, one of which should be a spirit
punchnep	nep (neep) is the old English word for root, a dish made with root vegetables WELSH
pungaji	usually means cooked in butter INDIAN
punta de espárrago	asparagus tip SPANISH
puntarelle	weed with a thick stalk and spiky leaves used in salads ITALIAN
punte di asparagi	asparagus tips ITALIAN
punto de nieve	dessert of whipped cream with beaten egg-whites SPANISH
puolikypsä	medium FINNISH
puolukka	lingonberry (type of cranberry) FINNISH
puolukkaliemi	fruit compote similar to the Russian kissel, made from cranberries thickened with potato flour FINNISH
puré	purée PORTUGUESE
püré	mash; purée HUNGARIAN
puré de patatas	mashed potatoes SPANISH
purè di patate	mashed potatoes ITALIAN
purée	fruit, vegetables, meat or fish pounded sieved or liquidised to a smooth pulp FRENCH
Püree	mash; purée GERMAN
puri	type of deep fried chapatti for special occasions INDIAN
purjo	leek FINNISH
purjolök	leek SWEDISH
purl	old fashioned winter drink of warm ale flavoured with bitters and spiked with whisky or brandy or mixed with sweetened milk and a measure of gin, whisky or brandy
purløg	chive DANISH
purple flowered choy sum	*see* brocoletto, choy sum, flowering pak choi, flowering white cabbage, hong tsoi sum, hon tsai tai, kozaitai, pak tsoi sum, rape
purre	leek NORWEGIAN
purslane	unusual lobster-shaped annual herb *Portulaca oleracea* with red stems and fleshy green leaves, used in salads or cooked as a vegetable

pusinky	small mounds of meringue CZECH
pusztadör	a semi-hard cow's milk cheese HUNGARIAN
Puter	turkey GERMAN
puuro	porridge FINNISH
pyroligneous acid	acid made by the destructive distillation of wood, poisonous and corrosive unless diluted; once used for pickling but today as an artificial smoke flavouring
pyttipanna	kind of bubble and squeak SWEDISH
pyttipanne	diced meat and potatoes fried with onions, sometimes topped with a fried egg NORWEGIAN
pyttipannu	kind of bubble and squeak made of diced meat, potatoes and onions, fried and served with raw egg yolk or fried egg FINNISH
pyy	hazel hen FINNISH
pyzy	meat pie POLISH

Q

qara baghii m'mimli	stuffed small marrows or courgettes MALTESE
qarita	octopus or cuttlefish stew MALTESE
qawwrama	mutton preserved in its own fat LEBANESE
quaglia	quail ITALIAN
quagliette de vitello	'little veal quails'; slices of ham laid on slices of veal, rolled up in a rasher of bacon, threaded on skewers with onion, sage and bread, baked and served with rice ITALIAN
quahog	a round clam found on the eastern seaboard AMERICAN
quail	small game bird of the genus *Coturnix*, now bred on farms
Quargel(käse)	small, sharp, whole sour milk cheese made in the Western Province of Austria AUSTRIAN
quark	soft curd cheese GERMAN
quart, le	a cow's milk cheese FRENCH
quartier	a quarter of a carcass of beef FRENCH
quartirolo	soft cow's milk cheese made in Lombardy ITALIAN
quas chawal	saffron rice fried in ghee INDIAN
quasi	cut of veal from the chump end of the loin FRENCH
quassia	bitter oil extracted from a tree of the genus *Quassia*, used for medicinal purposes and to flavour tonic wines, aperitifs and bitters
quatre épices	allspice; ground pepper, grated nutmeg, ground cloves and ground cinnamon FRENCH
quatre mendiants	old fashioned dessert of dried figs, raisins, filberts and almonds FRENCH
quatre-quarts	'four quarters'; a cake made from equal quantities of flour, butter, sugar and the weight of one ingredient in eggs, flavoured with orange, lemon or a liqueur FRENCH
queen cake	small light rich fruit cake, baked in patty pans or paper cases
queen of puddings	pudding of custard and breadcrumbs with meringue topping, usually flavoured with lemon zest or vanilla
Queensborough	the ugli fruit – discovered by Henry Queensborough Levy in the 1920s – Trout Hall Estate, Manchester, Jamaica

queijada small cottage cheese tart PORTUGUESE

queijinhos do céu marzipan balls rolled in sugar PORTUGUESE

queijo cheese PORTUGUESE

quenelle fish, meat or poultry blended to a fine forcemeat, bound and shaped into dumplings and cooked in liquid FRENCH

quente hot PORTUGUESE

quern stone hand mill for grinding corn

queso cheese SPANISH

queso de bola cow's milk cheese SPANISH

queso de cabra goat's milk cheese SPANISH

queso manchego ewe's milk cheese SPANISH

quetsche member of the plum family grown in Alsace-Lorraine

queue tail FRENCH

quiabo okra PORTUGUESE

quiche savoury custard tart, originally a regional dish from Lorraine FRENCH

quick freezing commercial process of freezing food

quignon wedge of bread from a large French loaf FRENCH

quillet sandwich cake filled with almond-flavoured crème pâtisserie (*see* fiouse) FRENCH

quinad vegetable stew traditionally eaten on Good Friday IBIZAN

quince pear-shaped fruit of the rosaceous tree *Cydonia oblonga,* with yellow skin and yellow scented flesh, which is too sour and hard to be eaten raw

quindim sweet of eggs and grated coconut PORTUGUESE

quinine bitter drug used as a malarial prophylactic and as a flavouring in Indian tonic water

quinnat salmon most common species of Pacific salmon, also called Chinook salmon

quinoa tiny, golden, delicately-flavour seed cooked as rice

quisquilla shrimp SPANISH

Quitte quince GERMAN

quofte meat balls made from minced mutton (*cf* kofta) ALBANIAN

quorn vegetarian meat substitute, a high quality protein developed from a fungus

R

rýže	rice CZECH
rýžový nákyp	rice pudding CZECH
rå	raw DANISH, NORWEGIAN, SWEDISH
raaka	raw FINNISH
raastettu	grated FINNISH
raavaanliha	heifer meat FINNISH
rabaçal, queijo de	mild creamy ewe's milk cheese from Coimbra PORTUGUESE
rabanada	slice of bread, dipped into a mixture of milk, egg, honey, sugar and cinnamon, fried, and served sprinkled with sugar PORTUGUESE
rabanete	radish PORTUGUESE
rábano	radish SPANISH
rabarbar	rhubarb POLISH
rabarbaro	rhubarb ITALIAN
rabarber	rhubarb DANISH, DUTCH, SWEDISH
rabarbra	rhubarb NORWEGIAN
rabbit and hare	two different species; rabbits are available all year and may be wild or farmed; hares are darker with a more gamey flavour and are available late summer to early spring
rabbit-fish	*Chimaera monstrosa*, a sea fish similar to mackerel, found in the Mediterranean and Atlantic
rabiole	variety of kohlrabi
râble	saddle, used exclusively in connection with hare FRENCH
rabotte	baked fruit dumpling from Normandy FRENCH
Rachel	garnish for tournedos and noisettes named after a famous 19th-century actress, made from artichoke bottoms filled with cooked meat decorated with ox marrow, chopped parsley and red wine sauce; method of cooking fish, stuffed with fish forcemeat and sliced truffle, poached in white wine and garnished with asparagus tips; chicken consommé thickened with tapioca, garnished with strips of artichoke bottom and served with ox marrow on toast FRENCH

rack	neck or rib section of lamb, pork or veal
raclette	traditional dish from the canton of Valais of melted cheese eaten with potatoes, pickled onions and gherkins; the name for the semi-hard cheese used to make the dish SWISS
raclette	small wooden scraper used in Brittany to spread crêpe batter on the griddle FRENCH
rac(c)oon	small edible mammal of the genus *Procyon*
rácponty	carp with potatoes and sour cream dressing HUNGARIAN
racuszki	fried potato puffs POLISH
racuszki drożdżowe	type of yeast doughnut POLISH
radicchie	radish ITALIAN
radicchio	salad vegetable with reddish purple, peppery leaves
Radieschen	radish GERMAN
radijs	radish DUTCH
radikia	wild plant found in mountainous areas, it is similar to a dandelion with pink tubers used in salads GREEK
radir	to seal or sear foods FRENCH
radis	radish FRENCH
rädisa	radish SWEDISH
radise	radish DANISH
radish	red, white or black root vegetable, popular in salads; in oriental cookery it is known as daikon
rådjurskött	venison SWEDISH
rådjurssadel	saddle of venison SWEDISH
rådjursstek	roast venison SWEDISH
rådyr	roe deer DANISH
raejuusto	cottage cheese FINNISH
raekjur	shrimp or prawn ICELANDIC
rafano	horseradish ITALIAN
raffiné	refined FRENCH
rafraîchir	to chill; to refresh FRENCH
råg	rye SWEDISH
raggmunk med fläsk	potato pancake with bacon SWEDISH
rágós	tough HUNGARIAN
ragot	wild boar over two years old FRENCH
ragoût	stew with meat or poultry and vegetables FRENCH
ragout z baraniny	mutton stew POLISH
ragù	the correct name for salsa bolognese, a meat sauce for pasta ITALIAN

ragusano	hard, slightly sweet whole cow's milk cheese from Ragusa SICILIAN
rahat lokum	Turkish delight
rahkapiirakka	vilipiimä cheesecake FINNISH
Rahm	cream GERMAN
Rahmkäse	farmhouse cream cheese AUSTRIAN
raia	skate PORTUGUESE
raie	skate; ray FRENCH
raifort	horseradish FRENCH
rainha-cláudia	greengage plum PORTUGUESE
raised pie	meat pie made with hot water crust pastry which becomes firm during baking
raisin	sun dried grape
raisin	grape FRENCH
raising agent	substance or method used to introduce air or gas into bread, cake, pastry or puddings to make them rise during cooking
raita	yoghurt-based vegetable or fruit side dish, an accompaniment to spiced food INDIAN
raiton	small skate FRENCH
raja	slice; portion SPANISH
rajčatový salát	tomato salad CZECH
rajce	tomato CZECH
rajská omácka	tomato sauce CZECH
rajská polévka	tomato soup CZECH
rák	crayfish, crab HUNGARIAN
räka	shrimp SWEDISH
räkcocktail	shrimp cocktail SWEDISH
raki	crayfish POLISH
räkor	shrimp; prawn SWEDISH
rakørret	national dish of half-fermented trout NORWEGIAN
råkost	uncooked shredded vegetables SWEDISH
rakott palacsinta	multi-layer filled pancakes HUNGARIAN
rakowa zupa	crawfish soup POLISH
rakvičky	meringue with whipped cream CZECH
râle	rail FRENCH
rallado	grated SPANISH
ram-boo-tan	(from ram-boot hair) a refreshing white fruit with a furry red skin BM
rambour	variety of apple from the Rambour district

rambutan	dark red-brown hairy fruit of the SE Asian tree *Nephelium lappaceum*, its flesh similar in taste and appearance to a lychee
ramekin	small, round, straight-sided ovenproof dish used to cook and serve individual portions
ramequin	ramekin FRENCH
ramereau	young wood pigeon FRENCH
ramínco	pork shoulder CZECH
rampion	herb – both leaves and roots can be used rampolla fish consommé flavoured with hock, garnished with julienne of eel pout, crayfish, oysters and mushrooms FRENCH
rån	small waffle SWEDISH
rana	alternative name for pescatrice; frog ITALIAN
rancid	said of butter, bacon, or other fat which has gone off
Rande	beetroot GERMAN
rangiport	cow's milk cheese from the Seine-et-Oise department FRENCH
rangoon bean	variety of lima bean
ranskalaiset pavut	French beans (US: green beans) FINNISH
ranskanleipä	white bread FINNISH
ransklaiset perunat	chips (US: French fries) FINNISH
rántott hús	breaded veal cutlet HUNGARIAN
rántott sajt	fried cheese HUNGARIAN
rántott zöldbab	fried string beans HUNGARIAN
raoule	common name for the edible fungus agaric FRENCH
rapa	turnip ITALIAN
raparperi	rhubarb FINNISH
rape	there are several varieties descending from a hybrid vegetable *Brassica napus*, cultivated partly as an animal fodder and partly for its seeds which are crushed to produce rape seed oil; also called colza, cole; there are edible varieties used in oriental cookery; *see* brocoletto, choy sum, flowering pak choi, flowering white cabbage, hong tsoi sum, hon tsai tai kozaitai, pak tsoi sum, choy sum
rape	turnip ITALIAN
rape	anglerfish SPANISH
râpe	grater FRENCH
rapphöna	partridge SWEDISH
rapphøne	partridge NORWEGIAN

rapusalaatti	salad with cooked crayfish FINNISH
rare	meat that is deliberately undercooked, presumably at the eater's request
rarebit	melted cheese with a variety of flavourings
rårörda lingon	lingonberry jam SWEDISH
ras al-hanout	spice mixture to flavour meat and game dishes, rice and couscous NORTH AFRICAN
rascasio	hogfish SPANISH
rascasse	hogfish FRENCH
rasgulla	semolina dumplings cooked in syrup INDIAN
rasher	single slice of bacon or raw ham
rashmi, reshmi kebab	minced-meat patty inside an omelette INDIAN
rasmali	rasgullas served in cream INDIAN
raspada	very thin tortilla MEXICAN
raspberry	soft juicy fruit with a central hull and a sweet, slightly acidic flavour
rassolnik	various soups containing salted cucumber RUSSIAN
rasstegay	savoury dish of small patties of yeast dough filled with a mixture of salmon, rice, hard-boiled eggs, butter and chopped parsley, baked and eaten hot RUSSIAN
rat	rodent, eaten during the siege of Paris in 1870, and famously served in a London restaurant (reported in *Oz* No 44, September 1972)
rata del mar	common stargazer, a fish with course flesh, mainly eaten in stews and soups or in rice dishes SPANISH
ratafia	cordial or liqueur flavoured with kernels of cherries, almonds, peaches or other fruits; essence made from oil of almonds; a small almond-flavoured macaroon
ratatouille	Provençal vegetable stew containing tomatoes, aubergine, sweet peppers and onions, courgettes and garlic FRENCH
raţe	duck ROMANIAN
rättika	black radish SWEDISH
rattleran	the next best cut of corned beef to fancy brisket AMERICAN
Räucheraal	smoked eel GERMAN
Räucherhering	smoked herring GERMAN
Räucherlachs	smoked salmon GERMAN
Rauchfleisch	smoked beef GERMAN
rauginti kopūstai	sauerkraut LITHUANIAN
rauw	raw DUTCH

ravanello	radish ITALIAN
ravani	cake with a syrup topping GREEK
ravier	flat plate used to serve hors d'œuvres
raviggiolo	Tuscan and Umbrian ewe's milk cheese ITALIAN
ravigote butter	aromatic herbs added to creamed butter and served with grilled meat FRENCH
ravigote sauce	vinegar sauce containing pounded hard boiled eggs, capers and herbs; a hot sauce is made by adding ravigote butter to a roux FRENCH
ravioles	ravioli SPANISH
ravioli	stuffed pasta envelopes
ravut	crayfish FINNISH
rawa halwa	semolina pudding INDIAN
raya	skate; ray SPANISH
razlevuša	cheese pastry YUGOSLAVIAN
raznjići	thin slices or cubes of pork, veal or lamb rolled, grilled on a skewer and served with rice and chopped raw onion YUGOSLAVIAN
razor shell	variety of sand-burrowing clam of the genera *Ensis* and *Solen* resembling an old-fashioned cut-throat razor when open, which can be served baked or as moules
razza chiodata	skate; ray ITALIAN
razzala, rezala	thick, mild, sweet, hot & sour sauce INDIAN
rebanada	slice SPANISH
rebarbara	rhubarb HUNGARIAN
rebarbora	rhubarb CZECH
Rebhuhn	partridge GERMAN
reblochon	semi-hard cow's milk cheese originating from the Haute-Savoie FRENCH
rebozado	breaded or fried in batter SPANISH
réce	teal HUNGARIAN
réchaud	small portable stove; dish heated by standing over hot water FRENCH
réchauffé	made-up dish of reheated food FRENCH
recheado	stuffed PORTUGUESE
recheio	stuffing; forcemeat PORTUGUESE
Rechnung	bill (US: check) GERMAN
recipe	list of ingredients and instructions for making a dish
récollet	cow's milk cheese from Alsace FRENCH

recuire	to recook; to bring to the right temperature; a term in sweet-making for annealing (softening) a jelly or syrup to add other foodstuffs FRENCH
recuite	cheese made with whey or skimmed milk
red cabbage	purple variety of cabbage
red fish, redfish	a male salmon that has recently spawned; sea fish of the genus *Sebastes* with a flattened body and bright orange-red skin with dark blotches
red herring	herring, cleaned and dried but not split
red mayonnaise	dressing served with lobster salad
red pepper	made from seeds and pods of capsicum peppers
red salmon	another name for blue-back salmon; sockeye (salmon)
red snapper	round sea fish with distinctive red skin and delicious white flesh
red-breasted bream	fresh water fish
redcurrant	form of currant from a hybrid plant
reddik	radish NORWEGIAN
redfin	small silvery freshwater fish
redfish	red or blue-back salmon AMERICAN
reducing	fast boiling a liquid in an uncovered pan to concentrate it by evaporation
ředkvička	radish CZECH
redware	edible seaweed, kelp
reebout, reerug	venison DUTCH
reedbird	finch-like bird, a delicacy in southern States AMERICAN
refeićão	meal PORTUGUESE
refogado	onions fried in olive-oil PORTUGUESE
reform sauce	brown sauce enriched by adding port wine and redcurrant jelly
refreshing	pouring cold water over blanched and drained vegetables to set the colour and stop the cooking process; reviving or keeping salad ingredients crisp by putting them back in the fridge after washing
refrigerating	storing food at a temperature low enough to arrest deterioration, at least for a short period
régence	garnish for fish of oysters and fish quenelles with beurre d'écrevisses, mushrooms, sliced soft roes and sauce normande; garnish for poultry, sweetbreads and vol-au-vent of truffled chicken quenelles, veal quenelles, goose liver, mushrooms and cocks' combs, with sauce allemande FRENCH

régence, sauce   classical sauce for fish of sauce normande with white wine, mushrooms and truffles; sauce for fowl of sauce suprême with white wine, mushrooms and truffles; sauce for poultry or veal of mirepoix and truffle-peelings reduced in Rhenish wine, added to demi-glace, boiled and strained FRENCH

Regensburger Braten   meat loaf made from half beef and half pork, suet, bread and seasoning AUSTRIAN, GERMAN

Regensburger Würst   spicy sausage from Lower Bavaria GERMAN

reggeli   breakfast HUNGARIAN

regnbueørret   rainbow trout NORWEGIAN

regning   bill (US: check) DANISH

Regulo™   control on a gas cooker used to set temperatures inside the oven

Regulo	°F	°C
0.5	250	121
1	275	135
2	300	149
3	325	163
4	350	177
5	375	190
6	400	204
7	425	218
8	450	232
9	475	246

When the Regulo was introduced (1922), it controlled gas flow, whose relationship to temperature could be uncertain; later the device used thermostatic control; also called gas mark

Reh   roe deer GERMAN

rehogada   sautéed SPANISH

Rehrücken   'haunch of venison'; an oblong chocolate cake covered in chocolate icing and spiked with blanched almonds so that it looks like a larded haunch of venison AUSTRIAN

Reibekuchen   potato pancake GERMAN

Reibgerstl   garnish for soup of strudel pastry trimmings left to dry, grated, dried in the oven and cooked in the soup for a few minutes AUSTRIAN

Reibkäse   grated cheese GERMAN

reikäleipä   ring-shaped rye bread FINNISH

reindeer	large Artic deer *Rangifer tarandus*; the meat is classified as venison and the milk can be used to make cheese
Reindlbiftek	speciality dish of fillet steak braised in demi-glace, garnished with fried egg, fried potatoes and sliced gherkins AUSTRIAN
reine	a chicken whose size is between poulet de grain and poularde FRENCH
reine des prés	meadowsweet FRENCH
reine, à la	dishes made from chicken FRENCH
reine-claude	greengage FRENCH
reinsdyr	reindeer NORWEGIAN
reinsdyrstek	roast reindeer NORWEGIAN
Reis	rice GERMAN
Réjane	garnish for entrées of tartlets of foie gras and asparagus tips covered in sauce madère; chicken consommé containing raw beaten eggs strained through a colander into hot soup, garnished with carrot and hazelnut royale; named after a famous actress, Gabrielle Réjane FRENCH
reje	shrimp DANISH
réjouissance	bones weighed in a joint of meat FRENCH
reke	shrimp NORWEGIAN
rekening	bill (US: check) DUTCH
rekling	thin fried strips of halibut NORWEGIAN
relâcher	to thin a sauce or purée by adding liquid FRENCH
relevé	the course after soup or fish, before the entrée FRENCH
reliefs	scraps of a meal FRENCH
religieuse	cake of filled, iced éclairs on a bed of pastry, decorated with cream; puff pastry apple tart FRENCH
relish	similar to chutney, a mixture of fruits or vegetables cooked with vinegar and spices
relleno	stuffing; forcemeat SPANISH
remolacha	beetroot SPANISH
remonter	to add condiment to a sauce or stew FRENCH
remoudou	a cheese made in the Hal country and in the region of Dolhain BELGIAN
rémoulade sauce	cold mayonnaise-based sauce usually served with cold meat, fish and shellfish
remuladesaus	mayonnaise with cream, chopped gherkins and parsley NORWEGIAN

ren	reindeer SWEDISH
renaissance, à la	garnish for meat or chicken of spring vegetables arranged round the dish FRENCH
rendang	hot, spicy, dry curry INDONESIAN
rendering	extracting fat from meat trimmings by cutting into small pieces and heating to 150°C until the fat runs out and can be strained
rengha	hors d'œuvre of olive oil and lemon juice containing small pieces of dried, smoked, boned herring GREEK
renklody	greengage POLISH
renklody w spirytusie	greengages preserved in alcohol POLISH
rennet	extract from the lining of calves' stomachs which causes protein in milk to curdle or coagulate, used to make junket and cheese
rensdyr	reindeer DANISH
renversé	turned out FRENCH
répa	carrots HUNGARIAN
řepa	turnip CZECH
repanakia	radishes GREEK
repas	meal FRENCH
repère	mixture of egg white and flour used to fix elaborate dishes to a plate FRENCH
repolho	green cabbage PORTUGUESE
repollo	cabbage SPANISH
reptiles	cold-blooded creatures – crocodilians, lizards, snakes, tortoises and turtles (and once dinosaurs) – some of which are edible, as are their eggs
requesón	fresh-curd cheese SPANISH
řeřicha	watercress CZECH
resin	substance that exudes from certain plants and trees; asafœtida resin is used in Indian cooking as seasoning and digestif INDIAN
restaurant	a commercial establishment, sometimes within an inn or hotel, where meals are prepared and served to customers
restaurateur	one who owns or runs a restaurant
restes	leftovers of a meal which can be recooked FRENCH
retek	radishes HUNGARIAN
rétes	strudel HUNGARIAN
retiisi	radish FINNISH
retsina	famous red or white wine flavoured with pine resin while in the cask GREEK

Rettich	black radish GERMAN
revani me kos	cake soaked in syrup and served with whipped cream ALBANIAN
revbensspjäll	spare-rib SWEDISH
réveillon	elaborate supper held after Midnight Mass on Christmas Eve, the chief dish usually boudin noir – black pudding FRENCH
revenir	to brown before cooking FRENCH
reverdir	to replace green colour in vegetables after they have been canned FRENCH
revithia	chick-peas GREEK
Rhabarber	rhubarb GERMAN
rhubarb	stem vegetable of the genus *Rheum* (especially *R.rhaponticum*), which must be cooked before eating, used in sweet dishes such as crumbles, fools, puddings and jams; the leaves contain the poisonous oxalic acid
rhubarb beet	variety of chard with bright red stems
rhubarbe	rhubarb FRENCH
rib steak	American name for entrecôte steak AMERICAN
riba	fish SERBO-CROAT
ribbenssteg	rib-roast of pork with crackling often served with red cabbage DANISH
ribbenssteg med æbler og svesker	rib-roast of pork stuffed with apples and prunes DANISH
ribes	currants ITALIAN
ribesneri	blackcurrants ITALIAN
ribesrossi	redcurrants ITALIAN
Ribisel	redcurrant GERMAN
ribs	currant (red or white) DANISH
ribs gelé	redcurrant jelly DANISH
ricci, riccio di mare	sea urchins ITALIAN
rice	*Oryza sativa* the most important cereal grain in the world, an aquatic plant grown in paddy fields in hot moist climates
rice bean	small dried bean similar in shape to the aduki, flavoured like rice when cooked
rice flour	very finely ground rice
rice paper	very fragile, sweet tasting, edible paper made from the pith of a Taiwanese tree *Tetrapanax papyriferum*
rice vinegar	mild-flavoured pale yellow vinegar made from rice
rice wine	potent wine resembling sherry CHINESE

riceys cendré, les   cow's milk cheese sometimes called champenois
FRENCH

riche, à la   sauce for fish made of sauce normande, beurre
homard, brandy and cayenne; dish of fish fillets with
sauce victoria garnished with lobster and truffle;
garnish for noisettes of médaillons of goose liver,
truffle and artichoke bottoms filled with asparagus
tips, masked with sauce madère; named after the
19th-century Paris café Riche FRENCH

Richelieu, à la   meat dish served with Richelieu sauce (rich brown
Madeira sauce) or garnished with mushrooms
potatoes or stuffed tomatoes; dishes dedicated to the
Duc de Richelieu, the 17th-century Cardinal's great-
nephew FRENCH

ricing   sieving potatoes or other vegetables through the
course mesh of a ricer AMERICAN

rickey   unsweetened long drink, liqueur or spirit and ginger
ale, flavoured with fresh fruit

ricotta   soft, fragrant ewe's or cow's buttermilk cheese;
ITALIAN

riddle   kitchen sieve with large holes

riekko   ptarmigan FINNISH

Riesengebirge-käse   soft goat's milk cheese from northern Bohemia
GERMAN

rieska   unleavened barley bread FINNISH

Riesling   white grape used to make wine with the same name

rifaki   kid GREEK

rigadelles   Atlantic coast name for small clams or cockles
FRENCH

rigaglie   giblets ITALIAN

rigani   wild marjoram GREEK

rigatoni   pasta similar to cannelloni; type of macaroni ITALIAN

rigodon   speciality dish from Burgundy similar to a bread
pudding, containing stale brioche and nuts FRENCH

rigottes   small round cheeses from the Rhône valley FRENCH

riisi   rice FINNISH

riista   game FINNISH

rijst   rice BELGIAN, DUTCH

rijstepap   rice porridge flavoured with brown sugar and
cinnamon BELGIAN

rijsttafel	'rice-table'; several dishes including stewed vegetables, spit-roasted meat and fowl served with rice, various sauces, fruit, nuts and spices DUTCH–INDONESIAN
rillauds	potted pork FRENCH
rillettes	same as rillauds except that the meat is lightly pounded after cooking
rillons	same as rillauds but using larger pork pieces
rim	kidney PORTUGUESE
rimmad	slightly salted SWEDISH
rind	outer skin of some fruits
Rinderbrust	brisket of beef GERMAN
Rindfleisch	beef GERMAN
ringdove	*see* wood pigeon
ringló	greengage HUNGARIAN
ring mould	a mould of toroidal shape
ringneck	freshwater duck also known as the black duck
ringneck pheasant	a common pheasant, *Phasiances colchius*, originating in Asia
riñón	kidney SPANISH
rinta	breast; brisket FINNISH
ripa	grouse; ptarmigan SWEDISH
ripieno	stuffing; forcemeat ITALIAN
Rippchen	pork chops; cutlets GERMAN
Rippe	rib GERMAN
rips	redcurrant NORWEGIAN
ris	rice DANISH, SWEDISH, NORWEGIAN
ris	sweetbreads FRENCH
ris de veau	veal sweetbread FRENCH
rising	said of baker's dough as it increases its volume before baking
risengrød	rice boiled in milk and served with cinnamon and butter DANISH
risengrynsgrøt	rice pudding sprinkled with cinnamon and sugar NORWEGIAN
risgrynsgröt	rice porridge served with cinnamon and sugar SWEDISH
risi e bisi	Venetian speciality dish made with green peppers and rice ITALIAN
risi-bisi	casserole of rice and peas POLISH

riskrem	boiled rice mixed with whipped cream, served with raspberry or strawberry sauce NORWEGIAN
rislapp	small sweet rice cake NORWEGIAN
riso	rice ITALIAN
risotto	rich, creamy rice boiled in stock, flavoured with wine, and served with mushrooms, onion, chicken, seafood and cheese added ITALIAN
rissois	speciality dish of fried shrimp patties from the north west of Lisbon PORTUGUESE
rissol	fritter with minced meat or fish PORTUGUESE
rissole	small roll or patty of cooked minced meat bound with mashed potatoes, coated in breadcrumbs and fried; there are also vegetarian versions
rissole	a small sweet or savoury pastry FRENCH
rissoler	to brown in fat or oil FRENCH
ristet	grilled, sautéed or toasted NORWEGIAN
ristretto, brodo	consommé ITALIAN
riven	grated SWEDISH
riverbank grape	wild vine with a black berry NORTH AMERICAN
rivierkreeft	crayfish DUTCH
riz	rice FRENCH
rizi	rice GREEK
rizibizi	rice with green peas HUNGARIAN
rizoto	risotto YUGOSLAVIAN
rizotto	rice casserole POLISH
rizs	rice HUNGARIAN
rizses libaaprólék	goose giblets with rice HUNGARIAN
rizzared haddock	sun-dried smoked haddock
rożna	grilled POLISH
roštěnky na pivě	carbonnade; beef and onion stew of cooked in beer CZECH
roach	small freshwater fish of the carp family, usually *Rutilus rutilus*
roasting	cooking by dry heat in the oven
roastit bubbly-jock	turkey stuffed with breadcrumbs, oysters, chestnuts, turkey liver and celery SCOTTISH
rob	old word meaning the juice extracted from fruits
Rob Roy's pleasure	haunch of venison braised with herbs, vegetables, stock and claret SCOTTISH
robalo	sea-bass PORTUGUESE
róbalo	haddock SPANISH

Robert sauce   a brown sauce said to have been invented by Robert Vino in the early 17th century

robert saus   brown sauce served with pork DUTCH

robin saus   apple sauce with mayonnaise or horseradish, an accompaniment to game dishes NORWEGIAN

robiola   soft cow's milk cheese from Lombardy, or a goat's milk cheese from Piedmont ITALIAN

robiolina   stronger version of robiola

rocamadour   goat's milk cheese from Guyenne FRENCH

rocambole   kind of onion grown in southern France, the fruit resembling garlic but not as pungent FRENCH

rochambeau, à la   garnish for meat of braised carrots, stuffed lettuce, boiled cauliflowers, pommes Anna and demi-glace
FRENCH

Rochen   skate; ray GERMAN

rock bass   North American freshwater fish, usually *Amboplites rupestus* AMERICAN

rock cakes   plain buns containing fruit and spices, made of a mixture thick enough for them to keep their rocky shape, baked in small heaps

rock cod   sea fish common off Spanish coasts

rock Cornish hen   hybrid breed of poultry

rock eel   species of catfish

rock hind   grouper with brown spots

rock medlar   small fruit of a European shad bush

rock salmon   large saltwater fish, similar to cod

rockefeller oyster   oyster in the shell, topped with puréed spinach sauce, onion and celery

rocket   green salad leaf, its flavour slightly bitter and peppery

rockfish   any large sea fish inhabiting rocky coasts

Rocky Mountain whitefish   species of whitefish NORTH AMERICAN

rodaballo   turbot; flounder SPANISH

rødbede   beetroot DANISH

rödbeta   beetroot SWEDISH

rødbeter   beetroot NORWEGIAN

rödbetssallad   beetroot salad SWEDISH

rodding   mountain trout SWEDISH

rode biet   red cabbage DUTCH

rodela   round slice PORTUGUESE

rødfisk   Norway haddock DANISH

rødgrød med fløde	fruit mould with cream DANISH
rødgrøt	fruit pudding with vanilla custard or cream NORWEGIAN
röding	char SWEDISH
rödkål	red cabbage SWEDISH
rødkål	red cabbage DANISH, NORWEGIAN
rødspaette	plaice DANISH
rödspätta	plaice SWEDISH
rødspette	plaice NORWEGIAN
rødstegt	underdone (US: rare) DANISH
rodzynki	raisins POLISH
roe	fish spawn or milt
roebuck	smallest European deer
roerei	scrambled egg DUTCH
rogaliki	crescent roll POLISH
rog(h)an josh	rich red-coloured marinated lamb or beef curry cooked in yoghurt, usually with peppers and tomatoes (literally red-juice meat) INDIAN
Rogen	roe (generally cod's roe) GERMAN
røget	smoked DANISH
røget sild	smoked herring on rye bread, garnished with chopped hard-boiled eggs, onions, radishes and chives DANISH
roggebrood	rye bread DUTCH
Roggenbrot	rye bread GERMAN
rogn	hard fish roe NORWEGIAN
rognon	kidney FRENCH
rognone	kidney ITALIAN
rognonnade	the loin cut of veal containing the kidneys FRENCH
rognons de coq	red kidney-shaped dried beans; gonads of a male fowl or cock FRENCH
rogon	creamy INDIAN
rogon roll	very soft creamy type of bread made with milk and butter or cream INDIAN
roh	raw, crude or unrefined GERMAN
Rohkost-Tomaten	stuffed tomatoes SWISS
rohlffky	crescent-shaped biscuits (cookies), often containing nuts CZECH
rohlík	roll CZECH
Rohschinken	cured ham GERMAN
roi, le	triple cream cheese from the Loire Valley FRENCH

rojoes à moda do Minho   chopped pork, Minho-style PORTUGUESE

rokadur   ewe's milk cheese similar to Roquefort YUGOSLAVIAN

røkelaks   smoked salmon NORWEGIAN

rokørret   salt-cured trout NORWEGIAN

rökt   smoked SWEDISH

røkt   smoked NORWEGIAN

röktfiskpudding   smoked fish pudding SWEDISH

rolada   stuffing; rolled slice of meat POLISH

roláda   roll-shaped cake CZECH

rolé   roulade ITALIAN

rolinhos de figado   baked stuffed liver rolls PORTUGUESE

rolling pin   long cylinder with a handle at each end for rolling out pastry

rollmops   method of preparing fresh herrings GERMAN

rollot   cow's milk cheese from the Somme FRENCH

rolls, bread   baked in numerous shapes from various types of dough

rolmops   Bismarck herring DUTCH

rolmops   marinated herring rolled around chopped onions or gherkins POLISH

rolo de carne picada   meatloaf PORTUGUESE

rolo de ovos   sponge rolled like a Swiss roll, served with port at the end of a meal PORTUGUESE

rolos de couve lombarda   Savoy cabbage leaves stuffed with minced or sausage meat PORTUGUESE

rolpens   fried slices of spiced and pickled minced beef and tripe, topped with apple slice DUTCH

roly-poly   steamed pudding of suet crust pastry spread with jam or mincemeat, rolled up and baked or steamed

rom   roe SWEDISH

romã   pomegranate PORTUGUESE

Romadur Käse   soft-ripened cow's milk cheese from southern regions of Austria and Germany AUSTRIAN, GERMAN

romaine   cos lettuce FRENCH

romaine, à la   garnish for roasted meat of spinach timbales and pommes Anna with tomato sauce and veal gravy; method of serving chicken FRENCH

romana   cow's milk cheese eaten with hot peppers and raw onion

romana, à la   dipped in batter and fried SPANISH

romana, alla	with vegetables, mint and sometimes anchovies ITALIAN
Romanoff	garnish for meat of stuffed cucumbers, pommes duchesse filled with salpicon of celeriac and mushrooms; fruit soaked in orange juice served with crème chantilly FRENCH
romans	goat's milk cheese produced in the Dauphiné FRENCH
romarin	rosemary FRENCH
rombo	turbot; brill ITALIAN
romero	rosemary SPANISH
rømme	thick sour cream NORWEGIAN
Roncal	hard cow's milk cheese from the Roncal Valley in Navarre SPANISH
rondin	metal cooking pot FRENCH
rönnbär	rowanberry SWEDISH
rönnbärsgelé	rowanberry jelly SWEDISH
rook	large black bird of the crow family; the young birds are edible
rookspek	smoked bacon DUTCH
rookworst	spice sausage DUTCH
room	cream DUTCH
roomboter	butter DUTCH
roomijs	ice cream DUTCH
root vegetables	group of vegetables with swollen roots such as carrots, parsnips, radishes, swedes, and turnips
ropa vieja	cooked, left-over meat and vegetables, covered with tomatoes and green peppers SPANISH
rope	bacterial contamination of bread dough; in tropical climates vinegar is sometimes added to dough to prevent infection
rophos	thick, reddish-brown grouper GREEK
Roquefort	blue ewe's milk cheese made during the lambing season in the village of Roquefort FRENCH
roquette	rocket FRENCH
roquille	candied orange peel FRENCH
roræg	scrambled eggs DANISH
rørt smør	butter beaten until soft DANISH
rørte tyttebær	cranberry jam NORWEGIAN
rosbief	roast beef DUTCH
rosbif	roast beef FRENCH, ITALIAN, SPANISH
rosca	ring-shaped white bread PORTUGUESE

roscón	ring-shaped cake SPANISH
roscón de boniatos	dessert of sweet potato, egg and almond mixture in a ring-mould, covered in sweet syrup and meringue and baked SPANISH
rose	plant grown now for decorative purposes but once widely eaten; pastry ornament used to cover the hole made in a pie
rose geranium	the leaves can be used to flavour fruit or cream
rose hips	fully-ripe dark red fruits of the wild rose, which can be made into a preserve or a syrup
rose petals	used to make jams, jellies, conserves and drinks and attractive decorations; can be frosted or crystallized
rosette pak choi	a variety of pak choi resembling endive, also known as taatsoi, tasai, flat black pak choi, flat pak choi
rose water	distilled from rose petals or prepared from rose oil, it is highly fragrant
rosefish	type of Norway haddock
róseibni	chips HUNGARIAN
rosemary	strong pungent herb with spiky leaves, it should be used sparingly as it tends to overpower other herbs
rosenkål	Brussels sprouts DANISH, NORWEGIAN
Rosenkohl	Brussels sprouts GERMAN
rosette	sausage made from shoulder meat of pork FRENCH
rosie	tomatoes ROMANIAN
rosin	raisin DANISH, NORWEGIAN
Rosine	raisin GERMAN
rosmarin	rosemary SWEDISH
Rosmarin	rosemary GERMAN
rosmarino	rosemary ITALIAN
rosół	broth; consommé POLISH
rosolio	bright red liqueur from Italy and France, flavoured with rose oil or tangerine rind, orange juice and orange blossom ITALIAN, FRENCH
rosolli	herring salad with pickles, beetroot, onions, hard-boiled eggs, capers and sour cream FINNISH
rosquilla	doughnut SPANISH
rossel	quartered raw beetroot placed in jars with lukewarm boiled water and left for two or three weeks; ingredient of borsch soup, a traditional Passover dish JEWISH

rossini, à la	garnish for tournedos and noisettes of médaillons of foie gras, truffle and demi-glace with truffle extract; method of serving chicken FRENCH
rostat bröd	toast SWEDISH
rostbef	roast beef POLISH
rostbiff	roast beef SWEDISH
Rostbraten	roast beef; thick, pan-fried sirloin steak GERMAN
rostélyos	steak HUNGARIAN
rösten	to roast; grill GERMAN
Rösti	grated, fried potatoes (US: hash-browns) SWISS
Röstkartoffel	roast potato GERMAN
roston sült	barbecued; grilled HUNGARIAN
rote Beete, Rübe	beetroot GERMAN
rote Grütze	fruit jelly served with cream GERMAN
ro-tee	bread BM
rotengle	freshwater fish also known as gardon rouge FRENCH
roti	unleavened bread INDIAN
rôti	roast meat; dish containing roast meat FRENCH
rôtie	slice of bread, toasted or baked FRENCH
rôtir	to roast FRENCH
rotisserie cooking	method of cooking developed from the spit over the open fire; the joint is secured on a shaft close to the source of heat and continuously rotated as the meat cooks
Rotkohl	red cabbage GERMAN
Rotkraut	red cabbage cooked with cider vinegar, cloves, apples, sugar, wine and water to cover SWISS
rötlax	smoked salmon SWEDISH
rotmos	mashed turnips SWEDISH
rotolo	rolled, stuffed meat ITALIAN
rött	redcurrant SWEDISH
Rotzunge	lemon sole GERMAN
roucaou	Mediterranean fish used in bouillabaisse rouelle butchery term for a thick slice cut across leg of veal FRENCH
rouennais	cow's milk cheese made in Normandy FRENCH
rouennaise, sauce	classical sauce served with roast Rouen duck made from sauce bordelaise and duck livers FRENCH
rougail	hot chutney served with Creole dishes
rouge de rivière	shoveller, a type of duck FRENCH
rouge-queue	redstart, a type of bird FRENCH

rouget	red mullet FRENCH
rouget-barbet	fish from the Mediterranean including mullets and gurnards FRENCH
rough puff pastry	variation of puff pastry which rises less than puff pastry
rouhesämpylä	wholemeal roll FINNISH
rouille, sauce	hot sauce from Provence containing chillies, sauce aëoli, lobster coral and sea urchin FRENCH
roulade	stuffed meat roll; galantine DANISH, FRENCH
roulé	sweet pastry spread with jam, rolled up and sprinkled with praline and toasted almonds before baking FRENCH
rouleau	rolling pin FRENCH
roulette	small-toothed wheel to cut pastry FRENCH
rouló	baked beef loaf GREEK
round	butchery term for the top part of the leg; cut of veal AMERICAN
roussette	a kind of fritter; dogfish FRENCH
roussir	to turn a piece of meat or poultry in hot fat FRENCH
rout cakes and biscuits	confections similar to petits fours which used to be served at 'routs' or evening parties
roux	equal amounts fat and flour cooked together to form the basis of a sauce or panada
rova	turnip SWEDISH
rowan	mountain ash, a tree of the genus *Sorbut*; the red berries (rowanberries) can be used alone or to make jelly or added to apple sauce to vary the flavour
royal icing	hard white icing made of egg whites and icing sugar, often used to decorate cakes that are kept for a long time
royal jelly	food given to bee larvae to cause them to become queen bees, claimed to have beneficial effects on human health
Royal Mint Chocolate	mint chocolate liqueur
royale	Duke cherry ; garnish for game soup of a type of custard which is chopped and added to soup before serving FRENCH
royan	delicately flavoured fish similar to sardine, caught near the town of Royan FRENCH
røykt kolje med gulrøtter og eggesmør	poached smoked haddock with boiled carrots NORWEGIAN
røyktlaks	smoked salmon NORWEGIAN

røykttorsk	smoked cod NORWEGIAN
rozbratlę	roasting a joint of beef or a large rib or sirloin steak POLISH
rozemarijn	rosemary DUTCH
rozijnen	raisins DUTCH
rozinky	raisins CZECH
rozmaring	rosemary HUNGARIAN
rozpeky	baked yeast cakes CZECH
roztrzepaniec	sour milk POLISH
rubané	dishes built up of ribbon-like layers FRENCH
rubbing in	incorporating fat into flour to achieve a short texture by rubbing the fat and flour lightly between the fingers until the mixture resembles breadcrumbs
rubets	tripe RUSSIAN
rubio	red mullet SPANISH
Rücken	chine; saddle GERMAN
rudd	*Scardinius erythrophthalamus*, a freshwater fish similar to roach
rudderfish	fish found in the Mediterranean
rue	hardy evergreen shrub with blue-grey foliage and a pungent aromatic smell, for culinary and medicinal use
Rüebli	carrot GERMAN
ruff	protected migratory bird which arrives in Britain in the summer, no longer eaten
ruffe	freshwater species of perch
ruffed grouse	ruffed game bird, prepared as partridge
rugbrød	rye bread DANISH
rughetta	weed with leaves similar to corn salad ITALIAN
Rührei	scrambled eggs GERMAN
ruibarbo	rhubarb SPANISH
ruijanpallas	halibut FINNISH
ruis	rye FRENCH
ruisleipä	rye bread FINNISH
ruivo	red gurnard PORTUGUESE
rukkileiva ja õuna	sharp-tasting pudding ESTONIAN
rullepølse	kind of sausage of rolled veal and pork, sliced and served on smørrebrød DANISH
rum	spirit distilled from molasses, principally from the West Indies and the Caribbean, which may be white

	but is often caramel coloured and may be flavoured with fruits
rum sauce	sauce served with steamed puddings BRITISH
rumbledethumps	border dish made from potatoes and cabbage SCOTTISH
rump	English hip or buttock cut of beef; American cut of veal
rump roast	joint of beef or veal from the end of the loin nearest the hip bone AMERICAN
rump steak	cut of beef
rumsztyk	rump steak POLISH
runderlap	beef steak DUTCH
rundstykke	poppy seed roll DANISH, NORWEGIAN
rundvlees	beef DUTCH
runner	amberfish; amberjack; jurel; a large fish of the genus *Seriola* whose young have golden markings AMERICAN
runner bean	climbing plant; the pods are eaten
ruohosipuli	chive FINNISH
ruoka	food FINNISH
rurki francuskie z bitą smietaną	tube-like waffles filled with whipped cream POLISH
rurki z kremem	puff pastry tubes filled with cream or syrup POLISH
rusina	raisin FINNISH
rusk	sweetened tea biscuit; piece of bread or cake crisped in the oven; commercially-made product for invalids, and to help young children's teeth
ruskea kastike	gravy FINNISH
ruskistettu	sautéed FINNISH
russe, à la	Russian-style
Russian dressing	dressing of mayonnaise, pimento, chilli sauce, green pepper and celery AMERICAN
Russian mayonnaise	mayonnaise of sauce velouté, sour cream and horseradish
Russian salad	salad containing diced beetroot, apple, potato, peas, green beans, cucumber and other vegetables in mayonnaise
russin	raisin SWEDISH
Russische Eier	Russian eggs; egg halves topped with caviar and served with remoulade sauce GERMAN

Russische eieren	Russian eggs; hard-boiled egg halves garnished with mayonnaise, herring, shrimps, capers, anchovies and sometimes caviar, served on lettuce DUTCH
rusztu	grilled POLISH
Rutherglen sour cakes	cakes traditionally eaten at St Luke's Fair on 18 October SCOTTISH
Rutherglen cream	sour cream from Rutherglen SCOTTISH
Rutland cheddar	cheddar cheese flavoured with beer, garlic and parsley
ruusukaali	Brussels sprouts FINNISH
ryż	rice POLISH
ryabchik	hazel hen RUSSIAN
ryba	fish POLISH, RUSSIAN
rydze	orange agaric; meadow mushrooms POLISH
rye	hardy cereal which grows in cold climates and poor soil
rye bread	dark-coloured bread often served with shellfish
ryngle	greengages CZECH
rype	ptarmigan, snow grouse DANISH, NORWEGIAN
rysk kaviar	caviar SWEDISH
rzepa	swede POLISH
rzewień	rhubarb POLISH
rzodkiewki	radishes POLISH

S

s kšřenem	with horseradish CZECH
s ledem	with ice CZECH
Saanenkäse	variety of Gruyère from the Saanen Valley SWISS
sábalo	shad SPANISH
sabayon	version of the Italian zabaglione, a sweet sauce served with rich sponge or fruit pudding FRENCH
sablé	biscuit or small cake from Normandy FRENCH
sabz	green herbs with yoghurt INDIAN
sabzi	vegetable INDIAN
saccharin	white crystalline powder, a product of coal tar, with remarkable sweetening properties but no food value
saccharometer	instrument to measure the density of sugar solutions
Sacher-torte	famous chocolate cake created by Franz Sacher, who founded the Hotel Sacher in Vienna and was pastry-chef to Prince Metternich AUSTRIAN
sack	old name for various white wines, particularly those from Spain and the Canaries, the only modern survivor being sherry
sacristains	twists of pâte feuilletée FRENCH
sada pulau	plain fried rice INDIAN
saddle of lamb	prime roasting joint, the whole of the back of the sheep from the end on the loin to the best end of neck, usually divided into smaller pieces sadella sardine GREEK
sádlo	lard CZECH
saetina	ground chillies ITALIAN
safflower	thistle-like plant *Carthamus ti.rictorius*, with large orange-red flower heads, the seeds producing a pale delicately-flavoured oil; colouring is obtained from the powdered dried flowers
saffran	saffron SWEDISH
saffransbröd	sweet saffron loaf or rolls SWEDISH
saffron	dried stigmas of purple flowering crocus *Crocus sativus*, the most expensive spice, with an aromatic, slightly bitter taste; only a few threads are needed for flavour and colour
saffron cake	saffron-coloured and flavoured yeast cake or sweet bread containing currants

safio	conger eel PORTUGUESE
safran	saffron FRENCH
Safran	saffron GERMAN
sáfrány	saffron HUNGARIAN
Saft	juice GERMAN
sag, saag	spinach INDIAN
saganaki	fried squares of féta cheese GREEK
sage	strong, slightly bitter large-leafed herb *Salvia officinalis*
sage derby	cow's milk cheese flavoured with sage leaves
sage grouse	game bird from the sage plains of North America
sago	dried starch granules from the pith of the sago tree
sago dana	equivalent of sago INDIAN
sagosuppe	Norwegian sago dessert NORWEGIAN
Sahne	cream GERMAN
Saibling	char, a type of fish GERMAN
saiga	antelope, *Saiga tatarica*, of the Capri variety
saignant	very underdone or rare meat FRENCH
saigneux	butchery term for neck of mutton or veal FRENCH
sailor's-choice	collective name for several types of fish, particularly the grunt and the pinfish AMERICAN
Saint Benoît	camembert-type cheese FRENCH
Saint Paulin	creamy yellow, semi-hard cheese, sometimes sold as Port Salut
Saint-Agathon	cow's milk cheese FRENCH
Saint-Claude	small goat's milk cheese FRENCH
Sainte Ménéhould	district of the Marne in France famous for its pork products
Sainte-Anne d'Auray	cow's milk cheese from Brittany FRENCH
Sainte-Maure	long, cylindrical, soft, creamy goat's milk cheese with a straw through the centre
Saint-Florentin	goat's milk cheese FRENCH
Saint-Germain	dishes served with green peas FRENCH
Saint-Honoré	cake which is a Parisian speciality FRENCH
Saint-Hubert	game soup FRENCH
Saint-Marcellin	soft cream cheese FRENCH
Saint-Michel	cake made from genoese mixture FRENCH
Saint-Nectaire	cheese from Auvergne FRENCH
saint-pierre	John Dory, a type of fish FRENCH
Saint-Rémi	a cow's milk cheese FRENCH

Saitenwürst	variety of frankfurter or wiener sausage GERMAN
saithe	coalfish, see cuddy, piltocks SCOTTISH
sajt	cheese HUNGARIAN
sajtos pogácsa	cheese scone HUNGARIAN
sake	alcoholic drink made from fermented rice JAPANESE
saksanpähkinä	walnut FINNISH
sal	salt PORTUGUESE, SPANISH
salaatti	salad FINNISH
salad	salad is most popularly made from raw vegetables such as lettuce, cucumber and tomato; it can be made from a variety of fruits and vegetables, raw or cooked, and can include cooked rice or pasta; fruit salads are served as dessert
salad dressing	sauce-like mixtures poured over salads; there are two main types – vinaigrette and mayonnaise
salad relish	cooked relish AMERICAN
salada	salad PORTUGUESE
salade	salad FRENCH
saladier	salad bowl FRENCH
salado	salted; salty SPANISH
salaison	to treat with salt, to preserve FRENCH
salám	salami CZECH
salamander	heavy metal instrument heated until red-hot, held over sugar-coated top of crème brûlée to caramelise the surface
salamandre	salamander; breadcrumbs fried in butter FRENCH
salambô	small cake made of choux pastry filled with kirsch-flavoured crème patisserie FRENCH
salame	salami ITALIAN
salami	dry finely chopped lean pork and pork fat sausage, highly seasoned and flavoured with garlic, moistened with red wine
Salamikäse	a full cream cheese AUSTRIAN
salamura	ewe's milk cheese TURKISH
salan	sesame INDIAN
salat	salad; lettuce DANISH, NORWEGIAN
salata	salad GREEK
saláta	salad HUNGARIAN
sałata	lettuce POLISH
sałatka	salad POLISH
salato	salted ITALIAN

Salbei sage GERMAN

salceson brawn POLISH

salchicha sausage SPANISH

salchichón salami SPANISH

sale salt ITALIAN

salé salted or pickled FRENCH

salep starchy tubers of *Orchis latifolia*, washed, dried and ground into pepper

salepi drink which looks like milk, made from orchid tubers GREEK

salgado salty; salted PORTUGUESE

sallad salad SWEDISH

Sally Lunn flat teacake made from plain yeast dough served hot, split and buttered or cold, topped with glacé icing (said to have been named after its 18th-century inventor)

Salm salmon GERMAN

salmagundi, salmagundy old English supper dish of meat, salad, eggs, anchovy, pickles and beetroot

salmão salmon PORTUGUESE

salmi, salmis stew of partly-roasted game cooked with wine or port

salmigondis ragoût of several meats FRENCH

salmon round fish of the family Salmonidae, especially *Salmo salar* of the Atlantic, and *Oncorhynchus* species (sockeye, Chnook *etc*), having silvery scales, deep pink flesh when raw and pale pink when cooked; classified as a freshwater fish, salmon spend much of their life in the sea and only return to freshwater to spawn

salmón salmon SPANISH

salmon trout large species of trout especially the brown trout or rainbow trout; the Dolly Varden trout from Alaska

salmon, smoked cold smoked for a long period of time; thin slices are considered a delicacy served with lemon, ground black pepper and brown bread and butter

salmonberry wild raspberry NORTH AMERICAN

salmone salmon ITALIAN

salmonella a genus of Gram-negative rod-shaped aerobic bacteria, many species of which cause food poisoning

salmonete red mullet PORTUGUESE, SPANISH

saloio, queijo de	goat's and ewe's milk cheese PORTUGUESE
saloop	infusion of aromatic herbs *etc* formerly used as a tonic or cure
salotai	salad of lettuce, tomatoes, onions, hard-boiled eggs, radishes and cucumber
salotas	salad LITHUANIAN
salpa	gilthead SPANISH
salpicão	sausage containing thick slices of pork fillet PORTUGUESE
salpicon	mixture of chopped fish, meat and vegetables in a sauce, used as stuffing or filling FRENCH
sal prunella	curing agent; saltpetre
salsa	parsley PORTUGUESE
salsa	sauce ITALIAN, SPANISH
salsiccie	usually a type of small pork cooking sausage ITALIAN
salsicha	sausage, usually smoked PORTUGUESE
salsifi	salsify SPANISH
salsifis	salsify FRENCH
salsify	Mediterranean plant, *Tragopogon porrifolius*, an unusual, slightly oyster-flavoured vegetable, with long tapering roots; also known as oyster plan or vegetable oyster
salt	mineral (sodium chloride) used for seasoning savoury dishes
salt beef	beef cured by soaking the whole joint in spiced brine to preserve it, it is then cooked and served hot or cold
salt substitute	a product containing potassium chloride instead of sodium chloride, in order to limit sodium in the diet
salta biten	salted boiled beef SWEDISH
saltad	salted SWEDISH
salteado	sautéed SPANISH
saltet	salted; cured DANISH
saltfiskur	cured fish ICELANDIC
saltgurka	salt-pickled gherkin SWEDISH
šalti baršrčiai	national soup LITHUANIAN
saltimbocca	veal slices with ham, sage, herbs and wine ITALIAN
salting	preserving food in dry salt or brine
saltpetre	potassium nitrate, a white crystalline substance with a piquant, fresh taste, used with common salt for preservation purposes and to give the meat a reddish colour

saltsa	sauce GREEK
salva	sage PORTUGUESE
salvia	sage ITALIAN, SPANISH
Salz	salt GERMAN
Salzburger Nockerl	dumpling of beaten egg yolks, egg whites, sugar and flour, fried in butter GERMAN
Salzgurke	pickled cucumber GERMAN
samak	fish MIDDLE EASTERN
sambal, sumbol	side dishes foods including chopped tomatoes, cucumber, chutneys and sliced bananas, served as accompaniments to curries INDIAN
sambal oelek	chilli-flavoured relish DUTCH-Indonesian sambar,
samber	curry from the south, originally made with lentils, but now prepared also with meat INDIAN
sambuca	elderberry and liquorice flavoured liqueur ITALIAN
sammakonreidet	frogs' legs FINNISH
sammenkogt ret	meat and vegetable stew DANISH
samosa	triangular, deep-fried savoury pastry filled with spicy meat or vegetable mixtures, served as a snack or starter INDIAN
samphire	green seashore umbelliferous plant, *Crithmum maritinum*, which may be pickled, used in salads or served as a vegetable accompaniment to fish
sämpylä	roll FINNISH
Samsoe	mild, nutty-flavoured cow's milk cheese with a few small irregular holes
San Simón	firm mild cheese from San Simón de la Cuesta in Lugo SPANISH
sand cake	Madeira-type cake made from cornflour, ground rice or potato flour
sand cherry	small shrub with a round sweet fruit
sand dab	saltwater fish of the genus *Citharichthys*, similar to plaice
sand eel, sand lance, sand launce	small snake-like fish of the family *Ammodytidae*, which buries itself on sandy beaches at low tide; also known as launce
sandacz	perch POLISH
sande	sandwich PORTUGUESE
sandía	watermelon SPANISH
Sandmuschel	clam GERMAN
sandre	giant perch FRENCH

Sandtorte	cake GERMAN
sandwich	two slices of bread, often buttered, with a filling of meat, cheese, egg, tomato etc or any of a myriad combinations, named after John Montagu, 4th Earl of Sandwich (1718–92) who took nourishment in this form so as not to have to leave the gaming table
sangaree	drink WEST INDIAN
sangler	to pack ice around a container of ice cream to freeze it FRENCH
sanglier	wild boar FRENCH
sangrante	underdone or rare meat SPANISH
sangue, al	underdone ITALIAN
sanguinante	underdone or rare meat ITALIAN
sanguine	dish from the Berry region made from onion cooked in butter, adding the blood of two chickens, adding seasoning to the dish which is shaken and cooked like an omelette FRENCH
sansonnet	young mackerel; colloquial French for starling FRENCH
san-tan	coconut milk BM
santé	soup containing potage purée parmentier, sorrel, egg yolks and cream, garnished with chervil butter FRENCH
santola	spider crab PORTUGUESE
sapodilla	delicious sweet, plum-sized fruit with reddish yellow granular flesh EAST INDIAN
sapota	name applied to a number of different fruits of tropical America
saracen corn	buckwheat
saragli	cake similar in taste to baklava GREEK
Sarah Bernhardt	chicken consommé thickened with tapioca with chicken quenelles, julienne of truffles, asparagus tips, sliced poached beef marrow and beurre d'écrevisses; the yolk of hard-boiled eggs mixed with chicken, raw yolk and breadcrumbs, replaced in the white, covered with sauce périgneux and baked; named after the French tragic actress Sarah Bernhardt (1844–1923) FRENCH
saramură	meat served in a broth of vinegar, salt and garlic ROMANIAN
šaran	freshwater bream SERBO-CROAT
sarapatel	fried liver and bacon PORTUGUESE

sarcelle	teal; culinary term for widgeon FRENCH
sarda	pilchard; sardine ITALIAN
sarda	mackerel PORTUGUESE
sarde, à la	garnish for meat of grilled or fried tomatoes, stuffed cucumber or courgettes, and rice croquettes FRENCH
sardell	anchovy SWEDISH
Sardelle	anchovy GERMAN
Sardellenring	rolled anchovy GERMAN
sardenera	pizza from San Remo in Liguria ITALIAN
sardin	sardine SWEDISH
sardina	small sardine ITALIAN
sardina	sardine; pilchard SPANISH
sardine	small round oily fish of the herring family, especially a young pilchard
sardinha	sardine PORTUGUESE
sardinky	pilchard CZECH
sardo	hard, aromatic sheep's milk cheese ITALIAN
sardynki	sardines POLISH
sárgabarack	apricots HUNGARIAN
sargasso	seaweed SPANISH
sargo	grey bream SPANISH
sarladaise, à la	garnish for lamb of pan-fried truffles and sliced potatoes, with thick meat gravy FRENCH
sarma	stuffed cabbage rolls popular in Serbia YUGOSLAVIAN
sarmades	cabbage leaves stuffed with chopped beef, pork, onions and rice GREEK
sarmale	stuffed cabbage rolls ROMANIAN
sarna	roe deer; venison POLISH
sarnina	venison POLISH
sarrasin	buckwheat FRENCH
sarsaparilla	from dried roots of a tropical American plant, it is used as a flavouring for carbonated drinks
sartadagnano	speciality of Provence, very small fish cooked in olive oil in a pan and pressed together so they can be turned like a pancake FRENCH
sartén	two-handled pot for cooking paella SPANISH
sartù	oven-baked rice with tomatoes, meat, chicken giblets, mushrooms and peas ITALIAN
sås	sauce SWEDISH
sa-sa-wee; mas-tad	mustard BM

sashimi   delicacy of raw seafood served as an hors d'œuvre
JAPANESE

sashuka   medium-heat sauce made from roasted spices, onions, tomatoes and green peppers INDIAN

sassafras   laurel tree; its roots and leaves produce spicy-flavoured lemon scented oil, and the dried leaves make filé powder

sassenage   cow's milk cheese from the Dauphiné FRENCH

satay, saté, sateh   originally from Indonesia, small pieces of marinated lamb, beef, pork, poultry or seafood, grilled or barbecued on skewers and served with peanut sauce

satsuma   small orange citrus fruit related to the tangerine

Sattel   chine; saddle GERMAN

saturated solution   solution containing as much of a substance as can be dissolved in that volume of water

Saubohne   broad bean GERMAN

sauce   used to flavour, coat or accompany a dish, to enhance foods with which they are served

sauce allemande   classical light-coloured sauce consisting of velouté blended with egg yolks, cream, and nutmeg; it is sometimes called sauce blonde or sauce parisienne
FRENCH

sauce américaine   sauce for fish and lobsters consisting of velouté, pounded lobster, lobster coral, butter, white wine and brandy FRENCH

sauce à la bigarade   orange sauce for roast duck FRENCH

sauce alone   local name for herb garlic mustard, a wild herb
ENGLISH

sauce béarnaise   classic sauce thickened with egg yolks, served with grilled meat or fish FRENCH

sauce blonde   *see* sauce allemande FRENCH

sauce choron   a classical sauce made from sauce béarnaise blended with tomato purée FRENCH

sauce normande   dishes from the Normandy area containing cream, seafood, apples, cider or calvados, for which Normandy is famous; fish braised in white wine and served with seafood and mushrooms and sauce normande; small cuts of meat served with a sauce of cider and calvados added to the pan juices; thick soup of potatoes, haricot beans, leeks, turnips and cream; French beans or salsify covered with cream and egg yolks; method of cooking potatoes; method of cooking pheasant FRENCH

saucepan	metal or enamel pan with a long handle used for cooking food, usually by boiling, with or without a lid
sauce parisienne	*see* sauce allemande FRENCH
sauce périgueux	sauce of demi-glace, truffle essence, truffles and Madeira FRENCH
sauce pérgourdine	classical sauce made of sauce périgueux with foie gras FRENCH
sauce provençale	classical sauce with shallots, garlic, meat stock and white wine FRENCH
sauce tartare	tartare sauce FRENCH
sauce tyrolienne	sauce béarnaise made with olive oil instead of butter
sauciaux	Bourbonnais name for pancakes FRENCH
saucijzebroodje	sausage roll DUTCH
saucisse	smaller types of fresh sausage, cooked and usually eaten hot FRENCH
saucisson	larger sausages, either lightly preserved and needing further cooking, or ready to eat FRENCH
sauer	sour GERMAN
Sauerampfer	sorrel GERMAN
Sauerbraten	pot roast marinated with herbs AUSTRIAN, GERMAN
Sauerkraut	cabbage fermented in salt often served with sausages GERMAN
sauge	sage FRENCH
saumon	salmon FRENCH
saumonette	a number of, shark-like sea fish in appearance FRENCH
saumure	brine FRENCH
saupiquet	mediaeval wine sauce FRENCH
saur	salted, smoked herring FRENCH
saurel	the horse mackerel, or scad AMERICAN
saus	sauce DUTCH, NORWEGIAN
sausage	minced pork or other meat, often mixed with bread or rusk and squeezed into a long thin case made from gut, linked (twisted) into regular cylindrical lengths when full; also known as links
sausage roll	roll of sausage meat encased in pastry and baked
sausagemeat	mixture similar to that used for sausages but not put into skins
saussiska	smoked sausage RUSSIAN
saussoun	sauce from the Var district which can be spread on bread FRENCH

sauté	to cook food in hot fat to brown it lightly FRENCH
sauter	to cook in oil or butter over a brisk heat FRENCH
Sauternes	sweet white wine from the vineyards of the Gironde, often served as a dessert wine
savanyú malac	sour pork HUNGARIAN
savanyú tojásleves	sour egg soup HUNGARIAN
savanyúkáposzta	sauerkraut HUNGARIAN
savarin	rich yeast mixture baked in a ring mould, served soaked in rum syrup with cream or fruit salad
sável	shad PORTUGUESE
saveloy	short, thick salted pork sausage, lightly seasoned and coloured red with saltpetre
savoie	sponge cake from the Savoy region FRENCH
savory	peppery flavoured summer herb, particularly good served with beans
savoury	titbits eaten with the fingers; highly seasoned dish, usually hot, served after the sweet course and before the dessert at a formal meal
savoy	one of the oldest of cabbages
savoy biscuits	small sponge fingers particularly used in dessert making
savoyarde, à la	sliced potatoes cooked with grated Gruyère cheese
savu kala	smoked fish FINNISH
savustettu	smoked FINNISH
sawrell	saurel MALTESE
Sbrinz-Käse	hard unpasteurised cow's milk cheese SWISS
scad	another name for horse mackerel
scalding	immersing tomatoes, etc in boiling water to make them easier to peel; pouring boiling water over or over pork to loosen hair from the skin or to treat the trotters; treating milk; bringing liquid to boiling point and cooking merrily at that temperature
scaling	removing scales from a fish
scallions	immature onions with a small bulb and lots of leaves
scallop	almost circular bivalve mollusc with ribbed shells (*see* pecten)
scalloped dishes	food baked in a scallop shell or similar container
scalloping	decorating the double edge of a pastry pie with small horizontal cuts, pushed up to produce a scalloped effect
scalogno	shallot ITALIAN
scaloppa	veal escalope ITALIAN

scaloppine	another name for piccate or small scaloppe ITALIAN
scamorza	soft, cow's milk cheese ITALIAN
scampi	Dublin Bay prawns ITALIAN
Scanno	ewe's milk cheese from Scanno in the Abruzzi ITALIAN
scapece	fried fish preserved in white wine vinegar and saffron ITALIAN
scappati	stuffed rolled slices of veal, a variation of saltimbocca
scarola	escarole; Batavian endive ITALIAN
scarus	Mediterranean species of parrot fish
scaup duck	wild duck common in northern and central Europe
schaaldier	shellfish DUTCH
schab	roast loin of pork POLISH
schab pieczony	roast pork tenderloin steak POLISH
schab po wiedeńsku	breaded pork chop POLISH
Schabzieger	unusual green soured skimmed milk cheese from the canton of Glarus, which has been made for 500 years SWISS
Schalentier	shellfish GERMAN
schaleth	dish made from noodle paste JEWISH
Schalotte	shallot GERMAN
schalottenlök	shallot SWEDISH
schapevlees	mutton DUTCH
scharàn sus orèhi	dish made from whole carp BULGARIAN
scharretong	lemon sole DUTCH
Schaschlik	chunks of meat, kidneys and bacon, grilled and braised in spicy tomato, onion and bacon sauce GERMAN
Schaumrolle	puff pastry rolls filled with whipped cream or custard GERMAN
Scheibe	slice GERMAN
Schellfisch	haddock GERMAN
schelvis	haddock DUTCH
schiacciala	Easter cake from Leghorn in Tuscany ITALIAN
Schildkrötensuppe	turtle soup GERMAN
schildpadsoep	turtle soup DUTCH
Schillerlocke	pastry cornet with vanilla cream filling GERMAN
Schinken	ham GERMAN
Schlachtplatte	cold meat, liver, sausage and sauerkraut GERMAN
Schlagober	Viennese term for whipped cream AUSTRIAN

Schlagobers	whipped cream GERMAN
Schlegel	leg; haunch GERMAN
Schleie	tench GERMAN
Schlesisches Himmelreich	'Silesian heaven'; pork chops fried with dried fruits GERMAN
Schlosserbuben	traditional sweet of soaked prunes stuffed with almonds, fried in batter and dusted with chocolate AUSTRIAN
Schlosskäse	soft cheese AUSTRIAN
schmal(t)z	rendered down chicken or goose fat AMERICAN, JEWISH
Schmarrn	a pudding AUSTRIAN
Schmelzkäse	soft pungent cheese, usually for spreading on bread GERMAN
Schmorbraten	pot roast GERMAN
Schmorfleisch	meat stew GERMAN
Schnapps	there are many varieties of this strong clear spirit, which has a flavour similar to gin GERMAN
Schnecken	snails; rectangular Austrian pastries AUSTRIAN, GERMAN
Schnittbohne	sliced French bean GERMAN
Schnitte	slice; cut GERMAN
Schnittkäse	collective term for German and Austrian semi-hard cheeses GERMAN, AUSTRIAN
Schnittlauch	chive GERMAN
Schnitzel	thin slice of meat, usually veal, coated with breadcrumbs and fried GERMAN, AUSTRIAN
Schöberl	garnish for clear soups AUSTRIAN
Schokolade	chocolate GERMAN
schol	plaice DUTCH
Scholle	plaice GERMAN
scholles	sun dried plaice BELGIAN
Schöps	mutton GERMAN
Schoten	green peas GERMAN
schuimomelet	fluffy dessert omelet DUTCH
schuka	pike RUSSIAN
Schulter	shoulder GERMAN
Schusterpfanne	'shoemaker's pot'; pork stew with pears, carrots and potatoes GERMAN
Schwäbische würste	sausages from Swabia GERMAN
Schwamm	mushroom GERMAN

Schwammerlsauce mushroom sauce AUSTRIAN

schwarze Johannisbeere blackcurrant GERMAN

Schwarzfisch method for cooking carp or other river fish AUSTRIAN

Schwarzwälder Kirschtorte Black Forest gateau GERMAN

Schwarzwälder Schinken variety of smoked ham from the Black Forest GERMAN

Schwarzwürste black sausages

Schwarzwurzel salsify GERMAN

Schwein pig GERMAN

Schweinefleisch pork GERMAN

Schweizer kraut marigold leaves cooked in salted water GERMAN

schweizerost Swiss cheese SWEDISH

schweizerschnitzel veal scallop stuffed with ham and cheese SWEDISH

scifers local Cornish name for Welsh onion

scirkeaprólék chicken giblets HUNGARIAN

sciroppo, alla in syrup ITALIAN

sciule piene Piedmontese dialect for cipolle ripiene - stuffed onions ITALIAN

scone small, light, plain cake, usually split and spread with butter or a filling

score to incise the outer surface of food as decoration

scorfano Genoese name for hogfish ITALIAN

scorza di noce moscata mace ITALIAN

scorzonera black salsify, once called 'viper grass' because it was used as a remedy for snake bites

Scotch blue hare a hare inhabiting mainly mountain districts

Scotch bonnet a very hot chilli, related to the habañero

Scotch broth barley broth, the national soup SCOTTISH

Scotch currant bun also known as black bun, a cake traditionally eaten at festivals SCOTTISH

Scotch egg cold shelled hard boiled eggs coated in seasoned flour and sausagemeat, wrapped in breadcrumbs and deep-fried

Scotch kale thick broth or soup containing shredded cabbage

Scotch pancake *see* drop scone

Scotch woodcock toast spread with anchovy paste and topped with scrambled eggs

scoter common black duck of the genus *Melanitta* from Europe and North America; only the young birds are edible

scouse a Liverpudlian stew, *see* lobscouse

Scoville	Wilbur Scoville devised a hotness unit for chillis expressed as the dilution required to reach the threshold of taste. Habanero chillis rate 200,000–300,000 Scoville; jalapeño averages a mere 3,000. A more accutate measure is now afforded using high-pressure liquid chromatography
scrag end	the lean end of neck of lamb or veal
scrapple	dish containing cornmeal and pork, eaten as brunch AMERICAN
scrippelle imbusse	pancakes filled with grated pecorino or Parmesan cheese and covered with chicken stock ITALIAN
scrod	baby cod or halibut AMERICAN
scrowled pichards	traditional Cornish dish of grilled pilchards
scum	froth which forms on top of boiling liquids
scup	sea bream; used in soups and stews AMERICAN
sea anemones	edible sea creatures (coelenterates) found mainly off Mediterranean coasts
sea beef	meat of a young whale SCOTTISH
sea cat	sailors' name for catfish
sea cow	another name for the manatee, a sea mammal
sea cuckoo	sailors' name for red gurnard
sea cucumber	marine echinoderm of the genus *Holothuroidea* that looks more like a plant with a cluster of tentacles at one end; it is dried and used in cooking CHINESE
sea date	tiny bivalve mollusc the size, shape and colour of a date, usually eaten raw
sea devil	sailors' name for angler fish
sea eagle	sailors' name for a large ray or skate
sea food	edible saltwater fish or shellfish
sea hen	sailors' name for the crooner
sea hog	sailors' name for the porpoise
sea owl	sailors' name for lumpfish
sea oxeye	fleshy European weed that grows near the sea
sea perch	white fish related to the sea bass
sea pie	beef stew with suetcrust lid
sea quince	small shellfish
sea robin	name for certain gurnards AMERICAN
sea rocket	a plant from beside the sea, whose young leaves can be used in salads
sea trout	silvery marine variety of the brown trout that spawns in fresh water

sea truffle	mollusc with a rigid shell
sea urchin	marine echinoderm such as the edible Echinus esculentus, with a soft body enclosed in a hard round shell or test
sea vegetables	a variety of seaweed used in cookery; some other seashore plants JAPANESE
sea water	sometimes used for cooking because of the many substances dissolved in it
sea wife	wrasse from the European coast of the Altlantic
sea wrack	membranous or filament-type edible seaweed
seakale	resembling blanched rhubarb or celery, it has crisp white stalks, tiny green leaves and a nutty flavour
seal	large marine mammal often eaten by Inuit
searing	quickly browning meat in hot fat before grilling, roasting or stewing
seasoned flour	flour mixed with a little salt and pepper, usually used to coat meat or fish before frying
seasoning	salt, pepper, herbs and spices added to flavour a dish
seaweed	marine plants, the most numerous of which are algae
seb	equivalent of apple INDIAN
sebadas	traditional dish often eaten as a sweet course of pastry and cheese sprinkled with orange and lemon juice, baked and served with sugar and honey SARDINIAN
sébille	wooden bowl FRENCH
sec	dry FRENCH
seco	dry; dried PORTUGUESE
secole	Venetian name for scraps of meat from bones of a joint of meat ITALIAN
sedano	celery ITALIAN
seed cake	type of Madeira cake flavoured with caraway seeds and lemon
seedless raisin	sultana AMERICAN
seetul	allspice, *Myrtus pimenta* INDIAN
Seezunge	sole GERMAN
segedínský	with sauerkraut and onion CZECH
sei	coalfish; coley NORWEGIAN
sei, seiti	black cod FINNISH
seigle	rye FRENCH
seisova pöytä	buffet with many hot and cold dishes, salads, cheeses and desserts FINNISH

seitan	processed form of wheat gluten, marinated in flavouring such as tamari, seaweed and ginger which turns it pale brown; a rich source of protein often found in health food shops
seiving	pushing edible material through a sieve
sekahedelmäkeitto	stewed dried fruit flavoured with cinnamon FINNISH
sękacz	layer cake POLISH
sekaná	pork and beef minced loaf CZECH
sel	salt FRENCH
Selchfleisch	smoked pork GERMAN
selderij	celery DUTCH
sele	suckling pig CZECH
sele na rožni	roast suckling pig CZECH
seledka	herring RUSSIAN
selery	celery POLISH
self-raising flour	commercially blended wheat flour containing a raising agent such as sodium bicarbonate
selinon	celery; celeriac GREEK
seljanka	salmon soup FINNISH
seljankakakeitto	fish soup usually made with two kinds of fish FINNISH
Selkirk bannock	yeasted fruit loaf SCOTTISH
selle	saddle FRENCH
selleri	celery DANISH, FINNISH, NORWEGIAN, SWEDISH
Sellerie	celery GERMAN
selles-sur-cher	goat's milk cheese from the Berry district FRENCH
selon grosseur, sg	price according to size (eg a lobster); often abbreviated FRENCH
selshcaree	trimmed back bacon cured in spiced brine and lightly smoked, popular in northern Europe
selvaggina	game ITALIAN
semi di finocchio	fennel seeds ITALIAN
Semmel	roll GERMAN
sémola	semolina SPANISH
sêmola	semolina PORTUGUESE
semolina	granular, hard wheat flour, often from durum wheat left after bolting, the main ingredient of dried pasta and milk puddings
semoule	semolina FRENCH
senap	mustard SWEDISH
senape	mustard ITALIAN
sencillo	plain SPANISH

Senf	mustard GERMAN
sennep	mustard DUTCH, DANISH, NORWEGIAN
sepia	cuttlefish SPANISH
seppia	cuttlefish; squid ITALIAN
septmoncel	blue-veined cheese from the Jura mountains FRENCH
sept-oeil	literally means 'seven eye'; lampern or river lamprey spawn FRENCH
sequillo	small cake like a macaroon, containing hazelnuts SPANISH
ser	cheese POLISH
seranno	sea bass SPANISH
serce	heart POLISH
sericá alentejano	cinnamon soufflé PORTUGUESE
sernik wiedeński	cheesecake POLISH
serpa, queijo de	regional farmhouse-made cheese PORTUGUESE
serra	most typical Portuguese cheese PORTUGUESE
serrano	sea bass SPANISH
serré	cheese from the Glaris district made from whey curdled a second time with rennet and pounded with herbs
sertésborda	pork chop HUNGARIAN
sertéshús	pork HUNGARIAN
sertéskaraj	cutlet of pork HUNGARIAN
sertészsír	lard HUNGARIAN
service tree	*Sorbus domestica*, a tree related to the rowan tree, whose fruit is the serviceberry; also called shad bush or sorb
sesame oil	strongly flavoured sesame seeds oil
sesame seeds	small, rich, sweet, spice seeds with a slightly burnt flavour enhanced by toasting or frying
sesos	brains SPANISH
seta	mushroom SPANISH
setsuuri	sweetened rye bread FINNISH
sev	equivalent of vermicelli INDIAN
sévigné, à la	garnish for tournedos and entrées of stuffed lettuce, grilled mushrooms, pommes château and sauce madère FRENCH
sevruga	grade of caviar, second only to beluga in cost (so presumably in quality)
sewaiian	dessert made from noodles, cream and nuts INDIAN

sfenci di San Giuseppe   small choux pastry buns flavoured with orange and lemon peel, filled with sweetened cottage cheese ITALIAN

sfogato   meat and vegetable custard or soufflé from the island of Rhodes GREEK

sfogliatelle   Neopolitan pastry shells filled with sweetened ricotta cheese and candied fruit ITALIAN

sfogliatelle   puff pastry with custard or fruit preserve filling ITALIAN

sformato   a cross between a soufflé and a pudding ITALIAN

sg   see selon grosseur

sgombro   mackerel ITALIAN

shad   European white fish of the herring family which migrates up river to spawn

shad bush   small tree native to North America

shaddock   largest citrus fruit of the tree *Citrus maxima* (or *decumana*), named after Captain Shaddock who introduced its seeds to Jamaica in 1696

shahi   royal INDIAN

shahi tukra   type of bread pudding INDIAN

shakar para   sweet crisp type snack INDIAN

shakarkhund   sweet potato INDIAN

shalgam   turnip INDIAN

shallot   small brown-cased member of the onion family

shami kebab   spiced minced meat patties TURKISH

shank   the lower part of the leg in pork, lamb and mutton

shape   blancmange, jelly etc shaped in a mould

shark   family of sea fish including dogfish and skate; edible sharks are smaller than the ferocious species

sharp-tailed grouse   North American bird similar to the prairie chicken

shashlyk, shashlik   lamb or mutton marinated and then threaded onto skewers with onions and bay leaves, grilled served on a bed of rice RUSSIAN

shchi   traditional green vegetable soup RUSSIAN

sheek kebab   spiced minced meat formed into sausages, skewered and grilled INDIAN

sheepshead   sea bream and porgies of the American Atlantic with strong, crussing teeth, especially *Archosargus rhomboidalis* ENGLISH

sheldrake   common wild duck found all over Europe

shellfish collective name for a wide variety of sea creatures, either molluscs or crustaceans, caught or farmed for their meat

shemis aromatic plant from the rocky shores of the Hebrides used locally as a green vegetable HEBRIDEAN

shepherd's pie well-flavoured cooked meat, usually minced (some say only lamb or mutton should be used), with mashed potato crust

sherbet a slightly effervescent powder with a fruit flavour eaten or made into a drink; another word for sorbet, especially in the US; Australian slang for beer

sherry blend of Spanish wines matured by the solera system

Sherwood cheese double Gloucester cheese flavoured with chives and onions

shikar pork (unclean to Moslems; a Portuguese influence) INDIAN

shin lower part of fore leg of beef

shirred eggs œufs en cocotte AMERICAN

shirring baking food (often eggs) in ramekins in the oven

shkubánky traditional potato cake made with potato and rye flour CZECH

shoat, shote recently-weaned piglet

shoo-fly pie a Pennsylvania-Dutch pie – a pastry shell containing a mollasses and brown sugar mixture AMERICAN

short-order cook one who cooks to order, as in a cafeteria

short ribs joint of meat from the lower ribs

short soup soup of chicken stock, noodle dumplings, minced meat and garnish CHINESE

shortbread thick, crisp cake, with a 'short', biscuit-like texture

shortcake dessert of two rounds of rich scone filled with fruit and cream

shortcrust pastry simple crumbly pastry used for pies and tart bases

shortening fat used in dough or cake mixture, so named because it makes the mixture 'short' or tender

shoulder joint of veal or lamb known as the forequarter

shoveller *Anas clypeata*, a wild duck found on ponds and marshes, with a spoon-shaped bill

shredding grating cheese or slicing raw vegetables into fine pieces or strips

Shrewsbury biscuit traditional biscuit of rolled dough cut into round shapes, flavoured with lemon or orange rind, mixed spice, dried fruit or cocoa powder

shrimp	in Britain, very small crustaceans of the genus *Cragnon* and their relatives are called shrimps, rather than prawns
shrimp paste	seasoning of sun-dried salted prawns
shrub	drink made from fruits, spices and sugar either to be added to rum, or with rum added
shunguki	Japanese for chrysanthemum greens, chop suey greens, Japanese greens
shurpa	soup from Uzbekistan with crushed raw onion and black pepper added before serving RUSSIAN
sianliha	pork FINNISH
siansorkka	pigs' trotters FINNISH
sidemeats	salt pork or bacon; offal AMERICAN
Siedfleisch	boiled meat GERMAN
siekane	minced; hashed POLISH
sielawa	whiting POLISH
sienet	mushrooms FINNISH
sieva bean	bean similar to the Lima bean
sieve	utensil with wire or nylon mesh through which foods can be poured or pressed to achieve a soft even texture
sieving	pouring or pressing foods through a sieve
sifting	shaking flour or other dry ingredients through a sieve to add air to the mixture for a better rise
sig	whitefish RUSSIAN
sigtebrød	rye and wheat flour bread DANISH
siianmäti	whitefish roe FINNISH
siika	whitefish FINNISH
sik	whitefish SWEDISH
sikotakia	liver GREEK
silakat	sprats FINNISH
silakka	Baltic herring FINNISH
silavapannukak-ku	pancake with diced bacon FINNISH
sild	small herring caught off the Norwegian coast DANISH, NOWEGIAN
sildekake	herring patty NORWEGIAN
sildesalat	herring and beetroot salad DANISH
sildesalat	salad of diced salt herring, cucumber, onions, vegetables, spices and mayonnaise NORWEGIAN
sill	herring SWEDISH
silli	herring FINNISH

sillocks	fry of coalfish SCOTTISH
silungur	trout ICELANDIC
silure	one of the largest European freshwater fish; catfish
silvano	chocolate tart; chocolate meringue ITALIAN
silver beet	leaf vegetable with large, spinach-flavoured leaves
silver hake	sea fish from the northern coast of New England AMERICAN
silver onion	very small silver skinned onion
silver sild	small sea fish related to the herring
silverside	cut of beef below the aitchbone and above the leg
silverside	atherine; sand smelt AMERICAN
silverweed	weed with starchy roots, eaten like parsnips
sima héjú öszibarack	nectarine HUNGARIAN
simla mirch	bell pepper INDIAN
simmering	keeping a liquid just below boiling point to cook dishes that require long slow cooking
simnel cake	spiced fruit cake served at Easter, it is made with a layer of marzipan on top and sometimes another baked in the centre, and may be decorated with eleven marzipan balls on top to represent the faithful apostles
simpukka	mussel FINNISH
sinaasappel	orange DUTCH
sinappi	mustard FINNISH
singeing	using a flame to burn off residual feathers on plucked birds
singin' hinny	type of griddle cake from Northumberland made from a currant scone mixture, turned on the griddle during cooking when it makes a hissing noise, hence the name
šípek	rosehip CZECH
sippets	19th-century name for triangular pieces of toast, served with minced beef or cheese dishes to soak up the gravy
sipuli	onion FINNISH
sir	cheese SERBO-CROAT
sirap	treacle; molasses SWEDISH
siréné	national cheese made from ewe's milk BULGARIAN
siri	crab PORTUGUESE
sirloin	joint of beef cut from the last rib to the sacrum
sirloin steak	cut of steak from the end of the loin

sirop	syrup FRENCH
sirup	syrup CZECH
sirupssnipp	ginger biscuit NORWEGIAN
šiškevap	beef or lamb rolled in paprika and grilled on skewers with potato and onion slices YUGOSLAVIAN
siskonmakkarakeitto	vegetable soup with diced veal sausage FINNISH
sitron	lemon NORWEGIAN
sitruuna	lemon FINNISH
sjampinjong	button mushroom NORWEGIAN
sjaslik	skewered chunks of meat, grilled and braised in spicy tomatoes, onions and bacon sauce DUTCH
sjokolade	chocolate NORWEGIAN
sjömansbiff	beef casserole with carrots, onions and potatoes braised in beer SWEDISH
sjøørret	salmon trout NORWEGIAN
sjötunga	sole SWEDISH
sjøtunge	sole NORWEGIAN
sjötungsfilé	fillet of sole SWEDISH
skabu kapostu supa	traditional sauerkraut soup LATVIAN
skaldjur	shellfish SWEDISH
skaldyr	shellfish DANISH
skalldyr	shellfish NORWEGIAN
skaltsounia	popular Cretan pasty containing féta cheese and eggs, fried in hot oil and sprinkled with honey, or containing a honey and nut mixture GREEK
skarp saus	sauce similar to Worcestershire sauce NORWEGIAN
skarpsås	cold sharp sauce served with fish SWEDISH
skate	flat bodied, kite-shaped sea fish found in warmer seas, a member of the ray family *Rajidae*
skembe	tripe GREEK
skewer	pointed instrument onto which meat and vegetables are threaded for cooking; or used for keeping joints etc firmly rolled
skillet	In England usually a saucepan; in American usually a frying pan
skilpaddesuppe	turtle soup NORWEGIAN
skimmed milk	milk with the cream removed
skimming	removing froth, fat or scum from the surface of stock, gravy, stews and jam
skink	essence; stew; soup SCOTTISH, IRISH
skinka	ham SWEDISH

skinke ham DANISH, NORWEGIAN

skinklåda ham and egg casserole SWEDISH

skinkomelett ham omelette SWEDISH

skinning removing skin from meat, fish, poultry, fruit or vegetables

skipperlabskovs lobscouse, a thick stew of beef, carrots and onions DANISH

skirlie mealie pudding, a dish of oatmeal and onion, an accompaniment or stuffing for poultry and meat SCOTTISH

skirret plant grown for its large white roots

skirt old name for flank of beef

skirts and bodices local name for fluted trimmings of pork and pickled spare ribs of bacon IRISH

skiva slice SWEDISH

skive slice DANISH, NORWEGIAN

skiver pan pan sold in Scandinavian stores in the US, especially for cooking a round fried cake AMERICAN

skořice cinnamon CZECH

sköldpaddssoppa turtle soup SWEDISH

skopové mutton CZECH

skordalia sauce similar to Greek skorthalia usually served with fried aubergine BULGARIAN

skórka peel POLISH

skorthalia classical sauce containing garlic, lemon and usually nuts GREEK

škraloup the skin on boiled milk CZECH

skrei large cod from Lofoten NORWEGIAN

skrubbe flounder DANISH

škubánky s mákem potato dumplings with poppy seeds and sugar cookies CZECH

skum saus 'froth or foam sauce'; whipped sweet sauce NORWEGIAN

škvarky crackling CZECH

sky meat and vegetable jelly used as a garnish DANISH

sky dripping; gravy SWEDISH

sky-blue and sinkers traditional Cornish recipe for a mixture of barley meal and scalded milk poured into water, cooked and poured into bowls containing pieces of barley bread, which rise in the light blue liquid and then sink – hence the name

skyr	soured skimmed milk dish similar to yoghurt, sweetened and eaten as a dessert ICELANDIC
Skyros	island cheese made from ewe's milk GREEK
sla	lettuce; salad DUTCH
slaboon	French bean (US: green bean) DUTCH
sladkosti	sweets (US: candies) CZECH
slagroom	whipped cream DUTCH
slak	snail DUTCH
slaking	liquefying cornflour or arrowroot with water ENGLISH
slaný	salted CZECH
slaneček	herring CZECH
slangeagurk	cucumber NORWEGIAN
slanina	bacon CZECH
slankekost	low-calorie food DANISH
slatko	jam or preserve made with raspberries, strawberries or watermelon rind, served with a glass of water SERBIAN
slätvar	brill SWEDISH
śledź	herring POLISH
śledźie	salted herring POLISH
sleeve-fish	calamary
šlehačka	whipped cream CZECH
šlehaný bílek	beaten egg white and sugar CZECH
slemp	spiced drink made for children on St Nicholas' Night DUTCH
slepičí polévka	chicken consommé CZECH
slepičí vývar s nudlemi	chicken broth with vermicelli CZECH
slepice na paprice	stewed fowl CZECH
šlimaki	snails POLISH
slim cake	traditional plain Manx fruit cake cooked on a griddle
sling	toddy made with gin and fruit, also known as gin sling
slipcote	Stilton which has burst after moulding
slipper	wedge-shaped cut of pork or ham from the corner of the fillet
slip sole	common name for sole weighing under half a pound
sliva	plum RUSSIAN
slivovitz	colourless, dry plum brandy RUSSIAN
slívy	greengages CZECH
śliwki	plums POLISH

słodkie	sweet POLISH
słodycze	sweets POLISH
słodzone	sweetened POLISH
sloe	small, bluish-black fruit of the blackthorn tree *Prunus spinosa*, used to make sloe gin and wines
sloke	laver IRISH, SCOTTISH
słonina	salt bacon POLISH
slot	fish liver dumplings SHETLAND ISLANDS
slottsstek	pot roast flavoured with brandy, molasses and marinated sprats Swedish
sloyanka	stew Russian
sly cakes	traditional Cornish pastry cakes containing currants and candied peel
små köttbullar	very small pork meat balls SWEDISH
småfranska	French roll SWEDISH
smažený řízek	breaded chop CZECH
smažený karbanátek	fried burger CZECH
smažený sýr	fried cheese in breadcrumbs CZECH
smažený sýr v těstíčku	cheese fried in butter CZECH
smažené brambůrky	fried potatoes CZECH
smažené květákové nočky	fried cauliflower dumplings CZECH
smažené syrové knedlíčky se smetanou	fried cheese dumplings CZECH
smažené, smažený	fried CZECH
småkager	small cakes; biscuits DANISH
småkaka	fancy biscuit SWEDISH
småkake	biscuit NORWEGIAN
smalec	lard POLISH
small salad	old fashioned name for watercress and white mustard when used for a salad AMERICAN
smallage	old name for wild celery
småvarmt	small hot dishes SWEDISH
smazené rybí filé	fried fillet of fish CZECH
smelt	very oily, silvery sea fish with a flavour similar to trout
smeltet smør	melted butter DANISH
smen	clarified butter MIDDLE EASTERN
smetana	soured cream, lower in fat than ordinary soured cream, much used in Eastern Europe and Russia RUSSIAN, FINNISH, CZECH
smetanový	creamed CZECH

śmietana	sour cream POLISH
smitane, sauce	classical sauce of Russian origin containing sautéed onion, white wine, sour cream and lemon juice FRENCH
smoborski sir	cheese YUGOSLAVIAN
smoked cheese	mild smoky-flavoured creamy-coloured cheese sold shaped as 'sausages'
smoked fish	may be hot or cold smoked; cold smoked fish other than salmon needs to be cooked before smoking, nowadays, the process is usually for flavour rather than for preservation
smokies	hot smoked whole haddock or whiting, gutted and with their heads removed SCOTTISH
smoking	preserving meat and fish by drying in the smoke of a wood fire
smolt	salmon when it is about two years old
smör	butter SWEDISH
smør	butter NORWEGIAN
smørbrød	'buttered bread'; open sandwiches NORWEGIAN
smörgås	open sandwich SWEDISH
smörgåsar	sandwiches SWEDISH
smörgåsbord	in Sweden, and to some extent the rest of Scandinavia, a traditional way of serving food resembling a buffet, starting with bread and butter and herring with boiled potatoes, followed by one or two small piquant dishes, egg dishes served with salads, cold meats, hot dishes such as kidneys and meatballs, and finally rye bread, cheese and coffee SCANDINAVIAN
smørrebrød	slices of buttered rye (or wheat) bread with a variety of garnishes such as shrimps, herring, ham, roast beef, cheese and salads DANISH
smultron	wild strawberry SWEDISH
snack	something quick and simple such as a sandwich served in place of a meal
snag	sausage AUSTRALIAN
snail	*Helix pomatia* is the cultivated variety of snail esteemed in France; in England, the common snail *H.aspersa* serves equally as well (if not better)
Snailcreep Hanging	place near Warminster (Wilts) where giant snails thrive
snake root	alpine grass, which can be used like spinach

snapper	different varieties of sea fish; freshwater turtle
sneboller	deep fried cakes DANISH
sneeuwbal	kind of cream puff DUTCH
sniadanie	breakfast POLISH
snídaně	breakfast CZECH
snidling	chives HUNGARIAN
sniglar	snails SWEDISH
snijboon	sliced French bean DUTCH
snipe	small long-billed bird of the genera *Gallinago* or *Capella* with striped plumage; should be eaten fresh
snittebønne	sliced French bean DANISH, NORWEGIAN
snitter	small snacks DANISH
snöbollar	biscuits, like macaroons SWEDISH
snoek	pike DUTCH
snöripa	ptarmigan SWEDISH
snow	mixture of sweetened fruit pulp and whisked egg white (hence apple, apricot etc snow)
só	salt HUNGARIAN
sočivo salata	salad of cooked lentils with a dressing of olive oil, vinegar, garlic, salt and paprika YUGOSLAVIAN
soaking	many foods need to be soaked before cooking, especially dried pulses, dried fruits and salty gammon joints
sobrasada	salami SPANISH
sobremesa	dessert PORTUGUESE
sobronade	country soup from the Périgord region containing pork, dried beans and vegetables FRENCH
socarat	the lumps of rice left at the bottom of a paella pan after it has been dished up, considered to be a delicacy CATALAN
socca	thick, chick pea flour pancakes from Nice FRENCH
socker	sugar SWEDISH
sockeye (salmon)	*Oncorhynchus nerka* of the Pacific, the red salmon
socle	solid shape of cooked, pounded rice used as a base for elaborate cold foods, to raise it above the dish to form a centrepiece
sød	sweet DANISH
soda bread	round bread, combining bicarbonate of soda, the raising agent, with buttermilk
soda fountain	counter where soft drinks etc are served by a soda jerk AMERICAN

soda water	water aerated with carbon dioxide under pressure
soep	soup DUTCH
soep van de dag	soup of the day DUTCH
soffritto	sautéed ITALIAN
sofrito	steak with garlic sauce GREEK
soft drinks	non-alcoholic bottled or canned drinks ready to drink or requiring dilution
soft roe	milt of the male fish
soft-shell turtle	turtle from slow-running rivers and lakes; both turtle and eggs are eaten
soft water	water containing very few minerals
sogan dolma	stuffed onions BOSNIA-HERCEGOVINAN
sogliola	sole ITALIAN
soir	sour milk curd cheese ESTONIAN
soissonnaise, à la	garnish for mutton made from haricot beans mixed with tomato sauce and garlic; puréed haricot beans mixed with cream, butter and thin tomato sauce FRENCH
soja	soya beans POLISH
sokeri	sugar FINNISH
sokeriton	sugarless FINNISH
sokeroitu	sweetened FINNISH
sól	salt POLISH
sola	sole POLISH
solbær	blackcurrant DANISH, NORWEGIAN
soldaatjes	'little soldiers'; fingers of fried bread DUTCH
sole	several species of flat fish of the family *Soleidae*, especially *Solea solea* resembling a shoe sole ENGLISH, FRENCH
solha	plaice PORTUGUESE
solimeme	yeast cake from the Alsace FRENCH
sológa	marinated sprats, onions, capers, pickled beetroot and raw egg-yolk SWEDISH
solomillo	fillet steak SPANISH
solomon's seal	the young shoots of this garden plant of the lily family are edible
solone	salted POLISH
solone śledzie	salted herring POLISH
soltetees	mediaeval cake with a surprise filling, served at a banquet

Somerset camembert mild, creamy English version of French camembert made from unpasteurised milk

somlói galuska sweet dumplings made with vanilla, nuts and chocolate, in orange and rum sauce HUNGARIAN

sonhos 'dreams'; type of doughnut PORTUGUESE

sonka ham; gammon HUNGARIAN

sont dry ginger, *Amonum zingiber* INDIAN

soo-kun breadfruit BM

soo-soo milk BM

sopa SOUP PORTUGUESE, SPANISH

sopp mushroom NORWEGIAN

soppa SOUP SWEDISH

soppressata sausage; preserved pig's head with pistachio nuts ITALIAN

soppresso pork and beef salami ITALIAN

sorbais, le cow's milk cheese from the Ardennes FRENCH

sorbapple fruit of the service tree; another name for the service tree

sorbet soft water ice flavoured with fruit or liqueur and sometimes containing whisked egg white; sometimes *sherbet* in the US

sorbitol naturally-occurring sugar substance which can also be synthetically manufactured, it is used as an artificial sweetener

sorges, sauce sauce from the Périgord region of vinaigrette, spring onions, shallots, parsley, and eggs FRENCH

sorghum staple cereal food in parts of Africa and Asia, cooked like rice

sorrel green leafy vegetable of the genus *Rumex* with distinctive acidic flavour, which can be eaten raw in salads, although it contains a high level of oxalic acid and should not be eaten in any quantity; it may also be served boiled like spinach

sorsa wild duck FINNISH

sort gryde pork or veal fried with mushrooms and served with a bacon, onion, and tomato sauce DANISH

sorvete ice-cream PORTUGUESE

sos sauce POLISH

sose mash; purée FINNISH

sosiski sausages POLISH

Soße sauce; gravy GERMAN

söt sweet SWEDISH

sotare	grilled Baltic herring SWEDISH
sot-l'y-laisse	'a fool leaves it'; the small piece of meat above the parson's nose in chicken or other birds FRENCH
sottaceto	pickled ITALIAN
søtunge	sole; tongue DANISH
soubise sauce	velvety onion sauce FRENCH
soubise, purée	purée of onions, rice, butter and cream
souchet	19th-century method of cooking fish, poached in the oven with onions and Hamburg parsley roots; the shoveller (a bird)
souchet, sauce	classical sauce of white wine, potatoes, carrots, leeks and celery FRENCH
soudzoukakia	spicy sausage from Smyrna GREEK
souf	aniseed, *Pimpinella anisum* INDIAN
sou-fassum	local speciality from Nice of stuffed cabbage with tomato sauce FRENCH
soufflé	fluffy sweet or savoury dish lightened by adding stiffly-beaten egg whites FRENCH
soufflé à la reine	soufflé with finely chopped poultry or meat FRENCH
soufflé rothschild	vanilla-flavoured souffle with candied fruit FRENCH
soumaintrain	whole milk cow's milk cheese from the Aube and Yonne departments FRENCH
soup	wide range of liquid dishes, from thin light consommés to thick, nourishing stews
soupa	soup GREEK
soupe	country style soup FRENCH
soup ladle	deep spoon with a long handle for serving soup
soupstone	legendary stone which makes a magic soup when boiled in water, provided that meat, vegetables etc are added
sour cream	cream which has been allowed to sour
sour milk	milk which has become sour has various culinary uses
sourdough	bread made from dough with a fermenting 'starter' WESTERN US, CANADA, ALASKA
souring	adding acid, possibly lemon juice, to cream to give it a sour taste
sourire	to simmer gently FRENCH
soursop	the spiny fruit of a West Indian tree *Annona muricata*, with a tart, edible pulp

sous	sauce DANISH
sóus	sauce RUSSIAN
sousing	pickling in brine or vinegar, especially fish
southern bisque	traditional soup containing vegetables, stewed corn and a ham bone garnished with corn kernels and green peppers AMERICAN
Southern Comfort	the most popular indigenous liqueur, Bourbon whiskey flavoured with peaches, oranges and herbs AMERICAN
souvarov	petit four of sweet pastry sandwiched with apricot jam FRENCH
souvarov, à la	method of cooking feathered game or poultry in an earthenware casserole with foie gras and butter; when half cooked, truffles cooked in Madeira are added FRENCH
souvlakia	dish of skewered lamb and vegetables grilled over charcoal GREEK
sovs	sauce DANISH
sow thistle	a weed, the leaves of which may be used for salad
sowans	old oatmeal dish similar to a fermented gruel SCOTTISH
soy sauce	light or dark brown salty, sweetish sauce made from fermented soya beans
soya bean	the most nutritionally valuable pulse, used in a variety of vegetarian dishes
spada	swordfish ITALIAN
spädgris	suckling pig SWEDISH
spagheto	spaghetti GREEK
spaghetti	the most common pasta, eaten with a wide variety of sauces
spaghetti marrow	winter squash shaped like a short yellow marrow; baked in its skin, its white flesh resembles spaghetti, and it is seasoned and eaten with butter or tomato sauce
spalla	shoulder ITALIAN
Spam™	a tinned luncheon meat launched in the US by Geo A Hormel & Co in 1937 (a contraction of spiced ham)
spanaki	spinach GREEK
Spanferkel	suckling pig AUSTRIAN, GERMAN
Spanische Soße	brown sauce with herbs GERMAN
Spanish mackerel	sea fish from American coasts AMERICAN

Spanish omelette	an omelette made with green peppers, onions, tomato, etc added to the egg mixture
Spanish onion	large, mild-flavoured onion, usually eaten raw
Spanish potato	large variety of potato used in Spain
spanyol paprika	pimiento HUNGARIAN
spare ribs	pork ribs with most of the meat trimmed off
spareribs	the ribs nearest the loin in pork or beef
	AMERICAN, IRISH
spárga	asparagus HUNGARIAN
Spargel	asparagus GERMAN
sparkakor	pastries sandwiched with redcurrant jelly SWEDISH
sparling	smelt SCOTTISH
sparris	asparagus SWEDISH
sparrow	bird of the finch family, once eaten in sparrow pie
spat	larva, or larvae, of bivalve molluscs when settled on the sea bed
spatchcocking	method of preparing a small whole bird for grilling, opening the body flat, and leaving the bones in
spatula	long metal or wooden strip with a handle for lifting, stirring, spreading or scraping in the kitchen
Spätzle	tiny noodles AUSTRIAN, GERMAN
spearmint	most commonly used member of the mint family
specialità	speciality ITALIAN
spécialité	speciality FRENCH
Speck	bacon, more specifically an extremely fatty type of bacon GERMAN
speculaas	popular biscuits flavoured with ginger, allspice and cinnamon DUTCH
spegepølse	raw sausage; salami DANISH
speilegg	fried egg NORWEGIAN
Speise	food GERMAN
Speise-eis	ice cream GERMAN
Speiß	spit GERMAN
spejlæg	fried egg DANISH
špekáčky	wieners CZECH
spek	bacon DUTCH
spekemat	cured meat NORWEGIAN
spekepølse	large air-dried sausage NORWEGIAN
spekesild	salted herring NORWEGIAN
spekeskinke	cured ham NORWEGIAN
Spekulatius	spiced biscuit GERMAN

spenat	spinach SWEDISH
špenát	spinach CZECH
špenátové smažemky s houbami	spinach rissoles with mushrooms CZECH
spenót	spinach HUNGARIAN
sperzieboon	French bean (US: green bean) DUTCH
spet	small barracuda, not often used for food spettekaka tall, cone-shaped cake cooked on a spit SWEDISH
Spezialität	speciality GERMAN
spezzatino	meat or fowl stew ITALIAN
spezztino di vitello	veal stew ITALIAN
spiced beef	mediaeval method of preserving beef
spiced cheese	salted version of Friesian cheese DUTCH
spiced salt	salt with added spices
spices	dried parts of aromatic plants used to flavour sweet and savoury dishes
spicken sill	salted herring SWEDISH
Spickgans	cured, smoked breast of goose GERMAN
spider crab	crab with a rough shell of such genera as *Libinia* and *Macropodia*
spiedini	skewers for cooking small meat balls or other food ITALIAN
spiedino	pieces of meat grilled or roasted on a skewer ITALIAN
spiedo	spit ITALIAN
Spiegelei	fried egg GERMAN
spiegeleier	fried egg DUTCH
spigola	fine-flavoured sea bass ITALIAN
spijskaart	menu; bill of fare DUTCH
spiked rampion	common herb, used for cooking BRITISH
spinach	green leafy vegetable *Spinacea oleracea*, whose leaves are rich in iron, available fresh or frozen
spinaci	spinach ITALIAN
spinat	spinach DANISH, NORWEGIAN
Spinat	spinach GERMAN
spinazie	spinach DUTCH
spirits	beverages made by distilling alcoholic liquor; the main spirits are brandy, gin, whiskey, rum and vodka
spit	thin metal bar for spearing meat, poultry or game, on which they are turned as they roast over an open fire
spit-roasting	originally, meat was roasted by turning on a spit over an open fire; today rotary attachments can be fitted

	to many cookers, but the need is less urgent as clean ovens are readily available
Spitzkäse	spiced, soured skimmed cow's milk cheese, containing caraway seeds GERMAN
špíz	mixed grilled meat CZECH
spleen	organ from mammals; ox spleen is sometimes used in stews
split	type of yeast bun, split and served with cream or butter and jam
split pea	variety of dried peas that splits naturally during the drying process
sponge cake	light cake of eggs, sugar, flour and flavouring, mixed by whisking
sponge fingers	airy finger-shaped biscuits made of sponge mixture
sponge pudding	baked or steamed pudding
spoom	water ice containing meringue mixture
spoonbill	wading birds of the family *Threskiornithidae*, related to herons and storks with a long horizontally-flattened bill
spot	small sea fish found off American coasts
spotted dick	steamed or boiled suet pudding containing currants, sultanas or other dried fruit
sprat	fairly round, small sea fish from the herring family
spring chicken	a chicken which is about 2–3½lbs in weight (US: fryer)
spring onion	member of the onion family
spring roll	layer of thin dough wrapped around a filling of cooked vegetables and meats
spritärter	green peas SWEDISH
sprits	kind of shortbread eaten on St Nicholas' Eve DUTCH
spritsar	almond ring-cakes SWEDISH
Sprossenkohl	Brussels sprout GERMAN
Sprotte	sprat GERMAN
sprouted seeds	seeds that have begun to sprout contain many more vitamins, particularly vitamin C
sprouting broccoli	a type of broccoli with flowerlets
spruce	coniferous tree; its essence flavours spruce beer; spruce oil flavours root beer, ice cream and chewing gum in the USA
sprue	fern used in England in soups and garnishes ENGLISH
spruitje	Brussels sprout DUTCH

spud	informal word for potato
spud bashing	peeling potatoes, especially in quantity
spuds and herring	traditional dish of potatoes, herrings and butter MANX
spugnola	morel mushroom ITALIAN
spumone	foamy ice-cream dessert with crystallized fruit, whipped cream and nuts ITALIAN
spurs of Bacchus	éperons bachiques ENGLISH
spurtle	wooden stick for stirring porridge SCOTTISH
squab	young pigeon; squab pie, a West Country dish made of squab meat, apples and onions
squash, fruit	drink of sweetened fruit pulp, intended to be diluted with water
squash, vegetable	the hard-rinded green fruit of edible curcurbitaceous plants such as *Curcurbita pepo* and *C.moschata*
squeteague	weakfish NARRAGANSETT, NATIVE AMERICAN
squid	several species of cephalopod, only tentacles and body pouch are eaten
squill fish	small shellfish prepared in the same way as prawn
squirrel	several species of small rodent, popular game in the US AMERICAN
srdce	heart CZECH
srikhand	saffron-flavoured yoghurt
srpske čufte na luku	meatball dish similar to the Turkish köfte YUGOSLAVIAN
St Ivel cheese	cream cheese from Somerset
St Lawrence dressing	dressing served with salads CANADIAN
stabburpølse	'stone house sausage'; blood sausage NORWEGIAN
Stachelbeere	gooseberry GERMAN
stamna	earthenware pot used for klephtes cooking GREEK
stamppot	vegetable hot pot, a national dish DUTCH
standing time	an essential part of microwave cooking, to complete the cooking by the conduction of the heat generated in the food to the centre
Stangenkäse	cream cheese from the Steiermark and in Salzburg AUSTRIAN
stangselleri	branch celery NORWEGIAN
stanley	method of serving chicken FRENCH
stap	traditional dish of haddock livers cooked until they dissolve, and flakes of haddock; the dish is eaten with bannocks

star anise	star shaped fruit of an evergreen tree, which tastes and smells of pungent aniseed
star fruit	fluted, yellow, waxy tropical fruit with a sweet and sour flavour
star gazer	hog fish
star gazey pasty (or pie)	type of Cornish pasty (or pie) made with herrings or pilchards
star of Bethlehem	*Ornithogalum umbellatum*, a small plant with edible roots
starch	complex form of carbohydrate; many units of glucose are joined in a long chain
starking alma	starking apple HUNGARIAN
starling	small black bird, occasionally eaten
staročeská (plzeňska) pivní polévka	old Czech or Pilsen-style beer soup, made from light beer thickened with bread cubes and egg yolks CZECH
steak	lean slices from the tenderest cuts of beef
steamboat	meal of small portions of meat and seafood CHINESE
steamed pudding	pudding cooked in a basin over boiling water
steaming	cooking food gently in the steam of boiling water
Steckrübe	turnip GERMAN
steelhead	rainbow trout AMERICAN
steeping	covering food with hot or cold water, and letting it stand, to soften it or extract its flavour and/or colour
stefanka	long layer cake filled with butter-cream POLISH
stegt	fried; roasted DANISH
stegt forskank	roasted forehock or shank of bacon DANISH
stehýnko	leg of fowl CZECH
Steinbuscher(käse)	strong, slightly bitter, semi-hard creamy cheese GERMAN
Steinbutt	turbot GERMAN
Steingarnele	prawn GERMAN
Steinpilz	boletus mushroom GERMAN
stek	roast NORWEGIAN
stek	steak, fillet POLISH
stekt	fried; roasted NORWEGIAN, SWEDISH
stellette	star-shaped pasta, used to garnish soups ITALIAN
Stelze	knuckle of pork GERMAN
stenbitssoppa	lumpfish soup SWEDISH
steppe	cheese similar to gouda RUSSIAN

sterilisation	destruction of bacteria in foods by heating to very high temperatures
sterlet	small sturgeon; the swimming bladder is used to make isinglass, the flesh is prized and the finest-quality caviar is obtained from the roe
sterlyad	sterlet RUSSIAN
steur	sturgeon DUTCH
stew	foods cooked with liquid; artificial oyster bed or fish tank
stewing	method of slow cooking in which food is simmered in a liquid to tenderize it
středna propečeno	medium rare CZECH
Stierenauge	fried egg GERMAN
stikkelsbær	gooseberry DANISH, NORWEGIAN
Stilton	semi-hard, white, full cream milk cheese; with blue veining caused by mould, usually natural
stinco	knuckle; shin ITALIAN
stint	the smaller species of sandpiper of genera such as *Calidris* or *Erolia* ENGLISH
stiphádo vothinó	thick beef stew GREEK
stir frying	cooking food rapidly in a little hot oil in a wok or frying pan
stirrer	many microwave ovens have a built-in stirrer, with the same effect as a turntable; this circulates microwaves evenly throughout the oven
stlek	old potato dish, eaten with bacon IRISH
stocaficada	Niçoise method of cooking stockfish
stoccafisso	stockfish ITALIAN
stock	liquid produced from simmering meat, bones and/or vegetables with herbs and flavourings in water for several hours
Stock	mashed potatoes GERMAN
stock cubes	flavouring in a crumbly block, convenient for making a quick stock
stock duck	mallard ORKNEY ISLANDS
stockfish	air-dried cod or haddock NORWEGIAN
stokvis	stockfish DUTCH
Stollen	Christmas cake made from sweetened yeast dough and dried fruits, almonds, nuts and candied lemon peel GERMAN
stone	the hard central seed case of a cherry, plum etc (US: pit)

stoning	removing the hard central seed case of a cherry, etc (US: pitting)
stonecrop	decorative rock garden plant of the genus *Sedum*, used in cooking
stoneware	strong form of heat-resistant, non-porous pottery
stoof	braised or stewed; diminutive of the word 'gestoofde' DUTCH
stoofsla	braised lettuce DUTCH
stoofvlees	braised stewing beef DUTCH
stør	sturgeon DANISH
store cheese	slang for Canadian cheddar cheese CANADIAN
storione	sturgeon ITALIAN
storioni	sturgeon GREEK
Stoßsuppe	caraway soup GERMAN
Stotzen	leg; haunch GERMAN
stout	dark, sweet, malt beer
stracchino	creamy, soft to medium-soft cheese, often used to flavour pasta ITALIAN
stracciatella	soup made from beef or chicken broth with semolina or breadcrumbs, eggs and grated cheese ITALIAN
stracotto	beef and pork sausage stew ITALIAN
strainer	kitchen utensil for straining sauces and soups
Strammer Max	slice of bread or a sandwich with spiced mince pork GERMAN
Strasbourgeoise, à la	consommé flavoured with juniper berries FRENCH
strascinati	shell-shaped fresh pasta ITALIAN
strava	meal; food CZECH
straw potatoes	deep fried, match-like strips of potato
strawberry	popular, red, juicy, summer fruit, growing round a central hull, and covered in tiny seeds
strawberry tomato	*see* physalis
strawberry, wild	smaller, more aromatic than the cultivated varieties
straws	strips of puff pastry
strega	aromatic herb liqueur, which contains about 70 herbs and barks ITALIAN
Streichkäse	soft cheese spread GERMAN
Streickwürst	sausage for use as a spread GERMAN
Streuselkuchen	coffee cake with cinnamon topping GERMAN
string beans	French beans AMERICAN
striped bass	Atlantic fish which may be cooked like salmon
strisciule	goat's meat stew CORSICAN

stroganoff	method of serving beef; method of serving fresh herrings RUSSIAN
strömming	fresh Baltic herring SWEDISH
strömmingsflundra	fried double fillets of Baltic herring, stuffed with dill or parsley SWEDISH
strömmingslåda	baked casserole of Baltic herring and potatoes SWEDISH
stroop	treacle (US: syrup) DUTCH
strouhaný	grated CZECH
struan Micheil	'St Michael's cake'; large, traditional bannock, eaten at harvest time HEBRIDES
strucla	long, white plain cake, eaten at Christmas POLISH
Strudel	paper-thin layers of pastry with a sweet or savoury filling AUSTRIAN, GERMAN
Strudelteig	dough used to make strudel AUSTRIAN, GERMAN
štrukli	sweet pudding of noodles, cream cheese and cream YUGOSLAVIAN
Stück	piece; slice GERMAN
studen	calf's feet mould RUSSIAN
studený nářez	cold cuts CZECH
studené předkrmy	cold appetizers CZECH
stuet	stewed (fruit); creamed (vegetables) NORWEGIAN
stufatino	meat stew from Rome ITALIAN
stufato	stewed; beef stew ITALIAN
stuffatu	mutton stew CORSICAN
stuffing	most commonly served with or in meat or poultry to help keep food moist, absorb fat and juices, and to bulk out the meal
sturgeon	large sea fish of the family *Acipenseridae*, not generally available in Britain, with flesh similar to veal; the roe is called caviar, and the air bladder provides isinglass
stuvad	cooked in white sauce; creamed SWEDISH
stuvet	creamed DANISH
sułtanki	sultanas; raisins POLISH
sušenky	biscuits; cookies CZECH
suave	soft SPANISH
subrics	a type of croquette FRENCH
suc	juice obtained from meat or vegetables when squeezed; juice reduced by boiling FRENCH
succotash	sweetcorn kernels and green or lima beans AMERICAN

succu tunnu	soup with semolina and saffron dumplings ITALIAN
sucées	petit fours containing crystallised fruits FRENCH
sucha kiełbasa	dried pork sausage POLISH
suchar	rusks (US: zwieback) CZECH
sucharki	crackers POLISH
suck cream	traditional Cornish dish made with cream, egg yolk, white wine and sugar
suck(l)ing pig	unweaned piglet
sucre	sugar FRENCH
sudak	pike/perch RUSSIAN
suédoise	fruit purée FRENCH
suer	to sweat FRENCH
suet	fat from around beef kidneys, shredded and floured, used to make traditional baked goods
suet pudding	a number of popular sweet and savoury puddings made with suetcrust pastry, steamed or boiled in a pudding basin
soufflé	soufflé ITALIAN, SWEDISH
Suffolk cheese	cheese from Suffolk, no longer made
suflé	soufflé SPANISH
suflet	soufflé POLISH
sugar	crystalline, sweet tasting substance, most commonly obtained from sugar cane and sugar beet
sugar beet	variety of beetroot with the highest sugar content
sugar boiling	basis of nearly all sweet making; used to produce caramel
sugar cane	thick grass cultivated for its sap, which can be turned into sugar
sugar pea	a type of pea; mange-tout
sugar plum	a crystallised plum
sugherello	a type of mackerel NORTHERN ITALIAN
sugo	juice; sauce ITALIAN
suiker	sugar DUTCH
suino	pork ITALIAN
suizo	bun SPANISH
suji, rawa	equivalent of semolina INDIAN
sukiyaki	dish cooked at the table like fondue; usually small strips of meat, vegetables and noodles, fried in a shallow pan JAPANESE
sukker	sugar DANISH, NORWEGIAN
suklaa	chocolate FINNISH

sůl	salt CZECH
sulatejuusto	processed cheese FINNISH
süllö	pike-perch HUNGARIAN
sulperknochen	a dish from Hesse, of boiled pickled pork leg, tail, ears and snout served with sauerkraut and pease pudding GERMAN
sulphuric acid	strong acid; used in very dilute form in some soft drinks
sült	baked, roast, fired HUNGARIAN
sultan hen	purple water-hen; prepared in the same way as a coot
sultana	dried fruit of a white seedless grape
sultane	large millefeuille pastry, decorated with feathers of spun sugar FRENCH
sultane, à la	garnish for fried chicken breasts of chicken forcemeat and tartlets filled with truffle, topped with cocks' combs and pistachio nuts, all covered in curry sauce suprême; dish containing pistachio nuts FRENCH
sulugun	Georgian cheese, often served fried in slices, and served with sour cream RUSSIAN
Sülze	jellied in aspic; brawn GERMAN
sum	sheat-fish POLISH
sumac	purple powder from petals and berries from a variety of the sumac shrub
sumbol	see sambal
sumec	sheat-fish CZECH
Sümegi torta	chocolate and hazelnut cake HUNGARIAN
summer pudding	dessert; bread lining filled with lightly cooked summer fruits, allowed to stand so the juices soak through the bread
summer snipe	sea lark
summer teal	one of the smallest members of the duck family, highly esteemed for its marshy flavour in the spring
sum-sum	another name for sesame
şuncă	unsmoked bacon ROMANIAN
sundae	an ice cream dish AMERICAN
sundew	insect eating plant, once used in potions
sunfish	brightly-coloured freshwater fish; tailless marine fish
sunflower	tall annual plant cultivated for its seeds, which are eaten or produce an oil suitable for cooking
šunka	boiled ham CZECH

sunka po štaročesku old Bohemian-style boiled ham, with plum, prune, walnut and wine sauce CZECH

šunkové fličky noodles with sliced ham CZECH

sunny side up of an egg, fried on one side only AMERICAN

suola salt FINNISH

suolattu salted; preserved in brine FINNISH

suomalainen pannukkakka pancakes, baked in the oven FINNISH

suomalaiset puikot biscuit sprinkled with chopped almonds and sugar FINNISH

suomi gruyère processed cheese FINNISH

suomuurain Arctic cloudberry FINNISH

sup soup RUSSIAN

supă soup ROMANIAN

supé supper SWEDISH

supp soup ESTONIAN

suppe soup DANISH, NORWEGIAN

Suppe soup GERMAN

suppevisk bouquet garni DANISH

suppion tiny squid FRENCH

supplì rice croquettes with mozarella cheese and meat sauce ITALIAN

suprême of fine quality FRENCH

suprême de volaille boned chicken breast with creamy sauce FRENCH

suprême, sauce white sauce like a velouté sauce, based on chicken stock; it can be enriched with cream, butter or egg yolks just before serving FRENCH

suprêmes breast and wings of chicken or game FRENCH

sur sour SWEDISH

sur commande to your special order FRENCH

suren equivalent of yam INDIAN

surkål sour cabbage and sauerkraut NORWEGIAN

surmullet red mullet AMERICAN

surówe raw POLISH

surówka salad POLISH

surprim sour milk cheese NORWEGIAN

sursild soused herring NORWEGIAN

sursød sweet-and-sour DANISH

surtido assorted SPANISH

sururu type of cockle PORTUGUESE

šušené svestky prunes CZECH

sushi	raw fish, usually raw fish or shellfish, moulded on to rice fingers, seasoned with vinegar and served cold with wasabi JAPANESE
susina	plum ITALIAN
suspiro	meringue PORTUGUESE
suspiros de freiras	'nun's sighs'; sweet flaky pastry, poached in syrup PORTUGUESE
süß	sweet GERMAN
Süßigkeit	sweet (US: candy) GERMAN
Süßspeise	dessert; pudding GERMAN
suszone grzyby	dried mushrooms POLISH
suszone owoce	dried fruit POLISH
sütemény	cakes HUNGARIAN
sutlyàsh	pudding made with rice and served with rosepetal jam BULGARIAN
suutarinlohi	sugar-salted sprats FINNISH
svamp	mushrooms DANISH, SWEDISH
svartsoppa	goose blood soup SWEDISH
svartvinbär	blackcurrant SWEDISH
svartvinbärsgelé	blackcurrant jelly SWEDISH
sveciaost	hard, pungent cheese SWEDISH
sveitsinleike	cordon bleu; breaded veal scallop stuffed with ham and Swiss cheese FINNISH
svekla	beetroot RUSSIAN
sveske	prune DANISH
svestkové knedlíky	plum dumplings CZECH
svid	lamb's head split in two with the brains removed, cooked; the meat is removed and served with mashed turnips ICELANDIC
svinekam med svesker	roast loin of pork stuffed with prunes DANISH
svinekjøtt	pork NORWEGIAN
svinekød	pork DANISH
svinekotelett	pork chop NORWEGIAN
svinemørbrad	fillet of pork (US: tenderloin) DANISH
svineribbe	spare-rib NORWEGIAN
svinestek	roast pork NORWEGIAN
svinina	pork RUSSIAN
svinjsko meso	pork SERBO-CROAT
sviske	prune NORWEGIAN

swan	large white bird of the genera *Cygnus* and *Coscoroba*, once eaten in large quantities, but now served only at appropriate banquets
sweating	gently cooking in a little fat until the juices run
swede	heavy, coarse-skinned root vegetable with orange flesh
sweet and sour sauce	sauce popular in Britain and America, combining for example the sweetness of pineapple and the sourness of vinegar CHINESE
sweet cicely	aromatic sweet herb *Myrrhis odorata*, also called myrrh; the flavour of the leaves resembles that of aniseed
sweet gale	*Myrica gale*, Dutch myrtle or bog myrtle; it can be used to flavour beef
sweet peppers	mainly mild, large fruits of *Capsicum frutescens grossum*
sweet potatoes	elongated tuber with orange or white, sweet, slightly perfumed flesh of the tropical American plant *Ipomoea batatas*
sweet woodruff	*Galium odoratum*, a white-flowering woodland herb; an essential ingredient in the young German wine Maibowle
sweetbreads	thymus gland or pancreas of calf or lamb, sold in pairs and considered a delicacy
sweetcorn	the unripe ear of *Zea mays saccharata*, it has a sweet nutty flavour, and deteriorates quickly after picking; also called sugar corn or green corn; baby sweetcorn is eaten whole
sweeteners	any substance, natural and artificial, adding sweetness to foods without adding energy sweets wide range of sweet confections and chocolates
swieży	fresh POLISH
Swiss cheese	hard cow's milk cheese made in the US, originally by Swiss immigrants; a hard white or pale yellow cheese with vacuoles, such as Emmenthal or Gruyère AMERICAN
Swiss roll	large, flat sponge cake, spread with filling and rolled up
Swiss steaks	slices of rump or round beef, flavoured and casseroled
Swiss Tilsiter cheese	cheese made and sold only in Switzerland SWISS
swordfish	*Xiphias gladius*, usually sold as steaks; it has a pale pink flesh and a firm texture

syllabub	a spiced drink made with milk added to rum, port, brandy or wine, often hot; dessert dating back to Elizabethan times of fresh milk poured in a thin stream from a height over wine, cider or ale, making a frothy mixture; cream whisked with wine, sugar and lemon zest until frothy, and skimmed; whisked egg whites mixed with whipped cream, flavoured with sugar, lemon juice, wine or spirit
sylt	jam SWEDISH
syltad	preserved; pickled SWEDISH
sylte	brawn NORWEGIAN
syltede agurker	gherkins (US: pickles) DANISH
syltekjøtti	jellied mutton chops NORWEGIAN
syltelabb	boiled, salt-cured pig's trotter NORWEGIAN
syltetøy	jam NORWEGIAN
syltlök	pickled pearl onion SWEDISH
synagrida	dentex GREEK
sy-or	vegetable BM
syr	cheese RUSSIAN
šyrecky	beer cheese CZECH
syrové pavézky	cheese cutlets CZECH
syrup	concentrated solution of sugar in water
szafran	saffron POLISH
szaharin	artificial sweetener HUNGARIAN
szalámi	salami HUNGARIAN
szalonna	smoked bacon HUNGARIAN
szardínia	sardine HUNGARIAN
szárított gyümölcs	dried fruit HUNGARIAN
szarlotka	apple cake POLISH
szárnyas	poultry HUNGARIAN
szarvas	deer HUNGARIAN
szaszłyk	shashlik POLISH
szczaw	sorrel POLISH
szczupak	pike POLISH
szczypiorek	chives POLISH
szechuan	large region of western China with its own style of hot, spicy cuisine CHINESE
szechwan pepper	fragrant spice of dried berries of the Chinese prickly ash CHINESE
szeder	mulberries; blackberries HUNGARIAN
szegedi halászlé	fisherman's soup HUNGARIAN

szegfűszeg	clove HUNGARIAN
székely sajt	ewe's milk soft cheese HUNGARIAN
szelet	slice HUNGARIAN
szelethús	escalope HUNGARIAN
szendvics	open sandwich HUNGARIAN
szerecsendió	nutmeg HUNGARIAN
szilva	plums HUNGARIAN
szilváslepény	plum pie HUNGARIAN
szív	heart HUNGARIAN
sznycel cielęcy	veal scallop POLISH
sznycel jarski	vegetarian scallop, a kind of potato fritter POLISH
sznycle	escalopes POLISH
szölö	grapes HUNGARIAN
szomjas	thirsty HUNGARIAN
szparag	asparagus POLISH
szparagi	asparagus tips POLISH
szpinak	spinach POLISH
szprotki	sprats POLISH
sztufada	marinated, larded roast beef POLISH
sztuka mięsa	boiled beef with root vegetables and horseradish sauce POLISH
szynka	ham POLISH
szynkowa	sausage which resembles ham in taste POLISH

T

taart	cake DUTCH
taatsoi	*see* flat black pak choi, flat pak choi, rosette pak choi, tasai
Tabasco sauce™	liquid seasoning, made with chillies, salt and vinegar AMERICAN
table d'hôte	menu offering a number of courses at a fixed price; usually with some choice of dishes within each course FRENCH
tabouli	salad made from bulgar wheat flavoured with tomatoes, parsley, lemon and mint
tacaud	common name for a variety of Atlantic cod FRENCH
tacchino	turkey ITALIAN
tàccula	small birds, simmered in stock, then put into a sack with myrtle leaves and allowed to cool SARDINIAN
taco	wheat or maizeflour pancake SPANISH
tacos	corn tortillas folded, fried until crisp and stuffed with a variety of savoury fillings MEXICAN
Tadcaster pudding	baked suet pudding from Tadcaster in Yorkshire
taetei cu nuci	broad, cooked noodles served hot with butter, sugar and chopped nuts ROMANIAN
Tafelspitz auf alt Wiener Art	Viennese speciality; a particular cut of beef simmered in stock and herbs AUSTRIAN
taffy	confection made from boiled syrup and butter; a word for toffee AMERICAN
Tagesgericht	special of the day GERMAN
Tagessuppe	soup of the day GERMAN
tagine	highly spiced stew of meat, vegetables or fruit MOROCCAN
tagliatelle	most common form of homemade pasta, consisting of long ribbon-like strips ITALIAN
taglierini	basic noodle dough ITALIAN
taglioline	fine, thin noodles ITALIAN
tahina	paste, made with sesame seeds and oil MIDDLE EASTERN
tahiri	rice and peas INDIAN
tahkojuusto	kind of Swiss cheese FINNISH

tail the tail of shellfish is the largest edible part; the tail in certain mammals can be used for food, mainly those of lamb, pig and ox

tailloir wooden board on which meat is cut FRENCH

taimen trout FINNISH

tainha grey mullet PORTUGUESE

taisin *see* Chinese celery cabbage, Chinese mustard (greens), Chinese mustard cabbage, Chinese white cabbage, chingensai, gai choy, green in snow, Indian mustard (greens), kai tsoi, leaf mustard, mustard cabbage

tajada slice SPANISH

talatourri salad of sliced cucumber and yoghurt CYPRIOT

taleggino stronger version of taleggio ITALIAN

taleggio medium hard, mild cheese ITALIAN

talerz plate POLISH

talkkuna traditional dish made with rye flour and peas FINNISH

tallarín noodle SPANISH

Talleyrand white sauce with cream and Madeira, garnished with vegetables, truffles and pickled tongue; garnish for meat and poultry, of macaroni with butter and Parmesan, goose liver, truffle and sauce périgourdine; sherry-flavoured chicken consommé with truffles cooked in sherry FRENCH

tallow wood *Eucalyptus microcorys*, a tree with sweet and aromatic fruit AMERICAN, AUSTRALIAN, MEXICAN

talmouses small tartlets with cheese-based fillings FRENCH

tamal flat cornmeal pancake, similar to tortilla

MEXICAN, SPANISH

tamale dish of minced meat, crushed maize and seasoning, wrapped in maize husks and steamed MEXICAN

tâmara date PORTUGUESE

tamarillo hard red or yellow fruit related to tomato and kiwi fruit

tamari Japanese soy sauce JAPANESE

tamarind spice derived from the large pod of the tamarind tree

tamboril anglerfish PORTUGUESE

tamie cow's milk cheese from Savoy FRENCH

tamis de crin drum hair sieve, with a very fine mesh FRENCH

tammy cloth used to press or strain a sauce or soup through

tanag hard-pressed cheese which used to be made in Ireland IRISH

tandoor	unglazed charcoal-heated clay oven used in India; the unique aroma of the clay and coals give the food its taste INDIAN
tandoori	dishes cooked in a tandoor oven INDIAN
tangelo	a hybrid fruit, the result of a cross between the tangerine and the grapefruit
tangerina	tangerine PORTUGUESE
tangerine	*Citrus reticulata*, a tree bearing easily peeled small oranges
tangine	spiced meat or vegetable stew, cooked in an earthenware pot of the same name NORTH AFRICAN
tangleberry	dark blue very sweet berry, related to huckleberry or blueberry; another name for dangleberry
tannin	group of strong acids, occurring in certain plants, that coagulate and toughen protein
tanrogan	scallops MANX
tansy	perennial plant with edible leaves
tapas	collection of hors d'œuvres, usually served with drinks SPANISH
tapénade	Provençal purée of capers, black olives, anchovies and olive oil, used as a dip or spread FRENCH
tapioca	obtained from the root of the cassava plant, sold in many forms; it is almost entirely made of starch, and is used chiefly to make milk puddings and moulds (shapes)
tapioka	tapioca POLISH
tara	cow's milk cheese IRISH
tarak	scallops TURKISH
tarama	dried grey mullet roe, used to make taramasalata
taramasalata	creamy dip of tarama, bread, garlic, onion, olive oil and lemon juice
taratòr	cold soup made from yoghurt, cucumber, nuts, garlic, olive oil, vinegar and seasoning BULGARIAN
taratouri	version of taratòr GREEK
tarbot	turbot DUTCH
tarhonya	staple food of the Alföld plain: an egg and flour dough, made into balls, browned with onions and boiled in water, served with meats, or eaten on their own; they may be dried and stored for use in winter HUNGARIAN
tarjoilupalkkio	service charge FINNISH
tarka dal	spiced lentil purée INDIAN

tarkari	mixed vegetables INDIAN
tárkony	tarragon HUNGARIAN
taro	a tuber, the staple crop of the Pacific Islands, which must be well cooked or fermented to detoxify it
tarragon	*Artemisia dracunculus*, a herb with a distinctive, aniseedish flavour
tarragon vinegar	mild vinegar flavoured with tarragon, a sprig of which usually appears in the bottle
tart	large or small open pastry case with a filling
tarta	cake; tart SPANISH
tårta	cake SWEDISH
tartaar	steak tartare DUTCH
tartaar speciaal	extra large portion/prime quality steak tartare DUTCH
tartan purry	old dish of chopped kale mixed with oatmeal SCOTTISH
tartare sauce	mayonnaise-based sauce with herbs, chopped capers and gherkins
tartaric acid	organic acid, common in sour fruits
tartarpihvi	steak tartare; raw, spiced minced beef FINNISH
tartaruga	turtle ITALIAN
tarte	tart FRENCH
tarte au suif	suet crust tart or pie filled with a mixture of nuts, eggs and maple syrup CANADIAN
tarte tatin	upside-down apple tart FRENCH
tartelette	small tart or tartlet FRENCH
tartina	open-faced sandwich ITALIAN
tartine	bread spread with butter, jam, honey, etc FRENCH, ITALIAN
tartines suisses	puff pastry, filled with a type of vanilla custard
tartufi de cioccolata	chocolate truffles ITALIAN
tartufi di mare	sea truffles ITALIAN
tartufo	truffles ITALIAN
tasai	*see* flat black pak choi, flat pak choi, rosette pak choi, taatsoi
tas kebab	thick meat stew cooked in an earthenware pot (tas) GREEK
Tascherl	pastry turnover with meat, cheese or jam filling GERMAN
taskurapu	crab FINNISH
tasse, en	served in a cup; particularly refers to soups FRENCH
Tatar	raw, spiced minced beef GERMAN

Tatarenbrot	open sandwich with tartare GERMAN
tatarský biftek	steak tartare CZECH
táth	early cheese, no longer produced IRISH
tattari	buckwheat FINNISH
tatti	boletus mushroom FINNISH
tatties an' herrin'	traditional dish from the Scottish Islands, made with new potatoes and herrings SCOTTISH
Taube	pigeon; dove GERMAN
tava	frying pan used to cook tortillas MEXICAN
tavar	griddle for cooking breads INDIAN
tavený sýr	cheese spread CZECH
tavuk	chicken TURKISH
tay	tea BM
tayglach	holiday confection eaten at Rosh Hashanah (Jewish New Year), made with honey, nuts and spices JEWISH
täyte	stuffing; filling FINNISH
täytetty	stuffed; filled FINNISH
T-benstek	T-bone steak SWEDISH
T-bone steak	cut of beef, which includes the tail of the fillet and sirloin AMERICAN
tea	leaf of a tropical evergreen shrub of the genus *Camellia*, used to make an infusion with boiling water; originally the steeped leaves were eaten; the word is now applied to a variety of infused beverages *eg* camomile tea, more properly described as a tisane
tea substitutes	tissanes are made from a variety of herbs and other plants
teacake	flat, round yeast cake, flavoured with currants, spices and peel, usually served split, toasted and buttered
teal	prized, small wild duck; one bird is usually served per person
tebirkes	bun with poppy seeds DANISH
teb-oo	sugar-cane BM
tebrød	rusks NORWEGIAN
tee-mun	cucumber BM
teeri	black grouse FINNISH
Teewürst	very fine spreading sausage GERMAN
teff	plant with very small grains which are ground to make bread ETHIOPIAN
tefteli	meat balls RUSSIAN
tegame, al	sautéed ITALIAN

tegamini	small, two-handled utensils for cooking eggs ITALIAN
teglia, alla	fried in a pan ITALIAN
Teigwaren	macaroni; noodles; spaghetti GERMAN
tej patha	equivalent of bay leaf INDIAN
tejberizs	milk and rice HUNGARIAN
tejföl	sour cream HUNGARIAN
tejszín	cream HUNGARIAN
tejtermék	dairy product HUNGARIAN
teleća janija od spanaća	popular dish, made with veal, spinach, onions, green peppers and stock YUGOSLAVIAN
telecí	veal CZECH
telecí brzlík	veal sweetbreads CZECH
telecí řízek	breaded veal cutlet CZECH
	veal stew CZECH
telecí játra	calf's liver CZECH
telecí maso na víně	veal braised with wine CZECH
telecí párek	veal sausage CZECH
telecí pečeně	roasted veal joint CZECH
telemes	féta-type cheese GREEK
tèleshko	veal BULGARIAN
Teller	plate; dish GERMAN
telli kadayif	noodles cooked in milk and sugar, served with raisins in syrup TURKISH
tel-or	egg BM
tel-or boo-soh	stale egg BM
tel-or go-ring	fried egg BM
tel-or mas-sah kras	hard boiled egg BM
tel-or reb-us	boiled egg BM
tel-or teng-a mas-sah	soft boiled egg BM
telyatina	veal RUSSIAN
tempeh	soya bean cake with a rich cheese-like flavour; it is sliced or cubed, shallow fried and eaten dipped in tamari INDONESIAN
temperature	measure of molecular activity (heat)
temperature probe	a means of measuring the temperature within a joint etc; it may be used as a thermostat to control oven temperature
tempero	seasoning PORTUGUESE
tempura	dish of pieces of seafood and vegetable dipped in batter and deep fried JAPANESE

tench	*Tinca tinca*, a small freshwater fish, a member of the carp family
tende de tranche	cut of beef equivalent to topside FRENCH
tenderising	beating raw meat with a spiked mallet or rolling pin; this breaks down the fibres to make it more tender
tenderloin	fillet of pork or beef AMERICAN
tendrons	cut of veal from ribs to sternum, the full width of breast FRENCH
tenro	tender PORTUGUESE
tepary bean	type of haricot bean MEXICAN
tepid	moderately warm, or lukewarm, liquid
tep-ong	flour BM
tequila	spirit distilled from pulque (agave juice) MEXICAN
terbiye	sauce served with stuffed vine leaves, eggplants, and courgettes, made from eggs, cornflour, lemon juice, and stock, which are beaten until frothy TURKISH
teriyaki	meat, poultry or fish marinated in mirin and soy sauce JAPANESE
tern	common inedible sea bird, whose eggs can be served hard-boiled
ternera	veal SPANISH
terrapin	small turtle of the family *Emydidae*, whose flesh is considered a great delicacy NORTH AMERICAN
terrine	china or earthenware dish used for pâtés amd potted meats; foods cooked in a terrine are often given the same name
terte	tart; cake NORWEGIAN
terveysruoka	health food FINNISH
testa di vitello	calf's head ITALIAN
tészták	pastries HUNGARIAN
teta	mild, pear shaped, cow's milk cheese made in Lugo and Coruña SPANISH
tête	head FRENCH
tête d'aloyau	the end of a rump of beef FRENCH
teterka	hazel grouse RUSSIAN
tetine	calf's or cow's udder FRENCH
tétras	grouse FRENCH
Tewkesbury saucer batters	traditional dish made by fruit pickers; batter is cooked on two saucers in the oven, one is filled with cooked fruit, and covered with the other
texturized vegetable protein	*see* TVP

thali, thalia	south Indian dining tray; a tray meal INDIAN
thé	tea FRENCH
thenay	soft, whole-milk type of camembert cheese FRENCH
thermidor	method of serving lobster
thermodynamics	an irrefutable reason for putting milk in the cup before pouring the tea
thermometer	instrument for measuring temperature
thickening	substance added to sauces, soups etc to make them thicker and bind them together
thimbleberry	wild raspberry AMERICAN
thon	tuna fish FRENCH
thonné	method of preparing veal, by marinading it in olive oil FRENCH
thornback	European skate; ray
thourins	white onion soup, made in the south of France FRENCH
Thousand Island dressing	salad dressing made with ketchup, chopped gherkins etc
Thracian cress	type of cress common in the Balkans
thrush	brown bird, which used to be eaten in England, still eaten in France, Italy and Corsica
Thunfish	tuna fish GERMAN
thym	thyme FRENCH
thyme	small-leafed herb of the genus *Thymus*, with a strong aromatic flavour; there are many varieties
Thymian	thyme GERMAN
Tia Maria	rum liqueur, containing coffee extracts and local spices JAMAICAN
tian	traditional Provençal dish of green vegetables, sautéd in olive oil, topped with breadcrumbs and grated Parmesan; it takes its name from the earthenware pot in which it is cooked FRENCH
tientsin pear	smooth, rounded, yellow fruit with crisp, sweet flesh and a grainy texture, rather like a pear
tiffin	light midday meal; a name not much used today ANGLO-INDIAN
tiganites	fritter GREEK
tigelada	eggs beaten with milk and cinnamon, baked in an earthenware bowl PORTUGUESE
tigiega mimlica	method of roasting chicken, stuffed with beef, pork, egg and breadcrumbs MALTESE
tiddy oggy	Cornish pasty

tignard blue-veined cheese from the Tigne valley FRENCH

tijelinhas de nata cakes made with puff pastry filled with cream custard PORTUGUESE

tijm thyme DUTCH

tikka meat marinated and cooked on a skewer in a tandoor INDIAN

tikva pumpkin BULGARIAN

til equivalent of sesame seed INDIAN

tile fish large deep-sea fish *Lopholatilus chamaelionticeps*

tilli dill FINNISH

tilliliha mutton with dill sauce FINNISH

tillisilli poached herring, with dill, white pepper and lemon juice FINNISH

Tilsiterkäse semi-hard cow's milk cheese, from the district of Tilsit GERMAN

tilslørte bondepiker apple charlotte NORWEGIAN

timartar tomatoes INDIAN

timbale round mould for moulding meat or fish mixtures; the name for dishes cooked in these moulds

timbale van ham ham timbale DUTCH

timian thyme DANISH, NORWEGIAN

timjan thyme SWEDISH

timo thyme ITALIAN

timpana popular dish of macaroni, liver, onion and cream cheese MALTESE

tinamou game bird, similar to partridge

tinca tench ITALIAN

tindaloo hotter version of vindaloo INDIAN

tioro fish stew with onions BASQUE

tipsy cake tall sponge cake made into a trifle, re-formed, decorated with almonds, and soaked in wine and fruit juice; it tends to fall drunkenly to one side

tiramisù rich dessert of sponge fingers topped with zabaglione, coffee-flavoured mascarpone cheese and whipped cream ITALIAN

tiri tiganismeno féta cheese GREEK

Tiroler Knödlsuppe beef soup with dumplings, from the Tyrol AUSTRIAN

Tiroler Leber liver recipe from the Tyrol AUSTRIAN

tiropeta phyllo pastry filled with cheese and eggs GREEK

tisane drink made by infusing herbs, such as camomile

Tiverton batter pudding   spiced batter pudding, steamed and served with butter and sugar originally from Tiverton (Devon)

tjäder   wood-grouse; capercaillie SWEDISH

tjap yjoy   chop suey; fried meat and vegetables served with rice DUTCH

tjur   capercaillie DANISH

tkemali   wild plums which grow in the Caucasus GEORGIAN

tlačenka   collared pork CZECH

tłuste   fat POLISH

T-luupihvi   T-bone steak FINNISH

toad-in-the-hole   sausages or chopped meat cooked in Yorkshire pudding batter

toadstools   common name for cap fungi

toast   bread browned on both sides under the grill, in a toaster or in front of a fire (using a toasting fork); it may also be prepared by toasting a slice of bread, cutting the crusts off, and slicing it into two half-toasts before toasting the untoasted faces thus revealed

toast soldiers   buttered toast cut into strips for dipping into a boiled egg

tocana   traditional onion and vegetable stew ROMANIAN

tocino   bacon SPANISH

toddy   drink of whisky, hot water, sugar and lemon;

toeristenmenu   tourist menu DUTCH

toffee   sweet confection, a sugar mixture boiled to 138–154°C

tofu   soybean curd, a white to cream coloured, smooth-textured and bland-flavoured food

Toggenburger Käse   a locally-sold Swiss cheese made mainly in the St Gall Alps, Toggenburg, in the Werdenberg district

toheroa   'long-tongued'; a shellfish found in the sand of beaches in New Zealand, with a tongue-like roe like a scallop MAORI

tojás   eggs HUNGARIAN

tök   pumpkin; squash; vegetable marrow HUNGARIAN

Tokay   the best known Hungarian wine HUNGARIAN

tökfőzelék   vegetable marrow with sour cream HUNGARIAN

tollo   dogfish SPANISH

töltelék   stuffing HUNGARIAN

töltött   stuffed HUNGARIAN

Tom and Jerry   hot drink of rum, brandy, egg, American nutmeg and sometimes milk

Tom Collins   cocktail of gin, lemon or lime juice, sugar or syrup, and soda water AMERICAN

tomaat   tomato DUTCH

tomaatti   tomato FINNISH

tomar   smoky-tasting farmhouse cheese from the Arrábida PORTUGUESE

tomat   tomato SWEDISH

tomatada à portugesa   fresh tomato sauce mixed with freshly cooked vegetables, served hot with scrambled eggs PORTUGUESE

tomate   tomato FRENCH, SPANISH

Tomate   tomato GERMAN

tomatillo   green tropical fruit, from the Cape gooseberry family; about the size of a tomato, with a papery calyx

tomato   a versatile fruit usually used as a vegetable; may be red or green, and tiny (eg cherry tomatoes), or large (eg beef tomatoes)

tomato purée   thick red tomato paste, used as flavouring

tomato sauce   sauce for table use, similar to tomato ketchup

tomatsuppe   tomato soup DANISH

tomber à glace, faire   to cook food, particularly a vegetable, in a little liquid which is boiled and reduced to nothing FRENCH

tomber, faire   to cook meat in its own juices FRENCH

tomcod   small freshwater fish resembling cod

Tomerl   cornmeal pancake AUSTRIAN

tomillo   thyme SPANISH

tomini del talucco   goat's milk cheese, made in Pinada, Piedmont ITALIAN

tomme   the name of a number of cheeses produced in Savoy, usually from skimmed cow's milk; a particular fermented buttermilk cheese from the Dauphiné region FRENCH

tomtate   another name for the grunt, a small fish found off Florida and the West Indies

Tonbridge brawn   a type of brawn from Tonbridge (Kent) made from pickled pigs' heads boiled with herbs, mace, onion and celery; once it is jellied it is chilled and sprinkled with breadcrumbs ENGLISH

tonfisk   tuna SWEDISH

tong   sole; tongue DUTCH

tongue   ox and lambs' tongues are the most common, and may be bought fresh or salted

tongue cress	species of cress
tonhal	tuna HUNGARIAN
tonijn	tunny (US: tuna) DUTCH
tonka bean	seed of a native South American tree, used for flavouring SOUTH AMERICAN
tonnarelle	matchstick noodles ITALIAN
tonnato	in tuna sauce ITALIAN
tonnellini	fine noodles ITALIAN
tonnetto	sea fish found in Italian waters ITALIAN
tonnikala	tunny (US: tuna) FINNISH
tonno	tuna ITALIAN
tonnos	tuna fish GREEK
toost	toast DUTCH
tope	small grey requiem shark *Galeorhinus galeus*
Topfen	dish containing curd or cottage cheese; fresh white cheese GERMAN
Topfkuchen	moulded cake with raisins GERMAN
topinambours	Jerusalem artichokes FRENCH
topinambur	Jerusalem artichoke ITALIAN
topiony ser	melted cheese POLISH
topknot	rare North Atlantic flat fish of the genus *Zeugopterus* and relations
topside	joint of beef cut from above the shin and round, presented without bone
toranja	grapefruit PORTUGUESE
Torbay sole	west country name for lemon sole (after Torbay, Devon)
torcik waflowy	waffle sandwich POLISH
tordo	thrush ITALIAN, SPANISH
torkad frukt	dried fruit SWEDISH
torma	horseradish HUNGARIAN
tornedó	round cut of prime beef PORTUGUESE
toro	bull SPANISH
toronja	variety of grapefruit SPANISH
torpille	large fish resembling skate FRENCH
torr	dry SWEDISH
torrada	toast PORTUGUESE
torrão de ovos	marzipan sweet PORTUGUESE
torrijas de nata	fritter made with very thick cream custard PORTUGUESE
torrone	nougat ITALIAN

torrons de xixona	type of nougat traditionally eaten in the village of San-Julià-de-Lória at the Saint's feast ANDORRAN
torsk	*Brosmius brosme*, a fish of northern coastal waters with a single long dorsal fin (US and Canadian: cusk) DANISH, NORWEGIAN, SWEDISH
torskerogn	cod roe DANISH, NORWEGIAN
torsketunge	cod tongue NORWEGIAN
tort	layer cake POLISH
torta	tart; cake ITALIAN, PORTUGUESE, SPANISH, HUNGARIAN
torta san Gaudenzio	layered Gorgonzola and Mascarpone cheeses, creating a gâteau effect ITALIAN
Törtchen	small tart; cake GERMAN
torte	international name for an open tart or rich cake type mixture, baked in a pastry case
Torte	bun; tart; light cake, sometimes layered, often filled with cream GERMAN
tortilla	soft unleavened bread containing maize flour MEXICAN
tortilla chips	deep fried segmented tortillas
tortelli	small fritters ITALIAN
tortelli di erbette	ravioli dish from Parma ITALIAN
tortellini	famous Bologna dish of stuffed coils of dough, poached and served with cheese, or eaten in broth ITALIAN
tortera de Sevilla	sweet tart from Seville, eaten at Christmas SPANISH
tortiglione	coiled almond cake ITALIAN
tortilha	omelette PORTUGUESE
tortilla	omelette; thin, maize pancake eaten throughout Mexico, cooked on both sides on a griddle until dry SPANISH
tortini	small round cakes; croquettes ITALIAN
tortino	savoury tart filled with cheese and vegetables ITALIAN
tortita	waffle SPANISH
tortoni	frozen dessert, named after the 18th-century Italian owner of a Paris restaurant FRENCH
torttu	tart; flan; cake FINNISH
tortue	sauce served with offal; turtle FRENCH
tortuga	turtle SPANISH
toscana, alla	with tomatoes, celery and herbs ITALIAN
tosta mista	toasted ham and cheese sandwich PORTUGUESE
tostada	toast SPANISH

tostadito	tortilla chip MEXICAN
tostato	toasted ITALIAN
tosti	grilled cheese and ham sandwich DUTCH
totano	young squid ITALIAN
tôt-fait	cake made with flour, sugar, eggs, lemon peel and butter FRENCH
totuava	variety of weakfish, found in the Gulf of California AMERICAN
toucinho	bacon PORTUGUESE
toucinhos	sweet of small light cakes or custards PORTUGUESE
touffe	herbs or vegetables with their stalks tied in a bundle FRENCH
toulon, à la	whitefish, stuffed and poached with mussels FRENCH
touloumotyri	variety of féta cheese, which is packed in goat skins GREEK
Toulousaine, à la	garnish of chicken quenelles, sweetbreads, white mushroom caps, cock's combs and truffles in mushroom-flavoured sauce allemande; ragoût à blanc bound with sauce béchamel; method of serving potatoes FRENCH
toupin	earthenware pot used in the Béarn district to cook daube FRENCH
tour de feuilletage	term for the series of turns given to puff pastry FRENCH
tourd	type of wrasse found in the Mediterranean FRENCH
tourlou	meat stew with various vegetables GREEK
tournedos	thick slices of meat from the middle of a fillet of beef DUTCH, FRENCH
tournée	old name for sauce allemande FRENCH
tourner	to shape vegetables FRENCH
tournesol	sunflower FRENCH
touron	sweetmeat similar to turrón FRENCH
toursi	pickled GREEK
tourte	round, shallow tart; puff pastry with a savoury filling; Corsican chestnut porridge, containing pignoli, aniseed and raisins FRENCH, CORSICAN
tourteau fromagé	speciality sweet cheese dish from the Poitou region, containing cream cheese or goats' cheese, flour, sugar, butter, egg yolks and stiffly beaten egg whites; the mixture is put into a mould, allowed to ferment slightly, baked, and eaten cold FRENCH
tourterelle	turtle dove FRENCH

tourtière Christmas pie eaten in Canada; French for a dish in which tourtes are eaten CANADIAN, FRENCH

toust toast CZECH

trace elements minerals needed in tiny amounts in the diet for good health, *eg* copper, iodine, iron, manganese and zinc

Tracey meal trade shorthand for prawn cocktail, steak, and Black Forest gâteau

tracklement condiment or chutney, a word supposedly invented by Dorothy Hartley in 1954, which she said was an old English word which has never been identified

trahana dough of goat's milk or yoghurt and ground wheat, dried and grated, and used to make a kind of porridge GREEK

trail entrails of game birds such as woodcock, snipe and plover and red mullet fish; they are all cooked without removing the entrails

tramezzino small sandwich ITALIAN

tranbär cranberry SWEDISH

tranche slice FRENCH

tranche au petit os cut of beef from the middle of silverside FRENCH

tranche grasse wedge-shaped cut from a leg of beef FRENCH

tranebær cranberry DANISH

transparent icing very thin icing used to give a professional finish to royal icing

Trappisten Käse cheese similar to port salut AUSTRIAN

traquet wheatear FRENCH

trás-os-montes famous smoked ham PORTUGUESE

Traube grape GERMAN

traut trout DANISH

travailler to beat, especially with a wooden spoon or spatula; relates in particular to batters and sauces FRENCH

treacle sticky sweet fluid obtained when processing sugar cane; black treacle and golden syrup

treccia plaited mozzarella cheese ITALIAN

tréfoil melilot FRENCH

treipen black pudding, sausages, and mashed potatoes, served with horseradish sauce LUXEMBOURG

tremoço salted lupine seed PORTUGUESE

tremper to soak bread in liquid FRENCH

trencher a wooden board upon which food was cut or served; turn the trencher – to turn the board over to use the other side rather than taking a clean one

trenette	Genoese form of tonnarelle pasta ITALIAN
treska	trout CZECH
tresse	plaited bread or cake FRENCH
triantafillo	rose petal GREEK
trichinosis	infestation with the slender unsegmented parasitic worm *Tricinella spiralis*; this infects pigs and other animals, and infested pork can infect humans
trifle	traditional dessert of sponge cake soaked in a liquid such as sherry or fruit juice, covering with layers of fruit, jelly, custard and whipped cream ENGLISH
triggerfish	brightly-coloured sea fish of the family *Balistidae*
tríglia	red mullet ITALIAN
tripa	speciality resembling a black pudding CORSICAN
tripas	tripe PORTUGUESE, SPANISH
tripe	stomach lining of the ox, cow or other ruminant prepared for cooking
tripes	intestines of ruminants FRENCH
triple sec	strong white curaçao
triple-crème	superior grade of Fontainebleau cheese FRENCH
tripletail	large sea fish of the *Lobortidae* family (especially *Lobotes surinamensis*) found in the brackish waters of Southeast Asia AMERICAN
trippa	tripe ITALIAN
tritato	minced ITALIAN
triticale	cross between wheat and rye
trøffel	truffle NORWEGIAN
trognon	edible heart of a vegetable FRENCH
trois frères	special shaped tin or mould with a well in the centre; cake baked in this special mould FRENCH
tronçon	'chunk'; food cut so that its length is greater than its width FRENCH
trôo	goat's milk cheese from Touraine, which is matured in ashes FRENCH
tropique	the hottest part of the oven FRENCH
trota	trout ITALIAN
trotter	foot of an animal, particularly the pig
trout	popular mainly freshwater fish, particularly *Salmo trutta*
trouxa de vitela	veal olive PORTUGUESE
trouxas de ovos	egg yolks poached in sweetened water, topped with syrup PORTUGUESE

třešne	cherries CZECH
trubičky se šlehačkou	puff pastry cream cornets CZECH
trucha	trout SPANISH
truckles	country name for different kinds of cheese ENGLISH
trufa	truffle PORTUGUESE, SPANISH
truffado, la	traditional potato dish from the Auvergne FRENCH
truffe	truffle FRENCH
truffel	truffle DUTCH
Trüffel	truffle GERMAN
truffiat	potato scone, traditional in the Berry province
trufflage	the addition of slices or pieces of truffle to foods FRENCH
truffle	highly prized edible, saprophytic, ascomycetous, subterranean fungi of the genus *Tuber*, known for their flavour and aroma; earthnut
truffle, chocolate	chocolate-based sweets with added flavourings such as rum, coffee, fruit and nuts
trufle	truffle POLISH
truite	trout FRENCH
truskawki	strawberries POLISH
trussing	tying or skewering into shape before cooking
truta	trout PORTUGUESE
truthahn	turkey GERMAN
tryffel	truffle SWEDISH
tsargana	small swordfish found in Greek waters GREEK
tsatsiki	salad of goat's milk yoghurt and cucumber GREEK
tsipoura	snapper GREEK
tsiros	a silver fish, similar to smelt GREEK
tsourekia	traditional plaited bread buns, eaten on Easter morning GREEK
tuňák	tuna CZECH
tučný	fatty; oily CZECH
tüdö	lung HUNGARIAN
tuńczyk	tuna POLISH
tufoli	large, thick cut macaroni ITALIAN
tuiles	'tiles'; biscuits shaped like curved tiles FRENCH
tuinboon	broad bean DUTCH
tükörtojás sonkával	bacon and eggs HUNGARIAN
tulum	popular, semi-hard ewe's milk cheese TURKISH
tumbada	pudding made from lemon custard and macaroons SARDINIAN

tumbet	sliced potaotes, aubergines, green peppers and garlic MALLORCAN
tumma leipä	dark bread FINNISH
tuna	the tunny, a very large, round, oily sea fish of the genus *Thunnus*; commonly available in cans or fresh to bake, poach, grill or fry
Tunbridge cherry batter	batter fritter from Tunbridge Wells in Kent
tunfisk	tunny (US: tuna) DANISH
tunfisk	tuna NORWEGIAN
tunga	tongue SWEDISH
tunge	tongue DANISH, NORWEGIAN
Tunke	sauce; gravy GERMAN
tunnbröd	unleavened barley bread SWEDISH
tunny-fish	another name for tuna fish
tuoni e lampo	'thunder and lightning'; country dish made from broken pasta mixed with chick peas, Parmesan and olive oil, butter or tomato sauce ITALIAN
tuore	fresh FINNISH
turban	circular arrangement of food on a plate; preparations cooked in circular moulds; an edible gourd FRENCH
turbot	*Scophthalmus maximus*, a flat, diamond shaped sea fish with very small scales
tureen	deep, wide dish from which soup is served
turfjes met bessensap	bread pudding with raspberry sauce DUTCH
turk's cap	an edible gourd
türkenkorn	maize GERMAN
turkey	*Meleagris gallopavo*, a large poultry bird which can have an excellent flavour, once especially popular at Christmas time but now available all the year round with an associated bland taste
Turkish delight	jelly-like sweet, flavoured and perfumed with flower essences
turlu	mutton stew TURKISH
turlu gyuvèch	mutton and vegetable stew BULGARIAN
turmeric	bright orange spice with a slightly bitter flavour; dried from the dried root of a plant of the ginger family, *Curcuma longa*
turn, on the	going off
turnip	*Brassica rapa*, a thick skinned root vegetable with yellow or white flesh
turnip tops	*see* kale, winter greens

turnover	piece of folded pastry containing mincemeat, jam or a savoury mixture
turnspit	the name for the dog who turned a spit by walking a treadmill, or the boy who turned it by hand
túró	cottage cheese HUNGARIAN
turrón	nougat-like sweetmeat, eaten at fiestas SPANISH
turshìya	mixed pickles BULGARIAN
turska	cod FINNISH
turtle	turtles, of the family *Chelonidae*, are found all over the world; however, turtle soup must be made from freshly-killed turtles and it is generally only made commercially
turtle dove	small member of the pigeon family
turtle herbs	mixture of basil, thyme and marjoram, sold commercially to flavour soups
tusk	alternative name for torsk
těsto	dough CZECH
těstoviny	pasta CZECH
tutano	marrow PORTUGUESE
tutti-frutti	mixture of soft fruits bottled in brandy; ice cream or other confection containing chopped fresh or candied fruit (Italian: all the fruits)
tutu à mineira	black bean purée mixed with cassava-root meal, served with cabbage and fried bacon PORTUGUESE
tuzlama	tripe cooked with calf's foot and root vegetables ROMANIAN
tvaroh	cottage cheese CZECH
tvarohové palačinky	cottage cheese pancakes CZECH
tvorog	curd cheese RUSSIAN
TVP	texturised vegetable protein; meat substitute made from vegetables, usually soya beans; it has no flavour of its own and takes on the flavour of foods it is cooked with (*cf* soupstone)
twaróg	fresh curd cheese POLISH
tweed kettle	salmon hash SCOTTISH
tybo	golden, brick-shaped cheese, from Ty DANISH
tykev	pumpkin; marrow; squash CZECH
tykmℙlk	kind of junket; thin yoghurt DANISH
tylżycki ser	firm, pale yellow, mild tasting cheese POLISH
tymián	thyme CZECH
tymianek	thyme POLISH
tyri	cheese GREEK

tyrolienne   sauce béarnaise made with olive oil; method of cooking fish, fried and served on pulped tomatoes, with fried onion rings; meat served on pulped tomatoes with onion rings and sauce tyrolienne

FRENCH

tyrolienne, sauce   mayonnaise and tomato purée sauce, for cold fish or meat FRENCH

tyttebær   kind of cranberry NORWEGIAN

tyúkhúsleves   chicken broth HUNGARIAN

tzatziki   salad of yoghurt and cucumber, flavoured with mint

GREEK

tzenios   collecting grounds of the roe of the grey mullet

GREEK

tzimmes   traditional Sabbath dish – there are many varieties; it can be made with or without meat, with fruit or with vegetables JEWISH

U

uborka   cucumber; gherkin HUNGARIAN

uccelletti   small birds, usually spit roasted ITALIAN

udder   a once popular fatty white meat, now rarely available

udruck   green ginger INDIAN

udziec   leg POLISH

ugli fruit   round, knobbly hybrid citrus fruit with a thick, coarse yellowish-brown skin, a cross between tangerine and grapefruit and orange (*see* Queensborough)

ugnsbakad   baked SWEDISH

ugnsomelett   baked omelette SWEDISH

ugnspannkaka   kind of batter pudding SWEDISH

ugnstekt   roasted SWEDISH

uhersky salám   Hungarian salami CZECH

uhor   eel CZECH

UHT milk. cream   method of sterilising milk by holding it at 147° (an 'ultra-high temperature') for a few seconds, to preserve it for up to six months without greatly altering the taste (or so they say)

ui   onion DUTCH

uitsmijter   two slices of bread, garnished with ham or roast beef and topped with two fried eggs DUTCH

Ujházi leves   soup first made by one of Hungary's most famous chefs HUNGARIAN

ukka   clear fish soup, usually made from the stock of freshwater fish RUSSIAN

ulloa   soft cheese from Galicia SPANISH

ulmer gerstlsuppe   traditional barley soup AUSTRIAN

umbelliferae   family of plants with umbrella-shaped clusters of flowers, including carrots, parsnips, chervil, parsley, anise and cumin

umble pie   edible entrails of a deer or other animal made into a pie, hence (h)umble pie

umbra   kind of minnow; Mediterranean fish resembling perch or sea bass

umeboshi plums   pickled plums with a tart, salty flavour

under roast   traditional Cornish steak dish

undercut	another name for fillet of beef
underground onion	another name for potato onion
unleavened bread	bread made without yeast or any rising agent; in Jewish diet it is eaten at Passover to commemorate the sparing of the Israelites in Egypt
uova	egg ITALIAN
uova de bufalo	egg-shaped mozzarella cheese ITALIAN
uova di pesce	hard fish roe ITALIAN
uovo	egg ITALIAN
upland cress	plant similar to American cress
upotettu muna, uppomuna	poached egg FINNISH
upside-down pudding	a baking tin is lined with fruit and covered in sponge mixture; when cooked the pudding is turned out, and the fruit is on top
Urbain-Dubois, à la	method of serving fish; scrambled eggs mixed with diced lobster FRENCH
ursuline, à la	œufs mollets served on slightly hollowed rounds of salmon forcemeat FRENCH
usquebaugh	Celtic form of the word whisky – meaning 'water of life'; an Irish liqueur made of whisky or brandy flavoured with spices, infused overnight GAELIC
ùsskùmrù	mackerel TURKISH
ustrice	oysters CZECH
usturoi	garlic ROMANIAN
uszka do barszczu	small ravioli POLISH
uszka do barszczu	dough envelopes in hot borsch POLISH
utka	duck RUSSIAN
uudet perunat	spring potatoes FINNISH
uunijuusto pihkamaidosta	cheese made in the oven from beestings FINNISH
uuniperuna	baked potato FINNISH
uunipuuro	barley pudding FINNISH
uunissa paistettu	baked FINNISH
uva	grape ITALIAN, PORTUGUESE, SPANISH
uzená krkovicka	smoked neck of pork CZECH
uzená sunka	smoked ham CZECH
uzené	smoked CZECH
uzeny	smoked CZECH
uzeny jazyk	smoked tongue CZECH
Uzès, sauce	sauce of sauce hollandaise beaten with anchovy essence and Madeira wine FRENCH

V

vaca	beef PORTUGUESE
vaca salada	corned beef SPANISH
vacherin	elaborate dessert; basket of meringues or macaroons built up in rings on a pastry base, filled with cream or ice cream and fruit; soft, runny Jura cheese FRENCH
vacsora	dinner; supper HUNGARIAN
vacuta	beef ROMANIAN
vad	game HUNGARIAN
vadasmártás	brown sauce HUNGARIAN
vaddisznó	wild boar HUNGARIAN
vadelma	raspberry FINNISH
vadételek	game HUNGARIAN
vadnyúl	hare HUNGARIAN
vaffel	waffle NORWEGIAN
våffla	waffle SWEDISH
vafle	waffle CZECH
vafler	waffles NORWEGIAN
vagens	runner beans PORTUGUESE
vagtel	quail DANISH
vähän paistettu	rare (under-done) FINNISH
väiksed heeringad piimä saustiga	national dish of small, salted herrings fried in butter ESTONIAN
vainilla	vanilla SPANISH
vaj	butter HUNGARIAN
vajas galuska	butter dumplings HUNGARIAN
vajassütemény	butter pastry HUNGARIAN
vajastészta	short pastry HUNGARIAN
vajency konak	egg brandy CZECH
vaktel	quail NORWEGIAN, SWEDISH
Valais reclette cheese	cheese made only in the canton of Valais SWISS
valencay	soft goat's milk cheese, usually made in a pyramid shape
valenciana	with rice, tomatoes and garlic SPANISH
Valenciennes, à la	garnish for tournedos, noisettes and poultry; chicken consommé FRENCH

valikoima	assorted; mixed FINNISH
välikyljys	entrecôte; rib-eye steak FINNISH
valkoinen leipä	white bread FINNISH
valkokaali	white cabbage FINNISH
valkokastike	white sauce FINNISH
valkoturska	whiting FINNISH
välling	soup made of cereal; gruel SWEDISH
valnød	walnut DANISH
valnöt	walnut SWEDISH
valnøtt	walnut NORWEGIAN
valois sauce	sauce béarnaise with a little meat jelly added FRENCH
valois, à la	garnish for fish of soft roes sautéed in butter; garnish for small pieces of meat or poultry FRENCH
välstekt	well done SWEDISH
van der hum	flavoured with the South African tangerine or naartje South African
vandmelon	watermelon DANISH
Vandyke	old English name for a dish made with toast, pastry or potato cut into pointed triangles (after the pointed beard of the painter Sir Anthony Vandyke 1599–1641)
vaniglia	vanilla ITALIAN
vanília	vanilla HUNGARIAN
vanilj	vanilla SWEDISH
vanilka	vanilla CZECH
vanilla	spice from dried pods of a climbing orchid of the genus *Vanilla*, especially *V. plonifolia*
vanilla essence	extracted from vanilla pods; vanilla flavouring is made from an ingredient in clove oil
vanilla sugar	made by leaving a vanilla pod in a jar of caster sugar
vanille	vanilla DUTCH, FRENCH, GERMAN
vannbakkels	cream puff NORWEGIAN
vanner	to stir a sauce constantly FRENCH
vannis	water-ice NORWEGIAN
vánočka	sweet bread usually eaten at Christmas CZECH
vanukas	pudding; custard FINNISH
vapeur	steam FRENCH
vaquito	fish from Spanish waters similar to serrano, but without taste SPANISH
varak	silver leaf, unique to Indian cooking; sheets of leaf silver are spread on finished desserts and festive meats INDIAN

varené	boiled CZECH
varené jídlo	cooked meal CZECH
varené maso	boiled meat CZECH
varené v páre	steamed CZECH
varenetzs	traditional country dish RUSSIAN
vareniki	type of ravioli made from noodle dough with various stuffings RUSSIAN
varenne, la	sauce made from mayonnaise FRENCH
vareschaga	national dish RUSSIAN
vargabéles	cobbler's delight HUNGARIAN
vargánya	chanterelle mushroom HUNGARIAN
varhaisaamiainen	breakfast FINNISH
variado	assorted PORTUGUESE
variado	varied; assorted SPANISH
varié	assorted FRENCH
variety meats	processed meat such as sausage, or offal AMERICAN
vario	assorted ITALIAN
varios	sundries SPANISH
vark	edible silver leaf INDIAN
varkensvlees	pork DUTCH
varm	warm SWEDISH
varme	warm DANISH
varme osteboller	hot cheese balls DANISH
varras	spit; skewer FINNISH
vasikan/kateenkorva	calf's sweetbread FINNISH
vasilopita	New Year's cake GREEK
vasque	shallow round bowl FRENCH
västerbottenost	pungent hard cheese, strong when mature SWEDISH
västerbottensost	slow-maturing hard cheese SWEDISH
västgötaost	semi-hard pressed cheese SWEDISH
västkunstsallad	seafood salad SWEDISH
västkustsallad	fish and vegetable salad SWEDISH
vatapá	fish and shrimp purée, flavoured with coconut milk and palm-oil, served with peanut and cashew sauce PORTUGUESE
vatkattu karpalohyytelö	whipped jelly with cranberries FINNISH
vatkattu marjapurro	dessert of berries, semolina, sugar and water FINNISH
vatkuli	beef stew flavoured with bay leaves FINNISH
vatrachopsaro	anglerfish or frog-fish GREEK
vatrushki s tvorogom	cheesecakes RUSSIAN

vattenmelon	watermelon SWEDISH
vautes	middle-English; fritter made with veal kidney, bone marrow, plums, eggs, ginger, cinnamon, saffron and salt
vaxbönor	butter beans SWEDISH
ve vlastní stáve	in brine CZECH
veado	venison PORTUGUESE
veal	meat of a young calf, often fed on a diet of nothing but milk so the meat will be pale
veau	veal FRENCH
vecere	dinner CZECH
vegan	follower of a strict form of vegetarianism; no animal products are eaten or used
Vegemite™	Australian vegetable extract used as a spread or flavouring
vegetable marrow	curcurbitaceous plant (*Curcurbita pepo*) with a large green, striped fruit
vegetable pear	another name for custard marrow
vegetable spaghetti	trailing vegetable marrow
vegetables	plants used for culinary purposes or for feeding animals
vegetal	relating to, or characteristic of, vegetables
vegetarian cheese	cheese made with non-animal rennet
vegetarian hierarchy	less strict vegetarians will eat, when 'necessary' they say, first fish, then poultry – though strict vegetarians argue – rightly – that either you are or you aren't
vegetarianism	wide range of eating habits based around avoidance of meat and fish
vegetarianská strava	vegetarian food CZECH
vegetáriánus	vegetarian HUNGARIAN
vegyeszöldség	mixed vegetables HUNGARIAN
vejce	eggs CZECH
velli	gruel FINNISH
velös leves	traditional brain soup HUNGARIAN
velouté sauce	rich white sauce based on white stock, which forms the basis of many other sauces FRENCH
venado	venison SPANISH
venaison	venison FRENCH
venäläinen silli	herring fillets with diced pickled beetroot and cucumber, hard-boiled eggs and lettuce, served with sour cream FINNISH

vendace	another name for pollan, used only in Scotland SCOTTISH
Vendée fressure	dish made from pig's pluck
vendôme	cow's milk cheese FRENCH
venecek	cream puff CZECH
venera	scallop; coquille St Jacques SPANISH
veneto	cow's milk cheese ITALIAN
veneziana	with onions or shallots, white wine and mint ITALIAN
venison	meat of the red, fallow or roe deer, which should be hung for 1–2 weeks before being cooked
venkel	fennel DUTCH
ventagli	pastry shaped like a horseshoe or fan ITALIAN
ventresca	speciality dish made with tuna fish stomach SARDINIAN
venus	another name for cockle
veprová krkovicka po selsku	neck of pork rubbed with garlic and roasted with onions CZECH
veprová pecene	pork roast CZECH
veprové klobásy	pork sausages CZECH
veprové koleno	pork knuckles CZECH
veprové kotlety na pive	pork chops in beer CZECH
veprové zebírko	stewed rib of pork CZECH
veprovy kotlet	pork chop CZECH
veprovy ovar s krenem	traditional dish of boiled pig's head served with horseradish sauce
veprovygulas se zelim	pork goulash with sauerkraut CZECH
verbena	herb of the genus *Verbena* with a faint lemon flavoured herb used for making a herb tea
verde, salsa	'green' sauce SPANISH, ITALIAN
verdura	green vegetables; green plant from the island of Ibiza SPANISH
verdura	green vegetables ITALIAN
verdura	greens SPANISH
véreshurka	black pudding HUNGARIAN
veriohukaiset	blood pancakes FINNISH
veripalttu	black pudding FINNISH
véritable Nantais dit du curé	small soft cow's milk cheese
verjuice	juice of unripe grapes, apples or crab apples, once used in sauces instead of lemon juice or vinegar
verjus	verjuice FRENCH
verlorenes Ei	poached egg GERMAN

vermicelli   thin noodles ITALIAN

vermicellisoep   consommé with thin noodles DUTCH

vermouth   dry, medium or sweet wine containing aromatic
                          herbs; may be served straight with soda water, or
                          mixed with gin

véron   beef consommé FRENCH

véronique, à la   garnish containing white grapes; method of baking
                          or poaching sole fillets in fish stock and white wine
                                                                      FRENCH

vers   fresh DUTCH

verte sauce   classical sauce served with fish, poultry and hard-
                          boiled eggs FRENCH

vert-pré, au   garnished with watercress and straw potatoes, often
                          served with maitre d'hotel butter and coated with
                          green mayonnaise FRENCH

verza   green cabbage ITALIAN

vese   kidney HUNGARIAN

vesepecsenye   tenderloin HUNGARIAN

vesiga   marrow from the backbone of the great sturgeon

vesimeloni   watermelon FINNISH

vesirinkelit   biscuits FINNISH

vesop   concentrated vegetable extract used in Chinese and
                          Eastern cookery CHINESE

vessie   bladder FRENCH

vetebröd   sweet bread SWEDISH

vetekrans   similar to vetebröd, but ring-shaped SWEDISH

vézelay   Burgundian goat's milk cheese FRENCH

viande   meat FRENCH

viande séchée   dried beef served as hors d'œuvre in paper thin slices
                                                                      FRENCH

viandes froids   cold slices of meat and ham (US: cold cuts) FRENCH

vic-en-bigorre   soft cow's milk cheese from the Béarn FRENCH

vichy carrots   young carrots, lightly scraped and cooked in water
                          and butter until the liquid has evaporated

vichy, à la   method of cooking carrots; garnish for meat; method
                          of serving potatoes FRENCH

vichyssoise   cold leek and potato cream soup

Victoria cheese   cream cheese made at Guildford in Surrey ENGLISH

Victoria sponge sandwich sponge cake containing fat, made in two tins,
                          then sandwiched together with a filling such as
                          butter cream icing, jam or cream

Victoria, à la	sauce for sole or other fish; garnish for sole and other fish; method of serving tournedos, noisettes or chicken breasts; iced bombe with strawberry ice cream; salad containing diced crawfish, cucumbers, truffles and asparagus tips FRENCH
videlle	wheel-shaped pastry cutter; small tool for removing stones (pits) from fruit FRENCH
vídensky rízec	Wienerschnitzel cutlet CZECH
vieille curé, la	sweet, brown, highly alcoholic liqueur with a distinctive aromatic flavour FRENCH
vieira	scallop PORTUGUESE, SPANISH
Vienna bread	long loaf made from a yeasted dough
Vienna flour	glattes mehl ENGLISH
Vienna sausage	sausage similar to frankfurter AUSTRIAN
Viennoise, à la	garnish for escalopes of veal, cutlets, chicken joints or fish FRENCH
vieras	scallops SPANISH
vierge	mixture of butter, lemon juice, salt and pepper which is served with vegetables FRENCH
vifter	pastries of the wienerbrød variety DANISH
vignettes	name for winkles in Brittany FRENCH
vihannes	vegetable FINNISH
vihreä salaatti	green salad FINNISH
vihreat pavut	French beans FINNISH
viili	processed sour milk FINNISH
viilokki	fricassée FINNISH
viini/kukko	chicken stewed in red wine FINNISH
viipale	slice FINNISH
viipurin	biscuit FINNISH
viiriainen	quail FINNISH
vijg	fig DUTCH
viking saus	sauce sometimes served with game NORWEGIAN
vildand	wild duck DANISH
vildfågel	feathered game SWEDISH
vildt	game DANISH
vilipiimä	clotted milk FINNISH
villalón	sheep's milk cheese SPANISH
villand	wild duck NORWEGIAN
villáreggeli	brunch HUNGARIAN
villedieu	cow's milk cheese FRENCH
villeroi, à la	sauce to coat foods before they are fried FRENCH

vilt	game NORWEGIAN, SWEDISH
vin	wine FRENCH
vin blanc, sauce	white wine sauce FRENCH
vinäger	vinegar SWEDISH
vinagre	vinegar PORTUGUESE, SPANISH
vinagreta	piquant vinegar dressing to accompany salads SPANISH
vinägrettsås	vinegar and oil dressing SWEDISH
vinaigre	vinegar FRENCH
vinaigrette	thin oil and vinegar dressing, to which may be added herbs and spices; French dressing FRENCH
vinaigretter, sauce	sauce usually served with cold vegetables FRENCH
vinbär	currant SWEDISH
vincent, sauce	sauce made from mayonnaise FRENCH
Vincisgras	a type of lasagne ITALIAN
vindaloo	exceptionally hot curry from Goa, containing potatoes; not as hot as tindaloo or as phall INDIAN
vindrue	grape DANISH
vindruva	grape SWEDISH
vine	the plant upon which grapes grow
vine fruits	currants, raisins and sultanas; types of dried grapes
vine leaves	young grape vine leaves, which can be stuffed, ie wrapped round a filling
vinegar	dilute acetic acid with various additives, arising from fermented beer, wine or cider, a condiment or preservative FRENCH
vinete	aubergine ROMANIAN
vinkort	wine list DANISH
vinny strik	wine diluted with water CZECH
vintage	there is a vintage (wine production) each year but the term usually applies to a 'vintage year', one in which the wine is of excellent quality
vintersallad	salad of grated carrots, apples and cabbage SWEDISH
violet	tiny, sweet scented perennial plant of the genus Viola with mauve and white flowers, used in soups, sauces, salads and desserts or crystallised and used as decoration
viper's bugloss	*Echium vulgare*, a hairy biennial plant with pink buds and edible blue flowers similar to borage
virgouleuse	variety of French pear FRENCH
virsli	sausage; frankfurter HUNGARIAN

virtiniai	ravioli LITHUANIAN
vis	fish DUTCH
visne	Morello cherry TURKISH
visne	Morello cherries CZECH
visniski	pasties RUSSIAN
vispgrädde	whipped cream SWEDISH
vissino	sour or Morello cherry GREEK
vitamins	natural substances essential for the metabolism, and hence growth and health of a body; most cannot be synthesised in the body, and so have to be ingested in foods such as vegetables, fruit juices and fish oils; a simplified list of the most common is as follows:

Vitamin A found in green and yellow vegetables, especially carrots; prevents, night blindness and protects epithelial tissue; also called dehydroretinol

Vitamin B complex, a large group containing such compounds as niacin, riboflavin and thiamine that promote healthy metabolism

Vitamin C, ascorbic acid, prevents scurvy

Vitamin D, calciferol, is essential for healthy bones and teeth

Vitamin E, tocopherol, is essential for promoting fertility and healthy muscles and blood vessels

Vitamin K is essential for producing the agents that cause blood to clot

Vitamin P regulates the permeability of the blood capillaries

vitela	veal PORTUGUESE
vitello	veal ITALIAN
vitellone	beef from an animal between 1 and 3 years old ITALIAN
vitkål	cabbage SWEDISH
vitling	whiting SWEDISH
vitlök	garlic SWEDISH
vive	weaver FRENCH
viveurs	seasoned with cayenne pepper or paprika FRENCH
vize	popular cow's milk cheese
vízitorama	watercress HUNGARIAN
vla	custard DUTCH
vlaa	fruit tart DUTCH
vlaamse karbonade	small slices of beef and onions braised in broth, sometimes containing beer DUTCH

vladimir	sauce of sauce suprême and liquid demi-glace FRENCH
vlasské orechy	nuts; walnuts CZECH
vlees	meat DUTCH
vodino	beef GREEK
vodka	strong, fiery, colourless spirit originating in Russia, distilled mainly from wheat or potatoes
vohveli	wafer; waffle FINNISH
voi	butter FINNISH
voileipä	sandwich, usually open faced FINNISH
voileipäpyötä	cold hors d'œuvres made with smoked or pickled fish FINNISH
voipavut	butter beans (US: wax beans) FINNISH
voissa paistettu	fried in butter FINNISH
voisula	melted butter FINNISH
voksbønne	butter bean NORWEGIAN
vol au vents	round or oval puff pastry cases filled with diced meat, poultry, fish or vegetables in sauce FRENCH
volaille	poultry; fowl FRENCH
volière, en	elaborate method of serving game birds FRENCH
Voltaire	oeufs en cocotte; the eggs are placed on a base of chicken purée, covered with sauce crème, sprinkled with Parmesan cheese and browned under the grill FRENCH
vongola	small clam ITALIAN
vongole	the name for little clams in Rome and southern Italy ITALIAN
voorgerecht	starter; first course DUTCH
voressen	meat stew GERMAN
vorschmak	minced lamb, herring fillets and fried onions cooked in broth, flavoured with catsup, mustard and marinated sprats, served with sour cream and baked potatoes FINNISH
vorspeise	starter; first course GERMAN
vørterkake	spiced malt bread NORWEGIAN
vredne unger	pastry filled with vanilla cream DANISH
vrucht	fruit DUTCH
vruchtensalade	fruit salad DUTCH
vuohenjuusto	goat's milk cheese FINNISH
vurt	sausage CZECH
vyvar	broth CZECH

W

Wacholderbeere	juniper berry GERMAN
Wachtel	quail GERMAN
wafel	wafer DUTCH
wafelki	waffles POLISH
wafer	very thin, crisp, sweetened biscuit
Waffel	waffle GERMAN
waffle	a chiefly US and Canadian pancake with indentations on each face, the result of the shape of the waffle iron, cooked golden brown and served with (maple) syrup
Wähen	pastry pie filled with fruits or vegetables SWISS
Waldmeister, Mariengras	woodruff GERMAN
Waldmeisterbraten	braised beef marinated in wine vinegar containing a bunch of woodruff AUSTRIAN
Waldorf salad	salad of apple, celery, mayonnaise and nuts named after the Walford Astoria Hotel in New York City AMERICAN
Waldorf sweetbreads	blanched sweetbreads sautéed in butter and served on artichoke bottoms covered in sauce allemande AMERICAN
Walewska, à la	fish poached in fish fumet, garnished with crawfish and truffle, coated with sauce mornay and lobster or crawfish butter FRENCH
Wallenbergare	steak made of minced veal, egg-yolks and cream SWEDISH
wall-eyed pike	freshwater fish from the pike-perch family
wally	giant pickled gherkin COCKNEY
walnoot	walnut DUTCH
Walnuß	walnut GERMAN
walnut	popular nut with round crinkly shell and wrinkled kernel from a tree of the genus *Juglans*, especially *J. regia*
walnut oil	fragrant, clear, pale golden oil made from walnut kernels
Wälschkorn	pickle made from young, unripe corncobs GERMAN
Walton Cheddar	cheese made from Cheddar and Stilton flavoured with walnuts

wanilia	vanilla POLISH
wapiti	*Cervus canadensis*, a deer found mainly in Canada
warm	moderately hot, *eg* a warm plate
warm	hot DUTCH
Warmbier	hot beer soup made from raw eggs are beaten into warm beer, flavoured with lemon GERMAN
warzywa	vegetables POLISH
wasabi	edible root similar to horseradish though more fragrant, served as a condiment with sushi JAPANESE
washed curd cheese	type of Canadian cheddar which is moister because water is run over it CANADIAN
wassail	a toast, or the wine in which it is drunk
wassail bowl	spiced ale, formerly served on Christmas Eve
Wassermelone	water melon GERMAN
Wasserteig	raised or hot water crust pastry GERMAN
water biscuit	thin, crisp plain biscuit usually served with butter and cheese
water chestnut	small tuber which tastes like sweet chestnut, used in Chinese and Eastern cookery; also called water calt(h)rop because of its four-pronged fruits
watercress	cruciferous plant *Nasturtium officinale*, with small green leaves, which grows in water
waterkers	watercress DUTCH
watermelon	*Citrus vulgaris*, an edible gourd, full of seeds which may also be dried and eaten
water ice	refreshing frozen dessert of sugar syrup flavoured with fruit juice or purée; sorbet
water parsnip	aquatic plant with edible leaves
water rail	*Railus aquaticus*, a game bird, which can be roasted or casseroled
waterfisch, patervisch	Dutch word used in France as a general term for freshwater fish; sauce served with freshwater fish FRENCH
waterzooi, waterzootje	famous speciality dish made with chicken or fish rubbed with lemon, simmered with vegetables, water and white wine; the meat is then cut into pieces and served with the vegetables and stock, on slices of toast BELGIAN, DUTCH
wàtróbka	liver POLISH
wax bean	American string bean with yellow, waxy pod
wax caps	edible fungi of the genus *Hygrophorus*

weakfish sea fish of the genus *Cynoscion* found along the North Atlantic coast of the Atlantic Ocean AMERICAN

wedding cake rich fruit cake usually with a number of tiers covered with marzipan and decorative royal icing; traditionally the top tier is stored as a christening cake for the couple's first child

wędlina plate of cold cooked meats or sausage POLISH

wędliny cured pork sausages and beef products POLISH

wędzone smoked POLISH

wędzonka smoked bacon POLISH

weenie diminution of wienerwurst AMERICAN

weever general name for a fish of the genus *Trachinus*; all species are edible and are used in soups and bouillabaisse EUROPEAN

węgorz eel POLISH

Weichkäse cream cheese GERMAN

Weichseltorte tart filled with Morello cherries AUSTRIAN Weinbeere grape GERMAN

weinerleipä Danish pastry FINNISH

Weinkraut, Weißkohl white cabbage, which may be braised with apples and simmered in wine GERMAN

Weißbrot white bread GERMAN

weiße Bohne haricot bean GERMAN

weisse Rübe turnip GERMAN

Weissfisch dace GERMAN

Weißkäse fresh white cheese GERMAN

Weisslackerkäse soft ripened cow's milk cheese BAVARIAN

Weißwurst veal and bacon sausage flavoured with parsley, onion and lemon peel GERMAN

Weizen wheat GERMAN

Wellington steak English and Irish method of serving a fillet steak by baking it in a pastry envelope, sometimes laying mushrooms or paté on top of the steak before covering in pastry

Welschkorn maize GERMAN

Welsh cakes small cakes WELSH

Welsh cawl 'cawl' is Welsh for soup; a national soup made from mutton and root vegetables, sometimes eaten as two dishes (pot-au-feu) – meat and vegetables – and broth WELSH

Welsh cheese pudding   cheese pudding made from bread toasted one side, buttered on the untoasted side and placed in a dish toasted side down, covered in grated cheese, more bread toasted side up, and more cheese; egg is beaten into milk and the mixture poured over the dish which is left for twenty minutes and then baked

Welsh onion   onion with bunching, leek-like bulb

Welsh rarebit   cheese, mustard and sometimes beer are melted and served on toast; it becomes buck rarebit if served with a poached egg on top

Wensleydale cheese   cylindrical double cream cheese, generally sold in its white form but it may be matured until blue, named from Wensleydale in north Yorkshire

wentelteefje   pain perdu – white bread dipped in egg batter, fried and sprinkled with cinnamon and sugar DUTCH

Westfälische Bohnensuppe   regional Westphalian soup made with kidney beans, vegetables and smoked sausage GERMAN

Westfälisher Schinken   well-known variety of cured and smoked ham

GERMAN

Wexford cheese   full-cream cheese from Wexford county in Leinster province IRISH

whale   a large marine mammal; now rarely used, it was once hunted for its oil and meat and was important in manufacturing margarine and oil

wheat   cereal of the genus *Triticum*, staple food for a third of the world's population; there are two main types of wheat: hard wheat is rich in gluten, and soft wheat is rich in starch

wheatear   a small bird of the genus *Oenanthe*, especially *O. oenanthe,* now protected in Britain

wheatgerm   the heart of wheat grain, available plain or toasted

whelk   molluscs with greyish-brown shells, usually sold ready cooked; running a whelk stall is proverbially easy

whey   watery liquid which separates from curd when milk clots

whig   whey from sour cream or butter milk SCOTTISH

whim-wham   pudding similar to syllabub SCOTTISH

whipping   beating air rapidly into a mixture, usually egg whites or cream

whisky   alcoholic spirit distilled from fermented cereal grains, chiefly barley, rye and maize (US and Irish: whiskey)

whitebait	tiny silvery fry of sprats or herring; they are fried and eaten whole – heads on and ungutted white basil climbing plant with edible stems and leaves
white beet	another name for chard
white cheese in brine	English name for the Bulgarian cheese siréné
whitefish	edible fish, members of the family *Coregonidae*
white flowering broccoli	*see* Chinese broccoli, Chinese kale, gai lan, kaai laan tsoi, kailan
white perch	small fish related to the sea bass from the eastern seaboard AMERICAN
white pudding	farmhouse sausages most commonly made from cooked pig offal mixed with pearl barley or breadcrumbs
white sauce	several sauces based on flour, butter, and milk or stock, all of which are white in colour
white wine sauce	sauce made in several different ways, with fish fumet or chicken stock, and white wine
white-headed duck	a wild duck; the eggs are more commonly eaten today
white-leaf beet	chard
whiting	fairly small sea fish with soft, white, delicately flavoured, flaky flesh
Whitley goose	traditional dish from Whitley Bay, not made from goose at all, but is a mixture of boiled onions, cheese and milk, baked in a hot oven until browned
Whitstable natives	particularly fine oysters cultivated at Whitstable (Kent)
wholemeal	flour which contains bran or wheat and rye
wi(d)geon	*Anas penelope*, a small bird of the wild duck family
Wiener Knödelsuppe	rich beef broth and dumplings AUSTRIAN
Wiener Koch	Viennese pudding similar to a soufflé AUSTRIAN
Wiener Krapfen	Viennese doughnuts AUSTRIAN
Wiener Schlagobers	Viennese whipped cream containing vanilla sugar AUSTRIAN
Wiener Schnitzel	veal escalope dipped in flour, beaten egg and breadcrumbs, and fried AUSTRIAN , GERMAN
Wiener Würst	small sausage resembling a frankfurter, the back-formation 'weenie' is appropriate AUSTRIAN
Wiener Zwiebelsauce	Viennese onion sauce AUSTRIAN
wienerbröd	Danish pastry SWEDISH
wienerbrød	Danish pastry DANISH, NORWEGIAN
wienerkorv	wiener; frankfurter SWEDISH

wienerschnitzel	breaded veal cutlet SWEDISH
wieninleike	wiener schnitzel; breaded veal scallop FINNISH
wieprzowina	pork POLISH
wijnikaart	wine list DUTCH
wijting	whiting DUTCH
wild	game DUTCH
wild duck	several species of duck
wild goose	barnacle goose; greylag
wild rice	annual water grass grown in North America and parts of Asia
wild zwijn	wild boar DUTCH
Wild (bret)	game; venison GERMAN
Wildente	wild duck GERMAN
Wildschwein	wild boar GERMAN
Williams pear	variety of pear with juicy yellow fruit; also called William's Bon Chrétien
Wilstermarschkäse	semi-hard cheese similar to Tilsiter GERMAN
wilted cucumber	peeled cucumber soaked in salted water or sprinkled with salt before serving AMERICAN
wilted lettuce	washed, crisp cos lettuce served with a sauce of onion, bacon, sugar and vinegar AMERICAN
Wiltshire cheese	cheese very similar to Gloucester cheese
Windbeutel	cream puff GERMAN
Windsor red cheese	mature Cheddar cheese flavoured with English fruit wine
Windsor soup	rich beef consommé; veal stock thickened with ground rice
windy pasty	left-over Cornish pasty pastry, cooked and eaten warm filled with ham
wine	product of alcoholic fermentation of fresh or dried grapes or grape juice
wine jelly	an old dessert made from lemon, redcurrant jelly, glucose, gelatine and port wine, often served to convalescents
wine sauce	sweet white wine sauce for serving with puddings; savoury sauce containing red wine or port
wineberry	fruit of wild raspberry grown in the far east
winkle, periwinkle	small mollusc of the genus *Littorina*, usually sold ready cooked
winogrona	grapes POLISH

winter berry	fruit of the evergreen shrub *Gaultheria procumbens*, related to the holly, the fruit of which is edible, cooked with sugar
winter cherry	*see* physalis
winter cress	herb of the watercress family
winter greens	kale; turnip tops
winterthur, à la	method of serving lobster or crawfish FRENCH
Wirsing (kohl)	Savoy cabbage GERMAN
wishbone	more popular name for the merrythought bone; fowl's furcula or fused clavicles; by custom, each of two people grasps an end in the little finger and pulls; the one getting the larger part makes a silent wish
witchetty grub	edible wood-boring caterpillar of Australian moth *Xyleutes leucomochla*
witch flounder	large, deep-sea flounder from the North Atlantic
witlof	chicory (US: endive) DUTCH
witlof op zijn Brussels	chicory rolled in a slice of ham, oven-browned with cheese sauce DUTCH
witloof	chicory, edible raw or cooked BELGIAN
witte bonen	dried white beans DUTCH
witte saus	white sauce used to accompany braised sweetbreads DUTCH
Wittling	whiting GERMAN
(z)wody	poached POLISH
wołowina	beef POLISH
wok	cooking pan of Chinese origin with sloping sides and well-rounded base, used for stir-frying CHINESE
wolf fish	sea fish of the family *Anarhichadidae* from the deep waters of the Arctic Ocean and other northern seas; also called catfish
wong bok	*see* bok choy, Chinese leaves, headless Chinese cabbage michihili, pe-tsai
wonton	snack made from a savoury filling inside a small square of paper-thin dough CHINESE
woodchuck	*Marmota monax*, rodent which can be eaten when young NORTH AMERICAN
woodcock	*Scolopax rusticola*, a small wild bird resembling the snipe, with mottled plumage, long bill and dark eyes, cooked without drawing or removing the head
wood grouse	another name for capercaillie

wood pigeon	most common form of wild pigeon, *Columba palumbus*, also called ringdove or cushat
wood sorrel	the leaves of this herbaceous plant are used in green salads
woodruff	old herb used in medicinal tea, German wine cup and Austrian cooking
Worcester(shire) sauce	pungent anchovy-flavoured sauce used to flavour sauces, meat, casseroles etc; the true Lea & Perrins sauce was first made to a secret recipe brought to England from India, but tasted so foul that it was shelved for some time, during which it matured deliciously
wormwood	bitter aromatic herb with grey foliage and yellow flowers, formerly used in aperitifs and herb wines but banned today as it is proven to cause blindness
worst	sausage DUTCH
wort	the liquid strained from a mash of malted grain, water, sugar, yeast and hops boiled with water, the basis of beer
wortel	carrot DUTCH
wortleberry	the blue or blackish berry of shrubs of the genus *Vaccinium*; another name for bilberry
wrasse	collective name for a number of sea fish of the family *Labridae* found on the European coasts of the Atlantic
Würst	sausage GERMAN
Würstchen	small sausage GERMAN
Würste von Kalbsgekröse	sausage made from calf's mesentery GERMAN
Würstkraut	herbs used to flavour sausages GERMAN
Würz	spice or seasoning GERMAN
würzig	spiced GERMAN
Würzkräuter	general term for aromatic herbs with a pungent smell GERMAN
wuzetka	small cake filled with chocolate, jam and custard POLISH

X

xavier classical beef consommé thickened with arrowroot, flavoured with Madeira and served with strips of unsweetened pancake; chicken-based potage velouté, blended with rice flour and served with diced chicken and royale garnish FRENCH

ximxim de galinha chicken braised in palm-oil served with a sauce of ground shrimp, sweet peppers, onions, peanuts and ginger PORTUGUESE

xiphios swordfish, usually grilled in slices GREEK

xouba small fish similar to sardine, usually charcoal-grilled SPANISH

Y

yabby small freshwater crayfish of the genus *Cherax* found in creeks, rivers, waterholes and dams AUSTRALIAN

yabloko apple RUSSIAN

yahni meat braised with onions and simmered in water with tomatoes GREEK

yahni meat stew TURKISH

yakitori small pieces of chicken grilled on skewers JAPANESE

yakni mutton INDIAN

yam tuber which originated in Africa

yaourt yoghurt FRENCH

yaourti yoghurt GREEK

yarrow common perennial herb; the young leaves can be used in salads and can replace chervil as a garnish

yaytsa eggs RUSSIAN

yeast microscopic single-celled plant of the genus *Saccharomyces*; in the right conditions it reproduces rapidly, breaking down starch and sugars by fermentation, converting them into carbon dioxide and alcohol

yeast extract made by treating yeast with acid, it is rich in B vitamins

yellow berry	Quebec name for the fruit of the cloudberry Canadian
yellow dock	curly-leafed plant for use as a vegetable or pot herb
yellowman	traditional toffee NORTHERN IRISH
yellow tail	*Seriola dorsalis*, a long sea fish with a yellow tail found off the costs of Southern California and Mexico, a member of the snapper family
yemas	egg yolks; dessert of whipped egg-yolks and sugar SPANISH
yemissis	stuffing GREEK
yemista	vegetables stuffed with minced meat and rice GREEK
yerba (maté)	a South American evergreen tree, *Ilex paraguariensis*, whose dried leaves are used to make 'Paraguay tea' SOUTH AMERICAN
yermades	a peach grown in Greece GREEK
yialandji	dish containing no meat, usually served cold GREEK
yiouvetsi	an Athens speciality of cubed lamb braised in tomato sauce or soup, served with noodles or macaroni GREEK
ymer	kind of sour milk DANISH
yoghurt	fermented milk product; harmless bacteria are introduced into whole or skimmed milk; they feed and produce an acid that causes the protein to coagulate, resulting in a semi-solid consistency and tart flavour; various fruits and flavours may be introduced for variety
yoğurt	yoghurt TURKISH
York cheese	soft farmhouse cow's milk cheese
York Club cutlets	method of serving lamb cutlets, devised at the York Club
York ham	famous smoked ham
Yorkshire apple pudding	made as Yorkshire pudding, with apples mixed into the batter and sprinkled with sugar before serving
Yorkshire boiled turkey	traditional method of cooking turkey, stuffed with a pig's tongue and a veal and suet stuffing, and simmered in seasoned giblet stock for several hours; originally, the turkey was boned, stuffed and sewn up to resemble the original shape of the bird
Yorkshire herring pie	traditional dish of herrings, potatoes and apples
Yorkshire pudding	batter pudding traditionally eaten with roast beef, but often served on its own especially in Yorkshire

Yorkshire sauce	sauce of orange, port, demi-glace sauce, redcurrant jelly, cinnamon and herbs
youngberries	sweet purple fruit, a cross between the blackberry and the dewberry named after the US fruit grower B M Young
yrttivoi	herb butter FINNISH
ysa	fresh haddock ICELANDIC
yufka böreği	pie containing minced meat or cheese TURKISH
yufkali kadayif	pudding made with puff pastry, vermicelli and syrup TURKISH
Yule log	traditional Christmas Swiss roll filled with chocolate and vanilla butter, and decorated to represent a log
yuyo	sauce flavoured with herbs or greens such as spinach SPANISH
Yvette	method for cooking fish, poached with herbs and stock, thickened, glazed and garnished with small tomatoes stuffed with sole purée; method of serving poached eggs on corn fritters, coated with sauce archiduc; method of serving scrambled eggs, mixed with crayfish tails, garnished with asparagus tips and served with shrimp sauce; method of serving potatoes; lobster soup; chicken consommé FRENCH

Z

zab	oat HUNGARIAN
zabaglione	frothy dessert containing wine, egg yolks and sugar, beaten over a gentle heat until it thickens ITALIAN
żabki	frogs' legs POLISH
żabki smażone	fried frogs' legs POLISH
zabpehely	oat flake HUNGARIAN
zachtgekookt ei	soft boiled egg DUTCH
zacierka	dry dough grated into soups as a garnish POLISH
zadělávané dršky	tripe cooked in a traditional style CZECH
zadělávany květák se syrem	cauliflower with cream sauce and cheese CZECH
za'faran	saffron MIDDLE EASTERN
zafferano	saffron ITALIAN

zaffrani, zafron	saffron INDIAN
Zährte	zarthe GERMAN
zając	hare POLISH
zakąska	appetizer POLISH
zákusek	piece of cake CZECH
zakuski	hors d'œuvres RUSSIAN
zakysaná smetana	sour cream CZECH
zalatina	type of brawn made from pig's head or lean pork or veal, flavoured with bitter orange or lemon juice, chilli, rosemary, cinnamon and cloves CYPRIOT
zalivnoe	cold jellied dish made from fish, meat, poultry or eggs, with vegetables, set with aspic RUSSIAN
zalm	salmon DUTCH
zamboriña	local name for the queen scallop, used by fishermen on the north west coast SPANISH
zampone di Modena	speciality meat dish; the bones from a pig's trotter and part of the leg are removed, leaving the skin intact; the meat, bacon, and truffles are seasoned, stuffed into the skin, cured, boiled and served in slices ITALIAN
zanahoria	carrot SPANISH
Zander	giant perch or pike-perch *Stizotedion lucioperca*, found in the rivers Elbe and Danube GERMAN
zanzarelle	a type of soup; an egg custard is seasoned with nutmeg, salt and pepper, poured through a colander into boiling stock so that it becomes like pasta, and a little Parmesan cheese is added ITALIAN
zapallito de tronco	small variety of vegetable marrow with a flavour not unlike that of avocado pear SOUTH AMERICAN
zapekanka	vegetable dish of potatoes, eggs, butter and fried onions, baked in the oven, often served with mushroom sauce RUSSIAN
zapiekane	baked POLISH
zaprażka biała	white roux of flour and butter POLISH
zardaloo	dried apricots in honey IRANIAN
zarthe	freshwater fish found in most European rivers except the Rhine
zarzamora	blackberry SPANISH
zarzuela (de mariscos)	savoury stew made from assorted fish and shellfish SPANISH
závin	paper-thin layers of pastry filled with fruit; strudel CZECH

zavináče	rollmops CZECH
zayats	young hare or leveret, popular in Russia RUSSIAN
zeberka wieprzowe	spare ribs POLISH
zébrine	variety of aubergine with violet and white stripes EUROPEAN
zedoary	spice from the dried rhizome of *Curcuma zeodaria*, a plant related to ginger and turmeric SOUTH EAST ASIAN
zeekreeft	lobster DUTCH
Zeeland oysters	oysters from the province of Zeeland DUTCH
zeera	cumin seed INDIAN
zeevis	saltwater fish DUTCH
zelèn fasùl	runner bean BULGARIAN
zelèn hayvèr	salad made from baked aubergines BULGARIAN
zelenina	vegetables CZECH
zeleninový salát	mixed salad CZECH
zeleninová polevka	vegetable soup CZECH
zeleninové karbanátky	fried vegetable rissoles in bread crumbs CZECH
zelí	cabbage CZECH
zeller	celery HUNGARIAN
zelná polévka s klobásou	cabbage soup with smoked sausage CZECH
zéphir	any light or frothy dish; mousseline forcemeat of game, poultry or white meat FRENCH
zèppola	fritter; doughnut ITALIAN
zèppole alla napoletana, seppole di San Giuseppe	small fried pastries from Naples, a St Joseph's Day speciality ITALIAN
Zervelat	seasoned, smoked pork, beef and bacon sausage GERMAN
zest	coloured outer layer of citrus fruit
zeste	ZEST FRENCH
zester	device for paring thin curls of citrus peel as flavouring
zhal farezi	marinated and charcoal grilled and served in a very hot green chilli and tomato sauce INDIAN
Zichorie	chicory GERMAN
Ziege	goat GERMAN
ziemniaki	potato dish POLISH
zimino	a Genoese fish stew, cooked in olive oil ITALIAN
ziminù	zimino SARDINIAN
zimne	cold POLISH
Zimt	cinnamon GERMAN

zinc	an essential trace element
zingara, à la	tomato-flavoured demi-glace sauce for small cuts of meat, poultry or eggs, garnished with a julienne of mushrooms, truffles, ham and tongue; garnish for poultry of ham, tongue, mushrooms and truffles, sautéed in butter and bound with tomato-flavoured demi-glace sauce; method of preparing chicken FRENCH
žirniai	peas cooked with butter and water LITHUANIAN
ziste	pith between the peel and fruit of a citrus fruit FRENCH
Zitrone	lemon GERMAN
zlato	goat's or ewe's milk cheese CZECH
zmrzlina	ice cream CZECH
znojemský gulás	stew of diced beef simmered in water with onion CZECH
zola	beef consommé garnished with chick-peas FRENCH
zöldbab	French beans; green beans HUNGARIAN
zöldpaprika saláta	green pepper salad HUNGARIAN
zöldség	vegetable HUNGARIAN
zónaadag	small portion HUNGARIAN
zouave	demi-glace sauce flavoured with tomato, garlic, mustard and tarragon FRENCH
zout	salt DUTCH
zrazy	originally a Polish dish, but now a Russian national dish, resembling beef olives but it may be made with other meats; Polish term for a chop or a slice of meat POLISH, RUSSIAN
zsálya	sage HUNGARIAN
zselé	jelly HUNGARIAN
zsemlegombóc	white bread dumplings HUNGARIAN
zsemlemorzsa	bread crumbs HUNGARIAN
zsenge	young HUNGARIAN
zsír	fat HUNGARIAN
zsömle	roll HUNGARIAN
zübdei hünkâri	'Imperial cream'; a sweet dish made from sugar, rose water, maraschino and gelatine mixed with whipped cream TURKISH
zucca	pumpkin; gourd ITALIAN
zucchero	sugar ITALIAN
zucchini	courgette; small vegetable marrow AMERICAN

zucchino	small vegetable marrow (US: zucchini) ITALIAN
Zucker	sugar GERMAN
Zuger Rötel	small red freshwater fish of the char family, served with egg sauce, except in Basel, where it is served with onion sauce SWISS
Zunge	tongue GERMAN
zupa	soup POLISH
zupa mleczna	cream soup POLISH
zupa owocowa	fruit soup POLISH
zuppa	soup ITALIAN
zuppa inglese	dessert of custard and sponge cake flavoured with rum or Marsala ITALIAN
żurawiny	cranberries POLISH
Zürcher Topf	boiled brisket of beef with root vegetables SWISS
zure saus	sour sauce flavoured with lemon, often served with boiled fresh tongue DUTCH
żurek	sour rye-flour soup usually containing cream POLISH
zuring	sorrel DUTCH
Zutat	ingredient GERMAN
zuurkool	sauerkraut, often served with bacon DUTCH
Zwetsch	member of the plum family used for drying into prunes GERMAN
zwezerik	sweetbreads DUTCH
Zwieback	small type of rusk, usually bought ready-made, to serve at cocktail parties GERMAN
Zwiebel	onion GERMAN
Zwischenrippenstück	rib-eye steak; entrecôte GERMAN
żytni chleb	rye bread POLISH